STUDENT SUPPLEMENT FOR BASIC STATISTICS IN BUSINESS AND ECONOMICS, THIRD EDITION

George W. Summers
University of Arizona

William S. Peters
University of New Mexico

Charles P. Armstrong
University of Rhode Island

Wadsworth Publishing Company
Belmont, California

A Division of Wadsworth, Inc.

ACKNOWLEDGMENTS

The authors wish to thank Roger Greenal and David Clayton of
the Academic Computer Center at the University of Rhode Island
for their assistance with computer-related matters. We also wish
to thank Judy Long and Elizabeth Flaherty, who are Instructors of
Management Science at the same institution, for their thoughtful
review of the *Student Supplement* for this text.

Editorial-Production: Phoenix Publishing Services, Inc.,
San Francisco

Printed in the United States of America
1 2 3 4 5 6 7 8 9 10—85 84 83 82 81

ISBN 0-534-00919-0

CONTENTS

1

HOW TO USE THIS BOOK

Learning statistics is much the same as learning other skills. You need to understand what techniques to acquire, to study the explanations of the techniques, to practice the techniques, and to test your proficiency in using the techniques. This supplement offers several aids to help you learn statistics. These include programmed learning sets, exercises (with solutions), and examinations. This self-instructional supplement is designed to be used in conjunction with *Basic Statistics in Business and Economics*, Third Edition, by Summers, Peters, and Armstrong, which we shall call the text.

Statistics is a cumulative subject and it is best to master small blocks of the subject at a time. Each chapter in the text has several blocks of material. As a general rule, the blocks of material should be learned sequentially. Thus you should master the first part of a chapter before going on to the next part.

Program sets have been provided for those topics that tend to give students the most difficulty. Each set, or module, covers one statistical concept or technique.

As you can see, the text and this supplement are designed to be used together as a learning system. The text provides the basic explanation of the statistical techniques. In some cases, you may master the techniques by reading the text and doing the exercises in the text. In other cases, you many wish to use the aids given in this supplement. In the following paragraphs, you will find an explanation of how to use each type of material presented in this supplement.

HOW TO USE THE DIAGNOSTIC TESTS

Learning statistics is largely a matter of practice. After you have studied a chapter in the text you will have mastered some concepts, but others will require additional work. Practice with the concepts you do not understand will help to grasp notions that are not clear.

In order to determine which skills you have acquired, we provide a Diagnostic Test for the first ten chapters. The test covers all of the major concepts in the chapter. Take the test after you have studied the text chapter. The test is self-scoring.

For each test, there is a Student Record Sheet. On this sheet, darken the squares corresponding to the questions that you answered *incorrectly*. Opposite the darkened squares you will find a reference to the text section or page which is the basis for the question. In addition, you will find references to Self-Correcting Exercises and Program Sets. These materials appear in this supplement. Directions for using these materials are given below. They provide additional practice problems and learning aids for the questions you have missed.

By analyzing the pattern of the darkened squares, you can determine which topics should be studied and in what detail. The test questions appear in the same order as the topics appear in the text. If you miss several questions from a particular section, you should study that portion of the text again. If you still feel uncomfortable with a topic, you may wish to work with the related Program Set or Self-Correcting Exercises. If your incorrect answers form a scattered pattern, you may only need to examine the solutions to the test questions. Patterns that are between these extremes may require a mixture of these strategies.

The Diagnostic Test is designed to indicate to you which topics you do not understand and how you can correct misconceptions in the most efficient manner. In order for the diagnostic test to do its job, you must be honest with yourself in interpreting the results. If you answer test questions incorrectly, accept the fact and take the necessary steps to correct the problem. Most students believe they know more than they actually do know after reading the material for the first time. This is cause for concern but not alarm. Often misconceptions can be corrected quickly. If they are not corrected as they are encountered, the misconceptions will persist and learning subsequent material will be more difficult or even impossible.

HOW TO USE THE ACHIEVEMENT TESTS

In order to measure your improvement, we have included a second test for chapters 2 through 8. The Achievement Test parallels the Diagnostic Test in terms of the number and difficulty of questions, as well as the topics covered by the test. You may wish to use

these after you have completed the study of each chapter or as an
aid in the preparation for examinations.

HOW TO USE THE PROGRAM SETS

You should use this supplemental material in a way that best suits
your particular needs. Three alternatives are:

1. After reading a section of the text you may feel that you need
   additional instruction before proceeding to the exercises.

2. You may wish to work through the program sets *before* reading
   the text.

3. If, after reading the text, you have difficulty working exercises, you may wish to work through the appropriate program
   set or sets.

   Each set contains a series of frames which you should complete.
The correct response is printed in the right margin directly below each frame. Cover the correct response with a card until you
have formulated your own response and are ready to compare it
with the correct one. The following examples will help you understand the format used here.

Example The mean of 3, 4, and 5 is ___.

$$4 \quad \frac{3 + 4 + 5}{3}$$

The material within asterisks provides a more detailed explanation about calculations involved in obtaining the correct response.
   When a verbal response is required, the number of blanks and
their lengths indicate the number of words and their lengths.

Example The *mean* is a short name for the _____ _____.

arithmetic mean

Some frames would require extensive calculations to obtain a numerical value. In these cases, we instruct you to "substitute but do
not solve," and we do the arithmetic for you.
   In some frames you are given a choice of responses.

Example The first step in computing the mean is to (add/subtract)
           the values.

add

In this type of frame indicate your response by circling one of the choices. The alternatives will appear within parentheses, separated by a slash, and they are underlined. In some frames, the choices are symbols, and the choices are separated by the word "or" instead of a slash.

Example The numerator in the formula for the mean is
(Σx or x^2 or N).

Σx

   We recommend that you proceed as follows to obtain full value from the program sets. Any shortcut you may be tempted to take will reduce your chance of mastering the statistical concepts and techniques covered.

1. Read each frame carefully and write in your response (circle your choice in multiple-choice frames).

2. Keep the correct response below *covered* until you have completed yours.

3. Check your response with the correct one. If it differs, review the preceding frames to discover where you went wrong before proceeding to the next frame.

HOW TO USE THE SELF-CORRECTING EXERCISES

Each chapter has a set of self-correcting exercises. The name *self-correcting* is used because detailed solutions (which have many intermediate steps) are given as opposed to a brief solution. The solutions for all Self-Correcting Exercises are given at the end of this supplement. The problems in the Self-Correcting Exercises have been selected to give you practice with the major points of the chapter. Each problem is labeled with a title similar to a chapter subheading in the text. This is done to enable you to find a problem concerning a technique which may be troubling you.
   Each exercise has several parts that guide you through a complex problem step by step. The solutions give you immediate feedback about your answers as you progress through a problem. This allows you to correct errors and misconceptions that can interfere with subsequent learning if they persist. It is very natural to make mistakes when learning a new technique. The fact that you make errors is not nearly so important as understanding *what* errors you have made and *why* you have made them. The immediate feedback mechanism of the Self-Correcting Exercises is specifically designed to assist you with the error detection-correction process.

Learning statistics is largely a matter of practice. The Self-Correcting Exercises offer you the opportunity to practice the important techniques in a step-by-step manner. Many students find it helpful to begin their practice with the Self-Correcting Exercises. In general, the degree of proficiency you attain in using statistical techniques is related to the number of problems you work. There are exercises at the end of each section in the text. By working these you improve your skill and confidence with the techniques and concepts. At the end of each chapter in the text, you will find more challenging exercises and exercises that integrate several concepts.

2

ORGANIZING AND PRESENTING DATA

The bar chart shows the number of male and female employees in a small corporation. Use this chart to answer Questions 1 through 3.

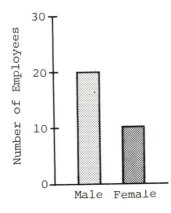

1. What is the absolute frequency of males?

2. What is the relative frequency of females?

3. Does the chart represent qualitative or quantitative data?

4. The pie chart shows the distribution of wages and fringe benefits budgeted for employees of a manufacturing firm. What

6

proportion of the total goes to state and federal taxes, including FICA?

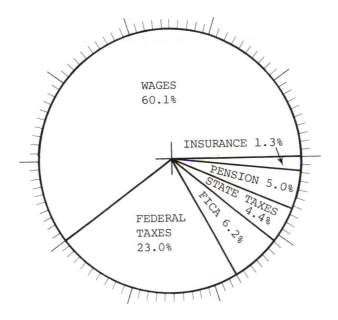

5. Figure 2-1 on page 8 shows the number of hospital admissions in three cities due to accidents. Describe the general movement of admissions for city B over time.

6. Are the data in Figure 2-1 cross-sectional or time series?

7. The following data represent the numerical grades of 15 history students.

    1,   3,   3,   4,   3,   2,   4,   1,   3,   5,   2,   3,   2,   3,   1

    What is the frequency of the grade 4?

8. For the data in Question 7, what is the relative frequency of the grade 1?

9. Use the frequency table to construct a frequency diagram.

Age	Number of Persons
4	2
5	3
6	2

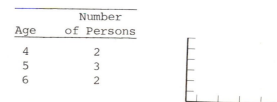

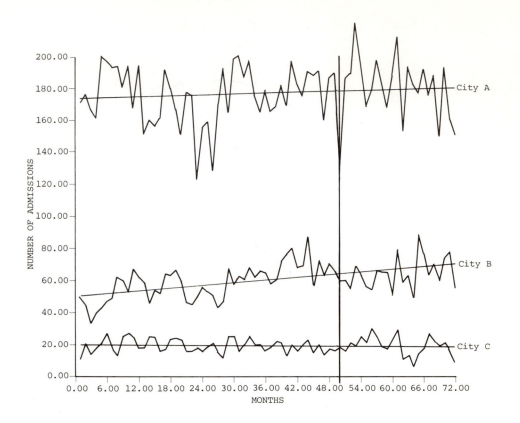

Figure 2-1

10. The table shows class limits for a data collection.

X
1-10
11-20
? -30

What value should replace the question mark?

11. For a frequency distribution with many-value classes, what is the major factor that determines the number of classes?

12. One hundred observations are to be used to determine a frequency distribution with many-value classes. If the average number of values per class is to be at least 7, what is the estimated maximum number of classes?

13. If a frequency distribution has positive skewness, does it have a longer tail to the left or to the right?

The following is a distribution of grades for 100 students. Use these data for Questions 14 through 17.

Grades	Number of Students	Cumulative Frequency
1	10	10
2	15	25
3	25	?
4	30	?
5	20	?
	100	

14. How many students had a grade of 2 or lower?

15. What is the cumulative frequency of the grade 3?

16. What is the cumulative relative frequency of the grade 2?

17. Is a cumulative frequency ogive a correct way of displaying the cumulative frequencies?

18. The following is a distribution of scores for an algebra test. Can you tell how many students had a score of 18 or less? Why or why not?

Scores	Cumulative Frequency
1-10	2
11-20	5
21-30	10
31-40	14
41-50	15

CHAPTER 2.   SELF-CORRECTING EXERCISES

2.1 Presenting Qualitative Data   The circulation department of a
newspaper is attempting to determine characteristics of the
circulation of its Sunday edition in 25 communities.   A sample
of households from each community is obtained; the results
for two of the communities are given here:

	Subscribers	Nonsubscribers
Community A	75	25
Community B	30	20

a. Plot the data in the space provided.   What type of scale is
implied by the graphs?

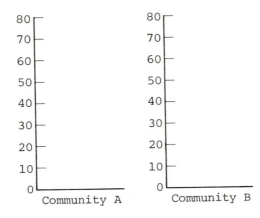

b. Plot the data using a relative scale.

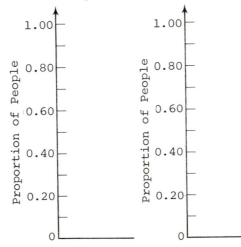

c. Which scale is the better choice for comparing these data? Why?

2.2 <u>Pie Charts</u>   The passage of Proposition 13 in California resulted in a $7,000,000,000 tax cut.   The beneficiaries of this tax cut for 1978 were as follows:*

Commercial, industrial, agricultural, and rental property	$2.9 billion
State of California and U.S. government	$2.6 billion
Homeowners	$1.7 billion
Total	$7.2 billion

*Source: *Consumer Reports*, September 1979.

Use the pie chart below to show the percent of the tax cut that went to each type of property owner. (The divisions on the chart are percentages, not degrees.)

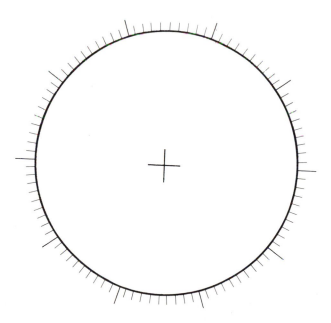

Pie Chart Grid

2.3 Horizontal Bar Charts   On the day Proposition 13 passed, voters were asked which services they would like to have cut if the proposition were passed.   The results of a CBS News Poll shown below gives the percentage of voters willing to have each type of service cut.*

Welfare	59%
Recreation	31%
Public Transportation	19%
City Libraries	19%
Schools	13%

The California Department of Finance estimates the percentage of revenues derived by each of these services from property taxes as follows:*

Welfare	13%
Recreation	15%
Public Transportation	5%
City Libraries	15%
Schools	50%

*Source: *Consumer Reports*, September 1979.

a. Complete the horizontal bar chart below to display these data.

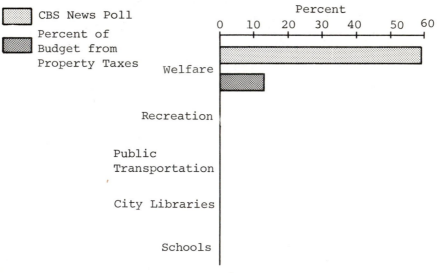

b. Does it appear that the voters' preferences for cutting services are in line with the actual uses of property taxes?

2.4 <u>Time Series</u> Figure 2-1 (page 8) shows the number of hospital admissions due to accidents for three cities. On the horizontal axis, month 1 is January 1972, month 2 is February 1973, and so forth. The data are for a 6-year period.

a. What do the data tell us about accidents for these cities?

b. How would your answer to (a) change if you had only the data for the month indicated by the vertical line on Figure 2-1?

2.5 <u>Distributions for Discrete Variables in Single-Value Classes</u> Forty homes in a certain city were surveyed to determine the number of radios in the home. Each number below is the number of radios in one home.

3	4	0	5	1
3	1	2	1	2
0	3	1	1	3
4	1	5	2	7
4	2	1	3	2
1	2	3	0	1
1	3	3	2	1
2	4	1	2	2

a. Treating every value in the range of observations as a class, tally the data into the classes.

b. Prepare a frequency distribution table from the tally.

c. Prepare a relative frequency distribution table.

d. Use the grid provided to plot a frequency diagram for the data in this exercise. Label each axis.

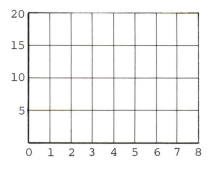

2.6 <u>Interpretation of a Frequency Diagram</u> The graph on the left shows the results of a consumer survey in the form of a frequency diagram. On the right is a relative frequency diagram for the same data.

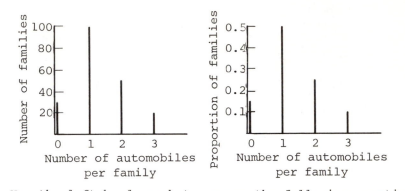

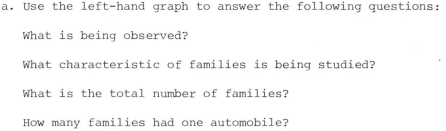

a. Use the left-hand graph to answer the following questions:

What is being observed?

What characteristic of families is being studied?

What is the total number of families?

How many families had one automobile?

b. Use the graph to the right to answer these questions:

What proportion of the families surveyed have no auto?

What proportion of the families have three autos?

c. Prepare a frequency distribution table from the frequency diagram.

d. Prepare a relative frequency distribution table from the relative frequency diagram.

2.7 Relative Frequency Distributions A data-processing firm employs a large number of keypunch operators. Each data processing card is punched by one operator and verified by another. In the verification process, any discrepancies can be ascribed to either the keypunch operator or the verifier operator. The company wishes to compare error rates for keypunch operators who have been working for 1 month against error rates for operators who have been working for 1 year. To measure error rates, the number of errors found per 100 cards punched by 500 new and by 100 experienced employees were tabulated. The results are given in the following frequency distributions.

| New Employees | | Experienced Employees | |
Error Rate	Number of Occurrences	Error Rate	Number of Occurrences
0	35	0	30
1	40	1	25
2	45	2	22
3	75	3	10
4	125	4	7
5	140	5	4
6	40	6	2
	500		100

a. From the frequency distributions, 35 new employees and 30 experienced employees had a zero error rate. Does this imply that new employees are more likely to have error-free work than experienced employees? Why or why not?

b. Find the relative frequency distributions for both groups. On the grids provided, plot the *relative* frequency distributions for both groups of employees.

c. Relative frequency distributions are preferable to frequency distributions for this situation. Why?

d. Do the relative frequency distributions found in (b) reflect differences you might expect to find between new and experienced operators? Discuss the differences shown by the relative frequency distributions.

2.8 Distributions for Discrete Variables in Many-Value Classes

A health maintenance organization recorded the number of out-
patient visits made during a one-year period by 50 patients.
The data are as follows.

0	2	5	9	15
0	2	5	9	17
0	2	5	9	18
1	3	6	10	18
1	3	7	10	19
1	4	7	12	21
1	4	7	13	22
1	4	8	13	22
1	4	8	14	24
2	4	8	15	25

a. How many value classes should be used if the average number
   of values per class is as near 7 as possible?

b. How many different values of the variables are included between the largest and the smallest observation—that is,
   what is the range of the variable indicated by the data?

c. If all classes are to have the same class length, what
   should be the class length?

d. Establish the value classes. Start the first class with
   the smallest observation. How many different values may be
   grouped in the first value class? What are these values?
   Is it correct to say the number of values of the variable
   grouped in the first class is equal to the upper limit
   minus the lower limit?

e. Use the value classes established in (d) to find the frequency distribution.

f. If you were given the frequency distribution developed in
   (e) (but not the original observations), could you say how
   many patients had zero visits? What can you say about the
   identity of the original observations that are grouped in
   the first class?

2.9 Cumulative Frequency and Cumulative Relative Frequency for Single-Value Classes

Note: Cumulative relative frequency is
cumulative frequency expressed on a relative scale. To find
cumulative relative frequency, divide the absolute frequency
by the total number of observations.

a. The frequency distributions describing the error rates for two groups of keypunch operators (Self-Correcting Exercise 2.7) are repeated for convenience.

	New Employees				Experienced Employees		
Error Rate	Occur-rences	Cumulative Frequency	Cumulative Relative Frequency	Error Rate	Occur-rences	Cumulative Frequency	Cumulative Relative Frequency
0	35			0	30		
1	40			1	25		
2	45			2	22		
3	75			3	10		
4	125			4	7		
5	140			5	4		
6	40			6	2		
	500				100		

In the space to the right of the frequency column, find the cumulative frequency and cumulative relative frequency distributions for both groups.

b. Suppose an error rate of two or less constitutes an acceptable quality level. What descriptive device (frequency, cumulative frequency, or cumulative relative frequency) would best serve to compare the two groups of employees? Why?

c. On the grids provided, plot the cumulative relative frequency distributions for both groups.

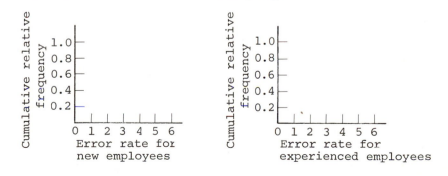

d. Do the graphs in (c) conform to your expectations for new and experienced operators?

e. Frequency, relative frequency, cumulative frequency, and cumulative relative frequency are alternative ways of describing a data collection. Briefly describe the functions of each type of distribution. Give one reason why the data collections for the two groups might be presented as cumulative relative frequency distributions.

2.10 Cumulative Frequency Distributions for Many-Value Classes   The following data are ages of 40 persons shopping in a supermarket on a certain day. Assume that ages are reported to the nearest birthday—that is, a person who will reach 20 in less than 6 months would have his or her age recorded as 20. Note that the data are arranged in order of magnitude for convenience.

4	19	31	39	47
7	20	32	39	48
10	21	33	39	52
10	21	33	39	52
12	21	34	40	53
13	24	37	40	58
13	28	38	42	61
16	31	38	43	64

The frequency distribution for these data is as follows.

Age	Number of Persons
4–13	7
14–23	6
24–33	7
34–43	12
44–53	5
54–63	2
64–73	1

a. Use the frequency distribution to find the cumulative frequency distribution table.

b. Use the grid provided to plot the results of (a).

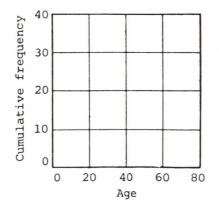

c. From (a), can you tell how many people are less than or equal to 23 years old?

d. From (b), can you tell how many people are less than or equal to 20 years old?

e. Answer (c) and (d) by examining the original observations. Explain why the answers agree or disagree.

CHAPTER 2. ACHIEVEMENT TEST

Use this diagram to answer Questions 1 through 3. The diagram is based on 100 parts that were classified as *good* or *defective*.

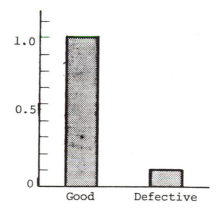

1. What is the absolute frequency of good parts?

2. What is the relative frequency of defective parts?

3. Does the graph show qualitative or quantitative data?

4. The pie chart on page 7 shows the distribution of wages and fringe benefits for a manufacturing firm. If the total budget for the items shown is $1,000,000, how much money is budgeted for state taxes?

5. What causes the fluctuations in the accident admission data shown in Figure 2-1 on page 8?

6. What quantity is presented in the horizontal axis of Figure 2-1?

7. The following data represent the values (in cents) of coins left in a cash drawer at the close of business.

   1,   5,   10,   10,   25,   50,   1,   1,   1,   10,   5,   50

   What is the absolute frequency of the 1-cent coins?

8. For the data in Question 7, what is the relative frequency of 10-cent coins?

9. Use the frequency diagram to find the relative frequency distribution.

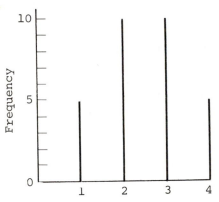

10. The following shows the frequency distribution of employee ages for a small firm:

Age	Number of Employees
21-30	3
31-40	5
41-50	10
51-60	8
61-70	2

What is the class interval length?

11. How many classes should be used for a frequency table that has ten observations?

12. A data collection has 10,000 observations. If the average number of values per class is to be at least ten, what is the estimated maximum number of classes?

13. A frequency distribution is symmetrical. What can be said about the skewness of the distribution?

The following shows the cumulative relative frequency of the grades of 100 students. Use this distribution to answer questions 14 through 17.

Grades	Cumulative Relative Frequency
1	0.10
2	0.25
3	0.70
4	0.80
5	?

14. How many students had a grade of 2 or lower?

15. What is the cumulative frequency of the grade of 3?

16. What is the cumulative relative frequency of the grade of 2?

17. If there are no grades higher than 5, what value should replace the question mark in the table above?

18. The following is a distribution of scores from a test. What proportion of students had a score of 31 or more?

Score	Cumulative Frequency
1-10	2
11-20	5
21-30	10
31-40	14
41-50	15

CHAPTER 2.   STUDENT RECORD AND REFERENCE SHEET

Darken the square corresponding to each test item you answered
incorrectly.   References indicate the topics you should study.
See Chapter 1 of this volume for details.

Item	Diagnostic Test	Achievement Test	Text References	Self-correcting Exercise References
1	☐	☐	25–32	2.1
2	☐	☐	25–32	2.1
3	☐	☐	25–32	2.1
4	☐	☐	25–32	2.2
5	☐	☐	19–26	2.4
6	☐	☐	19–26	2.4
7	☐	☐	32–39	2.5
8	☐	☐	32–39	2.5
9	☐	☐	32–39	2.6
10	☐	☐	32–39	2.8
11	☐	☐	32–39	2.8
12	☐	☐	32–39	2.8
13	☐	☐	41–46	—
14	☐	☐	41–46	2.9
15	☐	☐	41–46	2.9
16	☐	☐	41–46	2.9
17	☐	☐	41–46	2.9
18	☐	☐	41–46	2.10

3

SUMMARY DESCRIPTIVE MEASURES

CHAPTER 3. DIAGNOSTIC TEST

1. A random sample of sales in a variety store during a 2-hour period produced the following data: $1, $3, $5, $1, $10. What is the arithmetic mean of these data?

2. What symbol should be used to designate the answer to Question 1?

3. If the data in Question 1 were for *all* of the sales in the 2-hour period instead of a sample, would your answer to Question 2 change?

The following frequency table is to be used in answering Questions 4 and 5.

Age	Frequency	Midvalue	Estimated Class Total
11-20	3	?	
21-30	5	25.5	
31-40	2		
	10		

4. What is the midvalue of the class 11-20?

5. What is the estimated class total for the class 21-30?

6. Use this frequency table to determine the sample mean.

Hours	f	Midvalue (m)	Estimated Class Total (fm)
1-3	1		
4-6	8		
7-9	1		

7. In Question 6, would you necessarily obtain the same value for the sample mean if you had used the original observations instead of the frequency distribution?

8. What is the median of these data: 4, 5, 1, 2, 5?

9. What is the median of these data: 7, 8, 10, 12?

10. What is the mode of these data?   3, 1, 1, 5, 3, 1?

11. In this frequency diagram, is Y or Z likely to be the mean?

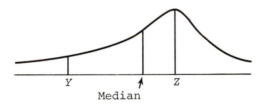

12. A population consists of the values 3, 2, 2, 1.   For this population, $\mu = 2$.   What is the variance of this population?

13. What symbol should be used to represent the quantity found in Question 12?

14. A sample variance is found to have a value of 16.   What is the sample standard deviation?

15. What symbol should be used to represent the quantity found in Question 14?

16. The following observations are the result of obtaining a sample.   Use this information to find the sample variance without computing the deviations from the mean.

x	x^2
3	9
5	25
10	100
18	134

17. Use the frequency table below to compute the sample mean.

Value Class	Frequency
0- 4	10
5- 9	50
10-14	40

18. The results of IQ tests have a mean of 100 and a standard deviation of 10. What is the standard score of a person who has an IQ of 95?

PROGRAM SET 3.1   Measuring Central Location: The Mean

1. We are usually interested in properties of a statistical population, rather than an individual value in the population. For example, the Dow-Jones average expresses a property of a collection of stock prices. A property of a population is associated with (one/all) value(s) in the population.

all

2. In order to see what we mean by a "property" of a statistical population, we shall examine two populations. These are purchases (rounded to the nearest dollar) made by a retail store's male and female customers.

$$\text{Males: } x = 1, 3, 3, 3, 5$$
$$\text{Females: } x = 4, 6, 8, 8, 10, 10, 10, 16$$

These values can be plotted on an axis as follows.

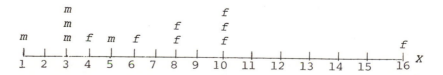

From the graph we can see that each of the two populations is centered at (the same/a different) value of X.

a different

3. The notion of the *center* of a statistical population is a property of a population that statisticians call *central location*. In the last frame, we saw that the data collections associated with male and female customers had (the same/different) central _____.

different, locations

4. We need some way to be more precise about the concept of central location; that is, we need to measure central location. One way to measure central location is to calculate the *arithmetic mean*. The arithmetic _____ is one way to _____ central location.

mean, measure

5. To calculate the arithmetic mean, we add the values in the population and divide their sum by the number of values in the population. For male customers,

$$x = 1, 3, 3, 3, 5$$

The sum of the values is

1 + 3 + ___ + ___ + ___ = ___

3, 3, 5, 15

6. Also, we can see that for x = 1, 3, 3, 3, 5, there are ___ members in the collection.

5

7. Knowing that the sum of the values in the foregoing population is 15, and that there are 5 values, we can calculate the arithmetic mean to be

$$\frac{\text{sum of the values in the population}}{\text{number of members in the population}} = \frac{\quad}{\quad}$$

$$\frac{15}{5} = 3$$

8. The procedure for calculating the arithmetic mean is to divide
   the (number of values/sum of the values) in the population by
   the (number of values/sum of the values) in the population.

                                    sum of the values, number of values

9. For the female customers,

                $x = 4, 6, 8, 8, 10, 10, 10, 16$

   the arithmetic mean is ___.

                                           9 *** 72/8 ***

10. We have found the arithmetic mean for male customers to be 3
    and the arithmetic mean for the female customers to be 9. On
    the diagram from Frame 2, draw arrows pointing to the center of
    the population for males and the center of the population for
    females.

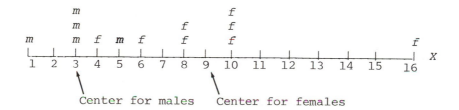

                Center for males   Center for females

11. The arithmetic mean is used so frequently as a measure of
    central location that statisticians have adopted a special
    symbol, μ (mu), to describe it. Whenever you see the symbol
    ___, you know that a reference is being made to the arithmetic
    _____.

                                                    μ, mean

12. It is also convenient to use the shortened form *mean* to indi-
    cate the full name *arithmetic mean*. The full name "arithmetic
    mean" is shortened to _____ and is represented by the symbol
    ___.

                                                    mean, μ

13. We shall use the symbol N to represent the number of values in
    the population. Instead of writing

         $$\mu = \frac{\text{sum of the values in the population}}{\text{number of members in the population}}$$

we can write

$$\mu = \frac{\text{sum of the values in the population}}{\underline{\qquad}}$$

N

14. Recall that we have used the symbol Σ to indicate that we are going to _____ some values.

add

15. If a collection has N values, we would use the compact notation $\sum_{i=1}^{N} x_i$ to indicate that we are going to _____ the values
in the collection starting with the first value and stopping
with the ___th value.

add, N

16. Instead of writing the formula for μ as

$$\mu = \frac{\text{sum of the values in the population,}}{N}$$

we may use the compact notation and write $\mu = \dfrac{\overline{\qquad}}{N}$.

$\sum\limits_{i=1}^{N} x_i$

17. When we calculate the mean, we always add all of the values
in the population. In order to simplify the notation, we
shall omit the upper and lower limits on the summation sign
and write the formula for the mean as

$$\mu = \frac{\Sigma X}{N}$$

In this formula, ΣX is understood to imply that we are to
add _____ of the values in the population.

all

18. Notice that the left side of the formula $\mu = \Sigma X / N$ tells us
that we are to calculate the mean and the right side tells how
to make the calculation. In other words, the left side tells
(how/what) to calculate and the right side tells us (how/what)
to calculate.

what, how

19. The formula for the mean is usually written as ___ = _____.

$$\mu = \Sigma X/N$$

20. Use the formula to calculate the mean of the population 4, 6, 8, 8, 8, and 14. _____

$$\mu = 8 \; \substack{* \\ * \\ *} \; 48/6 \; \substack{* \\ * \\ *}$$

21. So far, we have restricted our discussion to the population mean. The dollar purchases for the retail store's female customers are 4, 6, 8, 8, 10, 10, 10, 16. We found the population mean to be 9 and we use the symbol _____ to represent the population mean.

$$\mu$$

22. Suppose each value in the population is written on a card. The cards are thoroughly shuffled and three cards are selected at random without looking at the values written on them. The values selected are 6, 10, and 8. The total of these values is _____ and the number of values is _____.

24, 3

23. The average of these sample values is

$$\frac{}{} = $$

$$\frac{24}{3}, 8$$

24. Since the population mean is μ = 9, we conclude the mean of these sample values (is/is not) the same as the population mean.

is not

25. In order to maintain the distinction between the population mean and a sample mean, we must have a new symbol for the sample mean. We use $\overline{X}$ (pronounced X *bar*) for the (population/sample) mean and we use μ for the (population/sample) mean.

sample, population

26. The formulas for the population and sample means are

$$\mu = \frac{\Sigma X}{N} \quad \text{and} \quad X = \frac{\Sigma X}{n}$$

Here, N represents the number of values in the _____ and
n represents the number of values in a _____.

population, sample

PROGRAM SET 3.2   Measuring Dispersion: The Variance

1. Recall that we have learned how to measure the property of a
   population called *central location* by calculating the mean.
   The mean measures a _____ called _____ _____.

property, central location

2. Another property of a population is *dispersion*, which has to
   do with the variability of the values in a population. For example, we can see that the values 1, 3, 3, 3, and 5 (are/are not)
   all the same.

are not

3. Whenever the observations in the population are not all the
   same, we say that there is *variability*, or *dispersion*, in the
   population. There is no dispersion in a population when
   (all/some) of the observations in the population have
   (a different/the same) value.

all, the same

4. Let us consider two statistical populations. The first represents retail purchases (rounded to the nearest dollar) made by
   male customers of a certain store. The second represents the
   same information for female customers.

   $$\text{Males} \quad x = 1, 3, 3, 3, 5$$
   $$\text{Females} \quad x = 4, 6, 8, 8, 10, 10, 10, 16$$

   These collections are displayed in the following graph.

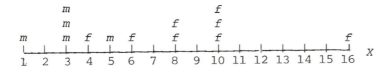

   It appears from the graph that there is more dispersion for
   (males/females).

females

5. Most people would be able to guess the answer to Frame 4 because the data collection for females has more values lying
farther from the center of the data. However, it is not always possible to guess correctly. We must refine the concept
of dispersion to eliminate guesswork. Statisticians have developed a measure called *variance* for measuring dispersion.
The variance is one measure of the property of _____
in a data collection.

dispersion

6. Variance is used to measure dispersion throughout the study of
statistics. It tells us how closely, on the average, the
values of a collection are clustered around the mean of a collection. For example, the values 3, 2, 2, and 1 have a mean
of $\mu = 2$. We see that the first value in the collection,
x = 3, is one unit greater than the mean. The second and
third values are exactly equal to the mean. The fourth value
is one unit (greater/less) than the mean.

less

7. We refer to the distance of each value (observation) from the
mean of the collection as its *deviation* from the mean. We
compute the deviation for each value of the collection by subtracting from it the mean of the collection. For example, we
see that *x* = 3, 2, 2, 1 has a mean of $\mu = 2$. In the table
below, we have started the computation of the deviation of
each observation from the mean, *X* - μ. Complete this table.

Observation		Deviation from the Mean
x	*x* - μ	*x* - μ
3	3 - 2	1
2	2 - 2	0
2	___ - ___	___
1	___ - ___	___

2 - 2 = 0; 1 - 2 = -1

8. The deviation from the mean tells us how far each observation
is from the mean. We calculate the deviation of each observation (*x*) by subtracting the mean from it. In symbols, we write
for the deviation *x* - ___.

μ

9. The mean of the collection 7, 8, 8, 10, 12, 12, and 13 is
   $\mu = 10$. Complete the table below by computing the deviation
   from the mean for each value.

x	$x - \mu$
7	-3
8	___
8	___
10	___
12	___
12	___
13	___

$-2, -2, 0, 2, 2, 3$

10. Recall that our objective is to develop a measure of dis-
    persion that will tell us how far, on the average, the members
    in the collection deviate from the mean of the collection. At
    first glance, it might appear that our desired measure of dis-
    persion could be obtained by averaging the deviations from the
    mean. However, from the above frame, we see that the average
    of the deviations from the mean is

$$\frac{(-3) + (-2) + (-2) + (0) + (2) + (2) + (3)}{7} = \underline{\quad}$$

0

11. In our example, the average of the deviations from the mean is
    zero. This is true for all data collections. In other words,
    it makes no difference whether a data collection has little
    dispersion or much dispersion, the average of the deviations
    from the mean is always equal to ___.

0

12. To avoid this difficulty, we measure dispersion by averaging
    the square of each deviation. The deviations for our example
    are given in the table below. Complete this table by com-
    puting the square of each deviation.

Observation x	Deviation $x - \mu$	Deviations Squared $(x - \mu)^2$
7	-3	9
8	-2	4
8	-2	____
10	0	____
12	2	____
12	2	____
13	3	____

4, 0, 4, 4, 9

13. The variance is defined as the average of the squared deviations from the mean. We see that the average of the squared
deviations just computed is

$$\frac{9 + 4 + 4 + 0 + 4 + 4 + 9}{7} = \frac{\underline{}}{7} = \underline{}$$

34, 4 6/7

14. One way to compute the variance for a data collection is by
means of a table such as the one in Frame 12. The first column
is for the values of the collection; the second is for the
deviation of each value from the mean; and the last is for the
_____ of each deviation.

square

15. Let us try another example, using 4, 5, 5, 6, and 10, which has
a mean of $\mu = 6$. Complete the following table.

Observation x	Deviation $(x - \mu)$	Deviations Squared $(x - \mu)^2$
4	-2	4
____	____	____
____	____	____
____	____	____
____	____	____

5	-1	1
5	-1	1
6	0	0
10	4	16

16. To compute the variance, we average the squared deviations.
    From the calculation in the last frame, we see that the
    variance is _____.

$$4\ 2/5 \quad \frac{(4 + 1 + 1 + 0 + 16)}{5} = \frac{22}{5}$$

17. The procedure for calculating the variance involves four
    steps:

    a. Compute the mean.

    b. Calculate the _____ of each value from the mean.

    c. Calculate the _____ of each deviation.

    d. Compute the _____ of the squared deviations.

                              deviation, square, average

18. Use the procedure in the last frame to compute the variance of
    4, 6, and 11: μ = ___ .

x	$x - \mu$	$(x - \mu)^2$
___	___	___
___	___	___
___	___	___

variance = _____

$$\mu = 7; \quad \begin{matrix} 4 & -3 & 9 \\ 6 & -1 & 1; \\ 11 & 4 & 16 \end{matrix}$$

variance = 8 2/3 $(9 + 1 + 16)/3$

19. Now find the variance of 7, 3, and 20 by the procedure
    we have developed.

x	$x - \mu$	$(x - \mu)^2$
7	-3	9
3	-7	49
20	10	100

$\mu = 10$; ; variance = 52 2/3 $\overset{*}{\underset{*}{*}}$ (9 + 49 + 100)/3 $\overset{*}{\underset{*}{*}}$

20. We now repeat the four steps that produce the variance.

   a. Compute the mean.

   b. Calculate the deviation of each value from the mean.

   c. Calculate the square of each deviation.

   d. Compute the average of the squared deviations.

   We calculate the variance so frequently that it is convenient to have a formula that enables us to write this procedure more compactly. We have already used symbols to represent the first three steps of the procedure. These symbols are

   a. μ

   b. ___ - ___

   c. (___ - ___)^2

$$X - \mu; \quad (X - \mu)^2$$

21. The fourth step tells us to average the squared deviations. If a collection contains N observations, we compute N deviations and N squared deviations. To complete the fourth step, we add the ___ (how many?) squared deviations and divide by ___.

$$N, N$$

22. Remember that Σ is used to indicate addition of quantities. To indicate the addition of the squared deviations, we write $\Sigma(X - \mu)^2$. The symbol(**s**) $\underline{(\Sigma \text{ or } (X - \mu)^2)}$ tell(s) us that we are to add the quantities $\underline{(\Sigma \text{ or } (X - \mu)^2)}$.

$$\Sigma, \quad (X - \mu)^2$$

23. To complete the fourth step, we write $\Sigma(X - \mu)^2/N$. The numerator of this expression tells us to ___ the _____ deviations

from the mean, and the denominator tells us to divide this sum by N, which represents the _____ of values in the collection.

add, squared, number

24. In order to see how the various elements of the formula relate to the computations, we shall indicate them in the table used for the computations. Using 4, 10, and 16, complete the following table.

x	$x - \mu$	$(x - \mu)^2$
___	___	___
___	___	___
___	___	___

$$\Sigma X = \underline{\quad} \qquad \Sigma(X - \mu)^2 = \underline{\quad}$$

$$\mu = \frac{\Sigma X}{N} = \underline{\quad} \qquad \text{variance} = \frac{\Sigma(X - \mu)^2}{N} = \underline{\quad}$$

4   -6   36
10   0   0
16   6   36

$\Sigma X = 30$, $\Sigma(X - \mu)^2 = 72$

$\mu = 10$, variance = 24 $\overset{*}{\underset{*}{*}}$ 72/3 $\overset{*}{\underset{*}{*}}$

25. Since we refer to variance frequently, we need to use a symbol to represent it. Statisticians use σ^2 (lower case Greek letter sigma, squared) to stand for variance. So, instead of saying

$$\text{variance} = \frac{\Sigma(X - \mu)^2}{N}$$

we can write

$$\underline{\quad} = \frac{\Sigma(X - \mu)^2}{N}$$

σ^2

26. We have seen that the formula for the variance is $\sigma^2 = \Sigma(X - \mu)^2/N$. Notice that the left side of the equation tells us (a procedure for calculation/what is to be calculated) and the right side tells us (a procedure for calculation/what is to be calculated).

what is to be calculated,
a procedure for calculation

27. We return now to the two statistical populations representing
retail purchases by male and female customers. The data collection for males is x = 1, 3, 3, 3, 5 with a mean of μ = 3.
Use the formula $\sigma^2 = \Sigma(X - \mu)^2/N$ to find the variance of this
set: σ^2 = _____.

$$1\ 3/5\quad\overset{*}{\underset{*}{*}}\quad (4 + 0 + 0 + 0 + 4)/5 = 8/5\quad\overset{*}{\underset{*}{*}}$$

28. If we calculate the variance for the female customers, we obtain σ^2 = 11. In Frame 4, when we looked at a graph of
the two data collections,

we guessed that the dispersion for females was greater than
that for males. Now, without guessing, we can say that the
data for females have (more/less) dispersion because these
data have a larger _____.

more, variance

29. In order to measure the dispersion, we calculate _____
by finding the average of the _____ deviations from the
_____.

variance, squared, mean

30. Next we shall examine an alternative method for computing the
variance. You should keep in mind that although the method of
computation is different, the same numerical result for the
variance will be obtained. One way to write the alternative
formula for the variance is

$$\sigma^2 = \frac{\Sigma X^2}{N} - (\mu)^2 .$$

Notice that the first term on the right-hand side ($\Sigma X^2/N$) tells
us to find the sum of the _____ of each observation and
divide this sum by ___.

square, N

31. The second term, $(\mu)^2$, tells us to _____ the mean.

square

32. In order to use the alternative formula for the variance, we must first compute two quantities Σx^2 and μ. Of course we must also know the numerical value of ___ .

N

33. One way to find Σx^2 and Σx is to make up a table listing each observation and the square of each observation. For 4, 5, 5, 6, and 10 we have started such a table; you should complete it.

Observation x	Observation Squared x^2
4	16
5	25
___	___
___	___
___	___

5	25
6	36
10	100

34. From the completed table we may find Σx, μ, and Σx^2.

x	x^2
4	16
5	25
5	25
6	36
10	100

$$\Sigma x = \underline{\quad\quad} \quad \underline{\quad\quad} = \Sigma x^2.$$

$$\mu = \underline{\quad\quad}$$

30, 202

$\mu = 6$

35. From the calculations made in the last frame, we may use the formula

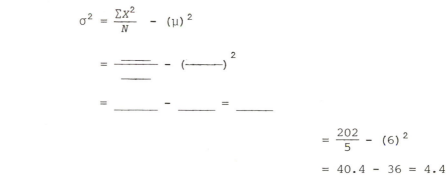

$$\sigma^2 = \frac{\Sigma X^2}{N} - (\mu)^2$$

$$= \frac{\underline{\hspace{1cm}}}{\underline{\hspace{1cm}}} - (\underline{\hspace{1cm}})^2$$

$$= \underline{\hspace{1cm}} - \underline{\hspace{1cm}} = \underline{\hspace{1cm}}$$

$$= \frac{202}{5} - (6)^2$$

$$= 40.4 - 36 = 4.4$$

36. In Frames 15 and 16, we computed the variance of 4, 5, 5, 6, and 10 by a different method. Turn back to these frames and study the method of computation and the numerical results. For the data collection of our example, we conclude the two methods of computing the variance produce (the same/a different) numerical value for the variance.

the same

37. Both formulas

$$\sigma^2 = \frac{\Sigma (X - \mu)^2}{N} \quad \text{and} \quad \sigma^2 = \frac{\Sigma X^2}{N} - (\mu)^2$$

produce the same numerical result for a given data collection. Notice the first formula requires us to compute the deviation of each observation from the mean. Unless these deviations are whole numbers, the (first/second) formula will be easier to use.

second

38. In a typical sampling situation we do not know the population mean nor the population variance; consequently we must alter the method of computing the variance when we work with sample data. The numerator for the formula for the population variance is $\Sigma (X - \mu)^2$. The numerator for the sample variance is $\Sigma (X - \overline{X})^2$. In the latter case, we use ($\overline{X}$ or μ) because the population mean usually (is/is not) known to us in a sampling situation.

$\overline{X}$, is not

39. The formulas for the population and sample variances are

$$\sigma^2 = \frac{\Sigma(X - \mu)^2}{N} \quad \text{and} \quad s^2 = \frac{\Sigma(X - \overline{X})^2}{n - 1} \; .$$

We use the symbol _____ to represent the sample variance.

$$s^2$$

40. The denominator in the formula for the sample variance is $n - 1$. In a later chapter, we shall see why the denominator is $n - 1$ rather than n. For now, it is important to remember that _(n or N)_ is the number of values in a sample.

$$n$$

41. The population of purchases for female customers in our sales example is 4, 6, 8, 10, 10, and 16. Suppose each of these values is written on a card. The cards are then shuffled with the numbers face down. Three cards are then selected at random and the following sample values are observed: 10, 16, 4. The sample mean of these values is $\overline{X} =$ _____ .

10

42. The sum of the squared deviations from the sample mean is:

$$\Sigma(X - \overline{X})^2 = (10 - 10)^2 + (\underline{} - \underline{})^2 + (\underline{} - \underline{})^2$$

$$= 0 + \underline{} + \underline{}$$

$$= \underline{}$$

$$= (10 - 10)^2 + (16 - 10)^2 + (4 - 10)^2$$
$$= \quad 0 + 36 + 36$$
$$= \quad 72$$

43. The formula for the sample variance is $s^2 = \dfrac{\Sigma(X - \overline{X})^2}{n - 1}$. Since there are three values in the sample, the sample variance is

$$s^2 \;=\; \frac{\overline{}}{\underline{}} \;=\; \underline{}$$

$$= \frac{72}{3 - 1} = 36$$

44. The formula in the last frame is easy to use when the deviations are whole numbers. When this is not the case, it is easier to

use the alternative formula $s^2 = \dfrac{\Sigma x^2 - n\overline{X}^2}{n - 1}$.   To assure ourselves that the two formulas produce the same result, we shall
calculate the sample variance with the same sample data, 10,
16, and 4.   For these data,

$$\Sigma x^2 = (10)^2 + (\underline{\quad})^2 + (\underline{\quad})^2$$

$$= 100 + \underline{\quad} + \underline{\quad}$$

$$= \underline{\quad\quad}$$

$$= (10)^2 + (16)^2 + (4)^2$$
$$= 100 + 256 + 16$$
$$= 372$$

45. Since $\overline{X} = 10$, $\Sigma x^2 = 372$, and $n = 3$, the sample variance is

$$s^2 = \frac{\Sigma x^2 - n\overline{X}^2}{n - 1} \quad = \quad \frac{\underline{\quad} - \underline{\quad}}{\underline{\quad}} = \underline{\quad\quad}$$

$$\frac{372 - 3(10)^2}{3 - 1} = \frac{72}{2} = 36$$

46. In Frame 43, we obtained (the same/a different) result using
(the same/a different) method.

                                          the same, a different

47. The standard deviation is another measure of dispersion. It
is the positive square root of the variance. For example, the
population standard deviation for the female sales data is the
positive square root of the variance ($\sigma^2 = 11$). Thus, the
standard deviation is $\sigma = \sqrt{11}$. The symbol for the population
standard deviation is (σ or σ^2).

                                                              σ

48. We found the sample variance to be $s^2 = 36$. The sample standard deviation is $s = \sqrt{\underline{\quad}} = \underline{\quad}$.

                                                    $\sqrt{36}$, 6

49. As we shall see in future chapters, we shall need to use both
the standard deviation and the variance. Remember, when you
need to compute the standard deviation, first compute the
_____ and then find the positive _____ _____ .

                                          variance, square root

CHAPTER 3.   SELF-CORRECTING EXERCISES

Note: In some of the exercises that follow, you should consider the data shown in Table 3-1 to be a population. For discussion purposes, you should consider the data on the patient records enclosed in rectangles as sample data. In practical problems, the number of values in a population is often much larger than the example shown here. For example, one hospital might have 20,000 patient records over a 1-year period. We use a small population for discussion purposes. (In later chapters, we shall see how some of the computations made in these exercises must be modified when the number of values in the sample is large in comparison with the number of values in the population.)

3.1 Measuring Central Location (the mean)

a. What is the arithmetic mean age of the population?

b. What is the arithmetic mean age of the female population?

c. What is the arithmetic mean age of the male population?

d. What is the sample mean age?

e. Compare your answers in (a) and (d). Explain any similarities or differences.

3.2 The Mean from Grouped Data

The ages of persons shopping in a supermarket on a certain day are shown below. We wish to consider these ages as a population. Use these data for parts a-d.

Age	f
4-13	7
14-23	6
24-33	7
34-43	12
44-53	5
54-63	2
64-73	1
	40

a. What formula for the mean should be used in this situation? Define each of the symbols in the formula.

TABLE 3-1 Patient Records for March 20, 1977

	Castro, J. E.	Palmer, R. A.	Barry, T. A.	Caruso, L. A.	Gonzales, T. F.	Smith, A. R.	LaSalle, R. O.
Social Security Number	843 756 123	256 732 190	735 421 930	302 465 120	125 673 491	742 124 394	563 732 542
Time of Admission	7:22 A.M.	8:30 A.M.	8:42 A.M.	9:00 A.M.	9:30 A.M.	10:32 A. M.	11:00 A. M.
Year of Birth	1967	1917	1917	1937	1957	1947	1947
Sex	Female	Female	Male	Male	Male	Female	Female
Age (Years)	10	60	60	40	20	30	30
Method of Admission	Emergency	Normal	Emergency	Normal	Normal	Emergency	Normal
Height (Inches)	54	64	67	70	72	61	60
Weight (Pounds)	52.01	184.50	173.49	173.50	173.51	140.09	122.72
Temperature	98.9	98.6	101.1	98.6	98.7	98.5	98.6
Status	Critical	Good	Fair	Good	Good	Critical	Fair
Primary Diagnosis	Laceration	Sprain	Diabetes mellitus	Appendicitis	Hypertension	Congestive heart failure	Infected ulcers
Disease Code	882	8478	2509	541	401	4270	7071

b. Use this formula to define the mean.

c. The original observations used to develop this frequency
   distribution (see page 18) indicate that $\Sigma x = 1302$. Compute
   the mean based on this information.

d. Compare your answers for (b) and (c). Give an explanation
   for the comparison.

e. We find that when data are grouped in many-value classes,
   measures of central tendency such as the mean are only approximations to the result that would be obtained if the
   original observations were used. The question of why we
   group data into many-value classes naturally arises. Give
   as many reasons as you can why grouping is useful. (For
   purposes of discussion, suppose your task were to analyze
   the ages of all persons living in the United States.)

f. Sometimes students are tempted to look at a distribution
   such as the following

x	f
1	98
2	1
3	1
	100

and claim (erroneously) that the mean for this distribution
is 2. What error is being made? How many 1's, 2's and 3's
were present in the original observations? What is the
actual mean of this distribution?

3.3 Measuring Central Location (the median)   (Refer to Table 3-1 on page 43.)

a. What is the median age of the population?

b. Compare the mean (see Question 1) and median ages of the
   population. In general, would you expect the mean and median to be equal? Why or why not?

c. What is the median age of the female population?

d. What is the median age of the male population?

e. What is the median age of patients admitted on a nonemer-
   gency basis?

3.4 Measuring Central Location (the mode)   (Refer to Table 3-1 on page 43.)

    a. What is the mode of the body temperatures for the population?

    b. What is the mode of the age data for the population?

3.5 Measuring Dispersion (the population variance)

    a. If the formula $\sigma^2 = \Sigma(X - \mu)^2/N$ is to be used in computing the variance, what is the first step in the computation?

    b. Use the formula in (a) and compute the variance for the population of male ages in Table 3-1 on page 43.

    c. If the formula $\sigma^2 = \dfrac{\Sigma x^2}{N} - (\mu)^2$ is to be used to find the variance, what quantities should be computed first?

    d. Use the formula in (c) to compute the variance for the population of male ages given in Table 3-1 on page 43.

    e. Compare the answers for (b) and (d).   Should your answers be the same or different?

    f. If you had to compute the variance for the collection of body temperatures, which formula would you use and why?

3.6 Measuring Dispersion (the sample variance)   (Refer to the sample age data given in Table 3-1 on page 43.   In Parts a and b, be sure to compute the value of $\bar{X}$ to two decimal places.   If you are not using a calculator, you may wish to use the table on pages 482-490.

    a. Use the formula $s^2 = \dfrac{\Sigma(X - \bar{X})^2}{n - 1}$ to compute the sample variance for the height data.

    b. Use the formula $s^2 = \dfrac{\Sigma x^2 - n(\bar{X})^2}{n - 1}$ to compute the sample variance for the height data.

    c. How do your answers for (a) and (b) compare?   Explain.

    d. Rework (b) using $\bar{X}$ computed to one decimal place.

    e. How do your answers for Parts c of Question 5 and b of this exercise compare?   Explain any similarities or differences.

3.7 Square Roots

a. Follow the instructions for the table on pages 482-490 to find the square roots of 4, 36, 144, 3600, 0.0144, and 0.0036.

b. Use the table to find the square roots of 3,159,431.4, 755,500, and 0.00000456501.

3.8 Measuring Dispersion (the standard deviation)

a. What computation must immediately precede the computation of the standard deviation?

b. Compute the population standard deviation of the age data used in Part b of Question 5.

3.9 Standard Scores After measuring the body weights and temperatures of a very large number of patients, the hospital staff determines the mean body temperature to be $98.6^{O}F$ with a standard deviation of $1/3^{O}F$. For body weights, the mean is 175 lb with a standard deviation of 25 lb. The hospital staff consider that any patient with a temperature or weight more than two standard deviations above the mean is "abnormal."

a. A patient is admitted with a temperature of $99.5^{O}F$ and a weight of 200 lb. Are this patient's temperature and weight normal? Explain.

b. Assume that the distribution of body weights follows the bell-shaped normal distribution shown in the diagram (page 74) in the text. What percentage of patients will have a body weight in the range of 150 to 200 lb? What percentage will be in the range of 125 to 225 lb?

3.10 The Meaning of Variance The following two populations (A and B) are to be used in this exercise.

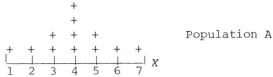

Population A

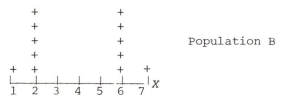

Both populations have the same mean, which is 4.

a. For integer data, the *range* of a population is the largest
   observation minus the smallest observation plus 1.   The
   range is sometimes used as a measure of dispersion.   What is
   the range for each population?

b. From the graphs, judge which population is clustered more
   tightly about its mean.

c. What is the variance for each population?

d. Which measure of dispersion (range or variance) more ade-
   quately describes the dispersion in the population?   Why?

CHAPTER 3.   ACHIEVEMENT TEST

1. A population of sales figures is $7, $10, $8, and $4.   What is
   the population mean?

2. What symbol should be used to designate the answer to Question
   1?

3. If the data in Question 1 were for a sample instead of a population, how would your answser to Question 2 change?

Use this frequency table to answer Questions 4 and 5.

Sales	Frequency	Midvalue	Estimated Class Total
1- 5	4	?	?
6-10	3	8	?
11-15	3	?	?

4. What is the midvalue of the class 1-5?

5. What is the estimated class total for the class 6-10?

6. Use this frequency table to determine the sample mean.

Age	f	Midvalue (m)	Estimated Total (fm)
1-10	3	5.5	?
11-20	5	15.5	?
21-30	2	25.5	?

7. In Question 6, three observations are in the class 1-10. From the frequency table, can you determine the numerical values of these observations?

8. What is the median of these data: 4, 7, 1, 0, 5?

9. What is the median of these data: 6, 9, 11, 14?

10. What is the mode of these data: 4, 1, 5, 1, 8, 3?

11. In this frequency diagram, is X, Y, or Z the mode?

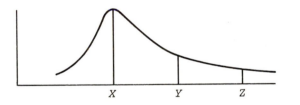

12. A population consists of the values 4, 3, 3, 0, 5. For this population, $\mu = 3$. What is the population variance?

13. What symbol should be used for the population standard deviation?

14. A sample variance is found to be 169. What is the sample standard deviation?

15. What symbol should be used to represent the quantity found in Question 14?

16. A sample of four observations produces $\Sigma X = 16$ and $\Sigma X^2 = 1084$. What is the sample variance?

17. Use the frequency table below to compute the sample mean.

Value Class	Frequency
0- 4	6
5- 9	2
10-14	2

18. The verbal portion of the Scholastic Aptitude Test is designed to have a mean of 500 and a standard deviation of 100. What is the standard score of students whose score on this test is 720?

CHAPTER 3.   STUDENT RECORD AND REFERENCE SHEET

Darken the square corresponding to each test item you answered *incorrectly*.   References indicate the topics you should study. See Chapter 1 of this volume for details.

Test Item	Diagnostic Test	Achievement Test	Text References	Self-Correcting Exercise References	Program Set References
1	☐	☐	51–56	3.1	3.1
2	☐	☐	51–56	3.1	3.1
3	☐	☐	51–56	3.1	3.1
4	☐	☐	51–56	3.2	——
5	☐	☐	51–56	3.2	——
6	☐	☐	51–56	3.2	——
7	☐	☐	51–56	3.2	——
8	☐	☐	58–60	3.3	——
9	☐	☐	58–60	3.3	——
10	☐	☐	62–63	3.4	——
11	☐	☐	64	—	——
12	☐	☐	66–75	3.5	3.2
13	☐	☐	66–75	3.5	3.2
14	☐	☐	66–75	3.6	3.2
15	☐	☐	66–75	3.6	3.2
16	☐	☐	66–75	3.6	3.2
17	☐	☐	66–75	—	3.2
18	☐	☐	73–75	3.9	——

4

PROBABILITY

CHAPTER 4. DIAGNOSTIC TEST

For the situations described in Questions 1-3, give the method used to assign probabilities.

1. The probability that the Bears will beat the Rams tomorrow is 0.60.

2. Since there are 52 cards in a deck of cards, the probability of drawing the ace of spades is 1/52.

3. The finished goods inventory of spark plugs has 1 million items. After examining 100 of these spark plugs, 2 were found to be defective. The probability of selecting a defective spark plug is 0.02.

The following table shows the classification of 1000 employees of a corporation by sex and method of wage payment (hourly or weekly). Use this table to answers Questions 4-10. For these questions, assume that an employee is to be selected at random.

	Male (M)	Female (F)	Totals
Hourly (H)	300	500	800
Weekly (W)	50	150	200
	350	650	1000

4. What is the probability that an employee selected at random is male and is paid on an hourly basis?

5. $P(W) = ?$

6. $P(W \text{ and } F) = ?$

7. What is the marginal probability of selecting a female?

8. What is the joint probability of selecting a weekly employee and a female?

9. An employee selected at random is a male.   What is the probability that he is paid on a weekly basis?

10. $P(M \mid W) = ?$

11. Two components in a stereo amplifier have the following characteristics.   The probability that the first component fails is $P(C_1) = 0.10$.   The probability that the first and second components fail is 0.08.   A technician examines an amplifier of this type and determines that the first component has failed. What is the probability that the technician will find the second component has failed?

12. A soft-drink machine dispenses three types of beverages (events A, B, and C).   The probabilities that a customer purchases each drink are $P(A) = 0.20$, $P(B) = 0.70$, and $P(C) = 0.10$.   What is the probability that a customer purchases A or C?

13. For the situation described in the last problem, what is the probability that a customer does *not* purchase A?

14. A contractor is bidding on two jobs.   The probability that the contractor gets job A is 0.10 and the probability of job B is 0.02.   The probability that the contractor gets both jobs is 0.04.   What is the probability that the contractor gets job A or job B?

15. If $P(C) = 0.2$ and $P(D \mid C) = 0.8$, what is the value of $P(D \text{ and } C)$?

16. The following joint probability table shows the relationship between sex and salary for a large corporation.

	Sex	
Salary	Male	Female
Above median for industry	0.450	0.300
Below median for industry	0.150	0.100

Are sex and salary independent or dependent events? Show the calculations to support your answer.

In a minor league in baseball, the league championship is determined by play-off series of two or three games. The champion is the team that wins two games. The tree diagram below shows the outcomes and appropriate probabilities for two teams, A and B. The notation A_1 means team A wins the first game, B_2 means team B wins the second game, and so on. Use this diagram to answer Questions 17-21.

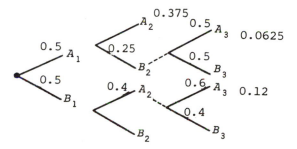

17. List all of the sequences of the mutually exclusive event that team A can win in exactly 3 games.

18. What is the probability that team A will not win in exactly 2 games?

19. What is the probability that team B only wins 1 game?

20. What is the probability that team B wins in exactly 2 games?

21. The probability that the play-offs last exactly 2 games is 0.575. If the series in fact lasts 2 games, what is the probability that team A will win?

CHAPTER 4.   SELF-CORRECTING EXERCISES

4.1 Views of Probability A die has 6 sides designated by the numbers 1 through 6. The experiment is *roll the die*. Event *A* is *side 1 is rolled*.

  a. What are the elements in the sample space? What is their relationship to the experiment?

  b. If all sample points are considered equally likely, what is the numerical value of $P(A)$?

c. The experiment is repeated 1000 times and the results are recorded as follows.

Side	Frequency
1	140
2	180
3	130
4	192
5	184
6	174
	1000

Use the relative frequency method to find $P(A)$. Is this value of $P(A)$ exact or approximate? Explain.

d. An observer believes the probability of rolling a 1 is related to the position of the roller's hand above the table and to which hand the roller uses. After assessing these factors, the probability 0.75 is assigned to event A for the next roll. What method of probability assignment is being made?

e. The three methods of assigning probabilities produced different numerical results. Is anything wrong? If so, what? What is required of all three methods of probability assignments?

f. Briefly discuss some of the circumstances under which you might use each of the three methods of probability assignments.

4.2 Joint, Marginal, and Conditional Probabilities The table shows a two-way classification of a 500-person labor force. Assume every person in the labor force has an equal chance of being selected in the experiment *select an individual from the labor force*.

Labor Force

	Skill Level		
Employment Status	Skilled (B_1)	Unskilled (B_2)	Total
Employed (A_1)	172	228	400
Unemployed (A_2)	28	72	100
Total	200	300	500

In this question, make all the computations based on the frequencies given in the table.

a. Find all of the joint probabilities for this experiment. Display your results in a table.

b. Find all the marginal probabilities for this experiment. Display your results in the table for your answer to (a).

c. In your own words, explain the meaning of the event A_2 and B_2. Does this differ from the event B_2 and A_2? What is the numerical value of $P(A_2 \text{ and } B_2)$?

d. Explain any difference between the statements: A_2 and B_2 and $P(A_2 \text{ and } B_2)$.

e. In your own words, describe the events in the probabilities $P(A_2 \mid B_2)$ and $P(B_2 \mid A_2)$. Are the events the same? What are the numerical values of these probabilities? Are the two values equal?

f. Compute the values of $P(A_1 \mid B_1)$, $P(A_2 \mid B_1)$ and $P(A_1 \mid B_2)$, and $P(A_2 \mid B_2)$. Display your results in a table similar to the one used in (a). Be sure to label the given events. What does the table tell you about unemployment for skilled and unskilled workers?

4.3 Joint, Marginal and Conditional Probabilities   A publisher of a weekly tax letter promotes this product by means of a brochure. The following table shows the joint probabilities of firms who subscribe and who do not subscribe to the tax letter with the firms who have and have not received the brochure.

	Received Brochure (R)	Did Not Receive Brochure (R')
Subscriber (S)	0.30	0.10
Nonsubscribers (S')	0.20	0.40

a. What is the probability that a firm is a subscriber? A nonsubscriber? Has received the brochure? Has not received the brochure? What are these probabilities called?

b. What event has the largest joint probability?

c. Equation 4-2 in the text shows how to compute conditional probabilities from joint and marginal probabilities.

Equation 4-2 is $P(A \mid B) = \dfrac{P(A \text{ and } B)}{P(B)}$. Use this equation to show how to compute $P(R \mid S)$, $P(R' \mid S)$, $P(R \mid S')$, $P(R' \mid S')$, $P(S \mid R)$, $P(S' \mid R)$, $P(S \mid R')$, and $P(S' \mid R')$ in terms of the appropriate joint and marginal probabilities. (In this part of the problem, you should record the values for the right-hand side of Equation 4-2. We shall find the numerical values in Part d.)

d. Use the results for (a) and (c) to find the numerical values of the eight conditional probabilities listed in (c).

e. What do the results of (b), (c) and (d) seem to indicate about subscription to the tax letter and the advertising brochure?

4.4 Addition Laws   A draw is to be made from an ordinary deck of playing cards. Let A be the event *an ace*, S be the event *a spade*, H be the event *a heart,* and A and S be the event *ace of spades*. Given the probabilities $P(A)$ = 4/52, $P(S)$ = 13/52, $P(A \text{ and } S)$ = 1/52, and $P(H)$ = 13/52, find the following probabilities:

a. $P(A \text{ or } S)$

b. $P(H \text{ and } S)$

c. $P(H \text{ or } S)$

d. Are the events A and S mutually exclusive?

e. Are the events H and S mutually exclusive?

4.5 Addition Laws   If a firm selects one of its employees at random, the probability of a female is 0.25, the probability of a college graduate is 0.15, and the probability of a female college graduate is 0.10.

a. What is the probability that the employee selected will be either a female or a college graduate?

b. Are the events *female* and *college graduate* mutually exclusive?

4.6 Multiplication Probability Relations   Students in a college are classified as seniors (S) or nonseniors (S') and as males (M) or females (F). The probability of selecting a male from this college is 0.60. One-third of the males are seniors and one-fourth of the females are seniors.

a. What is the probability of selecting a senior male?

b. What is the probability of selecting a senior female?

4.7 Independence   The marginal probabilities for the situation described in Question 4.3 are repeated here for convenience:

	Received Brochure (R)	Did Not Receive Brochure (R')
Subscribers (S)		0.4
Nonsubscribers (S')		0.6
	0.5	0.5

a. Assume the two classifications are independent and calculate the joint probabilities under this assumption.

b. The true joint probabilities for this situation are shown in Question 4.3.   Compare the true joint probabilities with the ones you found in (a). Was the assumption of independence correct?

4.8 Independence   An opinion poll asks the following two questions:

1. Do you agree or disagree that the president is doing a good job?

2. Do you agree or disagree that the vice president is doing a good job?

The results of both questions were cross-classified by sex and are presented below as joint probability tables:

		Males	Females
QUESTION 1:			
	Agree	0.225	0.525
	Disagree	0.075	0.175
QUESTION 2:			
	Agree	0.225	0.175
	Disagree	0.075	0.525

a. For the first question, compute the conditional probabilities of *agree* and *disagree* given *males*. Compute the conditional probabilities of *agree* and *disagree* given *females*. Compute the marginal probabilities of *agree* and *disagree.* Plot the probabilities on the appropriate grids below.

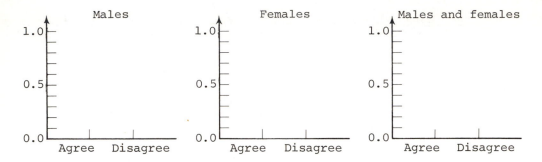

b. Repeat the calculatons for Part a using the joint probability table for the second question. Plot the results on the appropriate grids below.

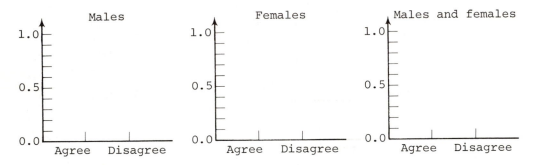

c. Are sex and opinion independent for the first question? For the second question?

d. If two variables are independent, what seems to be the relationship between conditional and marginal probabilities?

4.9 Aids in Probability Calculations   A manufacturer receives parts from three suppliers (S_1, S_2, or S_3). The parts are classified as defective (D) or nondefective (N). For this situation, the following probabilities are known: $P(D) = 0.11$, $P(S_1) = 0.30$, $P(S_2) = 0.40$, $P(D \text{ and } S_1) = 0.04$, and $P(D \mid S_2) = 0.15$.

a. Compute $P(D \text{ and } S_2)$.

b. In this cross-classified table, write all of the probabilities that are known or that you have computed so far.

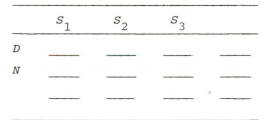

	S_1	S_2	S_3	
D	___	___	___	___
N	___	___	___	___
	___	___	___	___

c. Explain how to find any probabilities that are missing from the table.

d. For (a), could you have computed the joint probability of (D and S_2) by using $P(D$ and $S_2) = P(S_2 \mid D) * P(D)$?

4.10 <u>Aids in Probability Calculations</u>   A publishing house uses three firms, A, B, and C for typesetting. Twenty percent of the typesetting jobs are given to A and 50% are given to B. For jobs given to A, 1% will have errors. Six percent of the jobs given to B will have errors. Eight percent of the jobs given to C will have errors.

a. Draw a probability tree that describes this process. Use the first set of branches to describe the typesetter (A, B, or C). Use the second set of branches to describe whether or not a job from a typesetter contained an error (E) or no error (N).

b. Use the tree to help you list the mutually exclusive ways of obtaining a job with an error.

c. What is the probability that a job from A has no errors?

d. Indicate the appropriate marginal and conditional probabilities on the tree. Compute all of the joint probabilities.

e. What is the probability that a job has an error? What is the probability that a job has no error?

f. If a job has an error, what is the probability that it came from A? From B? From C?

g. Display the marginal and joint probabilities found in this exercise in a joint probability table. Explain how the tree diagram and the table are related.

CHAPTER 4.   ACHIEVEMENT TEST

For the events described in Questions 1-3, give the method (or methods) that might be used to assign probabilities to the given events.

1. John Jones will buy a new Cadillac next month.

2. A typist makes an error.

3. One draws the ace of spades.

The following table shows the results of an opinion survey in which employees were asked whether or not they favor flexible work schedules. The employees are cross-classified by method of compensation (hourly, weekly, or monthly).

	Hourly (H)	Weekly (W)	Monthly (M)	
Favor (F)	?	?	0.16	0.60
Oppose (O)	0.32	?	0.04	?
	0.40	0.40	?	

Use this table to answer Questions 4-10. For these questions, assume that an employee is to be selected at random.

4. What is the probability that an employee selected at random favors flexible work schedules and is paid hourly?

5. $P(M)$ = ?

6. $P(W$ and $F)$ = ?

7. What is the marginal probability of selecting an employee who opposes flexible work schedules?

8. What is the joint probability of selecting an employee who is paid weekly and opposes flexible schedules?

9. An employee selected at random is paid monthly. What is the probability that this employee favors flexible scheduling?

10. $P(M \mid F)$ = ?

11. An assembly has two components. The probability that the first component fails is $P(C_1)$ = 0.30. The probability that the first *and* second components fail is 0.06. If the first

component is found to have failed, what is the probability that the second component will fail?

12. A state agency is going to award a highway contract to one of three bidders, A, B, or C. If the probability that A wins the contract is 0.2, the probability that B wins the contract is 0.5, and the probability that B or C wins the contract is 0.8, what is the probability that A or C wins the contract?

13. For the situation described in Question 12, what is the probability that A does *not* get the contract?

14. The probability that a consumer will purchase product X is 0.25, the probability of product Y is 0.15, and the probability of both X and Y is 0.20. What is the probability that the consumer will purchase X or Y?

15. If $P(R) = 0.8$ and $P(S \mid R) = 0.2$, find $P(R$ and $S)$.

16. The following joint probability table shows the joint probabilities for the age and sex of employees of a government agency.

Age	Sex Male	Female
Below 45 years	0.125	0.250
Above 45 years	0.250	0.375

Are age and sex independent? Give calculations to support your answer.

Two computer files contain customer social security numbers, last names, and birthdays. The entries on the two files are to be matched. A match is considered valid if exactly two of the three variables (such as social security number and last name) have identical values. The process is shown in the probability tree. The notation M_1 means *social security numbers are the same in both files*, N_2 means *last names are not the same in both files*, and so forth. Use the tree diagram to answer the rest of the questions.

17. List all of the mutually exclusive event sequences in which a match of exactly two variables is made by examining all three variables.

18. What is the probability of obtaining *no* match by examining exactly two variables?

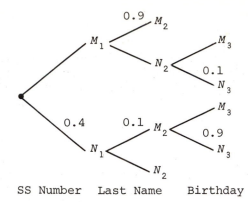

SS Number   Last Name   Birthday

19. What is the probability that social security numbers are not the same?

20. What is the probability that a match is made in examining exactly two variables?

21. The probability that exactly two variables are examined is 0.9. If exactly two variables are examined, what is the probability of a match?

CHAPTER 4. STUDENT RECORD AND REFERENCE SHEET

Darken the square corresponding to each test item you answered *incorrectly*. References indicate the topics you should study. See Chapter 1 of this volume for details.

Item	Diagnostic Test	Achievement Test	Text References	Self-Correcting Exercise References
1	☐	☐	88- 92	4.1
2	☐	☐	88- 92	4.1
3	☐	☐	88- 92	4.1
4	☐	☐	92- 95	4.2, 4.3
5	☐	☐	92- 95	4.2, 4.3
6	☐	☐	92- 95	4.2, 4.3
7	☐	☐	92- 95	4.2, 4.3
8	☐	☐	92- 95	4.2, 4.3
9	☐	☐	92- 95	4.2, 4.3
10	☐	☐	92- 95	4.2, 4.3
11	☐	☐	95- 95	4.2, 4.3
12	☐	☐	97-103	4.4
13	☐	☐	97-103	4.4
14	☐	☐	97-103	4.5
15	☐	☐	97-103	4.6
16	☐	☐	97-103	4.7, 4.8
17	☐	☐	105-111	4.10
18	☐	☐	105-111	4.10
19	☐	☐	105-111	4.10
20	☐	☐	105-111	4.10
21	☐	☐	105-111	4.10

5

DISCRETE PROBABILITY DISTRIBUTIONS

Suppose a group of people are seated in a lecture hall.   For
Questions 1-3, tell which situations involve the concept of a
random variable.   Justify your answers.

1. The eye color of a person selected at random.

2. The age of a person selected at random.

3. Your age.

Listed below are the names and grades for 5 students.   Use this
information to answer Questions 4-8.

Name	Letter Grade	Numerical Grade (x)
Angelo	A	4
Smith	C	2
Carpenter	A	4
Zimmer	D	1
Jones	C	2

4. If X is used to signify the numerical grade of a student selected at random, find the probability distribution of X.

5. Find the cumulative probability function of X.

6. Write an expression in terms of X for the event *a student selected at random has a grade of C or lower*.

7. What is the probability of the event described in Question 6?

8. $P(X = 2) = ?$

A manufacturer produces two products, A and B. The demands for the two products on any day are shown in the table below, together with their joint probabilities. Use this table to answer Questions 9 and 10.

Demand for B	Demand for A x_A		
x_B	1	2	3
0	0.21	0.04	0.02
1	0.04	0.24	0.12
2	0.03	0.10	0.20

9. Let T be the total demand for A and B. In terms of demand for A and B, what circumstances would cause a total demand of $T = 3$?

10. $P(T = 2) = ?$

11. For the probability distribution given here, find μ.

x	$P(x)$
10	1/2
20	1/4
30	1/4

12. For the probability distribution given in Question 11, find the value of $E(X)$.

13. The mean of the probability distribution given below is $\mu = 2$. What is the variance?

x	$P(x)$
1	1/2
2	1/4
4	1/4

14. For the situation in Question 13, what is the value of $E(X^2)$?

15. For a Bernoulli random variable, the probability of a success is 0.8. What is the standard deviation of this random variable?

16. Three trials are to be conducted from a Bernoulli process. List all of the possible sequences of outcomes that would produce exactly two successes.

17. 4! = ?

18. $_5C_3$ = ?

19. A Bernoulli process has a probability of a success of 1/3. If three trials are to be made, find the probability of exactly two successes.

20. Use the binomial table to find $P(3 \mid 10, 0.25)$.

21. Five trials of a Bernoulli process are to be observed. If the probability of a success on each trial is 0.25, what is the probability of two or fewer successes?

22. What is the mean of a binomial distribution for which $\pi = 0.25$ and $n = 20$?

23. What is the standard deviation of binomial distribution for which $\pi = 0.5$ and $n = 16$?

PROGRAM SET 5.1   Sample Space and Random Variables

1. Recall that a *sample space* is the set of all possible outcomes of an experiment. Suppose we have a die that is painted a different color on each side. If our experiment is to roll the die and see which face turns up, we may call the set

            red, blue, green, yellow, orange, black

   a sample _____.

                                                                    space

2. Notice that the elementary outcomes in the sample space (are/ are not) certain and they (are/are not) numerical.

                                                        are not, are not

3. Frequently, we need to assign numerical values to the elements of a sample space. Suppose the painted die is used in a game in which the following points are assigned for each color:

Color	Points
Red	0
Blue	1
Green	0
Yellow	2
Orange	0
Black	0

Notice that each element in the sample space is assigned a _____ _____.

numerical value

4. If the die is rolled and the outcome is *blue*, we know that the number of points scored is ____.

5. We frequently need to assign numerical values to the elements in the sample space. Whenever you assign numerical values to elements in a sample space, you must be particularly careful to assign a numerical _____ to each _____ in the sample space.

value, element

6. If we are to assign numerical values to the elements in a sample space, we must have a rule for doing so. In our example, the rule is given in Frame 3. This rule tells us to assign 0 to the element *red*, ____ to the element *blue*, ____ to the element *green*, and so on.

1, 0

7. When the die is tossed, it is (certain/uncertain) which color face will turn up. Therefore the numerical value that will occur is (certain/uncertain).

uncertain, uncertain

8. If the numerical values of a variable are uncertain events, the variable is called a random variable. In the following table for the die toss, the (color/value assigned) constitutes the random variable.

Elements in Sample Space	Value Assigned
Red	0
Blue	1
Green	0
Yellow	2
Orange	0
Black	0

value assigned

9. The random variable in the example of the die toss is (discrete/continuous). It can be defined as $X:x =$ _____ .

discrete; 0, 1, 2

10. Frequently, we are more interested in the assigned numerical values than we are in the elements of the sample space. In such cases, we collect all the elements in the sample space which are assigned the same numerical value. In the diagram here, draw arrows to indicate how the last three elements are collected.

Element	Value		$\underline{x}$
Red	0		
Blue	1		
Green	0		0
Yellow	2		1
Orange	0		2
Black	0		

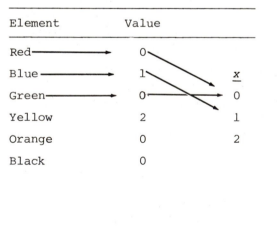

11. Thus, to say that the event $X = 0$ has occurred is exactly the same as saying either red or green or _____ or _____ has occurred.

orange, black

12. Thus, the probability that $X = 0$ (is/is not) the same as P(red
    or green or orange or black).

is

13. Since the elements in the sample space are mutually exclusive,
    we know that

$$P(\text{red or green or orange or black})$$
$$= P(\text{red}) + P(\underline{\hspace{1cm}}) + P(\underline{\hspace{1cm}}) + P(\underline{\hspace{1cm}})$$

green, orange, black

14. Suppose that each element in the sample space in Frame 8 is
    equally likely. Since there are ___ elements in the sample
    space, the probability that any particular element will occur
    is ____ .

6, 1/6

15. Using the results of the last two frames, we know that

$$P(\text{red or green or orange or black})$$
$$= \underline{\hspace{1cm}} + \underline{\hspace{1cm}} + \underline{\hspace{1cm}} + \underline{\hspace{1cm}} = \underline{\hspace{1cm}}$$

(1/6) + (1/6) + (1/6) + (1/6) = 4/6, or 2/3

16. In terms of the random variable X, we may say that the proba-
    bility that $X = 0$ is ____ .

2/3

17. The same result is shown in the diagram here. Use this diagram
    to find the probability that $X = 1$ and the probability that $X =$
    2.

Element	Value	x	$P(x)$	Probability of Element	Element
Red	0			1/6	Red
Blue	1			1/6	Blue
Green	0	0	4/6	1/6	Green
Yellow	2	1	____	1/6	Yellow
Orange	0	2	____	1/6	Orange
Black	0			1/6	Black

1/6, 1/6

18. The following table shows what is known as the *probability distribution of a random variable*. Notice the probability distribution of a random variable (does/does not) refer to the elements in the sample space. It (does/does not) refer to the numerical values assigned to the elements in the sample space.

x	P(x)
0	4/6
1	1/6
2	1/6

does not, does

19. In order to find the probability distribution of a random variable, we must have first assigned a _____ value to each element in the _____ _____.

numerical, sample space

20. We must also have assigned a _____ to each element of the sample space.

probability

21. Then we must collect the elements that have the same _____ value.

numerical

22. Finally, we find the probability of the collection of elements that have the same _____ _____.

numerical value

23. Let's consider another example. A salesperson determines that on any call, product A or B or C or D or E may be sold, or no sale may be made. The following table shows the commission for each product and the probability of each element. (Notice that the elements in this example do *not* have the same probability. On the right side of the table, A has the probability 0.1, B has the probability 0.2, and so forth.)

Element	Commission	x	$P(x)$	Probability of Element	Element
A	1	___	_____	0.1	A
B	3			0.2	B
C	2	___	_____	0.2	C
D	1	___	_____	0.1	D
E	3	___	_____	0.2	E
No Sale	0			0.2	No Sale

Use this information to find the probability distribution of the random variable *amount of commission*.

0	0.2
1	0.2 $\underset{*}{\overset{*}{*}}$ 0.1 + 0.1 $\underset{*}{\overset{*}{*}}$
2	0.2
3	0.4 $\underset{*}{\overset{*}{*}}$ 0.2 + 0.2 $\underset{*}{\overset{*}{*}}$

PROGRAM SET 5.2   Bernoulli Processes

1. Suppose we have a bin containing a very large number of parts of the same type. These parts are classified as "good" or "defective." We see that any part is in one of ____ possible classes.

2

2. Let us designate a random variable *x* to describe the two possible classifications. If the part is good, we will let *x* = 1; if the part is defective, we will let *x* = 0. We know that for a good part, *x* = ___ .

1

3. The following diagram gives the probabilities of selecting a good or defective part. In it, we can see that the probability of selecting a good part is _____ and the probability of selecting a defective part is _____ .

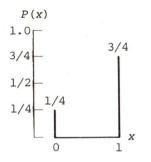

3/4, 1/4

4. Suppose the parts referred to in the last frames came from supplier A and that we also obtain parts from suppliers B and C.
   The following diagrams show the probabilities of selecting good
   or bad parts from the product of each supplier.

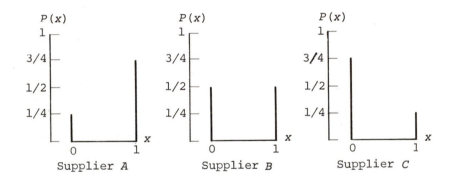

From the diagrams, we can see that the probability of obtaining
a good part from A is 3/4. The probability of obtaining a good
part from B is ____ and the probability of obtaining a good part
from C is ____.

1/2, 1/4

5. Since parts are classified as good or defective, the probability of a good part plus the probability of a defective part
   must equal ____.

1

6. If we know the probability of a good part from supplier A is
   3/4, then the probability of a defective part from this supplier must be ____.

1/4 ✻ 1 − (3/4) ✻

7. The diagrams in Frame 4 represent three different Bernoulli random variables. They are called Bernoulli random variables because there are only ____ (how many?) possible values of x.

2

8. Outcomes of random samples from large binary populations also constitute Bernoulli processes (after the mathematician Jacques Bernoulli). For each Bernoulli process, the values of $P(X = 0)$ and $P(X = 1)$ are related because $P(X = 0) + P(X = 1) = 1$. That is, if you are given $P(X = 1)$, you may compute $P(X = 0) =$ ___ - _____ .

$1 - P(X = 1)$

9. Since we may compute $P(X = 0)$ if we are given $P(X = 1)$, it is convenient to distinguish one Bernoulli random variable from another by the numerical value assigned to $P(X = 1)$. Let the numerical value assigned to $P(X = 1)$ be designated as π. Then $P(X = 1) = \pi$, and $P(X = 0) =$ _____ .

$1 - \pi$

10. From the diagrams in Frame 4, we see that for supplier B, $\pi =$ _____ and for supplier C, $\pi =$ ____ .

1/2, 1/4

11. Different Bernoulli random variables (do/do not) have the same numerical values assigned to x. Different Bernoulli random variables (may/may not) have different numerical values of π.

do *** x is always 0 or 1 ***, may

12. Evidently, we may distinguish one Bernoulli random variable from another by the numerical value of ___ .

π

13. Recall that the mean of a probability distribution is given by $\mu = \Sigma [x * P(x)]$. For the Bernoulli random variable,

x	$P(x)$
0	1/4
1	3/4

We see that $\mu =$ _____.

$$3/4 \; {}^{*}_{*} \; (0 * 1/4 + 1 * 3/4) \; {}^{*}_{*}$$

14. For supplier A, we see that μ (does/does not) equal π.

$$\text{does} \; {}^{*}_{*} \; \text{both values are } 3/4 \; {}^{*}_{*}$$

15. As we shall see, this result is always true. The following is the general form of the probability distribution for a Bernoulli random variable.

x	$P(x)$
0	$1 - \pi$
1	π

Use $\mu = \Sigma[x * P(x)]$ to find $\mu =$ _____.

$$\mu = \pi \; {}^{*}_{*} \; 0 * (1 - \pi) + 1 * \pi \; {}^{*}_{*}$$

16. The probability distributions for the three suppliers are given in Frame 4. Without making any computation, we know the mean for B is _____ and the mean for C is _____.

$$1/2, \; 1/4 \; {}^{*}_{*} \; (\mu = \pi = P(X = 1) \; {}^{*}_{*}$$

17. Evidently, π has two interpretations. These are _____ $= \pi$ and ____ $= \pi$.

$$P(X = 1), \; \mu$$

18. Recall the variance of a probability distribution is given by $\sigma^2 = \Sigma[(X - \mu)^2 * P(x)]$. For the distribution

x	$P(x)$
0	1/4
1	3/4

the variance is _____.

$$12/64, \text{ or } 3/16 \; {}^{*}_{*} \; (0 - 3/4)^2(1/4) + (1 - 3/4)^2(3/4) \; {}^{*}_{*}$$

19. As you may have guessed, we can find a formula for the variance of a Bernoulli random variable. In general, the distribution is given by:

x	$P(x)$
0	$1 - \pi$
1	π

We use $\sigma^2 = \Sigma[(X - \mu)^2 * P(X)]$ to find the variance. Since $\mu = \pi$,

$$\sigma^2 = (\underline{} - \underline{})^2 * (\underline{}) + (\underline{} - \underline{})^2 * \underline{}$$

$$(0 - \pi)^2 * (1 - \pi) + (1 - \pi)^2 * \pi$$

20. The result in the last frame may be simplified. Starting with

$$\sigma^2 = (0 - \pi)^2(1 - \pi) + (1 - \pi)^2\pi$$

we may factor $(1 - \pi)$. Thus

$$\sigma^2 = (1 - \pi)[(0 - \pi)^2 + (1 - \pi)\pi]$$

or

$$\sigma^2 = (1 - \pi)[\pi^2 + \pi - \pi^2]$$

Thus $\sigma^2 =$ \underline{}.

$$(1 - \pi)\pi$$

21. For supplier A, $\pi = 3/4$. Use $\sigma^2 = (1 - \pi)\pi$ to find $\sigma^2 =$ \underline{}.

$$3/16 \; {}^{*}_{*}\!\!{}^{*} \; (1 - 3/4)(3/4) \; {}^{*}_{*}\!\!{}^{*}$$

22. In Frame 18, we found (the same/a different) result by (the same/a different) method.

the same, a different

23. We may use the formula $\sigma^2 = (1 - \pi)\pi$ to find the variance for each distribution from the information given in Frame 4. For supplier B, $\sigma^2 =$ \underline{} and for supplier C, $\sigma^2 =$ \underline{}.

$$1/4 \; {}^{*}_{*}\!\!{}^{*} \; (1 - 1/2)(1/2) \; {}^{*}_{*}\!\!{}^{*}, \; 3/16 \; {}^{*}_{*}\!\!{}^{*} \; (1 - 1/4)(1/4) \; {}^{*}_{*}\!\!{}^{*}$$

24. One way to remember the formula for the variance of a Bernoulli random variable is to notice that it is the product of the probabilities $P(x = 0) * P(x = \underline{})$.

25. We may summarize our results to this point by noting that
    $P(X = 0) =$ _____ , $P(X = 1) =$ ___ , $\mu =$ ___ , and $\sigma^2 =$
    _____ * ___ .

$$1 - \pi, \ \pi, \ \pi, \ (1 - \pi)\pi$$

26. Evidently the mean μ and variance σ^2 of a Bernoulli random vari-
    able may be expressed in terms of ___ .

$$\pi$$

27. Suppose supplier D provides a batch of parts that contains
    9/10 good parts. Complete the following for this situation
    where $\pi =$ _____ .

x	$P(x)$
___	_____
___	_____

$$\mu \ = \ \text{_____}$$

$$\sigma^2 \ = \ \text{_____}$$

	0	1/10	$\mu = 9/10$ ***** $\mu = \pi$ *****
$\pi = 9/10$	1	9/10	$\sigma^2 = 9/100$ ***** $\sigma^2 = (1 - \pi)\pi$ *****

PROGRAM SET 5.3   The Binomial Probability Distribution

1. Suppose we are observing successive parts drawn from a very
   large number of parts of the same type. These parts are classified as "good" or "defective." Let us designate a random
   variable X to describe the two possible classifications. If
   the part is good, we shall let $x = 1$; if the part is defective,
   we shall let $x = 0$. We know that for a good part, $x =$ ___ .

1

2. If $P(X = 1)$ is constant throughout the successive draws and the
   outcomes of the draws are independent, then the draws can be described as trials from a _____ process.

Bernoulli

3. Suppose the process is a Bernoulli process. The diagram gives the probabilities of selecting a good or defective part. In it, we can see that the probability of selecting a good part is _____ and the probability of selecting a defective part is ____.

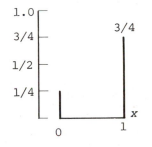

3/4, 1/4

4. Suppose four parts are selected from the bin. The results of the selection, in the order of selection, are:

First	Second	Third	Fourth
1	1	0	0

The total number of good parts is __.

2

5. Recall that under independence, we can find the probability of a joint event by *multiplying* the individual probabilities. Since the four draws constitute Bernoulli trials, we (may/ may not) consider the results of each selection to be independent of the others.

may

6. Thus we may compute the probability of the event

First	Second	Third	Fourth
1	1	0	0

to be $P(1, 1, 0, 0) = (3/4) * (3/4) *$ _____ $*$ _____ $=$ _____.

(1/4), (1/4); 9/256

7. Since we are interested in the total number of good parts, we add the values of x for each part. Call this sum r. Since the values x for the four parts are

	First	Second	Third	Fourth
x	1	1	0	0

we know that $r = 1 + $ ___ $ + $ ___ $ + $ ___ $ = $ ___ .

1, 0, 0; 2

8. It is important to understand that $P(R = 2)$ is *not* the same as $P(1, 1, 0, 0)$. In order to see this, look at the following event:

	First	Second	Third	Fourth
x	1	0	1	0

This event (is/is not) the same as the event in the previous frame, because the order in which the good and bad parts were selected (is/is not) the same.

is not, is not

9. Although the order in which the good parts occurred is not the same, we see that both events (do/do not) result in the same total number of good parts.

do

10. Thus, for both events, $r = $ ___ .

2

11. There are several ways of drawing the four parts so that $r = 2$:

First	Second	Third	Fourth
1	1	0	0
1	0	1	0
1	0	0	1
0	1	1	0
0	1	0	1
0	0	1	1

We see that there are ___ ways of having a sum of $r = 2$.

6

12. In order to find $P(R = 2)$, we must add the probabilities of the six mutually exclusive ways that $r = 2$ can occur. From the results of the last frame, we obtain

$$P(R = 2) = P(1, 1, 0, 0) + P(1, 0, 1, 0) + P(1, 0, 0, 1)$$

$$+ P(\_\_,\_\_,\_\_,\_\_) + P(\_\_,\_\_,\_\_,\_\_) + P(\_\_,\_\_,\_\_,\_\_).$$

$P(0, 1, 1, 0), \ P(0, 1, 0, 1), \ P(0, 0, 1, 1)$

13. In the table below, compute the probability of each of the six ways of obtaining $r = 2$.

$P(1, 1, 0, 0) = (3/4) * (3/4) * (1/4) * (1/4) = 9/256$

$P(1, 0, 1, 0) = $ _____ * _____ * _____ * _____ = _____

$P(1, 0, 0, 1) = $ _____ * _____ * _____ * _____ = _____

$P(0, 1, 1, 0) = $ _____ * _____ * _____ * _____ = _____

$P(0, 1, 0, 1) = $ _____ * _____ * _____ * _____ = _____

$P(0, 0, 1, 1) = $ _____ * _____ * _____ * _____ = _____

$(3/4) * (1/4) * (3/4) * (1/4) = 9/256$
$(3/4) * (1/4) * (1/4) * (3/4) = 9/256$
$(1/4) * (3/4) * (3/4) * (1/4) = 9/256$
$(1/4) * (3/4) * (1/4) * (3/4) = 9/256$
$(1/4) * (1/4) * (3/4) * (3/4) = 9/256$

14. Thus $P(R = 2) = $ ____ + ____ + ____ + ____ + ____ + ____ = ____.

$9/256 + 9/256 + 9/256 + 9/256 + 9/256 + 9/256 = 54/256$

15. Notice that each of the six ways of having a sum of $r = 2$ has (the same/a different) probability.

the same

16. An easier way to find $P(R = 2)$ is to say

$$P(R = 2) = \text{(number of ways of obtaining sum of 2)}$$

$$* \text{(probability of any one of the ways)}$$

Thus, for example, $P(R = 2) = $ ___ * _____ = _____.

$6 * (9/256) = 54/256$

17. Suppose we want $P(R = 1)$.   List here the events that will pro-
    duce $P(R = 1)$:

First	Second	Third	Fourth

1	0	0	0
0	1	0	0
0	0	1	0
0	0	0	1

18. The probability of obtaining the sum of 1 in the first way
    listed is _____ * _____ * _____ * _____ = _____ .

    $$(3/4) * (1/4) * (1/4) * (1/4) = 3/256$$

19. Then, the probability of a sum of 1 in any way is

    $$P(R = 1) = \underline{} * \underline{} = \underline{}$$

    $$4 * (3/256) = 12/256$$

20. We have been developing part of the probability distribution of
    r, the total number of good parts in a sample of four.   We know
    that r may be as small as zero if all the parts in the sample are
    (good/defective).   The largest value of r is ___ , which would
    occur if all of the parts are (good/defective).

    defective, 4, good

21. In order to compute the probability for a given value of R,
    we must first compute the _____ of ways the value of r can
    occur and then the _____ that any one of the ways will
    occur.   The probability of a given value of r is found by
    _____ these two quantities.

    number, probability, multiplying

22. One way to find the number of ways in which the values of r
    can occur is to draw a tree such as the one here.

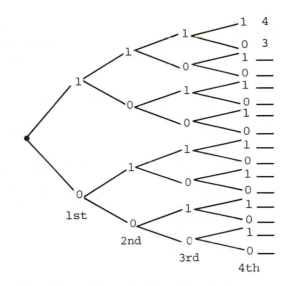

Compute the value of *r* for each branch of the tree.

3,2,3,2,2,1,3,2,2,1,2,1,1,0

23. Use the results of the tree in the last frame to complete the following table.

r	Number of Ways of Obtaining *r*
0	1
1	4
2	___
3	___
4	___

6, 4, 1

24. Use the probabilities for a good part (3/4) and a defective part (1/4) to find the probability of *any one way* that each value of *r* can occur. You may use the tree in Frame 22 to assist you in completing this table.

r	Number of Ways of Obtaining r	Probability of Any One Way
0	1	$(1/4)$ * $(1/4)$ * $(1/4)$ * $(1/4)$ = 1/256
1	4	$(3/4)$ * $(1/4)$ * $(1/4)$ * $(1/4)$ = 3/256
2	6	_____ * _____ * _____ * _____ = _____
3	4	_____ * _____ * _____ = _____
4	1	_____ * _____ * _____ = _____

$$(3/4)(3/4)(1/4)(1/4) = 9/256$$
$$(3/4)(3/4)(3/4)(1/4) = 27/256$$
$$(3/4)(3/4)(3/4)(3/4) = 81/256$$

25. We can find the probability of each of the possible values of r by completing the following table.

r	⎡Number of Ways⎤ ⎣of Obtaining r⎦	*	⎡Probability of Obtaining⎤ ⎣ Any One of the Ways ⎦	= $P(r)$
0	1		1/256	1/256
1	4		3/256	12/256
2	6		9/256	_____
3	4		27/256	_____
4	1		81/256	_____

54/256, 108/256, 81/256

26. Fortunately, there is an easier way to find probabilities of r. Notice that the probability 3/4 * 1/4 * 1/4 * 1/4 may be written as $(3/4)^1$ * $(1/4)^3$; the probability 3/4 * 3/4 * 1/4 * 1/4 may be written in exponential form as _____ _____ .

$$(3/4)^2 * (1/4)^2$$

27. Use this procedure to write "the probability of any one way" in exponential form. (Remember any number raised to the zero power is 1.)

r	Probability of Any One Way	Exponential Form
0	(1/4) * (1/4) * (1/4) * (1/4)	$(3/4)^0$ * $(1/4)^4$
1	(3/4) * (1/4) * (1/4) * (1/4)	$(3/4)^1$ * $(1/4)^3$
2	(3/4) * (3/4) * (1/4) * (1/4)	$(3/4)^{\underline{}}$ * $(1/4)^{\underline{}}$
3	(3/4) * (3/4) * (3/4) * (1/4)	$(3/4)^{\underline{}}$ * $(1/4)^{\underline{}}$
4	(3/4) * (3/4) * (3/4) * (3/4)	$(3/4)^{\underline{}}$ * (_____)$^{\underline{}}$

See table in next frame.

28. The results obtained in the last frame are summarized here.

r	Probability of Any One Way
0	$(3/4)^0$ * $(1/4)^4$
1	$(3/4)^1$ * $(1/4)^3$
2	$(3/4)^2$ * $(1/4)^2$
3	$(3/4)^3$ * $(1/4)^1$
4	$(3/4)^4$ * $(1/4)^0$

For $r = 0$, the sum of the exponents is $0 + 4 = 4$.
For $r = 1$, the sum of the exponents is ____ + ____ = ____.
For $r = 2$, the sum of the exponents is ____ + ____ = ____.

$1 + 3 = 4, \ 2 + 2 = 4$

29. The sum of the exponents is equal to 4 for each value of r.
Notice that the *exponent* for 3/4 (is/is not) equal to r.

is

30. Thus, the exponent for 1/4 must be 4 - ____.

r

31. In general, we may write the probability of any way of obtaining r as $(3/4)^r (1/4)^{4-r}$. Thus, the probability of any one way
of obtaining $r = 3$ is _____ * _____.

$(3/4)^3$ * $(1/4)^1$
(Verify your answer by referring to Frame 28.)

32. We also need to know the number of ways of obtaining a particular value of r. We will do this by means of our formula

for combinations. Recall that if we want to calculate the number of combinations of four things taken two at a time, we write

$$_4C_2 = \frac{4!}{(4 - 2)!2!} = \frac{4!}{(2!)!2!} = \underline{\quad}$$

6

33. In Frames 22 and 23, we found that the number of ways of finding a sum of $r = 2$ was also equal to ___ .

6

34. We may calculate the number of ways of finding a sum of r by using the formula $_4C_r = 4!/(4 - r)!r!$. If we want to find the number of ways of obtaining a sum $r = 3$, we could write

$$_4C\underline{\quad} = \frac{4!}{(4 - \underline{\quad})!\underline{\quad}!} = \underline{\quad}$$

3, 3, 3; 4

(Verify that $_4C_3 = 4$; check Frames 22 and 23.)

35. For our example, we may write:

$$P(r) = {}_4C_r * (3/4)^r * (1/4)^{4-r}$$

$$P(r) = \frac{\underline{\quad}!}{(\underline{\quad\quad})!\underline{\quad}!} * (3/4)^r * (1/4)^{4-r}$$

$$\frac{4!}{(4 - r)!r!}$$

36. The probability distribution for r has been developed for a fixed number of four Bernoulli trials and a fixed probability of 3/4 for a good part. In general, we use the symbol n to represent the number of trials. We use the symbol π to represent the fixed probability of one of the two possible events. In our example π represents the fixed probability of a good part on any draw. For our example, $n =$ ___ and $\pi =$ ____.

4, 3/4

37. If the probability of a good part is π, then the probability of a defective part is _____.

$1 - \pi$

38. Whenever we find the probability distribution of r, the values of π and n are (variable/fixed).

fixed

39. Even though n and π are fixed for a given probability distribution of r, we include the symbols n, π, and $1 - \pi$ in the
general formula.   Since we have found that for $n = 4$ and
$\pi = 3/4$, $P(r) = {}_4C_r(3/4)^r(1/4)^{4-r}$, we may write the general
formula as

$$P(r) = \underline{\hspace{3cm}}.$$

$${}_nC_r(\pi)^r(1 - \pi)^{n-r}$$

40. To illustrate the use of this formula, let us consider another
example.   Suppose that 4/5 of the voters of Usquepaug, Rhode
Island, are Republicans. We know that ____ of the voters are
not Republicans.

1/5

41. Suppose we want to find the probability that there are exactly
4 Republicans in a random selection of 5 voters.   In this example, n and π are fixed at $n =$ ___ and $\pi =$ ___.   We are
looking for $P(R =$ ___ $)$.

5, 4/5, 4

42. Use the general formula $P(r) = {}_nC_r(\pi)^r(1 - \pi)^{n-r}$ to find
$P(R = 4) =$ _____.

$$\frac{256}{625} \; \overset{*}{\underset{*}{\LARGE *}} \; \frac{5!}{(5 - 4)!\,4!} \ast \left(\frac{4}{5}\right)^4 \left(\frac{1}{5}\right)^{5-4} = \frac{5!}{1!\,4!}\left(\frac{4}{5}\right)^4\left(\frac{1}{5}\right)^1 = 5\left(\frac{4}{5}\right)^4\left(\frac{1}{5}\right)^1 \; \overset{*}{\underset{*}{\LARGE *}}$$

43. In the last frame, we found that $P(R = 4) = 256/625 = 0.4096$.
If we were to use the general formula with n fixed at 5 and
π fixed at 4/5 for all values of r, we would obtain the
probability distribution shown here (stated to four decimal
places).   A probability distribution such as this is an example of the *binomial probability distribution*. Thus we can
state that a binomial probability distribution gives the probability of obtaining any sum for fixed values of ___ and ___.

r	$P(r)$
0	0.0003
1	0.0064
2	0.0512
3	0.2048
4	0.4096
5	0.3277

π, n

44. It is important to distinguish between the binomial proba-
    bility distribution and the probability distribution for
    the Bernoulli process. For the present example, the proba-
    bility distribution for the Bernoulli process is:

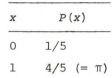

x	P(x)
0	1/5
1	4/5 (= π)

    The binomial probability distribution is used when there
    are ___ kinds of elements in the process.

                                                                    2

45. Remember, in order to describe a Bernoulli process of this
    kind, we must specify a numerical value for (n or π or r).

                                                                    π

46. Once we have described the Bernoulli process by specifying a
    numerical value for π, we can find a binomial probability by
    fixing (r or n) and calculating the probability of each value
    of (r or n).

                                                                    n, r

PROGRAM SET 5.4   Tabulated Values for the Binomial Probability Distribution

1. Consider the following Bernoulli random variables.

Classification	x	P(x)
Defective	0	1 - π
Good	1	π

We have learned that the binomial probability formula is

$$P(r) = \frac{n!}{(n - r)!r!} (\pi)^{r}(1 - \pi)^{n-r}$$

This formula gives us the probability of having r good parts in
n trials if the probability of having a good part on any trial
is ___ .

                                                                    π

2. Suppose we are given $n = 8$, $r = 2$, and $\pi = 0.4$. We may substitute these values into the formula

$$P(r) = \frac{n!}{(n - r)!r!}(\pi)^r (1 - \pi)^{n-r}$$

and find $P(R = 2)$. (Make the substitutions, but do not do the calculations.)

$$P(R = 2) = \frac{\overline{}}{\underline{}}(\underline{})^{\overline{}}(\underline{})^{\overline{}}$$

$$\frac{8!}{(8 - 2)!2!}(0.4)^2(1 - 0.4)^{8-2}, \quad \text{or} \quad \frac{8!}{6!2!}(0.4)^2(0.6)^6$$

3. For all but the smallest cases, the numerical calculation using the binomial formula is quite a job! Now, we will use tables that help avoid these calculations. First, a simple numerical example will familiarize you with the tables. Note that for a given number of trials, there are several possible outcomes. For $n = 2$ trials, we may observe no good parts, one good part, or two good parts. We know that for $n = 2$, the possible values of r are ____ or ____ or ____ .

0, 1, 2

4. Observe that r may be equal to zero. If $r = 0$, we know that all the parts selected are (good/defective).

defective

5. Now, suppose the probability of drawing a good part on any draw is $\pi = 0.5$. Suppose our number of trials is $n = 2$. (Recall that $0! = 1$.) We may use the formula

$$P(r) = \frac{n!}{(n - r)!r!}(\pi)^r (1 - \pi)^{n-r}$$

to find $P(R = 0) = $ _____ . (Express your answer in decimal form.)

0.25

6. Similarly, for $n = 2$ and $\pi = 0.5$, we may calculate $P(R = 1)$ from the formula

$$P(r) = \frac{n!}{(n - r)!r!}(\pi)^r (1 - \pi)^{n-r}$$

We know that $P(R = 1) = $ _____ .

0.50

7. Similarly, if $n = 2$ and $\pi = 0.5$, we find that $P(R = 2) = 0.25$. Let us tabulate our results:

r	$P(r)$
0	0.25
1	0.50
2	0.25

Remember, this table applies only when $n =$ ____ and $\pi =$ ____.

2, 0.5

8. Remember, to use the formula $P(r) = \dfrac{n!}{(n - r)!\,r!}(\pi)^{r}(1 - \pi)^{n-r}$,
we must know numerical values for ___, ___, and ___.

n, r, π

9. In order to use the tabulated values, we must also know the numerical values of n, π, and r. This excerpt from the binomial table shows several different distributions.

n	r	.05	.10	.15	.20	.25	.30	.35	.40	.45	.50
1	0	.9500	.9000	.8500	.8000	.7500	.7000	.6500	.6000	.5500	.5000
	1	.0500	.1000	.1500	.2000	.2500	.3000	.3500	.4000	.4500	.5000
2	0	.9025	.8100	.7225	.6400	.5625	.4900	.4225	.3600	.3025	.2500
	1	.0950	.1800	.2550	.3200	.3750	.4200	.4550	.4800	.4950	.5000
	2	.0025	.0100	.0225	.0400	.0625	.0900	.1225	.1600	.2025	.2500
3	0	.8574	.7290	.6141	.5120	.4219	.3430	.2746	.2160	.1664	.1250
	1	.1364	.2430	.3251	.3840	.4219	.4410	.4436	.4320	.4084	.3750
	2	.0071	.0270	.0574	.0960	.1406	.1890	.2389	.2880	.3341	.3750
	3	.0001	.0010	.0034	.0080	.0156	.0270	.0429	.0640	.0911	.1250
4	0	.8145	.6561	.5220	.4096	.3164	.2401	.1785	.1296	.0915	.0625
	1	.1715	.2916	.3865	.4096	.4219	.4116	.3845	.3456	.2995	.2500
	2	.0135	.0486	.0975	.1536	.2109	.2646	.3105	.3456	.3675	.3750
	3	.0005	.0036	.0115	.0256	.0469	.0756	.1115	.1536	.2005	.2500
	4	.0000	.0001	.0005	.0016	.0039	.0081	.0150	.0256	.0410	.0625

The top of the π columns is labeled π.

We can see that the circled distribution applies when $n =$ ____ and $\pi =$ ____.

2, 0.5

10. Earlier, from direct calculations with the binomial formula, we found the following values when $n = 2$ and $\pi = 0.5$.

r	$P(r)$
0	0.25
1	0.50
2	0.25

Look back at the tabulated values in the last frame. We see the tabular values (do/do not) agree with our calculated values.

do

11. The first thing to find when using the binomial table is the part of the table that applies to the required values of n and π.   In the table given in Frame 9, circle the distribution for $n = 4$ and $\pi = 0.45$.

							π					
n	r	.05	.10	.15	.20	.25	.30	.35	.40	.45	.50
1	0	.9500	.9000	.8500	.8000	.7500	.7000	.6500	.6000	.5500	.5000
	1	.0500	.1000	.1500	.2000	.2500	.3000	.3500	.4000	.4500	.5000
2	0	.9025	.8100	.7225	.6400	.5625	.4900	.4225	.3600	.3025	.2500
	1	.0950	.1800	.2550	.3200	.3750	.4200	.4550	.4800	.4950	.5000
	2	.0025	.0100	.0225	.0400	.0625	.0900	.1225	.1600	.2025	.2500
3	0	.8574	.7290	.6141	.5120	.4219	.3430	.2746	.2160	.1664	.1250
	1	.1364	.2430	.3251	.3840	.4219	.4410	.4436	.4320	.4084	.3750
	2	.0071	.0270	.0574	.0960	.1406	.1890	.2389	.2880	.3341	.3750
	3	.0001	.0010	.0034	.0080	.0156	.0270	.0429	.0640	.0911	.1250
4	0	.8145	.6561	.5220	.4096	.3164	.2401	.1785	.1296	.0915	.0625
	1	.1715	.2916	.3865	.4096	.4219	.4116	.3845	.3456	.2995	.2500
	2	.0135	.0486	.0975	.1536	.2109	.2646	.3105	.3456	.3675	.3750
	3	.0005	.0036	.0115	.0256	.0469	.0756	.1115	.1536	.2005	.2500
	4	.0000	.0001	.0005	.0016	.0039	.0081	.0150	.0256	.0410	.0625

12. From the preceding table, we can see that when $n = 4$ and $\pi = 0.45$, we have $P(R = 2) = $ _____.

0.3675

13. Using the table in Frame 11, we see that if $n = 3$ and $\pi = 0.15$, then $P(R = 1) = $ _____.

0.3251

14. Notice that we have been using the table by first fixing the sample size (n) and specifying the probability of having a good part on any draw (π). We shall now revise our probability notation to reflect the fact that n and π are *given*. Instead of specifying the values of n and π separately, we shall write

$$P(2 \mid n = 4, \ \pi = 0.15)$$

This notation is read "the probability that R = ___ *given* that n = ___ and given that π = _____.

2, 4, 0.15

15. In the notation $P(r \mid n = 4, \ \pi = 0.5)$, the known information is written to the (left/right) of the vertical line.

right

16. In the table below, we see that $P(5 \mid n = 12, \pi = 0.3)$ = _____.

						π					
n	r	.05	.10	.15	.20	.25	.30	.35	.40	.45	.50
12	0	.5404	.2824	.1422	.0687	.0317	.0138	.0057	.0022	.0008	.0002
	1	.3413	.3766	.3012	.2062	.1267	.0712	.0368	.0174	.0075	.0029
	2	.0988	.2301	.2924	.2835	.2323	.1678	.1088	.0639	.0339	.0161
	3	.0173	.0852	.1720	.2362	.2581	.2397	.1954	.1419	.0923	.0537
	4	.0021	.0213	.0683	.1329	.1936	.2311	.2367	.2128	.1700	.1208
	5	.0002	.0038	.0193	.0532	.1032	.1585	.2039	.2270	.2225	.1934
	6	.0000	.00005	.0040	.0155	.0401	.0792	.1281	.1766	.2124	.2256
	7	.0000	.0000	.0006	.0033	.0115	.0291	.0591	.1009	.1489	.1934
	8	.0000	.0000	.0001	.0005	.0024	.0078	.0199	.0420	.0762	.1208
	9	.0000	.0000	.0000	.0001	.0004	.0015	.0048	.0125	.0277	.0537
	10	.0000	.0000	.0000	.0000	.0000	.0002	.0008	.0025	.0068	.0161
	11	.0000	.0000	.0000	.0000	.0000	.0000	.0001	.0003	.0010	.0029
	12	.0000	.0000	.0000	.0000	.0000	.0000	.0000	.0000	.0001	.0002

0.1585

CHAPTER 5. SELF-CORRECTING EXERCISES

5.1 Random Variables and the Probability Distribution of a Random Variable A box contains 3 pennies and 3 nickels. Coins are to be drawn from the box with replacement. The random variable of concern is the monetary value of the coin drawn. Designate the pennies as P_1, P_2, and P_3 and the nickels as N_1, N_2, and N_3. Selection of each coin is considered equally likely.

a. Draw a diagram of the sample space. What assignment of probability should be made to each element in the sample space? What numerical value is assigned to each element in the sample space? Indicate both assignments on your diagram.

b. Let x represent the values of the random variable in cents. What are the probabilities of the events $X = 1$ and $X = 5$? What probability law is used in the computation of these events? Tabulate the probability distribution of the value of the random variable.

c. Explain any differences between the event P_1 and the event $X = 1$.

d. The following have been suggested as random variables for this situation: coin's weight, coin's color, coin's diameter, coin's metal, date of issue, and city where minted. Which of these could be random variables? Why?

e. For this sample space, how many random variables could possibly be defined? Does the choice of a particular random variable influence the assignment of probabilities to the elements in the sample space? If two random variables are defined on the same sample space, are they likely to have the same or different probability distributions? Illustrate the answers to the last two questions by finding the probability distribution of the random variable "date of issue" (Y). Assume P_1 was issued in 1975 and other coins in 1976.

f. What is the reason for selecting a particular random variable?

5.2 Sample Space and Random Variable   Suppose that a deck of 16 cards consists of the jack, queen, king, and ace of each of the four suits—spades, hearts, diamonds, and clubs. The sample space for the experiment *draw a card* is represented by the diagram at the left. Each card is equally likely to be selected. Suppose that in connection with the card drawn J, Q, K, and A count 1, 2, 3, and 4 points, respectively, and that an extra point is scored if a spade or heart is drawn.

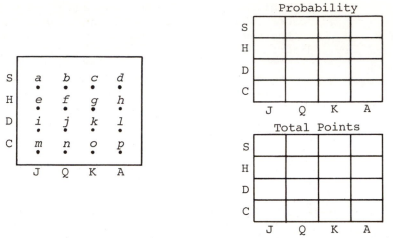

a. In the tables at the right of the sample space, record the
   probability and total points that should be assigned to
   each element in the sample space.

b. Let *x* represent the value of the random variable *total
   points*. Find the probability distribution of the random
   variable.

c. Find the cumulative probability function of X.

5.3 The Sum of Two Random Variables   A company makes two products,
A and B.   The random variable X_A is the number of demands per
day for product A and the random variable X_B is the number of
demands for product B.   The table at the left below shows the
joint probabilities for the demands for A and B.

	Demands for A					Demands for A		
Demands for B	x_B/x_A	1	2		Demands for B	x_B/x_A	1	2
	1	6/16	2/16			1	___	___
	2	3/16	1/16			2	3	4
	3	2/16	2/16			3	___	___

a. The table to the right above shows the possible total demands for both products.   Let T be defined as the total demands, so $T = X_A + X_B$.   For example, if $x_A = 1$ and $x_B = 2$,
   then $t = 1 + 2 = 3$ as shown in the table.   Compute the
   table for total demands.

b. In terms of x_A and x_B, what event or events will produce a total demand of $T = 3$.   What is the value of $P(T = 3)$?

c. Find the probability distribution of T.

5.4 Mean and Variance of a Random Variable   (Before starting this exercise, express the probabilities in Question 5.1b in halves and those in Question 5.2b in eighths.

a. Compute the mean and variance for the random variable in Questions 5.1 and 5.2.   Use $\sigma^2 = \Sigma (x - \mu)^2 P(x)$ to compute the variance.

b. For the random variables in (a), compute $E(X)$, $(E(X))^2$, and $E(X^2)$.   Does $(E(X))^2$ equal $E(X^2)$?

c. Find the variance of each variable in (a) by using $\sigma^2 = E(X^2) - (E(X))^2$.

5.5 Random Variables (Notation and Terminology)   A lumber wholesaler receives orders for construction grade 2 by 4 boards which are produced in 10, 12, 14, 16, 18, and 20 foot lengths. Let X represent the random variable length.

a. Write the definition of the random variable X.

b. Write the probability statements for these events:

   i. The next order is for a 10-foot length.
   ii. The next order is for a board longer than 10 feet.

c. Give a verbal description for the following statements:

   i. $P(X = 16)$.
   ii. $P(X \geq 14)$.

5.6 The Bernoulli Process   The following information is recorded for a large number of patients admitted to a hospital.   Identify which items might be considered as the basis for defining a Bernoulli random variable.

a. Sex.

b. Age.

c. Weight.

d. Whether or not the patient has health insurance.

e. Whether the patient's weight is below normal, normal, or above normal.

f. Whether the patient's weight is normal or abnormal.

5.7 Binomial Distribution   When in the home office a salesperson must place long-distance calls through a central operator. During morning hours, the operator is busy 2/3 of the time. Consider the experiment *the salesperson attempts to place three calls with the operator*.   Use B for *busy* and S for *Succeeds in getting operator*.

a. Assume we are interested in counting the number of times the salesperson succeeds.   What is the value π?   Write down the probability distribution for the Bernoulli random variable.   Find the mean and variance of this probability distribution.

b. Draw a tree diagram showing the possible outcomes of 3 calls.   Put probabilities on the branches and multiply them to show probabilities for the different outcomes of three attempts.

c. From your results in (b), find the following probabilities.

Number of Successful Calls r	Probability $P(r)$
0	
1	
2	
3	

d. Are the distributions in Parts a and c the same?   Are they related?   If so, how?

e. In the space at the right of the table in Part c, find the binomial distribution by substituting appropriate values in the binomial formula $P(r) = {}_nC_r\, \pi^r (1 - \pi)^{n-r}$ and carry out the calculations.   The results should agree with the probabilities you determined in (c).

f. From the probability distribution found in Part c, determine the probability of *at least two successful calls* and the probability of *no more than one successful call*.

g. If we were interested in the number of *busy* calls, how would (a) change?   Without making any computations, could you find the binomial distribution for $n = 3$?   (Assume the results of (c) are known to you.)

5.8 Binomial Formula and Binomial Table

a. Solve the following by using the binomial formula.   Check your answers by looking up the same probabilities in the binomial table (Apendix B, Table B-1).

  i. $P(R = 2 \mid n = 3, \pi = 0.6)$

  ii. $P(R = 0 \mid n = 4, \pi = 0.2)$

  iii. $P(R = 3 \mid n = 3, \pi = 0.3)$

b. Use the binomial table to find the probabilities necessary to show that the following equations are correct.

  i. $P(R \geq 2 \mid n = 3, \pi = 0.6) = 0.6480$

  ii. $P(R < 2 \mid n = 3, \pi = 0.6) = 0.3520$

  iii. $P(R \leq 3 \mid n = 9, \pi = 0.3) = 0.7296$

  iv. $P(R > 12 \mid n = 15, \pi = 0.50) = 0.0037$

5.9 Application   A random sample of four parts is to be taken from a large lot of parts that has unknown defective proportions. Use the binomial formula to find the following and check your answer by looking up the required probability in the binomial table.

a. The probability of observing two defective parts if the proportion defective in the lot is 0.20.

b. The probability of observing two defective parts if the proportion defective in the lot is 0.10.

5.10 Concepts and Terminology

a. Explain the difference between the probability distribution for a Bernoulli random variable and binomial probability distribution.   What distinguishes one Bernoulli random variable from another?

b. For a *given* Bernoulli random variable, how many different binomial distributions are there?   In this case, what distinguishes one binomial distribution from another?

c. For a Bernoulli random variable, $\pi = 0.5$, is the state-
ment $P(X = 1) = P(R = 1 | n = 3, \pi = 0.5)$ true or false?
Explain.

d. Without making any calculation, explain whether each of the
following statements is true or false.

i. $P(R \geq 1 | n = 2, \pi = 0.5)$ $= 1 - P(R = 0 | n = 2, \pi = 0.5)$

ii. $P(R \geq 1 | n = 2, \pi = 0.5)$ $= P(R = 1 | n = 2, \pi = 0.5)$

iii. $P(R \geq 2 | n = 4, \pi = 0.5)$ $= P(R > 1 | n = 4, \pi = 0.5)$

iv. $P(R = 1 | n = 2, \pi = 0.5)$ $= P(R = 1 | n = 2, \pi = 0.1)$

v. $P(R = 1 | n = 2, \pi = 0.5)$ $= P(R = 1 | n = 10, \pi = 0.5)$

vi. $P(R = 0 | n = 8, \pi = 0.75) = 0$ (exactly).

5.11 A Potpourri of Binomial Applications

a. An inspection sampling procedure has been designed in which
5 items from each large production lot are to be classed as
good or defective. Any lot yielding a sample with 1 or
more defective items is to be rejected as not meeting
quality specifications.

i. Find the probability of rejecting a lot that has 5%
defective items.

ii. Find the probability of accepting a lot that has 15%
defective items.

b. Ten wine tasters are given brand X and three other brands
in unmarked glasses. They are asked to identify brand X.
If the tasters are making their identification of brand X
at random (that is, by guessing), what is the probability
that 6 or more of the wine tasters will correctly identify
brand X?

c. Nine out of 12 customers were observed to choose a 2-pound
can of coffee over two 1-pound cans when offered at the
same price. What is the probability of a result as uneven
as this (that is, 9 or more or 3 or less) if among all
customers there were an equal number preferring either alternative?

d. An acceptance sampling plan called for lots to be accepted
if a random sample of 10 items yielded 2 or fewer defectives.

i. What is the probability of rejecting a lot with proportion defective of 0.05?

ii. What is the probability of accepting a lot with proportion defective of 0.40?

5.12 The Mean and Variance of a Binomial Probability Distribution

a. For the situation in (i) and (ii) of Question 5.11d find
the mean and variance of the Bernoulli random variable.
What determines the numerical values?

b. For the situation described in (i) and (ii) of Exercise
5.11d, find the mean and variance of the binomial distributions. What determines these values?

c. If the sample size were doubled, would your answer to (a)
change? Would your answer to (b) change?

5.13 The Bernoulli Random Variable and the Binomial Distribution— A Summary

a. Use Table B-1 to find the binomial distribution for three
different Bernoulli random variables if $\pi = 0.1$, $\pi = 0.5$,
and $\pi = 0.9$. Use $n = 4$ for all three distributions. List
the results below.

	$\pi = 0.1$		$\pi = 0.5$		$\pi = 0.9$
r	$P(r)$	r	$P(r)$	r	$P(r)$
0		0		0	
1		1		1	
2		2		2	
3		3		3	
4		4		4	

b. Find the mean and standard deviation for each Bernoulli
random variable. Find the mean and standard deviation for
each binomial distribution.

c. On the grids below, plot each of the probability distributions for each Bernoulli random variable and the corresponding binomial distribution. Indicate the locations of
the means found in (b).

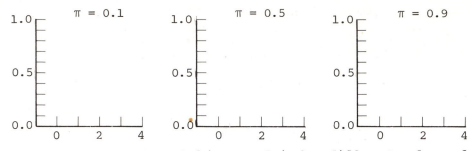

d. Use the results of (c) to explain how different values of
π influence the mean, standard deviation, and skewness of
bionomial distributions having a fixed value of n.

e. Listed below are binomial probability distributions for a
Bernoulli random variable with π = 0.1. Compute the means
and standard deviations for these distributions.

π = 0.1, n = 4		π = 0.1, n = 16	
r	P(r)	r	P(r)
0	0.6561	0	0.1853
1	0.2916	1	0.3294
2	0.0486	2	0.2745
3	0.0036	3	0.1423
4	0.0001	4	0.0514
		5	0.0137
		6	0.0028
		7	0.0004
		8	0.0001
		9	0.0000
		10	0.0000
		11	0.0000
		12	0.0000
		13	0.0000
		14	0.0000
		15	0.0000
		16	0.0000

f. On the grids below, plot the binomial distributions. Indicate the locations of their means. (A third binomial for
   $\pi = 0.1$ and $n = 64$ is shown for comparison.)

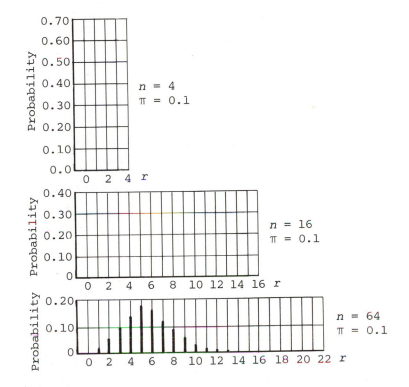

CHAPTER 5. ACHIEVEMENT TEST

In a survey, households are selected at random. The pollster asks
the following three questions about the household. Indicate which
questions involve the concept of a random variable. Justify your
answer.

1. What is middle initial of the head of household?

2. How many persons live in this household?

3. Whom would you favor as the next President of the United
   States?

Listed below are the number of semester hours taken by a group of
5 students. Use this information to answer Questions 4-8.

Name	Semester Hours
Angelo	30
Smith	15
Carpenter	30
Zimmer	45
Jones	45

4. If H is used to signify the semester hours of a student select-ed at random, find the probability distribution of H.

5. Find the cumulative probability distribution of H.

6. Write an expression in terms of H for the event a *student se-lected at random has 30 semester hours or less*.

7. What is the probability of the event described in Question 6?

8. $P(H = 15) = ?$

A car ferry boat takes automobiles one at a time to the east or west bank of a river. Only one ferry is employed in this service. The joint probability table for the number of vehicles waiting to go east and waiting to go west is shown in the table below. Use this table to answer Questions 9-10.

Waiting to Go West x_W	Waiting to Go East x_E		
	0	1	2
0	0.05	0.05	0.05
1	0.05	0.20	0.15
2	0.05	0.10	0.30

9. Let T be the total number of cars waiting. In terms of x_E and x_W, what circumstances would cause a value of $T = 3$ to occur?

10. $P(T = 2) = ?$

11. Find the mean of this distribution.

x	$P(x)$
5	5/8
6	2/8
7	1/8

12. For the probability distribution in Question 11, what is the expected value of X?

13. The mean of the distribution given below is 5. What is the variance?

x	$P(x)$
3	1/2
5	1/4
9	1/4

14. For the probability distribution given in Question 13, what is the value of $E(X^2)$?

15. A Bernoulli random variable has a mean of 0.2. What is the standard deviation of this variable?

16. There are to be 4 trials of a Bernoulli process. List all of the outcomes that would produce exactly 3 successes.

17. $5! = ?$

18. $_6C_3 = ?$

19. A Bernoulli process has $\pi = 1/6$. If three trials are to be made for this process, find the probability of exactly two successes.

20. Use the binomial table to find $P(5 \mid 15, 0.8)$.

21. Five Bernoulli trials are to be observed. If the probability of a success on each trial is 0.45, what is the probability of 2 or fewer successes?

22. What is the mean of the binomial distribution for which $\pi = 0.3$ and $n = 20$?

23. What is the standard deviation of a binomial distribution for which $\pi = 0.1$ and $n = 100$?

CHAPTER 5.   STUDENT RECORD AND REFERENCE SHEET

Darken the square corresponding to each test item you answered *incorrectly*.   References indicate the topics you should study. See Chapter 1 of this volume for details.

Test Item	Diagnostic Test	Achievement Test	Text References	Self-Correcting Exercise References	Program Set References
1	☐	☐	116–119	5.1	5.1
2	☐	☐	116–119	5.1	5.1
3	☐	☐	116–119	5.1	5.1
4	☐	☐	119–124	5.1	5.1
5	☐	☐	119–124	5.2	5.1
6	☐	☐	119–124	5.2	5.1
7	☐	☐	119–124	5.2	5.1
8	☐	☐	119–124	5.2	5.1
9	☐	☐	119–124	5.3	5.1
10	☐	☐	119–124	5.3	5.1
11	☐	☐	126–129	5.4	—
12	☐	☐	126–129	5.4	—
13	☐	☐	126–129	5.4	—
14	☐	☐	131–137	5.4	—
15	☐	☐	131–137	5.12(a)	5.2
16	☐	☐	131–137	5.7	5.2
17	☐	☐	131–137	5.7	5.2
18	☐	☐	131–137	5.7	5.2
19	☐	☐	131–137	5.7	5.2
20	☐	☐	131–137	5.8	5.3
21	☐	☐	131–137	5.8	5.2, 5.3
22	☐	☐	137–141	5.12	—
23	☐	☐	137–141	5.12	—

6

CONTINUOUS RANDOM VARIABLES AND THE NORMAL DISTRIBUTION

The graphs below, which represent two different probability processes, are to be used to answer Questions 1-4.

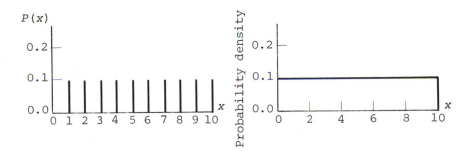

1. Identify the random variable for each graph as discrete or continuous.

2. Use the graphs to compute $P(X = 2)$ for both probability processes.

3. Use the graphs to compute $P(X = 6.5)$ for both probability processes.

4. Use the graphs to compute $P(7 \leq X \leq 9)$ for both probability processes.

The graphs below are related: The one on the left is the probability density function and the one on the right is cumulative
density function of the continuous random variable shown on the
left.

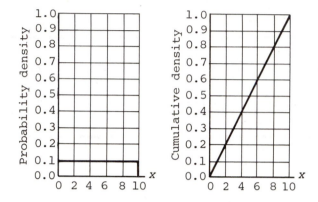

5. Use the graph on the left to compute these probabilities:

   a. $P(X \leq 2)$

   b. $P(X \leq 3)$

   c. $P(2 \leq X \leq 3)$

6. Use the graph on the right to compute the probabilities requested in Question 5.

7. Use both graphs to find $P(X \leq 10)$.

8. What information is required to distinguish one normal distribution from another?

9. The distribution of IQs is normal with a mean of 100 and a
   standard deviation of 10. The probability of finding an individual with an IQ between 100 and 110 is 0.3413. Without
   making any calculations or using the tables, state the probability of finding an individual with an IQ between 90 and 100.

10. What are the mean and standard deviation of the standard normal
    distribution?

11. How many different normal distributions are there? Do we need
    a separate table for each?

12. How do we make two different normal distributions look alike?

13. An individual has an IQ of 125. If IQs are normally distributed with a mean of 100 and a standard deviation of 10, what is the individual's standard score?

14. Use Table B-2 in Appendix B to find these standard normal probabilities.

   a. $P(Z \leq 0.65)$

   b. $P(Z \leq 0.6)$

   c. $P(0.6 \leq Z \leq 0.65)$.

15. Use Table B-2 in Appendix B to find these standard normal probabilities.

   a. $P(Z \leq -2.34)$

   b. $P(Z \geq -2.34)$

16. For the standard normal, what is the value of $P(Z \leq 6.41)$?

Questions 17-21 refer to a normal distribution with a mean of 100 and a standard deviation of 10.

17. $P(X \leq 92) = ?$

18. $P(80 \leq X \leq 105) = ?$

19. $P(X \geq 75) = ?$

20. Find the 25th percentile of this distribution.

21. We wish to construct an interval of X for this distribution that contains 80% of the values. Ten percent of the values are to lie above the interval and 10% are to lie below. Determine the interval.

22. Does the normal approximation to the binomial apply to a binomial distribution which has $\pi = 0.10$ and $n = 20$? Why or why not?

23. Find the mean and standard deviation of a binomial distribution with $\pi = 0.5$ and $n = 10,000$.

Questions 24-26 apply to finding normal approximations to the binomial distribution that has $\pi = 0.5$ and $n = 100$. For this distribution, $\mu = 50$ and $\sigma = 5$.

24. In order to find the normal approximation to $P(R = 53 \mid n = 100, \ \pi = 0.5)$, what interval on the normal distribution should be used? What is the corresponding interval on the standard normal?

25. Find the normal approximation to $P(R = 53 \mid n = 100, \ \pi = 0.5)$.

26. Find the 25th percentile of the binomial distribution.

PROGRAM SET 6.1   Areas of the Standard Normal Distribution

1. The graph here shows the *standard normal distribution.*

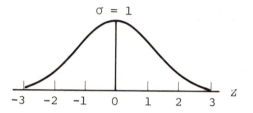

$\sigma = 1$

-3 -2 -1 0 1 2 3 z

As you can see, the letter used to represent the random variable in the standard normal distribution is ___.

z

2. From the graph in the last frame, we see that the standard normal distribution has a mean of ___ and a standard deviation of ___.

0, 1

3. A normal distribution having a mean of zero and a standard deviation of one is called the _____ normal distribution. The letter ___ is used to designate the random variable in the distribution.

standard, z

4. The standard normal distribution, like all normal distributions, is symmetric about its mean. Due to this symmetry, 1/2 of the area under the curve will be to the left of $z = 0$ and 1/2 of the area under the curve will be to the _____ of $z = $ ___.

right, 0

5. Recall that the total area under any probability density function must be equal to one. Thus, the area to the left of $z = 0$ must be ____.

0.5

6. The area under the density function corresponding to some interval on the Z-axis is the same as the probablity that Z occurs in this interval. To indicate the probability that Z is less than 0, we would write $P(Z \leq$ ___$)$.

0

7. Since half the area lies to the left of $z = 0$, we know that $P(Z \leq 0) =$ _____.

0.5

8. When working with statements such as $P(Z \leq 0)$, you should keep in mind that a normal distribution extends an infinite distance to the left and to the right of its mean. Thus $P(Z \leq 0) = 0.5$ implies that the area to the left of $z = 0$ that extends an infinite distance to the (right/left) is 0.5.

left

9. Table B-2 in the text gives areas that are to the left of a specified value of z. Turn to Table B-2 and examine the sketch on the right side of the table. Evidently, the shaded area of 0.8413 is to the (right/left) of $z =$ ____.

left, 1.0

10. In terms of probability, we would write $P(Z \leq$ ____$) = 0.8413$.

1.0

11. Table B-2 displays pairs of numbers in a two-column format. The first column in a pair of columns gives values of Z. The second column gives the area which is to the ____ of the corresponding value of z.

left

12. To see how Table B-2 works, locate the z-column that contains the value -1.00. The area to the left of this value is in the second column and has the value ____.

0.1587

13. Figure 6-1(a) shows a graph of the value pairs shown in Table
    B-2.   From Figure 6-1(a), we see that the values in this table
    are for a (density function/cumulative density function).

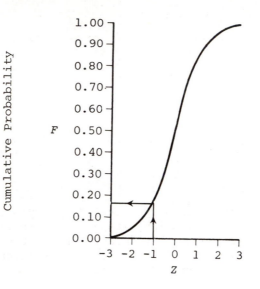

Figure 6-1(a)

cumulative density function

14. Figure 6-1(b) shows a graph of the corresponding density func-
    tion.   In order to see the relationship between these graphs
    and Table B-2, we shall use the graphs to find the approximate
    area.   In Figure 6-1(a), the vertical line shows the location
    of the value z = -1.00.   The horizontal line shows the cor-
    responding left-tail area.   In this case, the left-tail area
    read from the graph is ___ (state to two decimal places).

0.16

15. Figure 6-1(b) shows these values on the corresponding proba-
    bility ____ function.

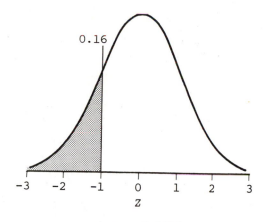

Figure 6-1(b)

density

16. Use Figure 6-1(a) to find the cumulative probabilities for these values of Z.   State your results in two decimal places.

z	Cumulative Probability
-1.0	0.16
0.0	_____
1.0	_____
2.0	_____
3.0	_____

z	Cumulative Probability	Value From Table B-2
-1.0	0.16	0.1587
0.0	0.50	_____
1.0	0.84	_____
2.0	0.98	_____
3.0	1.00	_____

17. Verify each value you found in the last frame by using Table B-2.   Write your responses in the space provided with the answers to the last frame.

0.5000, 0.8413,
0.9772, 0.9986

18. Use Figure 6-1(b) to show the values of Z and the corresponding areas from Table B-2 in the text.

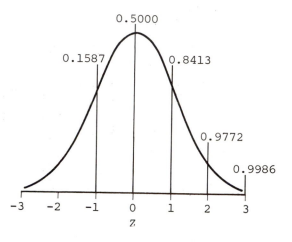

19. As you can see, all of the areas in Table B-2 are left-tail areas. These left-tail areas are associated with probabilities called *lower-tail probabilities*. Thus, these tabulated areas are always for an area that is to the ____ of a specified value of z.

                                                              left

20. To obtain a right-tail area (or upper-tail probability), we need to remember that the *total* area under the curve is 1. Thus the area to the right of $z = 0.5$ is 1 *minus* the area to the left. Thus $P(Z \geq 0.5) = 1 -$ _____ = _____.

                                               0.6915, 0.3085

21. The probability that z exceeds 0.15 is $P(Z > 0.15) =$ _____.

                              0.4404 *** 1 - 0.5596 ***

22. Use the normal curve here to shade in the approximate area for the probability that $z > 0.15$.

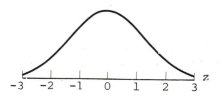

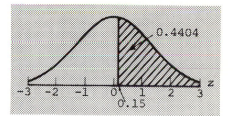

23. Sometimes we need to find the area between two values of z.
Suppose we want to find the area between $z = 1.0$ and $z = 0$.
Earlier we found the area to the left of $z = 1.0$ to be 0.8413
and the area to the left of $z = 0$ to be 0.5. The area between $z = 1.0$ and $z = 0.0$ is $0.8413 - 0.5000 =$ _____.

0.3413

24. In symbols, we write $P(0 \leq Z \leq 1) = P(Z \leq 1) - P(Z \leq$ ___$)$.

0

25. The probability $P(-1.96 \leq Z \leq 1.96)$ may be written
$P(-1.96 \leq Z \leq 1.96) = P(Z \leq$ _____$) - P(Z \leq$ _____$)$.

1.96, -1.96

26. From Table B-2, we see $P(Z \leq 1.96) =$ _____ and
$P(Z \leq -1.96) =$ _____.

0.9750, 0.0250

27. Thus $P(-1.96 \leq Z \leq 1.96) =$ _____.

0.9500 ✱ 0.9750 - 0.0250 ✱

28. Since the area within the interval $-1.96 \leq Z \leq 1.96$ is 0.9500,
we know the area outside this interval must be _____.

0.0500 ✱ 1 - 0.9500 ✱

29. Notice that the largest positive value of z in Tables B-2
is $z = 3.09$ and this table gives $P(Z \leq 3.09) = 0.9990$.
The largest negative value of z given in the tables is $z =$
-3.09. From the table, $P(Z \leq -3.09) =$ _____.

0.0010

30. From the results of the last frame, $P(-3.09 \leq Z \leq 3.09) =$
_____.

0.9980 ✱ 0.9990 - 0.0010 ✱

31. The probability that z lies outside the interval
    $-3.09 \leq z \leq 3.09$ is _____.

$$0.0020 \overset{*}{\underset{*}{*}} 1 - 0.9980 \overset{*}{\underset{*}{*}}$$

32. Although the normal density function extends an infinite dis-
    tance to the left and right of the mean, the probability that
    a value of z will be outside the range tabulated in Table B-2
    (is/is not) large.

                                                                is not

PROGRAM SET 6.2   Areas for a Normal Distribution of X

1. The figure shows several different normal distributions.

   $\mu = 17, \sigma = 1$ $\mu = 36, \sigma = 1$
   $\mu = 24, \sigma = 2$
   $\mu = 8, \sigma = 2$
   $\mu = 36, \sigma = 3$

   0 4 8 12 16 20 24 28 32 36 40 44 48 x

   One normal curve appears to be distinguished from another by
   the numerical values of ____ (symbol) and ____ (symbol).

                                                                μ, σ

2. It is necessary for us to find areas under any normal distribution. Recall that we have learned to do this for a
   particular normal distribution called the _____ normal distribution.

                                                                standard

3. Lower-tail areas for the standard normal distribution are given
   in Table B-2 in the text. From this table, you can see that
   the area to the left of $z = 1$ under the standard normal distribution is _____. In other words, $P(Z < 1) = $ _____.

                                                        0.8413, 0.8413

4. Now consider a normal distribution with $\mu = 36$ and $\sigma = 3$. For
   this distribution, we wish to find the area to the left of
   $x = 39$. From our work with standard scores, we know that the
   standard score for a given value of x is computed from

$z = (x - \mu)/\sigma$. Thus for our normal distribution with $\mu = 36$ and $\sigma = 3$, the standard score for $x = 39$ is $z =$ ___.

1 ***** (39 - 36)/3 *****

5. As you may have guessed, the area to the left of $x = 39$ under the normal distribution with $\mu = 36$ and $\sigma = 3$ *is the same as* the area to the left of $z = 1$ under the _____ normal distribution.

standard

6. Since $P(Z < 1) = 0.8413$, $P(X < 39) =$ _____.

0.8413

7. To find the area to the left of a particular value of x, we must first find the _____ score corresponding to the particular value of x by using the formula $z =$ _____.

standard, $(x - \mu)/\sigma$

8. Consider $x = 42$ for the normal distribution with $\mu = 36$ and $\sigma = 3$. The standard score corresponding to $x = 42$ is $z =$ ___.

2 ***** (42 - 36)/3 *****

9. From Table B-2, $P(Z < 2) =$ _____.

0.9772

10. Since the area to the left of $z = 2$ (is/is not) the same as the area to the left of $x = 42$, $P(X < 42)$ (is/is not) equal to $P(Z < 2)$.

is, is

11. To find the probability that x is less than a particular value, we first convert the particular value of x to the corresponding value of ___ (symbol).

z

12. Next, we find the area to the left of this value of z from Table B-2. This is (less than/equal to/greater than) the area to the left of the particular value of x in our original problem.

equal to

13. Let us consider another example. Suppose for the normal curve with μ = 36 and σ = 3, we wish to answer the question: $P(X < 37.5)$ = ? Our first task is to convert x = 37.5 to z = _____.

$$0.5 \; \ast\ast\ast \; (37.5 - 36)/3 \; \ast\ast\ast$$

14. Next, from Table B-2, we find $P(Z < 0.5)$ = _____.

0.6915

15. Finally, we state the results in terms of x.   Thus $P(X < 37.5)$ = _____.

0.6915

16. Use this procedure for a normal curve having μ = 36 and σ = 3 to find $P(X < 42.3)$.

a. z = _____
b. $P(Z <$ _____ $)$ = _____
c. $P(X < 42.3)$ = _____

a. 2.1 $\ast\ast\ast$ (42.3 - 36)/3 $\ast\ast\ast$
b. $P(Z < 2.1)$ = 0.9821
c. $P(X < 42.3)$ = 0.9821

17. For a normal curve with μ = 36 and σ = 3, $P(X < 37.2)$ = _____.

0.6554

$\ast\ast\ast$ z = (37.2 - 36)/3 = 0.4, $P(Z < 0.4)$ = 0.6554 $\ast\ast\ast$

18. For the same normal curve in the last frame, $P(X < 34.8)$ =

_____.

0.3446

$\ast\ast\ast$ z = (34.8 - 36)/3 = -0.4, $P(Z < -0.4)$ = 0.3446 $\ast\ast\ast$

19. When converting x to z, we must be very careful to obtain the correct *sign* for z.   In the last frame, z is negative which implies that x = 34.8 is to the (right/left) of μ = 36.

left

20. We can compute an area under a normal curve that is within a given interval.   For the normal curve having μ = 36 and σ = 3, we wish to find $P(34.8 \leq X \leq 37.2)$.   The equivalent problem expressed in terms of z is $P($ _____ $\leq Z \leq$ _____ $)$.

-0.4, 0.4

21. Recall that $P(-0.4 \leq Z \leq 0.4) = P(Z \leq 0.4) - P(Z \leq \underline{\hspace{1cm}})$.

-0.4

22. Using Table B-2, $P(-0.4 \leq Z \leq 0.4) = \underline{\hspace{1.5cm}} - \underline{\hspace{1.5cm}} =$
    $\underline{\hspace{2cm}}$.

$0.6554 - 0.3446 = 0.3108$

23. Consequently, $P(34.8 \leq X \leq 37.2) = \underline{\hspace{1.5cm}}$.

0.3108

24. For a normal curve with $\mu = 36$ and $\sigma = 3$, $P(32 \leq X \leq 42) =$
    $\underline{\hspace{2cm}}$.

0.8854

$\begin{matrix} * & & & * \\ * & P(-1.33 \leq Z \leq 2) = 0.9772 - 0.0918 & * \\ * & & & * \end{matrix}$

PROGRAM SET 6.3   Percentiles of the Normal Distribution

Before studying this set, you should examine Figures 6-1(a) and
6-1(b), which show how we find a left-tail area associated with
a given value of z.   In this set, we shall learn how to find the
values of z associated with a given left-tail area.

1. Figure 6-2(a) shows the cumulative density function for the
   standard normal distribution.   This figure shows that for a
   left-tail area of 0.1000, the associated value of z is $\underline{\hspace{1cm}}$.

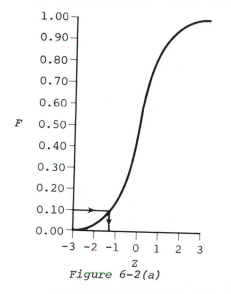

Figure 6-2(a)

-1.3

2. Figure 6-2(b) shows the same results on the standard normal
   (density/cumulative density) function.

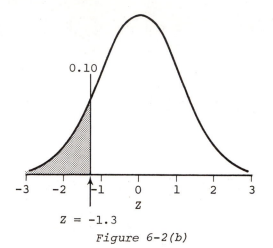

Z = -1.3

Figure 6-2(b)   density

3. Use Figure 6-2(a) to determine the z-values for the left-tail
   areas listed below.   Display your results on Figure 6-2(b).
   State your answers to one decimal place.

Left-tail Area	z-Value
0.10	-1.3
0.20	_____
0.30	_____
0.40	_____
0.50	_____
0.60	_____
0.70	_____
0.80	_____
0.90	_____

0.10	-1.3	-1.28
0.20	-0.8	_____
0.30	-0.5	_____
0.40	-0.2	_____
0.50	0.0	_____
0.60	0.2	_____
0.70	0.5	_____
0.80	0.8	_____
0.90	1.3	_____

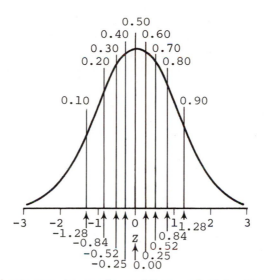

4. A more convenient way to work problems of this type is to use
   tabulated values. Table B-3 in Appendix B gives values of z
   for given left-tail areas. This table has a two-column format.
   The first column in each pair of columns lists the left-tail
   area and the second column gives the corresponding z-value.
   Turn to Table B-3 and find the left-tail area 0.100. The associated z-value for this area is _____.

                                                                    -1.28

5. Use Table B-3 to find the z-values requested in Frame 3. Use
   the space provided in the response to Frame 3.

                                                     0.10   -1.28
                                                     0.20   -0.84
                                                     0.30   -0.52
                                                     0.40   -0.25
                                                     0.50   0.00
                                                     0.60   0.25
                                                     0.70   0.52
                                                     0.80   0.84
                                                     0.90   1.28

6. In Table B-3, left-tail areas less than 0.100 and greater than
   0.900 are stated to three decimal places. Areas between these
   two values are stated to _____ decimal places.

                                                                    two

7. The reason for this is that we need to have (more/less) accuracy
   in the extremes of the normal distribution.

                                                                    more

8. In terms of probability notation, the problems we have been doing may be stated as $P(Z \leq ?) = 0.975$. This problem says, given the lower-tail probability 0.975, what value should replace the question mark so that the probability statement is true? Use the tables in Appendix B-3 to determine this value.
   _____

   1.96

9. The notation $P(Z \leq ?) = 0.975$ is cumbersome. Instead, we write the probability using a subscript: $z_{0.975}$. This notation means find a value of z that has an area of 0.975 to its (right/left).

   left

10. From the results of Frames 8 and 9 we know $z_{0.975} =$ _____.

    1.96

11. Values such as $z_{0.44}$ are called *percentiles* of the standard normal distribution. In other words, $z_{0.44}$ is the _____ percentile of the standard normal.

    44th

12. Thus, 44% of the standard normal is to the left of $z_{0.44} =$ _____.

    -0.15

13. So far we have worked with percentiles of the standard normal distribution. To obtain percentiles of any other normal distribution, we must solve the equation $z = (x - \mu)/\sigma$ for x. Thus $x = \mu +$ ____.

    $z\sigma$

14. If we wanted to find the 44th percentile of a normal distribution with a mean of 100 and a standard deviation of 10, we would first write:

    $$x_{0.44} = \mu + z_{0.44}\sigma$$

    The value of $x_{0.44}$ is $x_{0.44} =$ ____ + (____)(____) = ____.

    $100 + (-0.15)(10) = 98.5$

15. For a normal distribution with a mean of 100 and a standard
    deviation of 10, 44% of this distribution lies to the (left/
    right) of $x_{0.44}$ = 98.5

    left

16. For a normal distribution with a mean of 100 and a standard
    deviation of 10, $x_{0.975}$ = _____.

    119.6 $\begin{array}{l} x_{0.975} = \mu + z_{0.975}\sigma \\ = 100 + 1.96(10) \end{array}$

17. Tables B-2 and B-3 both refer to the standard normal. We use
    Table B-2 when we are given a value of (for) (z/probability) and
    need to determine a value of (for) (z/probability).

    z, probability

18. We use Table B-3 when we are given a value of (for) _____
    and need to determine a value of (for) _____.

    probability, z

PROGRAM SET 6.4   Normal Approximation to the Binomial

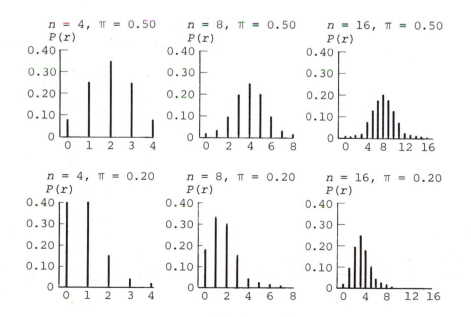

Figure 6-3   Selected Binomial Distributions

1. Figure 6-3 shows the binomial distributions from two Bernoulli processes. The top half of the figure presents binomial distributions
   for a process in which π = ____.   The bottom half of the figure
   presents binomial distributions for a process in which π = ____.
   In each half of this figure, the different distributions represent
   different sample sizes, 4, 8, and ____.

                                                          0.5, 0.2, 16

2. In Figure 6-3, all of the distributions for π = 0.5 (are/are not)
   symmetrical.

                                                                    are

3. All of the distributions for π = 0.2 are skewed.   The skewness is
   greater for n = (4 or 16) than it is for n = (4 or 16).

                                                                  4, 16

4. If π = 0.5, the binomial distribution (is/is not) symmetrical
   for any size n.

                                                                    is

5. We noted that as π departs from 0.5, skewness (decreases/
   increases).

                                                              increases

6. Also, we noted that the skewness will decrease as n _____.

                                                              increases

7. In fact, for π = 0.2, the shape of the distribution begins to
   resemble the shape of the normal distribution for n = (4 or 16).

                                                                    16

8. As suggested by Figure 6-3, for any value of π, the limit of the
   binomial distribution as n increases is a _____ distribution.

                                                                normal

9. The normal distribution can be used as an approximation of the
   binomial distribution.   It is a better approximation for any
   fixed value of π as ___ is increased.

                                                                     n

10. The generally accepted rule is that the normal distribution is a
    good enough approximation of the binomial if $n\pi/(1 - \pi)$ and

$n(1 - \pi)/\pi$ both equal or exceed 9. If we had a sample of four
with $\pi = 0.5$, this would be (sufficient/insufficient) to permit us to use the normal approximation.

$$\text{insufficient} \quad 4(0.5)/(0.5) = 4, \text{ which is less than } 9$$

11. Under this rule, for $\pi = 0.50$, a sample size of _____ is sufficient for use of the normal approximation of the binomial.

9

12. This rule indicates that if $\pi = 0.20$, we would need to have a
sample size of at least ____.

36

13. We have learned that the binomial probability distributions
are (discrete/continuous). The normal probability distribution is (discrete/continuous).

discrete, continuous

14. In using the normal distribution as an approximation of the
binomial distribution, we have to use normal probabilities
for intervals centered on integer values. That is, we need
to specify the limits associated with each _____.

integer

15. Suppose we want to use the normal approximation to the probability of a given value of r. The limits on the integer r are
$r + 0.5$ and $r - 0.5$, as illustrated in the following diagram.
To approximate a binomial probability for $P(R = 20)$, we use a
normal probability for $P(\_\_\_\_\_ \leq X \leq \_\_\_\_\_)$.

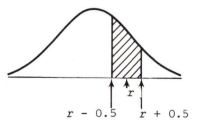

$r - 0.5 \qquad r + 0.5$

19.5, 20.5

16. As an example, suppose we wish to use the normal distribution
as an approximation of the binomial distribution for the case
$\pi = 0.4$ and $n = 15$. Before using the approximation, we must
calculate $n\pi/(1 - \pi)$ and $n(1 - \pi)/\pi$ to see if these values are

equal to or greater than 9. By the rule governing the appropriate use of the normal distribution for such an approximation, the binomial distribution with $\pi = 0.4$ and $n = 15$ (may/may not) be approximated by the normal distribution.

may

```
*
* $n\pi(1 - \pi)$ and $n(1 - \pi)/\pi$ are both greater than 9 for this example *
*
```

17. Suppose in the above example we wish to use the normal distribution to estimate $P(R = 9)$. The lower and upper limits in this case are ____ and ____.

8.5, 9.5

18. Now, if we find the normal probability for $P(8.5 \leq X \leq 9.5)$, we will approximate the exact binomial probability $P(R = \_\_\_)$.

9

19. Before finding $P(8.5 \leq X \leq 9.5)$, we need to know the mean and standard deviation for the normal distribution. Recall that the mean and standard deviation of the binomial sampling distribution are $\mu_r = n\pi$ and $\sigma_r = \sqrt{n\pi(1 - \pi)}$. In our example, these values are determined by $\mu_r =$ (____)(____) and $\sigma_r = \sqrt{(\_\_\_)(\_\_\_)(1 - \_\_\_)}$ (substitute, but do not solve).

$15(0.40)$, $\sqrt{15(0.40)(1 - 0.40)}$

20. Solving the equations, we obtain $\mu_r = 6$ and $\sigma_r = 1.9$. These are also the mean and standard deviation for the normal distribution. In order to find $P(8.5 \leq X \leq 9.5)$ on the normal distr˙˙ution, we need to find two z-values. These are

$$z = \frac{9.5 - 6}{1.9} \quad \text{and} \quad \frac{\_\_\_ - \_\_\_}{\_\_\_}$$

$\dfrac{8.5 - 6}{1.9}$

21. After doing the arithmetic, we find that $x = 9.5$ corresponds to $z = 1.84$ and $x = 8.5$ corresponds to $z = 1.32$. Thus $P(8.5 \leq X \leq 9.5) = P(\_\_\_\_ \leq Z \leq \_\_\_\_)$.

1.32, 1.84

22. Notice that $P(1.32 \leq Z \leq 1.84) = P(Z \leq 1.84) - P(Z \leq 1.32)$. From Table B-2, we find $P(Z \leq 1.84) = 0.9671$ and $P(Z \leq 1.32)$ _____.

0.9066

23. Thus $P(1.32 \leq Z \leq 1.84) =$ _____.

$$0.0605 \overset{*}{\underset{*}{*}} 0.9671 - 0.9066 \overset{*}{\underset{*}{*}}$$

24. Therefore $P(8.5 \leq X \leq 9.5) =$ _____.

0.0605

25. Thus $P(R = 9)$ is (exactly/approximately) equal to 0.0605.

approximately

26. As a check on how close our normal probability approximation is to the exact binomial probability, we may check the table of exact binomial probabilities. Table B-1 reveals that for $n = 15$, $\pi = 0.40$, and $r = 9$, the exact binomial probability is _____.

0.0612

CHAPTER 6.   SELF-CORRECTING EXERCISES

6.1 Probability Density Function   The following sketch shows a density function.

a. Explain how to use the density function to find probabilities.

b. What is the area under this density function between 0 and 10? What must be the total area under any density function? Why?

c. Use this density function to find the following probabilities.

   i. $P(1 \leq X \leq 4)$ v. $P(0 \leq X \leq 10)$

   ii. $P(X \leq 4)$ vi. $P(X \leq 10)$

  iii. $P(X \leq 1)$ vii. $P(X \leq 0)$

   iv. $P(X \geq 4)$

d. Use the results of (c) to verify the following
statements. Give an explanation for each.

i. $P(1 \leq X < 4) = P(X \leq 4) - P(X \leq 1)$

ii. $P(0 \leq X \leq 10) = P(X \leq 10) - P(X \leq 0)$

iii. $P(X \geq 4) = 1 - P(X \leq 4)$

What name is given to probabilities such as
$P(X \leq 4)$ and $P(X \leq 1)$?

e. Compute the following probabilities.

i. $P(3 \leq X \leq 4)$ iii. $P(3.375 \leq X \leq 3.625)$

ii. $P(3.25 \leq X \leq 3.75)$ iv. $P(3.4375 \leq X \leq 3.5625)$

f. The intervals for X in (e) are all centered on 3.5. What
happens to the probability as the interval decreases? What
would you conclude about the probability of X being in an
interval having no width? Thus what is $P(X = 3.5)$? For a
continuous random variable, what is the probability that X
is exactly equal to any given value?

6.2 Standard Normal Probability Distribution For the standard
normal probability distribution find the following probabilities using Appendix B in the text. Show your solution on
the accompanying graph.

a. $P(Z \leq -1.5)$ b. $P(Z > 1.80)$

c. $P(1.2 \leq Z \leq 2.5)$ d. $P(Z \leq 1.28)$

e. $P(Z \leq -1.64)$

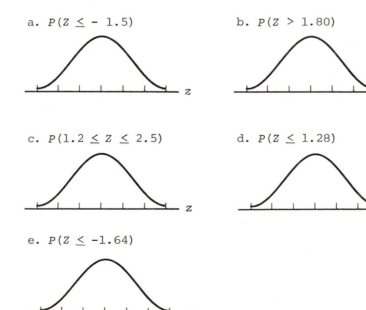

6.3 Normal Probability Distribution of X Use the three-step procedures developed in the text to solve the following.   Show your solution on the accompanying graph.   Here X = automobile speeds, μ = 55 mph, and σ = 6 mph.

  a. The probability of an automobile traveling less than 52 mph.

     1.

     2.

     3.

  b. The probability of an automobile traveling over 70 mph.

     1.

     2.

     3.

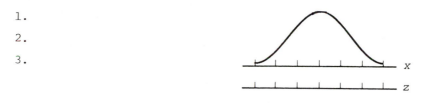

  c. The probability of an automobile traveling between 50 and 60 mph.

     1.

     2.

     3.

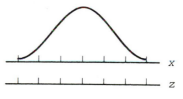

  d. The probability of an automobile exceeding 62.68 mph.

     1.

     2.

     3.

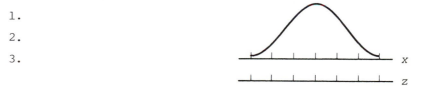

6.4 Percentiles of the Normal Distribution

  a. Use the tables in Appendix B-2 or B-3 to find the following: $z_{0.005}, z_{0.010}, z_{0.025}, z_{0.05}, z_{0.10}, z_{0.90}, z_{0.95}, z_{0.975}, z_{0.99}$, and $z_{0.995}$.

  b. Use the answers for (a) to answer the following questions.

    i.   What value of z cuts off an area of 0.025 to its *left*?

    ii.   What value of z cuts off an area of 0.975 to its *right*?

    iii.   What value of z cuts off an area of 0.975 to its *left*?

    iv.   What is the area between $z_{0.01}$ and $z_{0.99}$?

    v.   What is the area *outside* the interval $z_{0.01}$ to $z_{0.99}$?

    vi.   Construct a symmetrical interval around $z = 0$ such that the area *inside* the interval is 0.90.

    vii.   Construct a symmetrical interval around $z = 0$ such that 0.01 of the area is *outside* this interval.

    viii.   Construct a symmetrical interval around $z = 0$ such that 0.05 of the area is *outside* this interval.

c. Given X = Brand A **tire** mileage, $\mu = 40$ thousand miles, and $\sigma = 5$ thousand miles,

    i.   Construct a symmetrical interval around $\mu = 40$ such that the area *inside* the interval is 0.4514.

        1.

        2.

        3.

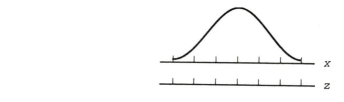

    ii.   The 25th percentile of the distribution of tire mileage.

        1.

        2.

        3.

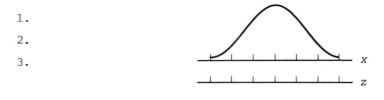

iii. The 80th percentile of the distribution of tire mileage.

1.

2.

3.

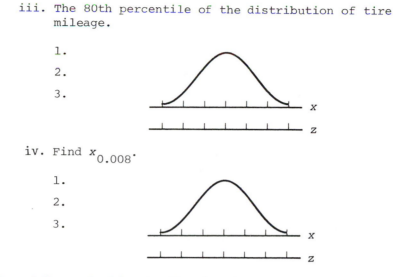

iv. Find $x_{0.008}$.

1.

2.

3.

6.5 Normal Approximation to the Binomial

a. Given a binomial probability distribution with n = 16 and π = 0.5, find each normal approximation.

   i. $P(R = 9)$

  ii. $P(R = 4)$

 iii. $P(R \leq 6)$

  iv. $P(R \geq 4)$

b. Find the exact binomial probabilities for (i) and (ii) of Part a in the binomial table.

CHAPTER 6.   ACHIEVEMENT TEST

The graphs below are to be used to answer Questions 1-4.   The graphs represent two different probability processes.

1. Identify the random variable for each graph as discrete or continuous.

2. Use the graphs to compute $P(X = 2)$ for both probability processes.

3. Use the graphs to compute $P(X = 6.5)$ for both probability processes.

4. Use the graphs to compute $P(7 \leq X \leq 9)$ for both probability processes.

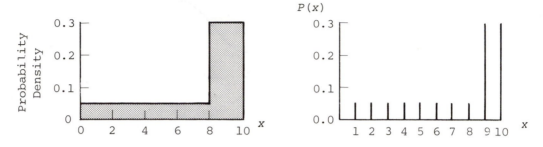

The graphs below are related. The one on the left is the probability density function and the one on the right is the cumulative density function of the random variable shown on the left.

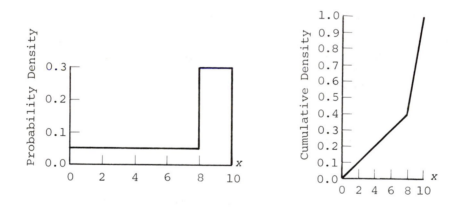

5. Use the graph on the left to compute the following probabilities:

   a. $P(X \leq 6)$

   b. $P(X \leq 9)$

   c. $P(6 \leq X \leq 9)$

6. Use the graph on the right to compute the probabilities requested in Question 5.

7. Use both graphs to find $P(X \geq 10)$.

8. Two normal distributions have the same mean. Are these distributions necessarily the same?

9. The distribution of IQs is normal with a mean of 100 and a standard deviation of 10.   The probability of finding an individual with an IQ greater than 110 is 0.1587.   Without making any calculations or using the tables, state the probability of finding an individual with an IQ less than 90.

10. How is the standard normal different than all other normal distributions?

11. Although there are an infinite number of normal distributions, we need to have tabulated values for only one distribution. Why?

12. How do we make two different normal distributions look alike?

13. An individual has an IQ of 152.   If IQs are distributed normally with a mean of 100 and a standard deviation of 10, what is this individual's standard score?

14. Use Table B-2 to find these standard normal probabilities:

   a. $P(Z \leq 0.85)$

   b. $P(Z \leq -0.6)$

   c. $P(-0.6 \leq Z \leq 0.85)$

15. Use Table B-2 to find these standard normal probabilities:

   a. $P(Z \leq 2.34)$

   b. $P(Z \geq 2.34)$

16. For the standard normal, what is the value of $P(Z \geq 6.41)$?

Questions 17-21 refer to a normal distribution with a mean of 100 and a standard deviation of 10.

17. $P(X \leq 82) = ?$

18. $P(70 \leq X \leq 115) = ?$

19. $P(X \geq 85) = ?$

20. Find the 75th percentile of this distribution.

21. We wish to construct an interval of X for this distribution that contains 90% of the values.   Five percent of the values are to lie above the interval and 5% are to lie below.   Determine the interval.

22. Does the normal approximation to the binomial apply to a binomial distribution that has $\pi = 0.10$ and $n = 200$? Why or why not?

23. Find the mean and standard deviation of a binomial distribution with $\pi = 0.5$ and $n = 1600$.

Questions 24-26 apply to finding normal approximations to the binomial distribution that has $\pi = 0.5$ and $n = 100$. For this distribution, $\mu = 50$ and $\sigma = 5$.

24. In order to find the normal approximation to $P(R = 47 | n = 100, \pi = 0.5)$, what interval on the normal distribution should be used? What is the corresponding interval on the standard normal?

25. Find the normal approximation to $P(R = 47 | n = 100, \pi = 0.5)$.

26. Find the 75th percentile of the binomial distribution.

CHAPTER 6. STUDENT RECORD AND REFERENCE SHEET

Darken the square corresponding to each test item you answered *incorrectly*. References indicate the topics you should study. See Chapter 1 of this volume for details.

Test Item	Diagnostic Test	Achievement Test	Text References	Self-Correcting Exercise References	Program Set References
1	☐	☐	149–151	6.1	—
2	☐	☐	149–151	6.1	—
3	☐	☐	149–151	6.1	—
4	☐	☐	149–151	6.1	—
5	☐	☐	151–152	6.1	—
6	☐	☐	151–152	6.1	—
7	☐	☐	151–152	6.1	—
8	☐	☐	152–155	6.1	—
9	☐	☐	152–155	6.1	6.1
10	☐	☐	152–155	6.2	6.1
11	☐	☐	156–161	6.2	6.1
12	☐	☐	156–161	6.2	6.1
13	☐	☐	156–161	6.2	6.1
14	☐	☐	156–161	6.2	6.1
15	☐	☐	156–161	6.2	6.1
16	☐	☐	156–161	6.2	6.1
17	☐	☐	156–161	6.3	6.2
18	☐	☐	156–161	6.3	6.2
19	☐	☐	156–161	6.3	6.2
20	☐	☐	156–161	6.4	6.3
21	☐	☐	156–161	6.4	6.3
22	☐	☐	163–168	6.5	6.4
23	☐	☐	163–168	6.5	6.4
24	☐	☐	163–168	6.5	6.4
25	☐	☐	163–168	6.5	6.4
26	☐	☐	163–168	6.5	6.4

7

SAMPLING METHODS AND SAMPLING DISTRIBUTIONS

CHAPTER 7. DIAGNOSTIC TEST

An auditor wishes to obtain a sample of balances from 10 accounts. The account numbers and balances are listed below.

Account Number	Balance	Account Number	Balance
1	$ 61.00	6	$ 35.00
2	$ 30.00	7	$150.00
3	$ 25.00	8	$ 20.00
4	$110.00	9	$ 60.00
5	$ 40.00	10	$ 20.00

A random number table produces the following single-digit random numbers.

7	4	0	4	1
5	7	2	2	2
7	4	0	1	1
6	7	7	8	8
5	4	5	0	6

These values were selected sequentially from a table of random numbers and they are to be used to obtain the sample.

Use this information to answer Questions 1-5.

1. Assume the first random number selected is in the first column. The second, third, fourth, and fifth random numbers appear in order in the first column. Use these random numbers to obtain a random sample of five accounts. Assume sampling *without* replacement.

2. What is the sample mean of the sample data obtained in Question 1? What symbol is used for this mean?

3. Rework Question 1 assuming sampling *with* replacement.

4. What is the sample mean for the sample data obtained in Question 3?

5. What is the mean of the population of 10 balances? Is this value equal to the mean found in Question 2? What symbol is used for the population mean?

6. There are 10(9)(8)(7)(6) sequences of 5 balances that can be selected without replacement from a population of 10 balances. What is the mean of the 30,240 sample means?

7. The standard deviation of the population of 10 balances is σ = \$40.88. What is the standard error of the mean if 5 values are used in a random sample *with* replacement?

8. Rework Question 7 assuming five values are used in a sample *without* replacement.

9. If a random sample of 100 balances is taken *with* replacement, what is the standard deviation of the distribution of sample means? What is the shape of this distribution?

10. How would a sample size of 400 influence the answers to Question 9?

11. Intelligence quotients are normally distributed with a mean of 100 and a standard deviation of 10.0. What is the probability that an individual selected at random will have an IQ greater than exactly 106?

12. For the situation described in Question 11, what is the probability that a random sample of 25 individuals selected from a very large population will have an average IQ greater than exactly 106?

13. For a random sample of 16 IQs, find the value of the sample mean that has a probability 0.05 of being exceeded.

14. Fifty percent of the admissions for a large hospital are for patients who will have surgery. What are the mean and standard deviation of the sampling distribution of the proportion for random samples of 16 observations?

15. Explain any differences between the quantity represented by p and by π.

16. In a population, 40% of the consumers prefer Brand A. In a random sample of 10 observations from this population, what is the probability of observing 20% or fewer who prefer Brand A?

17. For the population described in Question 16, could you use the normal approximation for the sampling distribution of the proportion if $n = 10$? If $n = 20$?

18. Ten percent of the items in a production run are defective. For a random sample of 400 items, what is the probability that 15% or more of the items in the sample are defective?

PROGRAM SET 7.1   Sampling from Normal Populations

1. Suppose a lumber yard owner knows that the dollar value of all orders received is normally distributed with a mean μ = $150 per order and a standard deviation of σ = $10. If we want to write an expression referring to the probability that any single order selected at random is less than $180 but more than $120, we write $P($_____$)$.

$$120 \leq X \leq 180$$

2. By converting x to z and using Table B-2 in the text, we may find $P(120 \leq X \leq 180) =$ _____.

$$0.9972 \; {}^{*}_{*} \; P(-3 \leq Z \leq 3) = 0.9986 - 0.0014 \; {}^{*}_{*}$$

3. You must be very careful to notice that the statement $P(120 \leq X \leq 180) = 0.9972$ refers to the probability that any single order selected at random from the population of (some/ all) orders will lie in the specified interval.

all

4. Thus we know the population of orders is _____ distributed with $\mu =$ _____ and $\sigma =$ ____.

normally, 150, 10

5. In statistics, we are often concerned with a collection of observations taken from a population. If we selected 4 orders at random from the population, the four orders would constitute a sample for which n = ____.

4

6. Suppose these 4 observations were obtained from this population: $100, $140, $160, and $120. The mean of these observations is computed from $\overline{X} = (\Sigma X)/n$ and in this case $\overline{X}$ = ____.

$$130 \;\ast\ast\; 520/4 \;\ast\ast$$

7. Of course, $\overline{X}$ = 130 is only one of many possible values of the sample mean that could be obtained from four observations in this population. The distribution of all sample means is an important consideration in statistics. We have seen that the mean and variance of the distribution of sample means are given by $\mu_{\overline{X}} = \mu$ and $\sigma^2_{\overline{X}} = \sigma^2/n$. In these relationships, μ and σ^2 refer to the mean and variance of the _____.

population

8. Since μ = 150, σ^2 = 100, and n = 4, $\mu_{\overline{X}}$ = ____ and $\sigma^2_{\overline{x}}$ = ____.

$$150, 25 \;\ast\ast\; 100/4 \;\ast\ast$$

9. In other words, the mean and standard deviation of the distribution of sample means are $\mu_{\overline{x}}$ = 150 and $\sigma_{\overline{x}}$ = ____.

$$5 \;\ast\ast\; \sigma_{\overline{x}} = \sqrt{\sigma^2_{\overline{x}}} = \sqrt{25} \;\ast\ast$$

10. As you may have guessed, the distribution of sample means from a normal population is also _____ distributed.

normally

11. Since the distribution of sample means is normal with $\mu_{\overline{X}}$ = 150 and $\sigma_{\overline{X}}$ = 5, we may use Table B-2 in the text to compute the probability that the sample mean will be less than some specific value. Suppose we wish to determine $P(\overline{X} \leq 162)$. Our first task is to solve the equivalent standard normal distribution problems; that is, we should find $P(Z \leq$ ____$)$.

$$2.4 \;\ast\ast\; (162 - 150)/5 \;\ast\ast$$

12. From Table B-2, $P(Z \leq 2.4)$ = _____.

0.9918

13. Thus $P(\overline{X} \leq 162)$ = _____.

$$0.9918$$

14. For our example, $P(140 \leq \overline{X} \leq 160) = P(\_\_\_\_ \leq z \leq \_\_\_)$.

$$-2 \; \substack{* \\ * \\ *} \; (140 - 150)/5 \; \substack{* \\ * \\ *}, \; 2 \; \substack{* \\ * \\ *} \; (160 - 150)/5 \; \substack{* \\ * \\ *}$$

15. From Table B-2, $P(-2 \leq z \leq 2)$ = _____ - _____ = _____.

$$0.9772 - 0.0228 = 0.9544$$

16. In other words, a sample mean of 4 independent observations taken from this population will fall in the interval ____ to ____ 95.44% of the time.

$$140, 160$$

17. When working with the distribution of $\overline{X}$ where observations are taken from a normal population, you should remember that the distribution of $\overline{X}$ has a _____ distribution.

$$normal$$

PROGRAM SET 7.2   Sampling from Nonnormal Populations

1. We have seen that the distribution of sample means follows a normal distribution when the population has a _____ distribution.

$$normal$$

2. The question naturally arises regarding the distribution of sample means from a nonnormal population. The sketch shows the probability distribution for a population.

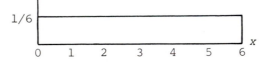

As you can see this population (is/is not) normally distributed.

$$is \; not$$

3. Our concern is with the distribution of sample means from this population. The mean and standard deviation of the distribution of sample means are given by $\mu_{\overline{X}} = \mu$ and $\sigma_{\overline{X}}^2 = \sigma^2/n$. For the popula- shown in the last frame, $\mu = 3$ and $\sigma^2 = 3$. Thus we know $\mu_{\overline{X}} = \_\_\_$.

3

4. In order to find $\sigma^2_{\overline{X}}$, we need to specify a sample size. Suppose we decide to use $n = 300$. Thus $\sigma^2_{\overline{X}} =$ _____ .

0.01 or 1/100 ✳ 3/300 ✳

5. In other words, the distribution of sample means has $\mu_{\overline{X}} =$ ____ and $\sigma_{\overline{X}} =$ _____ .

3, 0.1 ✳ $\sigma_{\overline{X}} = \sqrt{\sigma^2_{\overline{X}}} = \sqrt{1/100}$ ✳

6. Since the population has a rectangular shape, you may be tempted to say the distribution of sample means has the same shape as the population. This is not correct. The central limit theorem tells us that for a population whose probability distribution has *any* shape, the probability distribution of sample means is approximately normal provided n is sufficiently large. Since our population has a rectangular probability distribution, it (is/is not) normal. The central limit theorem tells us the distribution of sample means from this population will be (rectangular/normal/approximately normal).

is not, approximately normal

7. The sketch shows the population for our example. To the right of this sketch, draw a sketch of the distribution of sample means for $n = 300$. On your sketch, indicate the location and value of the mean of this distribution and give the value of the standard deviation. Be sure to label the axis.

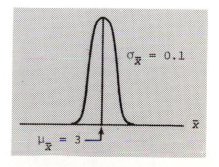

8. It is extremely important that you understand the meaning of the central limit theorem. It tells us that the distribution of sample means from a population having any shape is (normal/the same shape as the population/approximately normal) provided n is sufficiently large.

approximately normal

9. The accuracy of the approximation depends on the sample size. As a rule of thumb, there must be at least 30 observations to make the approximation reasonably accurate. As you might suspect, the accuracy of the approximation increases as n (increases/decreases).

increases

10. In our example $n = 300$. Thus we would expect a normal distribution of sample means to be a (poor/good) approximation.

good

11. Since the distribution of sample means is approximately normal, we may use Table B-2 in the text to answer probability problems concerning the sample mean. In our example, $\mu_{\overline{X}} = 3$ and $\sigma_{\overline{X}} = 0.1$. Thus, $P(2.85 \leq \overline{X} \leq 3.15) = $ _____ $-$ _____ $= $ _____ .

0.9332 - 0.0668 = 0.8664

$$* \atop * \atop * \quad P(2.85 \leq \overline{X} \leq 3.15) = P(-1.5 \leq Z \leq 1.5) \quad {* \atop * \atop *}$$

12. For the same example, $P(2.81 \leq \overline{X} \leq 3.26) = $ _____ $-$ _____ $=$ _____ .

0.9953 - 0.0287 = 0.9666

$$* \atop * \atop * \quad P(2.81 \leq \overline{X} \leq 3.26) = P(-1.9 \leq Z \leq 2.6) \quad {* \atop * \atop *}$$

13. In statistics we frequently work with populations that *are* and *are not* normally distributed. If a population has a normal distribution, then the distribution of sample means will be (exactly/approximately) normally distributed.

exactly

14. If a population is not normally distributed, the distribution of sample means will be (exactly/approximately) normally distributed if $n \geq$ ____ .

approximately, 30

15. Since the central limit theorem applies to a probability distribution of any shape, we (may/may not) apply this theorem when the population has a probability distribution of an unknown shape.

may

16. Provided we make the sample size large enough, the central limit theorem assures us that the probability distribution of the (population/sample mean) is approximately normal.

sample mean

CHAPTER 7.   SELF-CORRECTING EXERCISES

7.1 Simple Random Sampling   These data represent the incomes (nearest thousand dollars) of 20 families living in a garden apartment. The apartments are numbered serially by building (apartment numbers appear in parentheses). There are four buildings—A, B, C, and D. Some of the apartments in each building face a center court, some face a major arterial street, and some face a residential street.

Facing	Building			
	A	B	C	D
Court	(1) 9	(6) 9	(11) 12	(16) 13
	(2) 8	(7) 10	(12) 14	(17) 13
	(3) 10			(18) 13
Residential	(4) 4	(8) 8	(13) 9	(19) 12
		(9) 8		
Arterial	(5) 5	(10) 5	(14) 6	(20) 9
			(15) 5	

a. Give a brief explanation of how to use a table of random numbers to draw a simple random sample.

b. Use the table of random numbers (Table B-8 in the text) to select an unrestricted simple random sample of 8 families without replacement. (For the sake of definiteness, start with the left-most column of two-digit numbers reading the numbers consecutively from top to bottom. Discard numbers not in the interval 1-20). Display your results in a table such as Table 7-2 in the text. Include the value of income for each unit selected.

c. Is this sampling technique done with or without replacement?

d. What is the sample mean?

e. Suppose you "ran out" of random numbers at the end of the first column. What would you do?

f. State whether you think the following statements are true or false and explain your answers.

    i. Two persons acting independently of each other take random samples of 8 families in the garden apartment. The two sets of data should be exactly the same.

    ii. Every time a table of random numbers is used, start in the same place in the table.

7.2 The Mean and the Standard Deviation of the Sampling Distribution of the Mean

a. Was the sample found in Question 7.1 selected with or without replacement?

b. The mean and standard deviation of all 20 incomes are $9.1 thousand and $3.0 thousand, respectively. What symbols should be used to describe these values?

c. What are the mean and standard deviation of the distribution of sample means if a simple random sample of 8 families is selected without replacement? What symbols should be used to represent these quantities?

d. How would your answers to (c) change if a simple random sample of 16 families were selected without replacement? If 4 families were selected without replacement?

e. How would your answers to (c) and to (d) change if a simple random sample of 8 families were selected *with* replacement?

f. Use the results of (c), (d), and (e) to explain the influence of n and $(\frac{N - n}{N - 1})$ on the standard deviation of the distribution of sample means.

g. Is the sample mean you found in Question 7.1 equal to the population mean? Would you expect these quantities to be equal?

7.3 Development of the Sampling Distribution of the Mean

a. There are 4 pool balls in an urn—a two-ball, a four-ball, a six-ball, and an eight-ball. Find the mean and variance of X, where x is the value associated with a ball.

b. Listed below are all of the possible sample results for the experiment *draw 2 balls from the urn with replacement and find the sample mean*. Complete the table by finding the rest of the sample means.

Sample	$\bar{x}$	Sample	$\bar{x}$	Sample	$\bar{x}$	Sample	$\bar{x}$
2, 2	2	4, 2	3	6, 2	___	8, 2	___
2, 4	3	4, 4	4	6, 4	___	8, 4	___
2, 6	4	4, 6	5	6, 6	___	8, 6	___
2, 8	5	4, 8	6	6, 8	___	8, 8	___

c. Find the frequency distribution of the sample means found in (b). List your results in the table below:

$\bar{x}$	$f(\bar{x})$
2	1
3	2
4	
5	
6	
7	
8	

d. Convert the frequencies in (c) to probabilities and find the mean and the standard deviation of the distribution of sample means.

e. Use Equations 7-1 and 7-2 in the text to compute the mean and the standard deviation of the distribution of sample means. How do your results compare with those obtained in (d)?

f. Now suppose a sample of 2 is taken *without* replacement. On the list given in (b), cross off the samples and sample means that are not possible with this sampling procedure. Find the distribution of sample means.

g. Use the distribution in (f) to find the mean and the standard deviation of the distribution of sample means. Compare these results with those found in (d).

h. Use Equations 7-1 and 7-2 in the text to find the mean and standard deviation of the distribution of sample means for sampling without replacement. Compare your results with those obtained in (g).

i. On the grids below, plot the sampling distribution of the mean for sampling with and without replacement.

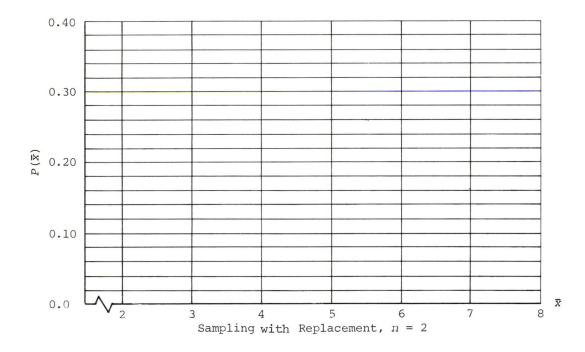

Sampling with Replacement, $n = 2$

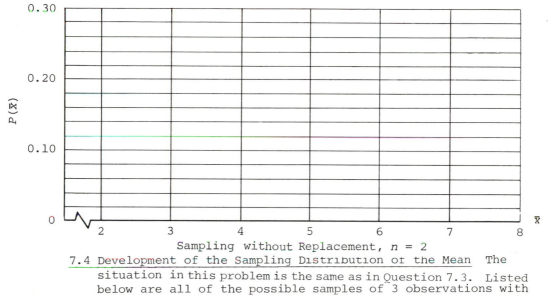

Sampling without Replacement, $n = 2$

7.4 Development of the Sampling Distribution of the Mean   The situation in this problem is the same as in Question 7.3.   Listed below are all of the possible samples of 3 observations with replacement.

Sample	Sample Mean	Sample	Sample Mean	Sample	Sample Mean	Sample	Sample Mean
2, 2, 2		2, 2, 4		2, 2, 6		2, 2, 8	
2, 4, 2		2, 4, 4		2, 4, 6		2, 4, 8	
2, 6, 2		2, 6, 4		2, 6, 6		2, 6, 8	
2, 8, 2		2, 8, 4		2, 8, 6		2, 8, 8	
4, 2, 2		4, 2, 4		4, 2, 6		4, 2, 8	
4, 4, 2		4, 4, 4		4, 4, 6		4, 4, 8	
4, 6, 2		4, 6, 4		4, 6, 6		4, 6, 8	
4, 8, 2		4, 8, 4		4, 8, 6		4, 8, 8	
6, 2, 2		6, 2, 4		6, 2, 6		6, 2, 8	
6, 4, 2		6, 4, 4		6, 4, 6		6, 4, 8	
6, 6, 2		6, 6, 4		6, 6, 6		6, 6, 8	
6, 8, 2		6, 8, 4		6, 8, 6		6, 8, 8	
8, 2, 2		8, 2, 4		8, 2, 6		8, 2, 8	
8, 4, 2		8, 4, 4		8, 4, 6		8, 4, 8	
8, 6, 2		8, 6, 4		8, 6, 6		8, 6, 8	
8, 8, 2		8, 8, 4		8, 8, 6		8, 8, 8	

a. Find the probability distribution of sample means and plot this distribution on the grid. What are the mean and the standard deviation of this distribution?

b. On the list of samples given above, cross off the sample
   that would be impossible if sampling were done without replacement. Find the probability distribution of the sample
   means. What are the mean and standard deviation of this
   distribution? Plot the distribution on the grid.

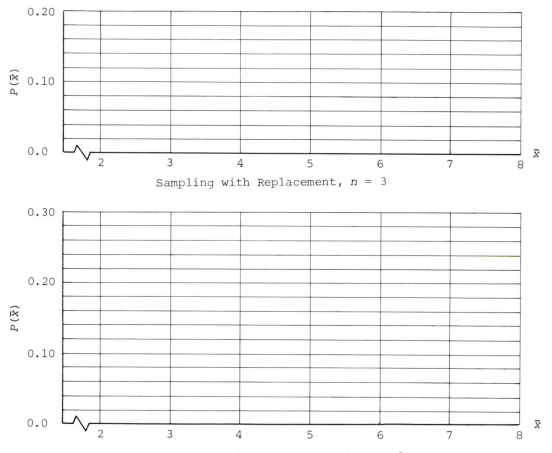

Sampling with Replacement, $n = 3$

Sampling without Replacement, $n = 3$

c. For a fixed sample size, what is the influence of sampling without replacement on the standard deviation of the
   distribution of the sample means? Use your graphs and
   computations from (a) and (b) to justify your answers.

d. If samples of 4 observations without replacement were drawn
   from the population, how many different sample sequences
   would be possible? What would be the value of the standard
   deviation of the distribution of sample means? What would
   be the standard deviation of the distribution of sample
   means if the sampling were done with replacement?

e. Explain the influence of the sample size on the standard deviation of the distribution of sample means. Use your answers for Questions 7.3 and 7.4 to justify your answer.

f. What is the influence of the sample size on the mean of the distribution of sample means?

7.5 <u>Sampling from Normal Distributions</u>   Verbal SAT scores are normally distributed with a mean of 500 and a standard deviation of 100. The graph of the distribution is shown below.

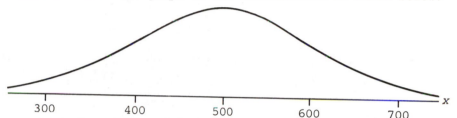

a. A random sample of 4 observations is drawn from this population. The observations are 610, 490, 525, 505. What is the sample mean? How many such samples are possible?

b. What are the mean and standard deviation of the sampling distribution of which the sample mean in (a) is a member?

c. One thousand random samples such as the one in (a) were drawn from the population. The frequency distribution for the sample mean is shown below. On the grid, plot the histogram of the relative frequencies.

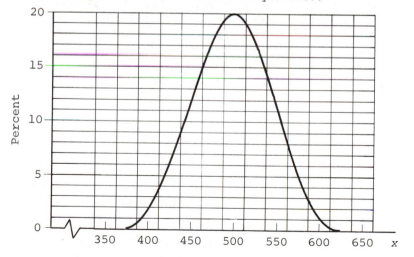

Sample Mean $(\bar{x})$	f
338 - 362	7
363 - 387	8
388 - 412	27
413 - 437	71
438 - 462	117
463 - 487	167
488 - 512	198
513 - 537	173
538 - 562	119
563 - 587	71
588 - 612	30
613 - 637	8
638 - 662	4
	1000

d. Does the distribution of sample means appear to be normally distributed? Does the shape of the sampling distribution appear to be in accordance with sampling theory? Does the sample size influence the normality (or nonnormality) of the distribution?

7.6 The Central Limit Theorem The distribution of repair times for electronic components being repaired is shown in the figure below. The mean repair time for all components is 1 hour and the standard deviation is 1 hour.

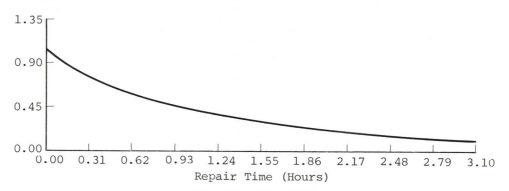

a. A random sample of repair times (in hours) for 4 components produces the following sample data: 0.90, 1.10, 1.21, 0.86. What is the sample mean? How many sample means are possible?

b. A thousand samples such as the one in (a) were selected. What is the mean of the 1000 sample means? What is the standard deviation?

c. Table 7-1 shows the distribution of the values of the 1000 means. Plot the relative frequency distribution for these means using the class limits given in Table 7-1. Does the distribution of sample means appear to be a normal distribution?

Table 7-1   *Distribution of Sample Means for n = 4*

Sample Means ($\bar{x}$)	f
-0.02 - 0.21	8
0.22 - 0.45	110
0.46 - 0.69	188
0.70 - 0.93	207
0.94 - 1.17	170
1.18 - 1.41	129
1.42 - 1.65	78
1.66 - 1.89	57
1.90 - 2.13	20
2.14 - 2.37	12
2.38 - 2.61	14
2.62 - 2.85	2
2.86 - 3.09	3
3.10 - 3.33	2
	1000

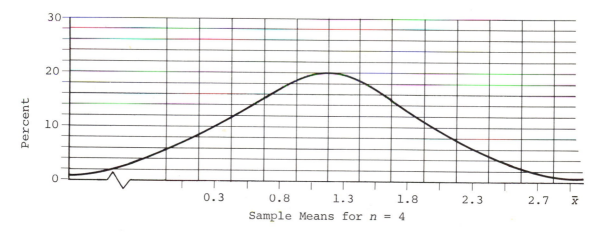

Sample Means for *n* = 4

d. A thousand sample means are selected from the population of repair times. Each sample mean is based on 16 observations. What are the mean and standard deviation of these sample means?

e. The frequency distribution of the 1000 sample means is shown in Table 7-2. Plot the relative frequency distribution of these means using the class limits stated below. Does this distribution of sample means appear to be a normal distribution?

Table 7-2   Distribution of Sample Means for n = 16

Sample Means ($\bar{x}$)	f
0.37 - 0.48	10
0.49 - 0.60	41
0.61 - 0.72	87
0.73 - 0.84	158
0.85 - 0.96	190
0.97 - 1.08	183
1.09 - 1.20	134
1.21 - 1.32	95
1.33 - 1.44	50
1.45 - 1.56	26
1.57 - 1.68	15
1.69 - 1.80	10
1.81 - 1.92	1
	1000

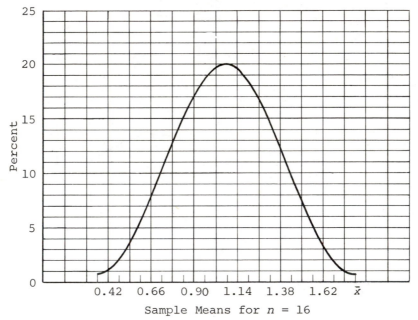

Sample Means for *n* = 16

f. The relative frequency distribution in Table 7-3 is for a thousand sample means each based on 64 observations. What are the mean and standard deviation of this distribution? Does this distribution of sample means appear to be a normal distribution?

Table 7-3   Distribution of Sample Means for n = 64

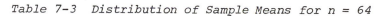

Sample Means ($\overline{x}$)	f	Sample Means ($\overline{x}$)	f
0.68 – 0.73	11	1.10 – 1.15	110
0.74 – 0.79	28	1.16 – 1.21	61
0.80 – 0.85	90	1.22 – 1.27	33
0.86 – 0.91	128	1.28 – 1.33	8
0.92 – 0.97	159	1.34 – 1.39	2
0.98 – 1.03	221	1.40 – 1.45	4
1.04 – 1.09	143	1.46 – 1.51	2
		total f =	1000

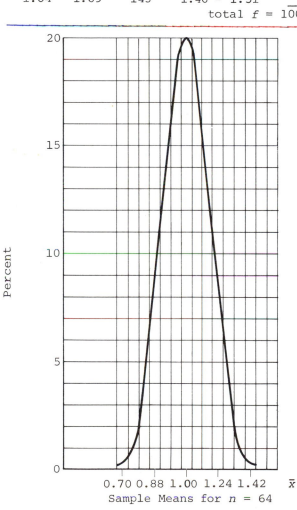

Sample Means for *n* = 64

g. Were the samples drawn from a normal population? What happened to the shape of the sampling distribution as the sample size is increased? Why?

7.7 Mean and Variance of the Distribution of Sample Means Over the past year, the manager of a large department store knows that the mean dollar value of all purchases is $15 per purchase and the standard deviation is $2. Consider these purchases to be a normal population.

a. For a random sample of nine observations, compute the mean, variance, and standard deviation of the distribution of sample means.

b. Assume a random sample of 36 observations is to be taken. Repeat the computations in (a). How does an increase in sample size influence each of these values?

c. On the same axis, sketch the population and the distribution of sample means for $n = 9$ and $n = 36$. What is the shape of these distributions?

7.8 Finding Probabilities on Normal Sampling Distributions The situation in this exercise is the same as in Question 7.7.

a. What is the probability that a single purchase will be more than $16?

b. What is the probability that a random sample of 9 purchases will have an average greater than $16?

c. What is the probability that a random sample of 36 purchases will have an average greater than $16?

d. What is the probability that the mean of a random sample of 9 observations will be within ±$0.50 of the population mean?

e. What is the probability that the mean of a random sample of 36 observations will be within ±$0.50 of the population mean?

7.9 Percentile of a Normal Sampling Distribution The situation in this exercise is the same as in Question 7.7.

a. For a situation involving a random sample of 9 observations, what sample mean has a probability of 0.05 of being exceeded? What sample mean has a probability 0.01 of being exceeded?

b. Answer (a) assuming a random sample of 36 observations.

7.10 <u>The Sampling Distribution of the Mean</u> Assume a population has a normal distribution with a mean of 100 and a standard deviation of 10.

a. If 25 observations are to be taken from this population, find the mean and standard deviation of the distribution of sample means from this population.

b. i. What value of $\overline{x}$ cuts off an area of 0.025 to its left?

   ii. What value of $\overline{x}$ cuts off an area of 0.975 to its right?

   ii. What value of $\overline{x}$ cuts off an area of 0.975 to its left?

   iv. What is the area between $\overline{x}_{0.01}$ and $\overline{x}_{0.99}$?

   v. What is the area outside the interval $\overline{x}_{0.01}$ to $\overline{x}_{0.99}$?

   vi. Construct a symmetrical interval around $\mu_{\overline{x}} = 100$ such that the area inside the interval is 0.90.

   vii. Construct a symmetrical interval around $\mu_{\overline{x}} = 100$ such that 0.01 of the area is outside this interval.

   viii. Construct a symmetrical interval around $\mu_{\overline{x}} = 100$ such that 0.05 of the area is outside this interval.

c. Discuss the following statements.

   i. The mean of 25 observations taken from this population must always be 100.

   ii. The mean of all possible sample means, each of which is based on 25 observations from this population, must equal 100.

7.11 <u>The Sampling Distribution of the Proportion</u> When in the home office, a sales representative must place long-distance calls through a central operator. During morning hours, the operator is busy 2/3 of the time. The binomial sampling distribution for the number of times the representative succeeds in getting the operator is shown below. This distribution was developed in Self-Correcting Exercise 5.6 and is based on a Bernoulli process for which $\pi = 1/3$.

r	P(r)	p	P(p)
0	8/27		
1	12/27		
2	6/27		
3	1/27		

a. From the bionomial distribution, determine the value of n.

b. In the space to the right of the binomial distribution, find the corresponding sampling distribution of the proportion. What is the largest and the smallest value of the random variable?

c. In what ways are the two distributions similar? In what ways are they different?

d. Would you judge the two distributions to have the same mean? The same variance? Explain your answers.

e. Compute the mean of each distribution using $\mu = \Sigma[x * P(x)]$.

f. Verify your answer to (e) using formula 7.5 in the text.

g. Compute the standard deviation of each distribution using formula 7.6 in the text.

h. How would your answers to (f) and (g) change if the sales representative placed 49 calls?

i. Consider the situation in which the representative attempts to place three calls. What is the probability of *one successful call*? What is the probability of *one third of the calls being successful*? Are the events for these probabilities the same?

7.12 The Normal Approximation for the Sampling Distribution of the Proportion One-fourth of the persons contracted in a fundraising drive for a public FM radio station will make a contribution. A random sample of 300 persons will be contacted.

a. What is the mean and standard deviation of the distribution of the sample proportion?

b. Can the normal approximation be used for this sampling distribution? Why or why not?

c. What is the probability that the proportion of persons contacted who contribute is less than or equal to 0.20?

(Include the continuity correction factor as in Equation 7-7.)

d. Work (c) again, neglecting the correction factor. How do the answers compare?

e. Find the mean and standard deviation for the binomial sampling distribution with n = 300 and π = 0.25.

f. For the distribution in (e), find the probability that $R \leq 60$. Include the continuity correction factor as in Equation 7-7.

g. Compare your answers for (c) and (f). Explain any similarities or differences.

CHAPTER 7. ACHIEVEMENT TEST

A town manager wishes to obtain a sample of four tax bills from 10 accounts. The account numbers and amounts are listed below:

Account Number	Amount	Account Number	Amount
1	$ 1010	6	$ 890
2	$ 715	7	$ 780
3	875	8	$ 810
4	550	9	$ 960
5	1210	10	$ 1050

A random number table produces the following single-digit random numbers.

6	4	0	4	1
4	7	2	2	2
3	4	0	1	1
4	7	7	8	8
5	4	5	0	6

These values were selected sequentially from a table of random numbers and they are to be used to obtain the sample. Use this information to answer Questions 1-5.

1. Assume the first random number selected is in the first column. The second, third, fourth, and fifth random numbers appear in order in the first column. Use these random numbers to obtain

a random sample of four accounts. Assume sampling *without* re-placement.

2. What is the sample mean of the sample data obtained in Question 1? What symbol is used for the mean?

3. Rework Question 1 assuming sampling *with* replacement.

4. What is the sample mean for the sample data obtained in Question 3?

5. What is the mean of the population of 10 accounts? Is this value equal to the mean found in Question 2? What symbol is used for the population mean?

6. There are 10(9)(8)(7) sequences of 4 balances that can be selected *without* replacement from a population of 10 balances. What is the mean of these 5040 sample means?

7. The standard deviation of the population of 10 balances is $\sigma = \$177$. What is the standard error of the mean if 4 values are used in a random sample *with* replacement?

8. Rework Question 7 assuming $n = 10$ and sampling *without* re-placement.

9. If a random sample of 144 accounts is taken *with* replacement, what is the standard deviation of the distribution of sample means? What is the shape of this distribution?

10. How would a sample size of 9 influence the answers to Question 9?

11. Incomes in a city are normally distributed with a mean of $20,000 and a standard deviation of $1000. What is the probability that an individual selected at random will have an income less than $19,000?

12. For the situation described in Question 11, what is the probability that a random sample of 25 individuals will have an average income less than $19,000?

13. For a random sample of 16 incomes, find the value of the sample mean that has a probability 0.10 of being exceeded?

14. Fifty percent of the admissions for a large hospital are for patients who will have surgery. What are the mean and standard deviation of the sampling distribution of the proportion for a random sample of 64 observations?

15. Which of the following parameters is *not* influenced by the sample size: the mean or standard deviation of the binomial, the mean or standard deviation of the distribution of the proportion?

16. In a population, 60% of the consumers prefer brand A. In a random sample of 12 observations from the population, what is the probability of observing 75% or fewer who prefer brand A?

17. For the population described in Question 16, could you use the normal approximation for the sampling distribution of the proportion if n = 10? If n = 20?

18. Thirty-six percent of the items in a production run have a minor flaw. For a random sample of 400 items, what is the probability that 30% or less of the items in the sample have minor flaws?

CHAPTER 7.   STUDENT RECORD AND REFERENCE SHEET

Darken the square corresponding to each test item you answered *incorrectly*. References indicate the topics you should study. See Chapter 1 of this volume for details.

Test Item	Diagnostic Test	Achievement Test	Text References	Self-Correcting Exercise References	Program Set References
1	☐	☐	176–180	7.1	—
2	☐	☐	176–180	7.1	—
3	☐	☐	176–180	7.1	—
4	☐	☐	176–180	7.1	—
5	☐	☐	181–189	7.2	—
6	☐	☐	181–189	7.2–7.4	—
7	☐	☐	181–189	7.2–7.4	—
8	☐	☐	181–189	7.2–7.4	—
9	☐	☐	181–189	7.2–7.4	7.1, 7.2
10	☐	☐	181–189	7.6	7.1, 7.2
11	☐	☐	190–192	7.8	7.1, 7.2
12	☐	☐	190–192	7.9	7.1, 7.2
13	☐	☐	190–192	7.9	7.1, 7.2
14	☐	☐	194–197	7.11	—
15	☐	☐	194–197	7.11	—
16	☐	☐	194–197	7.11	—
17	☐	☐	194–197	7.12	—
18	☐	☐	194–197	7.12	—

8

ESTIMATION OF MEANS AND PROPORTIONS

CHAPTER 8. DIAGNOSTIC TEST

1. The sketch shows two sampling distributions for an estimator of the population mean μ. Is the estimator unbiased?

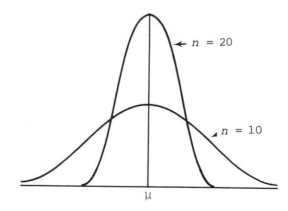

2. An estimator for the population mean has an expected value of 50. If the population mean is 40, is the estimator biased or unbiased?

3. The standard normal is to be used in the computation of a symmetrical confidence interval. If the level of confidence will be 0.8, what is the absolute value of z that should be used in the computation?

For Questions 4-6, assume a random sample of 3 observations produces the values 15, 10, and 20.

4. What is the point estimate of the population mean?

5. What is the estimated population variance?

6. What is the estimated population standard deviation?

A population is normally distributed with a standard deviation of 20. The population consists of 10,000 values. In Questions 7-11, you are to use this information with respect to the computation of 0.95 confidence interval estimates of the population mean.

7. For a random sample of 100 observations, what is the half-width of the confidence interval?

8. Would your answer to Question 7 change if a sample of 2500 observations without replacement were used? If so, how?

9. Would it be permissible to compute the confidence interval based on 4 observations?

10. A sample of 64 observations is selected from the population. The sample mean is computed and found to be 43. What is the 0.95 confidence interval estimate of the population mean?

11. Assume the population is *not* normal. Would it be permissible to form a confidence interval estimate based on 10 observations? Based on 50 observations?

12. For a *t*-distribution with 2 degrees of freedom, find a symmetrical interval around the mean of the distribution that includes 90% of the distribution.

13. How would your answer to Question 12 change for a *t*-distribution with 20 degrees of freedom? For a *t*-distribution with 200 degrees of freedom? For the standard normal?

14. A population is normally distributed with an unknown standard deviation. A random sample of 4 observations produces the values 8, 4, 6, and 10. What is the estimated population standard deviation? What is the estimated standard error of the mean?

15. A population consists of 100,000 values and is normally distributed. A random sample of nine observations produces $\bar{X} = 20$ and $s = 30$. What is the 0.90 confidence interval estimate for the population mean?

16. Would it be permissible to compute the confidence interval in Question 15 using 9 observations if the population were *not* normal?

A production run consists of 10,000 items. In a random sample of 400 items, 80 are defective. Use this information to answer Questions 17-19.

17. What proportion of the sample is defective?

18. Is it permissible to use the normal approximation to compute the 0.90 confidence interval estimate for the population proportion? If so, find the intervals.

19. If a random sample of 400 items from this population produced 40 defectives, would it be permissible to use the normal approximation to compute the 0.90 confidence interval estimate of the sample proportion? If so, compute the interval.

20. A population is normally distributed with a standard deviation of 20. How many observations will be required to find the 0.95 confidence interval of the population mean if the half-width of the interval is to be 10? If the half-width is to be 1? Assume an infinite number of values in the population.

21. It is desired to compute the 0.95 confidence interval estimate for the population proportion. The confidence interval half-width is to be no more than 0.10. Assume no value for the population proportion can be ruled out in advance and that there are an infinite number of values in the population. Find the required sample size. Does the normal approximation apply?

22. How would your answer to Question 21 change if the maximum value for the confidence interval half-width were 0.01?

23. How would your answer to Question 21 change if a population proportion of more than 0.10 could be ruled out in advance?

PROGRAM SET 8.1 Interval Estimation for Normal Populations with σ Known

1. Suppose we do *not* know the mean (μ) but we do know that the standard deviation (σ) of a normally distributed population is 18. If we take a sample of 36 and obtain $\overline{x} = 60$, we (do/do not) know where this value lies with respect to the distribution's mean ($\mu_{\overline{x}} = \mu$).

do not

2. We are in the situation of knowing that the shape of the population distribution is _____ and that the standard deviation
   of the population is ____. But we do not know the value of
   ($\overline{x}$ or $\mu_{\overline{x}}$).

                                          normal, 18, $\mu_{\overline{x}}$

3. Knowing the standard deviation of the population and the sample
   size, we can determine the standard deviation of the sampling
   distribution of sample means for samples of a given size by
   using the formula for the standard error of the mean, $\sigma_{\overline{x}} = \sigma/\sqrt{n}$.
   The standard error of the mean is another designation for the
   standard deviation of the (population/sampling distribution).

                                          sampling distribution

4. In our example, the standard error of the mean is

$$\sigma_{\overline{x}} = \frac{\rule{2cm}{0.4pt}}{\rule{1cm}{0.4pt}} = \rule{1.5cm}{0.4pt}$$

                                          $18/\sqrt{36} = 3.0$

5. Our sample mean ($\overline{x}$) could be well above or below the population
   mean ($\mu_{\overline{x}}$). However, from our work with normal probabilities, we
   know we (can/cannot) be highly confident that $\overline{x}$ lies within, for
   example, three standard errors of $\mu_{\overline{x}}$.

                                          can

6. If we assume that our sample mean lies exactly three standard errors above the population mean, we could determine that value of
   $\mu_{\overline{x}}$ by using the equation $z = (\overline{x} - \mu_{\overline{x}})/\sigma_{\overline{x}}$. In this equation,
   we would substitute $z =$ ___ .

                                          3

7. For our example, substitution of the known numerical values in
   the above equation gives

$$\rule{1.5cm}{0.4pt} = \frac{\rule{1.5cm}{0.4pt} - \mu_{\overline{x}}}{\rule{1.5cm}{0.4pt}}$$

                                          $3 = \dfrac{60 - \mu_{\overline{x}}}{3.0}$

8. If we solve for $\mu_{\overline{x}}$ in the above equation, we obtain $\mu_{\overline{x}} =$ ____ .

                   $51 \ \ 3(3.0) = 60 - \mu_{\overline{x}}$

9. Thus if $\mu_{\overline{x}} = 51$, our sample mean $(\overline{x} = 60)$ lies exactly ____ standard errors above $\mu_{\overline{x}}$.

3

10. Table B-2 of Appendix B in the text indicates that the probability of a sample mean falling three or more standard deviations above $\mu_{\overline{x}}$ is _____.

0.0014

11. Similarly, if we had assumed that our sample mean lies exactly three standard errors below the population mean, we could again determine the value of $\mu_{\overline{x}}$ by using $z = (\overline{x} - \mu_{\overline{x}})/\sigma_{\overline{x}}$. But in this case, $z =$ ____.

−3

12. For this example, substituting the known numerical values in the equation of Frame 11, we have

$$\underline{\quad} = \frac{\underline{\quad} - \mu_{\overline{x}}}{\underline{\quad}}$$

$-3 = \dfrac{60 - \mu_{\overline{x}}}{3.0}$

13. If we solve for $\mu_{\overline{x}}$ in the preceding equation, we obtain $\mu_{\overline{x}} =$ ____.

$69 \quad \overset{*}{\underset{*}{*}} \quad -3(3) = 60 - \mu_{\overline{x}} \quad \overset{*}{\underset{*}{*}}$

14. Thus, the interval centered on $\overline{x} = 60$ and running three standard errors below to three standard errors above it has ____ as its lower limit and ____ as its upper limit.

51, 69

15. This interval, 51 to 69, is called an *interval estimate* of the (sample/population) mean.

population

16. For any given interval estimate, we can construct a measure of our degree of confidence. This is called the _____ coefficient.

confidence

17. To determine the value of the confidence coefficient, we must use Table B-2. From it, we determine that the probability of a randomly selected observation falling three standard deviations or more below the mean is _____.

0.0014

18. The following sketch shows the sampling distribution of the mean with the lower limit μ_L and $\sigma_{\bar{x}}$ = 3.0. On this figure, sketch the curve depicting the sampling distribution of the mean with upper limit μ_U = 69 and $\sigma_{\bar{x}}$ = 3.0.

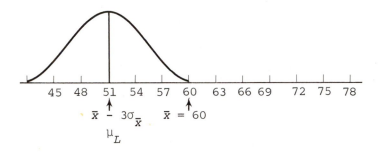

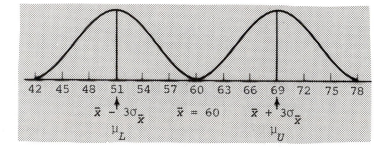

19. For a curve with μ_L = 51, we know that the probability of obtaining a mean that is 60 or larger is _____. Similarly, for the curve with μ_U = 69, the probability of obtaining a mean that is 60 or smaller is _____.

0.0014, 0.0014

20. We find the confidence coefficient by subtracting the sum of the tail areas from 1. In our example, the confidence coefficient is 1 - (_____ + _____) = _____.

1 - (0.0014 + 0.0014) = 0.9972

21. If we set the limits of our interval estimate at two standard errors rather than at three, the sum of the tail areas would (increase/decrease).

increase

22. This would result in a (larger/smaller) confidence coefficient.

smaller

23. Thus in this situation the larger the width of the interval estimate, the (more/less) confidence we have that $\mu_{\bar{x}}$ lies within it.

more

24. In considering the formula for the standard error of the mean, $\sigma_{\bar{x}} = \sigma/\sqrt{n}$, it is apparent that, for a given σ, the $\sigma_{\bar{x}}$ will decrease if the size of the sample is (decreased/increased).

increased

25. It follows that with a larger sample the length of an interval estimate, at a given confidence level, will become (larger/smaller).

smaller

26. By increasing the sample size, we can maintain a given degree of confidence while (narrowing/broadening) the length of an interval estimate.

narrowing

27. In the first example, we found a confidence interval and a confidence coefficient that corresponds to three standard errors. Frequently, we are given a confidence coefficient and asked to find the confidence interval. Suppose we wish to form an interval estimate where the confidence coefficient $(1 - \alpha)$ is 0.95. From a population of normally distributed observations, where $\sigma = 27$, we select a sample of 81 and compute $\bar{x} = 100$. In this example, we know that $1 - \alpha =$ _____. Thus $\alpha =$ _____ and $\alpha/2 =$ _____.

0.95, 0.05, 0.025

28. From Table B-3, we find that the magnitude of the standard normal deviate (z) which cuts off the tail area equal to $\alpha/2$ is _____ (ignore the sign of z).

1.96

29. Next, find the standard error of the mean ($\sigma_{\overline{x}}$) using

$$\sigma_{\overline{x}} = \frac{\sigma}{\sqrt{n}} = \frac{\underline{\hspace{1cm}}}{\underline{\hspace{1cm}}} = \underline{\hspace{1cm}}$$

$27/\sqrt{81} = 3$

30. Find the lower limit (μ_L) of the interval estimate using

$$\mu_L = \overline{x} - z_{\alpha/2} * \sigma_{\overline{x}} = \underline{\hspace{1cm}} - \underline{\hspace{1cm}}(\underline{\hspace{1cm}}) = \underline{\hspace{1cm}}$$

$100 - 1.96(3) = 94.12$

31. Also, find the upper limit μ_U of the interval estimate,

$$\mu_U = \overline{x} + z_{\alpha/2} * \sigma_{\overline{x}} = \underline{\hspace{1cm}} + \underline{\hspace{1cm}}(\underline{\hspace{1cm}}) = \underline{\hspace{1cm}}$$

$100 + 1.96(3) = 105.88$

32. For our example, the interval having a confidence coefficient of _____ has a lower limit of _____ and an upper limit of _____.

0.95, 94.12, 105.88

33. In the foregoing examples, we have assumed that the population was normally distributed. In such cases, the sampling distribution of the mean is normally distributed for (only small/only large/any) sample size.

any

34. If we could not assume the population to be normally distributed, we could use the central limit theorem, provided our sample size is at least 30. For such cases, we can assume that the sampling distribution of the _____ will be essentially _____ distributed even though the parent _____ is not.

mean, normally, population

35. Usually we will write the formula for this confidence interval as $\overline{x} \pm z * (\sigma/\sqrt{n})$. Thus $\overline{x} + $ _____ is the formula for the (upper/lower) limit of the confidence interval and $\overline{x} - $ _____ is the (upper/lower) limit of the confidence interval.

$z * (\sigma/\sqrt{n})$, upper, $z * (\sigma/\sqrt{n})$, lower

PROGRAM SET 8.2   The Family of t-Distributions

1. Suppose we have a population that is normally distributed with a mean μ and a known standard deviation σ. We have seen that the distribution of sample means for a fixed n from a normal population (is/is not) normally distributed.

is

2. The distribution of sample means from a normal population with a known standard deviation has a mean that (is/is not) equal to the population mean and a standard deviation of $\sigma_{\overline{x}} =$ _____.

is, $\sigma/\sqrt{n}$

3. We have seen that *any* normal distribution can be transformed to the standard normal distribution through the formula for z. For the normal distribution of $\overline{x}$, the formula for z is written $z = (\overline{x} - \mu)/\sigma_{\overline{x}}$. Since $\sigma_{\overline{x}} =$ _____, we may substitute this value in the formula for z and write $z =$ _____.

$\sigma/\sqrt{n}$, $\dfrac{\overline{x} - \mu}{\sigma/\sqrt{n}}$

4. Let us consider this formula in light of the experiment *take a random sample of n observations from a normal population that has a mean μ and a known standard deviation σ*. From the random sample, compute $\overline{x}$ and, using this value of $\overline{x}$, compute $z = \dfrac{(\overline{x} - \mu)}{\sigma/\sqrt{n}}$. Suppose you were to repeat this experiment a very large number of times. For each random sample, you would compute the quantities ___ and ___.

$\overline{x}$, z

5. We know that the results of this experiment would give a distribution of z that follows the _____ normal distribution.

standard

6. From the formula $z = \dfrac{(\overline{x} - \mu)}{\sigma/\sqrt{n}}$, we see that the numerator (does/does not) vary from sample to sample and the denominator (does/does not) vary from sample to sample.

does, does not

7. The reason the denominator does not vary from sample to sample is because the population standard deviation is (known/unknown).

known

8. Now we will change one aspect of the situation. We will still assume the population is normally distributed with a mean μ, but now we will assume the population standard deviation is unknown and must be estimated from a random _____.

sample

9. From a random sample, we will now have to compute $(\underline{\mu \text{ or } \overline{x}})$ and $(\underline{\sigma \text{ or } s})$.

$\overline{x}$, s

10. When the population standard deviation was assumed to be known, we computed the quantity $\dfrac{(\overline{x} - \mu)}{\sigma/\sqrt{n}}$ for each random sample. As you might suspect, when the population standard deviation is unknown, we will need to modify the computation of this quantity by using the estimated value of *s*. Thus, we would compute

$$\dfrac{(\overline{x} - \mu)}{\underline{\hspace{2cm}}}$$

$s/\sqrt{n}$

11. From a random sample of *n* observations from a normal population with an unknown standard deviation, we must compute $\overline{x}$, *s*, and the quantity $\dfrac{(\overline{x} - \mu)}{s/\sqrt{n}}$. For the latter quantity, $\underline{\text{(the numerator/}}$ $\underline{\text{the denominator/both the numerator and the denominator)}}$ will vary from sample to sample.

both the numerator and the denominator

12. In the quantity $\dfrac{(\overline{x} - \mu)}{s/\sqrt{n}}$, there are two sources of variations. One is caused by $\overline{x}$ and the other is caused by ___.

s

13. Suppose we repeat the experiment many times and compute the value $\dfrac{(\overline{x} - \mu)}{s/\sqrt{n}}$ for each random sample. The distribution of the value $\dfrac{(\overline{x} - \mu)}{s/\sqrt{n}}$ does not follow the standard normal distribution. Instead the distribution of this quantity follows a distribution known as the *t-distribution*. Evidently, the *t*-distribution is useful to us when the population standard deviation is $\underline{\text{(known/}}$ $\underline{\text{not known)}}$.

not known

14. As we have seen, the distribution of $z = \dfrac{(\overline{x} - \mu)}{\sigma/\sqrt{n}}$ follows the standard normal distribution which has a mean of zero and a standard deviation of one. The distribution of $t = \dfrac{(\overline{x} - \mu)}{s/\sqrt{n}}$ also has a mean of zero. Since there are two sources of variation in each value of t, there is more variation in the t-distribution than in the standard normal distribution. Thus we know the t-distribution has a standard deviation that is (less than/equal to/greater than) 1.

greater than

15. Although we have referred to "the" t-distribution, there is actually a family of t-distributions. One t-distribution is distinguished from another by a parameter known as *degrees of freedom* (*df*). Thus, the t-distribution with 9 *df* is (the same as/different than) the t-distribution with 25 *df*.

different than

16. The diagram shows the t-distributions for three different degrees of freedom and the standard normal distribution. The t-distribution that differs the most from the standard normal distribution is that for ___ degree(s) of freedom.

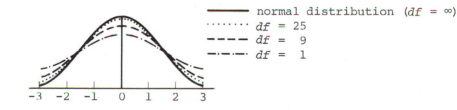

1

17. The t-distribution becomes more like the standard normal distribution as the degrees of freedom (increase/decrease).

increase

18. In Frame 16, the t-distribution that most nearly approximates the normal standard distribution is the distribution for (25 or 1) *df*.

25

19. As the degrees of freedom become very large, the t-distribution becomes similar to the _____ _____ distribution.

standard normal

20. As you may have guessed, the degrees of freedom is related to the number of observations (n). For inferences about μ, the degrees of freedom is $n - 1$. Thus, for 26 observations, there are _____ df.

$$25 \overset{*}{\underset{*}{*}} n - 1 = 26 - 1 \overset{*}{\underset{*}{*}}$$

21. As we have seen, there is a different t-distribution for each value of degrees of freedom. If we were to use the same type of table as we did for the standard normal distribution, we would need a different table for each t-distribution. In other words, we would need a different t-table for each different numerical value of _____ ___ _____.

degrees of freedom

22. Fortunately, each t-distribution may be "summarized" by giving a few commonly needed values. To see how this is accomplished, we shall see how we could summarize the standard normal distribution. From Table B-3 in the text, we see that a value of z having an area of 0.0049 to its left is $z = -2.58$. In symbols we write $z_{0.0049} =$ _____.

−2.58

23. To three decimal places, the area is 0.005; we write $z_{0.005} = -2.58$. We may use Table B-3 to find the closest value of z that cuts off 0.0100 to its left. Thus $z_{0.010} =$ _____.

−2.33

24. Similarly $z_{0.025}$ means a value of z that cuts off an area of 0.025 to its (left/right).

left

25. From Table B-3, $z_{0.025} =$ _____.

−1.96

26. It would be convenient to arrange these values in a table such as this:

$z_{0.005}$	$z_{0.010}$	$z_{0.025}$
−2.58	−2.33	−1.96

The table heading gives (a left-/a right-) tail area and the entry in the table gives (an area/a value of z).

a left-, a value of z

27. Use Table B-3 to complete the table.

$z_{0.005}$	$z_{0.010}$	$z_{0.025}$	$z_{0.050}$	$z_{0.100}$	$z_{0.900}$	$z_{0.950}$	$z_{0.975}$	$z_{0.990}$	$z_{0.995}$
-2.58	-2.33	-1.96	-1.64	_____	_____	_____	_____	_____	_____

-1.28, 1.28, 1.64, 1.96, 2.33, 2.58

28. Although this table does not give all of the values for the standard normal distribution, it does give the more commonly used values. The important thing to remember about this table is that the (left/right) tail area is given in the (body/heading) of the table and the corresponding value of z is given in the (body/heading) of the table.

left, heading, body

29. A similar method of tabulation is used for the family of t-distributions given in Table B-4 of Appendix B. Each row in this table summarizes a different t-distribution. In other words, each row in this table is for a different numerical value of

_____ ___ _____.

degrees of freedom

30. The following table is for a t-distribution with 1 df. Complete this table by using Table B-4.

$t_{0.005}$	$t_{0.010}$	$t_{0.025}$	$t_{0.050}$	$t_{0.100}$
-63.6574	-31.8207	-12.7062	_____	_____

$t_{0.900}$	$t_{0.950}$	$t_{0.975}$	$t_{0.990}$	$t_{0.995}$
_____	_____	_____	_____	_____

-6.3138, -3.0777
3.0777   6.3138   12.7062   31.8207   63.6574

31. From the last frame, we can see that for a t-distribution with 1 df, $t_{0.025} =$ _____.

-12.7062

32. The notation $t_{0.025} = -12.7062$ means that the area to the (left/ right) of -12.7062 is 0.025.

left

33. For 1 df, we know that $t_{0.975}$ = _____ .

+ 12.7062

34. For 1 df, $P(-12.7062 \leq t \leq 12.7062)$ = _____ - _____ = _____ .

0.975, 0.025, 0.950

35. For 1 df, $P(-6.3138 \leq t \leq 6.3138)$ = _____ .

0.90 $\overset{*}{\underset{*}{*}}$ 0.95 - 0.05 $\overset{*}{\underset{*}{*}}$

36. For 9 df, Table B-4 tells us $t_{0.025}$ = _____ and $t_{0.975}$ = _____ .

-2.2622, 2.2622

37. For 9 df, $P(-2.2622 \leq t \leq 2.2622)$ = _____ .

0.95 $\overset{*}{\underset{*}{*}}$ 0.975 - 0.025 $\overset{*}{\underset{*}{*}}$

38. As we saw in the diagram in Frame 16, the dispersion in the family of t-distributions decreases as the numerical value of the parameter degrees of freedom (increases/decreases).

increases

39. One way you can see the relationship between dispersion and degrees of freedom is to look at a column in Table B-4. For example, look at the column for $t_{0.975}$. As the degrees of freedom increase, the values of t (increase/decrease).

decrease

40. For an infinite number of degrees of freedom, the value of $t_{0.975}$ = 1.96, which is the same as the corresponding value on the _____ normal distribution.

standard

41. For practical purposes, *all* t-distributions with more than 30 degrees of freedom are very nearly normal. For a t-distribution with 150 degrees of freedom, we know that $t_{0.975}$ is very nearly equal to _____ .

1.96

42. Earlier we discussed taking a random sample from a normal population having an unknown standard deviation. The quantity

$$\frac{(\overline{x} - \mu)}{s/\sqrt{n}}$$

which is computed from the sample, has a t-distribution with
_____ (symbol) degrees of freedom.

$(n - 1)$

43. If we use $n = 10$ for our experiment and repeat the experiment
many times, we know that 5% of the computed quantities
$(\overline{x} - \mu)/(s/\sqrt{n})$ will be less than _____ .

-1.833 ⁑ for $n - 1 = 9df$, $t_{0.05} = -1.833$ ⁑

44. When using the t-table you should be careful to remember the
values in each (column/row) are for a given t-distribution with
a fixed number of _____ ___ _____ .

row, degrees of freedom

CHAPTER 8. SELF-CORRECTING EXERCISES

8.1 Properties of Estimators (Consistency, Efficiency, and Minimum Variance)

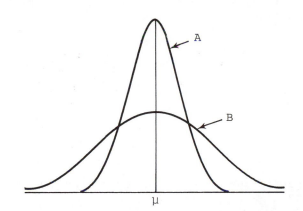

The sketch shows two sampling distributions used to estimate
the population mean μ of a normal distribution. Distribution
A is for the distribution of the sample mean $\overline{X}$ and distribution B is for the distribution of the sample median (Md). Both
distributions are based on samples of 10 observations.

a. Which sample statistic is a more efficient estimator of μ? Which estimator has the smaller variance?

b. What other property is illustrated by these distributions?

8.2 Properties of Estimators (Bias)   A population consists of the values 0, 1, and 2.

a. Find the population mean and variance.

b. The table below shows the results of obtaining samples of $n = 2$ observations from this population.   Sampling is *with* replacement.   The sections of the table show the sample values, sample means, and sample variances.   The sample variances are computed using $s^2 = \Sigma(X - \overline{X})^2/(n - 1)$.   Complete this table.

	Sample Values			Values of $\overline{X}$			Values of s^2		
Second draw	0	1	2	0	1	2	0	1	2
First draw									
0	0, 0	0, 1	0, 2	0	0.5	1	0	0.5	2
1	___	___	___	___	___	___	___	___	___
2	2, 0	2, 1	2, 2	1	1.5	2	2	0.5	0

c. The table below shows the probability distributions of $\overline{X}$ and s^2 from Part (b).   Complete these tables and find $E(\overline{X})$ and $E(s^2)$.

$\overline{X}$	$P(\overline{X})$
0	1/9
0.5	2/9 = 1/9 + 1/9
1.0	___
1.5	___
2.0	___

s^2	$P(s^2)$
0	3/9 = 1/9 + 1/9 + 1/9
0.5	___
2	___

d. What is the bias for the estimator $\overline{X}$?   For the estimator s^2?

e. Another estimator for the population variance is $S^2 = \Sigma(X - \overline{X})^2/n$.   Find the value of S^2 for the sample values 2, 1.

f. The probability distribution of the values of S^2 is shown below. Find $E(S^2)$ for this distribution.

S^2	$P(S^2)$
0	3/9
0.25	4/9
1	2/9

g. What is the bias for the estimator S^2?

h. When computing the sample variance, why do we usually divide the sum of the squared deviations by $n - 1$ rather than n?

8.3 Point Estimates

a. A random sample of cash balances in a savings institution produces the following results: $100, $150, $50. Find unbiased point estimates of the population mean and variance.

b. A random sample of 250 items from a production run produces 75 defectives. What is the point estimate for the proportion of defectives in the population?

(*Note*: In the exercises that require the computation of a confidence interval, you should assume the sample size is small relative to the number of values in the population unless the information in the problem indicates this is not the case.)

8.4 Interval Estimation: Normal Population In an industrial process, steel bars are cut to a specified length by an automatic cutting machine. An inspector selects a sample of four bars cut by the machine, measures them, and finds a confidence interval estimate for the mean bar length that has been cut by the machine. From the machine's past performance, the inspector knows that the standard deviation of the cut lengths is 0.6 ft. The 4 lengths from the most recent sample are 9.16, 10.08, 10.50, and 10.56, to the nearest hundredth of a foot. Assume the population is normally distributed.

a. What is the unbiased point estimate of the population mean?

b. What is the standard error of the mean?

c. What is the 0.95 confidence interval estimate for the population mean?

d. Is the population mean the same as your answer to (a)? Do you know the value of the population mean? If so, what is its value? If not, what do you know about the population mean? If the population mean is unknown, how might the inspector determine the exact value?

e. Which is more useful, the information found in (a) or the information found in (c)?

f. In answer to (c), one person stated that the 0.95 confidence interval is $10.075 \pm (1.96)(0.6)$ ft. On what point in the procedure is this person confused?

g. What is the half-width of the confidence interval? What would be the half-width of the confidence interval if 16 observations were used to compute $\overline{X}$?

h. How would your answer to (g) change for a 0.90 confidence coefficient and $n = 4$?

i. What do you conclude about the influence of n on the confidence interval width? About the influence of the confidence coefficient?

8.5 Interval Estimation: Unspecified Population Distribution   An auditor must get a quick estimate of the mean dollar amount per sale during the past year for a certain retail store. It can be assumed that the distribution of all these sales has positive skewness. A random sample of 144 sales tickets has a mean of $7.50 per sale. Detailed follow-up studies of all sales tickets for each of the past 5 years have shown that the standard deviation remains nearly constant at $3.

a. Find the 0.9545 confidence interval estimate of this year's mean sales.

b. In view of the skewness of the population distribution, what justifies the use of the procedure adopted in (a)?

c. If the auditor were required to use no more than 10 observations for the estimate, would the confidence interval be valid? Why or why not?

8.6 Finite Population Correction   For the situation described in Question 8.5, assume the sample of 144 observations were selected *without* replacement from a population of 1000 sales.

a. Find the 0.9545 confidence interval estimate of the population mean.

b. Compare your answer for (a) with the answer obtained in 8.5(a). Explain any similarities or differences.

8.7 Development of the *t*-Distribution The scores of the mathematics portion of the SAT are normally distributed with a mean of $\mu = 500$ and a standard deviation of $\sigma = 100$. In this problem, we shall consider samples of $n = 3$ from this population.

a. Two samples of $n = 3$ produce the following data:

Sample 1:	480, 610, 550
Sample 2:	510, 520, 420

For each sample, compute the sample mean. How many sample means for $n = 3$ are possible for this population?

b. For each sample mean, compute the standardized mean score using $z = (\overline{X} - \mu)/(\sigma/\sqrt{n})$. How many values of Z are possible for this situation?

c. One thousand sample means, including the two given in (a), were drawn from this population. Each mean was standardized using the formula in (b). The frequency distribution of these standardized mean scores is given in the table.

z	Frequency
−3.0 — −2.6	9
−2.5 — −2.1	15
−2.0 — −1.6	57
−1.5 — −1.1	103
−1.0 — −0.6	156
−0.5 — −0.1	176
0.0 — 0.4	188
0.5 — 0.9	138
1.0 — 1.4	95
1.5 — 1.9	43
2.0 — 2.4	13
2.5 — 2.9	7
	1000

Plot the relative frequency histogram for these data on the grid.

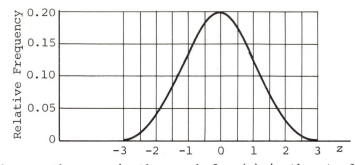

d. The smooth curve in the graph for (c) is the standard normal.   How well do the data correspond to the standard normal?   What do you conclude about the distribution of sample means (in standardized form) when the parent population is normal and σ is known?

e. Suppose we want to compute the standard scores for the sample means, but the population standard deviation is *not* known.   Use the formula

$$t = \frac{(\overline{X} - \mu)}{s/\sqrt{n}}$$

to find the standard scores for the two samples given in (a).

f. Are the standardized scores found in (e) the same as those found in (b)?   Why or why not?

g. The standardized scores for the 1000 samples are displayed in Figure 8-1 (page 177). What happens to the distribution of sample means when the population standard deviation is not known?

h. Is the smooth curve in Figure 8-1 the standard normal?   If not, what is this curve?

i. What do you conclude about the distribution of sample means (in standardized form) when the parent population is normal with σ unknown?

j. Would Figure 8.1 change if *n* were changed to 4?   If *n* were changed to 100?   If so, how?

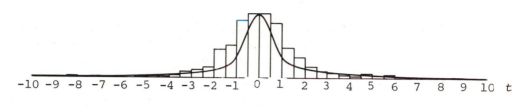

Figure 8-1

8.8 The Family of *t*-Distributions

a. For a *t*-distribution with 5 *df*, find $t_{0.005}$, $t_{0.01}$, $t_{0.025}$, $t_{0.05}$, $t_{0.10}$, $t_{0.90}$, $t_{0.95}$, $t_{0.975}$, $t_{0.99}$, and $t_{0.995}$.

b. For a *t*-distribution with 6 *df*, would $t_{0.95}$ be slightly larger or slightly smaller than $t_{0.95}$ found in (a)? Why?

c. For the values found in (a), what does the subscript on $t_{0.01}$ mean? What does the subscript on $t_{0.99}$ mean? What is the relationship between $t_{0.01}$ and $t_{0.99}$? Why?

d. For a *t*-distribution with 10 *df*, find a value of *t* such that 0.005 of the area under this distribution lies to its left. For the same distribution, find a value of *t* such that 0.005 of the distribution lies to its right. What proportion of the area under the distribution lies between these two values?

e. What is the mean of every *t*-distribution?

f. Consider a *t*-distribution with 11 *df*. Find a symmetric *t*-interval around the mean of this distribution that cuts off an area of 0.95.

g. What is the standard deviation of the standard normal distribution? Will a *t*-distribution have a standard deviation that is less than, equal to, or greater than this value?

h. A confidence interval estimate is to be computed using a *t*-distribution with 20 *df*. If the confidence coefficient is 0.90, what is the value of *t* that should be used in the computation?

i. How would your answer to (h) change for 40 *df*? For 132 *df*?

j. How would your answer to (h) change for a confidence coefficient of 0.95?   For a confidence coefficient of 0.99?

8.9 Variance Estimation   Two students are asked to find unbiased
point estimates of the mean and variance of the ages of residents in Kingston, Rhode Island.   Both students are to use 4
observations.   The random sample collected by the first student is 49, 48, 50, 49.   The random sample collected by the
second student is 50, 34, 60, 40.

a. Using the data collected by each student, find two unbiased
point estimates of the population mean and variance.   What
symbols should be used to identify these quantities?

b. Should each student obtain the same numerical values for
the estimated mean and variance?   Why or why not?

c. Find the estimated population standard deviation using the
data collected by each student.

d. Find the estimated standard error of the mean using the
data collected by each student.

e. For the population in Question 8.7, the variance is $\sigma^2 =$
10,000.   For the 1000 samples, the sample variance was computed in two ways.   First, the sample variance was computed
using $s^2 = \Sigma(X - \overline{X})^2/(n - 1)$.   The relative frequency
histogram for these values is shown in the top part of
Figure 8-2.   Next the sample variances were computed using
$s^2 = \Sigma(X - \overline{X})^2/n$; these results are shown on the bottom
part of Figure 8-2 (page 179).   On the average, which
method of computing the sample variance produces estimates
closer to the true variance?

8.10 Confidence Interval Estimates   Assume the second student in
Question 8.9 wishes to find the 0.95 confidence interval estimate of the population mean.

a. If the population is not normal, can the confidence interval be found?   How?

b. Assume the population is normally distributed and find the
confidence interval.

8.11 Interval Estimation   On the basis of a random sample of 36
observations, the population mean age for Kingston residents
is estimated to be 48 years.   The variance estimated from this
sample is 25 (years)^2.   The population is assumed to be relatively free of skewness.

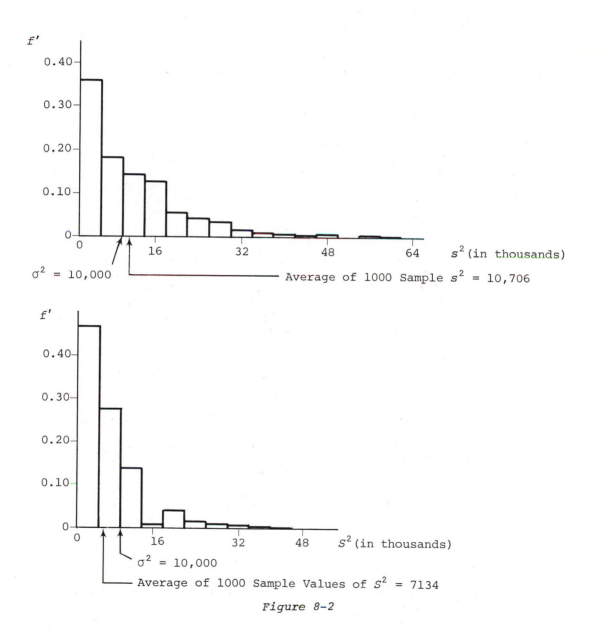

Figure 8-2

a. How many degrees of freedom apply to the estimated population?

b. What is the estimated population standard deviation? What is the estimated standard error of the mean?

c. Find the 0.95 confidence interval estimate for the population mean.

d. Is the confidence interval computed in (c) useful in view of the fact that the population mean is estimated to be 48 years? Why or why not?

e. Could this computation have been made if modest skewness were present in the population? Why or why not?

8.12 Confidence Interval for a Proportion (Normal Approximation)

a. Construct the 0.95 confidence interval for the true probability of heads for a coin that produced 40 heads in 100 tosses.

b. On the basis of a random sample of 300 citizens who intend to vote in a school bond referendum, 170 indicate they will vote approval. Find the 0.98 confidence interval estimate for the true proportion who will vote approval.

c. Do the situations in (a) and (b) meet the sample size requirements for normal approximations to confidence intervals for proportions?

8.13 Confidence Interval for the Proportion (Small Sample)   In a random sample of 20 shoppers, 8 prefer brand A.

a. What is the point estimate of the population proportion that prefers brand A?

b. Use Figure 8-6 in the text to find the 0.95 confidence interval estimate for the population proportion.

8.14 Determining Sample Size   For the situation described in Question 8.4, the inspector wishes to maintain the same confidence coefficient and specify the confidence interval length.

a. If the confidence interval length is to be $\bar{x} \pm 0.5$ ft, how many observations will be required? How many observations will be required if the confidence interval is to be $\bar{x} \pm 0.1$ ft? $\bar{x} \pm 0.01$ ft?

b. What do you conclude about the influence of n in determining a confidence interval for a fixed confidence coefficient?

8.15 <u>Determining the Sample Size with a Correction Factor</u>   For the situation described in Question 8.5, assume the sample of 144 observations were selected without replacement from a population of 1000 sales. How many observations would be required to find the 0.9544 confidence interval $\overline{X} \pm 0.25$?

8.16 <u>Determining Sample Size for Proportions</u> A state legislature committee wishes to determine what proportion of citizens favor tax credits for property owners who install solar heating equipment. They decide to make this determination by mailing a survey to a random sample of citizens. They desire a 0.95 degree of confidence and they wish to keep the error of estimation to no more than ± 0.01. Assume all surveys are returned.

a. How large should the sample be in each of the following cases?

   i.   If they have no idea of the value of the true proportion favoring the tax credit?

   ii. If they are sure that at least 80% favor the tax credit?

b. Suppose that the measured sample proportion is $p = 0.90$. Do the sample sizes found in (a) meet the minimum requirements for normal approximation to confidence intervals for a proportion?

8.17 <u>Selecting the Correct Formula</u>   This exercise is designed to help you select the correct formula for confidence interval calculations. For each situation, state the required formula. Indicate any instances in which the computation is not valid. No computations are required.

a. The mean dry weight of a large shipment of canned peaches is to be estimated based on 100 observations. The population standard deviation is not known and the population is thought to be skewed.

b. The proportion of persons in a small town of 1000 persons who favor candidate A is to be estimated based on a random sample of 300 persons.

c. The situation is the same as (b) except a sample of 60 is to be used.

d. The situation is the same as (a) except 5 observations are to be used.

e. The situation is the same as (a) except $\sigma = 0.2$ oz.

CHAPTER 8. ACHIEVEMENT TEST

1. The figure shows two sampling distributions for an estimator of the population mean μ. Is the estimator unbiased?

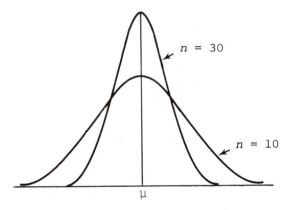

2. An estimator for the population mean has an expected value of 40. If the population mean is 40, is the estimator biased or unbiased?

3. The standard normal distribution is to be used in the computation of a symmetrical confidence interval. If the level of confidence will be 0.85, what is the absolute value of z which should be used in the computation?

For Questions 4-6, assume a random sample of three observations produces the values 12, 10, 8.

4. What is the point estimate of the population mean?

5. What is the estimated population variance?

6. What is the estimated population standard deviation?

A population is normally distributed with a standard deviation of 10. The population consists of 10,000 values. In Questions 7-11, you are to use this information with respect to the computation of 0.90 confidence interval estimates of the population mean.

7. For a random sample of 100 observations, what is the half-width of the confidence interval?

8. Would your answer to Question 7 change if a sample of 5000 observations without replacement were used? If so, how?

9. Would it be permissible to compute the confidence interval based on four observations?

10. A sample of 25 observations is selected from the population. The sample mean is computed and found to be 40. What is 0.90 confidence interval estimate of the population mean?

11. Assume the population is *not* normal. Would it be permissible to form a confidence interval estimate based on 10 observations? Based on 32 observations?

12. For a *t*-distribution with 4 *df,* find a symmetrical interval around the mean of the distribution which includes 95% of the distribution.

13. How would your answer to Question 12 change for a *t*-distribution with 10 *df*? For a *t*-distribution with 300 *df*? For the standard normal?

14. A population is normally distributed with an unknown standard deviation. A random sample of 4 observations produces the values 10, 6, 8, and 12. What is the estimated population standard deviation? What is the estimated standard error of the mean?

15. A population consists of 100,000 values and is normally distributed. A random sample of 16 observations produces $\overline{X} = 20$ and $s^2 = 0.16$. What is the 0.95 confidence interval estimate for the population mean?

16. Would it be permissible to compute the confidence interval in Question 15 using 16 observations if the population were *not* normal?

A storage bin contains 10,000 items. In a random sample of 200 items, 80 are defective. Use this information to answer Questions 17-19.

17. What proportion of the sample is defective?

18. Is it permissible to compute 0.95 confidence interval estimate for the population proportion? If so, find the interval.

19. If a random sample of 200 items from this population produced 40 defectives, would it be permissible to compute the 0.95 confidence interval estimate of the sample proportion? If so, compute the interval.

20. A population is normally distributed with a standard deviation of 20. How many observations will be required to find the 0.90 confidence interval of the population mean if the half-width of

the interval is to be 20? If the half-width is to be 2? Assume an infinite number of values in the population.

21. It is desired to compute the 0.90 confidence interval estimate for the population proportion. The confidence interval half-width is to be no more than 0.10. Assume no value for the population proportion can be ruled out in advance and that there are an infinite number of values in the population. Find the required sample size.

22. How would your answer to Question 21 change if the maximum value for the confidence interval half-width were 0.2?

23. How would your answer to Question 21 change if a population proportion of more than 0.30 could be ruled out in advance?

CHAPTER 8.   STUDENT RECORD AND REFERENCE SHEET

Darken the square corresponding to each test item you answered *incorrectly*. References indicate the topics you should study. See Chapter 1 of this volume for details.

Test Item	Diagnostic Test	Achievement Test	Text References	Self-Correcting Exercise References	Program Set References
1	☐	☐	212-219	8.1-8.3	—
2	☐	☐	212-219	8.1-8.3	—
3	☐	☐	221-226	—	—
4	☐	☐	212-219	8.1-8.3	—
5	☐	☐	212-219	8.1-8.3	—
6	☐	☐	212-219	8.1-8.3	—
7	☐	☐	221-226	8.4-8.6	8.1
8	☐	☐	221-226	8.4-8.6	8.1
9	☐	☐	221-226	8.4-8.6	8.1
10	☐	☐	221-226	8.4-8.6	8.1
11	☐	☐	221-226	8.4-8.6	8.1
12	☐	☐	227-230	8.7-8.8	8.2
13	☐	☐	227-230	8.7-8.8	8.2
14	☐	☐	227-230	8.9-8.11	—
15	☐	☐	227-230	8.9-8.11	—
16	☐	☐	227-230	8.9-8.11	—
17	☐	☐	231-234	8.12-8.13	—
18	☐	☐	231-234	8.12-8.13	—
19	☐	☐	231-234	8.12-8.13	—
20	☐	☐	235-239	8.14-8.16	—
21	☐	☐	235-239	8.14-8.16	—
22	☐	☐	235-239	8.14-8.16	—
23	☐	☐	235-239	8.14-8.16	—

9

HYPOTHESIS TESTS FOR MEANS AND PROPORTIONS

Last year the average account receivable per month for a bank credit card company was $25. All accounts receivable are normally distributed with a standard deviation of $5. Using a random sample of data from the accounts from this year, the bank wishes to use the data to draw a conclusion about the average account receivable this year. Three possible hypotheses are as follows:

	Form A	Form B	Form C
H_0:	$\mu = 25$	H_0: $\mu \geq 25$	H_0: $\mu \leq 25$
H_A:	$\mu \neq 25$	H_A: $\mu < 25$	H_A: $\mu > 25$

Use this information to answer Questions 1-10.

1. If the bank wishes to detect an increase in the average account receivable but does not care about a decrease, which form of the hypothesis should be used?

2. If the bank wishes to detect either an increase *or* a decrease, which form of the hypothesis should be used?

3. If the bank is only concerned with a decrease, what form should be used?

186

4. What, if anything, is wrong with the following form of the hypothesis test?

$$H_0: \quad \mu \geq 25$$

$$H_A: \quad \mu < 20$$

Suppose the bank selects form A and decides to use a random sample of 9 observations. Use this information for Questions 5-10.

5. What is the standard error for this situation?

6. Suppose the hypothesis $\mu = 25$ is true. What is the probability that the sample mean is within two standard errors of $\mu = 25$? What is the probability that the sample mean is within three standard errors of $\mu = 25$?

7. For the situations described in Question 6, what are the action limits in terms of z? In terms of $\overline{X}$?

8. If a level of significance of 0.05 is selected, what are the action limits in terms of z? In terms of $\overline{X}$?

9. A random sample of 9 accounts produces these data: 28, 30, 14, 17, 21, 35, 12, 0, 40. The sum of these values is $197. For the 0.05 level of significance, what conclusion should be reached about the null hypothesis?

10. Is the null hypothesis true or false?

A machine is designed to fill soft drink cans with a mean of 12 oz of soda. When the machine is correctly adjusted, the mean fill weight is 12 oz. If the machine is not in adjustment, the mean fill weight drops to 11.5 oz. It is desired to test the hypothesis $H_0: \mu \geq 12$ versus the alternative $H_A: \mu < 12$. For a fixed sample size, the diagram on page 188 shows the possible distributions of sample means. Use this information to answer questions 11-14. The action limit is 11.59.

11. If the null hypothesis *is* true, what is the probability of a correct decision? What is the probability of an error?

12. If the null hypothesis is *not* true, what is the probability of a correct decision? What is the probability of an error?

An advertising executive is considering a new package label for a client's product. With its present label the product produces a mean sales revenue of $10,000 per market area. The executive knows the sales revenue is normally distributed with a standard deviation of $1000. The executive plans to test market the

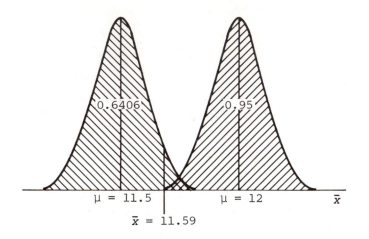

$\mu = 11.5$ $\mu = 12$ $\bar{x}$

$\bar{x} = 11.59$

new package in four market areas selected at random to determine
if a significant increase in sales is produced by the new package.
Use this information to answer Questions 13-16.

13. State the null and alternative hypotheses.

14. For a level of significance of 0.10, state the action limits or
    limit in terms of z.

15. For a level of significance 0.10, state the action limit in
    terms of $\bar{X}$.

16. The test data for the four markets are $12,000, $8000, $5000,
    and $16,000. What conclusion should be reached about the null
    hypothesis using a 0.10 level of significance?

For Questions 17-20, give the formula that should be used to
determine the action limits in terms of $\bar{X}$ in order to test the
hypothesis under the conditions described. If a test is not
permissible, indicate this in your answer. In each case assume the sample size is small relative to the number of values
in the population and that the random variable is manufacturing
cost. Assume two-tailed tests.

17. A population is normally distributed with an unknown standard
    deviation. A random sample of 5 observations is available for
    the test.

18. The situation is the same as Question 17, except the popula-
    tion is *not* normal.

19. A population is normally distributed with a known standard deviation.   Three observations are available for the test.

20. A population has a known standard deviation and it may or may not be normally distributed.   Sixty observations are available for the test.

21. Would your answer to Question 20 change if the population consisted of 300 values and the sampling was done without replacement?   If so, how?

22. A production run consists of 10,000 items.   It is desired to test the null hypothesis that the proportion defective is less than or equal to 0.10.   In a random sample of 1000 items, 250 are defective.   What is the value of the test statistic?

23. For the situation discussed in Questions 11 and 12, what is the power of the test when $\mu = 11.5$?

The sketch shows the power curves for three sampling plans (A, B, and C).   Use this sketch to answer Questions 24-27.

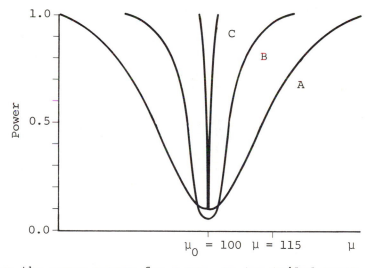

24. Are the power curves for a one- or two-tailed test?

25. Which plan has the probability of a type I error of 0.05?

26. Which sampling plan, A or C, is more powerful?   Which involves the larger sample size?

27. Suppose sampling plan A is used.   If $\mu = 115$, what is the probability of a type II error?

28. The figure below shows a hypothesis testing situation for a
    one-tailed test. The population is assumed to be normally dis-
    tributed with a standard deviation of 50. The test designer
    desires a level of significance of 0.05 and a probability of a
    type II error to be 0.20 for the indicated distribution. How
    many observations will be required to implement the test?

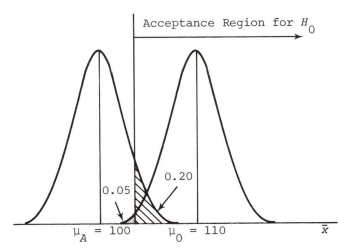

PROGRAM SET 9.1 Two-tailed Tests

1. One application of statistics is the use of sample data in
   estimating the values of a population parameter. Sample data
   also are used for testing statistical hypotheses. When we make
   a conjecture about the value of a parameter, we are making one
   type of statistical _____.

                                                          hypothesis

2. The process of hypothesis testing involves making a statement to
   be tested, collecting sample data, and, by using relevant portions of sampling theory, making a decision whether to accept or
   _____ the hypothesis.

                                                          reject

3. There is always a risk that we are wrong in our conclusion about
   a statistical hypothesis regarding a population parameter when
   our decision is based upon data obtained from a _____ drawn
   from that population.

                                                          sample

4. Only if we had the complete population at our disposal could we avoid the risk. Thus, in concluding either to accept or to reject a statistical hypothesis, we (do/do not) run the risk of choosing the wrong conclusion.

do

5. One type of statistical inference involves the examination of sample data in order to determine whether to accept or reject the hypothesis that it came from a given statistical population. Consider this example:

> A manufacturer of iron rods has, over the years, established that the mean length of all rods produced by machine is 60 mm. The standard deviation of the lengths of these rods has consistently been 7.5 mm. This distribution of lengths has been normal. Having moved the machine from one building to another, the manufacturer is now concerned with whether or not the length gauge is still accurately set. To check its accuracy, we take a sample of 49 rods and determine that their mean length is 57.6 mm.

In this example, the population mean is hypothesized to be ___, and the population standard deviation is taken as ____.

60, 7.5

6. We want to know whether or not it is reasonable that the sample of iron rods having a mean length of _____ mm came from a population having a mean of ____ mm and a standard deviation of _____ mm.

57.6, 60, 7.5

7. This is a typical test, which begins with a statement of a *null hypothesis*. When we hypothesize a value for the population mean, we give the hypothesized mean the symbol, μ_0. In our example, μ_0 = ____.

60

8. The statement that the μ_0 = 60 is called the _____ hypothesis.

null

9. Thus, the hypothesized value of the population mean (μ_0) determines the mean of the distribution of _____ means ($\mu_{\bar{x}}$). In symbols, this is μ_0 = ___ (symbol).

sample, $\mu_{\bar{x}}$

10. In order to examine the tenability of the hypothesis that $\mu_0 = 60$, where $\overline{x} = 57.6$, we must determine the sampling distribution of the test statistic. To do this, we begin by recalling that $\sigma =$ _____ .

                                                                7.5

11. Given the numerical values of these two parameters, μ_0 and σ, it is possible to determine the test statistic's sampling distribution. Recall that the test statistic in this case is the _____ _____ .

                                                    sample mean

12. Recall also that the sampling distribution of the sample mean has a standard deviation that is called the standard _____ of the mean.

                                                            error

13. The formula for the standard error of the mean is

$$\sigma_{\overline{x}} = \frac{\rule{2em}{0.4pt}}{\rule{2em}{0.4pt}}$$

    and its value for our example is _____ .

                        $\sigma/\sqrt{n}$, 1.07 $\genfrac{}{}{0pt}{}{*}{\genfrac{}{}{0pt}{}{*}{*}}$ 7.5/$\sqrt{49}$ $\genfrac{}{}{0pt}{}{*}{\genfrac{}{}{0pt}{}{*}{*}}$

14. If the assumptions stated in our example are true, then the distribution of sample means has three characteristics:

    a. It is _____ distributed.

    b. Its mean ($\mu_{\overline{x}}$) is (the same as/different from) the mean (μ) of the parent population.

    c. It has a standard deviation, called the standard _____ of the _____ , denoted by _____ .

                    a. normally b. the same as c. error, mean, $\sigma_{\overline{x}}$

15. In our example, the numerical values of $\mu_{\overline{x}}$ and $\sigma_{\overline{x}}$ are $\mu_{\overline{x}} =$ _____ and $\sigma_{\overline{x}} =$ _____ . These are the parameters of the assumed normal distribution of the test statistic, $\overline{x}$.

                                                    60, 1.07

16. Since the possible values of $\overline{x}$ are normally distributed, we know that the probability of getting a sample mean ($\overline{x}$) from this

distribution that is three or more standard errors (in either direction) from $\mu_{\overline{x}}$ is _____ (see Appendix B-2).

0.0026

$*$
$*$ $P(-3 \leq Z \leq 3) = 0.9987 - 0.0013 = 0.9974,\ 1 - 0.9974 = 0.0026$ $*$
$*$ $*$
                                                                             $*$

17. Thus it stands to reason that the probability of getting a value of $\overline{x}$ from this distribution that is four or more standard errors from the population mean is (less/more) than 0.0026.

less

18. The question then becomes: How far will we permit the sample mean, $\overline{x}$, to deviate from the assumed population mean, μ , and still accept the hypothesis that μ = 60? We need to establish limits within which ___ must lie in order for the null hypothesis to be accepted.

$\overline{x}$

19. We need to establish an acceptance region centered on the hypothesized mean. As we have seen from a normal distribution, the probability that a random draw will be within ±1.96 standard deviations of the mean is ____ .

0.95

20. If the null hypothesis is true, the probability is 0.95 that the particular sample mean we obtain will lie between a lower critical value which is _____ $\sigma_{\overline{x}}$ below μ_0 and an upper critical value which is _____ $\sigma_{\overline{x}}$ above μ_0.

1.96, 1.96

21. Thus, for our example, the values that enclose this acceptance region are as follows:

Lower critical value: ____ - 1.96(_____) = _____

Upper critical value: ____ + 1.96(_____) = _____

$60 - 1.96(1.07) = 57.90$
$60 + 1.96(1.07) = 62.10$

22. Thus, we know that when the hypothesis and the accompanying assumptions are true, $\overline{x}$ will fall within this acceptance region ____ % of the time.

23. Such a region provides a reasonably (low/high) level of pro-
    tection against erroneously concluding that μ is not 60 when,
    in fact, it is 60.

                                                            high

24. Recall that in our example we obtained a sample mean of 57.60
    mm and computed an acceptance region of 57.90 to 62.10 mm.
    This sample mean (does/does not) fall within the acceptance
    region under the null hypothesis.

                                                         does not

25. It follows that we should (accept/reject) the hypothesis that
    μ_0 = 60.

                                                          reject

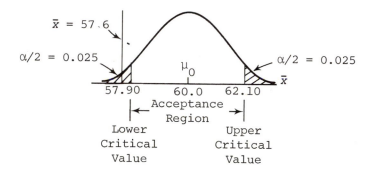

Figure 9-3

26. In Figure 9-3, the acceptance region is centered on μ_0 = _____
    and runs from a lower critical value of _____ to an upper
    critical value of _____.

                                              60, 57.90, 62.10

27. In Figure 9-3, note that $\bar{x}$ = 57.60 lies outside the acceptance
    region. Thus, the hypothesis that μ_0 = 60 is (accepted/
    rejected).

                                                         rejected

28. Because $\bar{x}$ = 57.60 lies outside the $(1 - \alpha)$ acceptance region,
    the null hypothesis was rejected. In so rejecting the null
    hypothesis, we are expressing a preference for the belief that
    μ (is/is not) equal to 60.00.

                                                          is not

29. However, we must remember that there is a small probability that our particular sample statistic is one of those extreme deviations which, though rare, *do occur* and that the null hypothesis may in fact be _____.

                                                                    true

30. The acceptance region for our example was based on $\alpha = 0.05$. Of course, α can be set at any value. The expression $\alpha/2$ indicates that half of α is assigned to one tail of the sampling distribution and the other half is assigned to the other tail. Thus, this particular test is called a (one-/two-) tailed test.

                                                                    two-

31. We used a two-tailed test in the foregoing example because we were testing the hypothesis that the mean length of the iron rods did not deviate from $\mu = 60$ mm in *either* direction. Thus, we were asking whether the sample $\overline{X}$ came from a sampling distribution where $\mu_{\overline{X}}$ was (smaller/larger/either smaller or larger) than 60 mm.

                                                    either smaller or larger

32. If we reject the null hypothesis (which in this case we did), we do so in favor of the _____ _____.

                                                    alternative hypothesis

33. A hypothesis test may also be expressed in terms of standardized scores instead of $\overline{X}$. On the sketch, indicate the values of Z associated with the given probabilities.

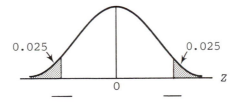

                                                                -1.96, 1.96

34. The portion of the z-axis between $z = -1.96$ and $z = 1.96$ forms the (acceptance/rejection) region for the null hypothesis when the level of significance is _____.

                                                    acceptance, 0.05

35. To decide whether to accept or to reject the null hypothesis,
we must compute the value of the test statistic. In this case,
we use $z = (\overline{x} - \mu_{\overline{x}})/\sigma_{\overline{x}}$. Recall that $\overline{x} = 57.6$ and $\sigma_{\overline{x}} = 1.07$.
For example, we compute the value of the test statistic to be
$z =$ _____.

$$-2.24 \quad {}^{*}_{*}{}^{*} \quad \frac{(57.6 - 60)}{1.07} \quad {}^{*}_{*}{}^{*}$$

36. Since $z = -2.24$ (does/does not) lie in the acceptance region,
we (accept/reject) the null hypothesis.

does not, reject

37. Evidently we (shall/shall not) reach (the same/a different) conclusion about the null hypothesis whether we work with $\overline{X}$ or
____.

shall, the same, Z

PROGRAM SET 9.2   One-tailed Tests

1. In the two-tailed test situation, we want to reject the null
hypothesis when the true mean lies substantially above or
_____ the hypothesized value.

below

2. Two-tailed tests guard against a bad decision in (one/either)
direction.

either

3. We are now going to examine one-tailed tests, wherein our only
concern is whether or not the true mean differs from the
hypothesized value in (one/either) direction.

one

4. A building contractor purchases large quantities of iron rods
from the manufacturer of our example in Program Set 9.1, Frame
5. Although the contractor cannot use rods that are shorter
than 60 mm, the rods can be longer than 60 mm, because they can
be trimmed to fit the construction. We shall assume that the
rod-manufacturing equipment produces a normally distributed
population of rod lengths and that the standard deviation of
lengths is known to be 7.5. An inspector wants to make certain
that the rods delivered to the contractor are at least 60 mm

in length, almost without exception.   Now, if the mean length
of the rods (μ) is 60 mm, then the lengths will be _____
distributed around this value.

normally

5. This indicates that if $\mu = 60$, (less than half/half/more than
   half) of the rods will be less than 60 mm in length.

half

6. This is unacceptable to the inspector, who requires that the
   mean length of rods be (greater than/exactly/less than) 60 mm
   in length so that the majority of rods will measure at least
   _____ mm.

greater than, 60

7. To make sure that virtually all of the rods are at least 60 mm
   long, the manufacturer should set the equipment to produce rods
   with mean length slightly more than 60 mm.   The inspector's job
   is to see that this is indeed the case.   A test that will indicate whether the mean length of rods is (shorter than/exactly/
   longer than) 60 mm is needed.

longer than

8. To perform a one-tailed test, the inspector begins with the
   supposition that the mean length of rods is equal to or less
   than 60 mm.   This is the _____ hypothesis, which it is hoped
   can be (accepted/rejected).

null, rejected

9. Thus, the inspector states that the hypothesized mean (μ_0)
   is equal to or less than 60 mm.   The null hypothesis in this
   case is written as:

   Null hypothesis (H_0): μ ($\leq$ or $=$ or $\geq$) μ_0

$\leq$

10. The alternative hypothesis, therefore, must be:

    Alternative hypothesis (H_A): μ _____ μ_0

$>$

11. This indicates the null hypothesis is that the mean length of
    rods is equal to or less than 60 mm.   The alternative

hypothesis is that the mean length of rods is (less than/
equal to/greater than) 60 mm.

greater than

12. Suppose the inspector selects a sample of 49 rods.   Recall
    that the population standard deviation is assumed to be 7.5.
    If the null hypothesis is true, his assumption concerning the
    population of rod lengths will result in a sampling distribu-
    tion of $\bar{x}$ for a sample of 49 that is normal in shape, with
    $\mu =$ _____, at most, and a standard error ($\sigma_{\bar{x}}$) of

$$\sigma_{\bar{x}} = \frac{\sigma}{\sqrt{n}} = \frac{\rule{1cm}{0.4pt}}{\sqrt{\rule{0.8cm}{0pt}}} = \rule{1.5cm}{0.4pt}$$

60, $7.5/\sqrt{49} = 1.07$

13. Suppose that the inspector has chosen a significance level of
    0.05 ($\alpha = 0.05$), as indicated in the following diagram.

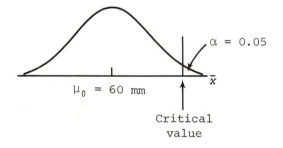

To determine the critical value, we need first to use Table
B-3 to determine $z_{1-\alpha}$.   The area to the left of the critical
value is _____.   For this area $z_{1-\alpha} =$ _____.

0.95, 1.65

14. Notice that for a one-tailed test we look up the magnitude of
    ($z_{1-\alpha}$ or $z_{1-\alpha/2}$) because we are concerned with values in (one/
    two) tail(s) of the sampling distribution.

$z_{1-\alpha}$, one

15. In our example, given the conditions: the hypothesized population
    mean is 60 mm; the standard error of the mean is 1.07; and the
    distribution of sample means is normal. We can state that only 5
    in 100 times will we get a random sample of 49 rods with a mean

length that falls 1.65 standard errors or more above 60 mm. In this case, the critical value of $\bar{x}$ is 60 + _____ (_____) = _____ .

$$60 + 1.65(1.07) = 61.77$$

16. For this situation and a 0.05 level of significance, we have the following hypothesis statement for a one-tailed test.

Null hypothesis (H_0): $\mu \leq 60$ mm
Alternative hypothesis (H_A): $\mu > 60$ mm

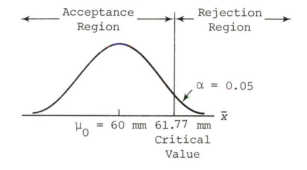

The diagram indicates that values of the sample mean $(\bar{x})$ that are larger than _____ lie in the rejection region for the null hypothesis.

61.77

17. The key point in the rationale of the one-tailed test is that if the inspector selects a random sample of 49 rods and finds that its mean $(\bar{x})$ is equal to or less than the critical value, 61.77, he or she will (accept/reject) the null hypothesis that $\mu \leq \mu_0$.

accept

18. If the sample yields a mean $\bar{x}$ that exceeds the critical value, 61.77, then the inspector can (accept/reject) the hypothesis that the machine is set to produce rods that are too short.

reject

19. If $\bar{x}$ exceeds 61.77, the inspector can accept the alternative hypothesis that the machine is producing rods of a mean length which is (less than/equal to/greater than) 60 mm.

greater than

20. In summary, the critical value of 61.77 mm in our example is 1.6 standard errors above the hypothesized mean μ_0 of 60 mm. Suppose the inspector obtained a sample of 49 rods which had a mean of 61.1 mm. This value falls within the (acceptance/rejection) region of the null hypothesis. Therefore, the inspector (should/should not) require the manufacturer to adjust the machines to produce a greater mean length of rods.

acceptance, should

21. Thus the inspector should (accept/reject) the shipment.

reject

22. If the sample of 49 rods had a mean of 62.3, the inspector would (accept/reject) the null hypothesis and (accept/reject) the shipment.

reject, accept

23. In the foregoing example, we made an upper one-tailed test. By requiring the critical value (61.77) to be above the hypothesized mean (60), the inspector is assured that the mean rod length is (no more than/at least) 60.

at least

24. In other problems, we might wish to assure ourselves that a parameter were no more than a hypothesized value. In such cases, we would use (an upper/a lower) one-tailed test.

a lower

25. Thus to perform a lower one-tailed test, the hypothesis statement is

$$\text{Null hypothesis } (H_0): \mu \underline{\quad\quad} \mu_0$$
$$\text{Alternative hypothesis } (H_A): \mu \underline{\quad\quad} \mu_0$$

$\geq$, $<$

CHAPTER 9. SELF-CORRECTING EXERCISES

9.1 Statement of the Hypothesis Last year the national average on the mathematics SAT exam was 478. A random sample of this year's scores is selected to test a hypothesis about the mean score for this year. The mean score for last year is the basis of the hypothesis. For each of the following situations, state the appropriate form of the null and alternative hypothesis.

a. A test to detect an increase in the mean score.

b. A test to detect a decrease in the mean score.

c. A test to detect any change in the mean score.

9.2 The Sampling Distribution and Action Limits for a Two-Tailed Test Steel shafts for an automobile part must be cut so that they are neither too long nor too short. The cutting machine, when properly adjusted, cuts shafts that have a mean length of 10 in. The distribution of all shaft lengths from this machine is a normal distribution with a standard deviation of 0.5 in. A quality control program is based on a random sample of 16 shafts. The program is designed to detect maladjustments in the machine that would produce shafts that are either too long or too short.

a. State null and alternative hypothesis for the two-tailed test.

b. What is the standard error for this situation?

c. If the acceptance region for the null hypothesis is ±2 standard errors, what is the acceptance region in terms of $\overline{X}$?

d. If the acceptance region for the null hypothesis is ±3 standard errors, what are the action limits in terms of $\overline{X}$?

e. If the probability of a type I error (level of significance) is 0.05, what is the acceptance region in terms of Z? In terms of $\overline{X}$?

f. Rework (e) assuming a level of significance of 0.10.

g. The level of significance is set at 0.05. The inspector claims the acceptance region in terms of Z is $-1.645 \leq Z \leq 1.645$. What mistake has the inspector made, if any?

9.3 Two-Tailed Tests for Normal Populations A package-filling machine is set to put 112 oz of dry dog food in packages. The standard deviation of fill weights for any setting of the machine is known to remain constant at 6 oz. Fill weights are normally distributed. To decide if the process is remaining in control, an inspector will select a random sample of nine such weights from time to time and compare the sample mean with upper and lower acceptance limits. The probability of declaring the process out of control (when it is actually in control) is 0.0456.

a. What is the null hypothesis? What is the alternative hypothesis?

b. What is the level of significance?

c. What is the standard error of the mean?

d. What values of the sample mean define the acceptance region for the null hypothesis? How would these values be used to formulate a set of instructions (that is, a decision rule) for determining whether the machine is or is not in control?

e. Do we need to actually obtain a random sample to establish the null hypothesis, the level of significance, or the acceptance region? What is the basis for establishing these quantities?

f. The results of a random sample of nine observations are 110, 118, 111, 110, 109, 110, 117, 108, and 106. Based on these observations what should be concluded about the null hypothesis? About the filling process?

g. Another random sample of 9 observations is taken several days later. The sum of these 9 observations is 963 oz. What should be concluded about the null hypothesis and filling process now?

h. On the basis of the results of (g), the quality control inspector orders the machine to be stopped and examined for improper adjustment. After doing so, the machine is found to be in perfect order. Is anything wrong with the test procedure? How frequently would you expect an outcome such as this to occur?

i. State the acceptance region in terms of standard scores. Express the results of (f) and (g) in standard scores. What would you conclude about the null hypothesis in each case? How do these conclusions compare with those reached in (f) and (g)?

9.4 Type I and Type II Errors   The Environmental Protection Agency sets a standard for an industrial process such that average water pollutant discharge must be no more than 100 parts per million (ppm). A plant operator wishes to detect mean pollutant discharges that exceed 100 ppm. The pollution control equipment works in such a way that the pollutant in the discharge is normally distributed with a standard deviation of 10 ppm. A random sample of 16 observations are taken at randomly selected times during each shift. Assume a 0.05 level of significance.

a. State the null and the alternative hypothesis for the manufacturer.

b. What is the acceptance region for the null hypothesis?

c. If the process mean is actually 100 ppm, what type of
statistical error is possible? What is the probability of
this error?

d. Suppose that a sample mean falls in the rejection region
for the null hypothesis when the process mean is 100. What
is the implication for the manufacturer?

e. Suppose that the process mean is actually 105 ppm. What
type of statistical error is possible? What is the probability of this error?

f. Answer (e) if the process mean is 110 ppm.

g. Suppose a sample mean falls in the acceptance region for
the null hypothesis when the process mean is actually 105
ppm. What is the implication for the manufacturer?

h. Suppose the level of significance is kept at 0.05, but the
sample size is increased. What would be the impact on the
probabilities computed in (e) and (f)? What would be the
impact if the sample size were decreased?

9.5 One-tailed Test Action Limits

a. Use this diagram to show the action limits and acceptance
regions for the null hypothesis of an upper one-tailed test
in terms of the standard normal. Show these results for
the 0.10, 0.05, and 0.01 levels of significance.

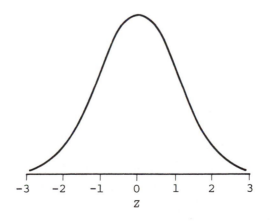

b. Repeat (a) for a lower one-tail test.

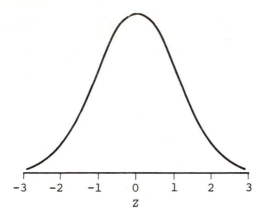

c. On the diagram below, show the action limits and acceptance region for an upper one-tail test and a two-tail test. Use a 0.05 level of significance for both tests. Give an explanation of why the action limits are the same or different.

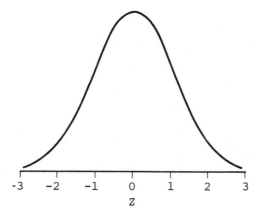

d. Find the acceptance region for the null hypothesis and the action limits in terms of $\overline{X}$ for the null hypothesis H_0: $\mu \geq 80$. Assume the population from which the sample is drawn is normally distributed with a standard deviation of 5. Assume $n = 16$ and $\alpha = 0.05$.

9.6 One-Tailed Test—Normal Population   In an effort to control expenses, the management of a firm has requested that long-distance telephone calls be kept to less than 5 min. To test whether this request has resulted in a mean call length of less than 5 min, a random sample of the lengths of 225 long-distance calls will be collected. The standard deviation of all calls is known to be 1.5 min. The firm wishes to test the null hypothesis that its request to keep calls under 5 min is not being honored versus the alternative that its request is being honored. Assume a 0.025 level of significance and a normal distribution.

a. State the null and the alternative hypotheses in terms of the population mean.

b. What is the standard error of the mean?

c. Find the acceptance region in terms of the sample mean and in terms of standard scores.

d. The total time for 225 randomly selected calls is 1080 min. What do you conclude about the null hypothesis? Show your conclusion in terms of the sample mean and in terms of standard scores.

e. Would a two-tailed test be appropriate in this case? Why or why not?

9.7 Two-Tailed Test for Unspecified Population Distribution

During the past yeat, the 30 traveling salespeople employed by a certain company have submitted a combined total of nearly 1000 travel expense vouchers. Two years ago, the mean expenditure per voucher was $160. The standard deviation has remained virtually constant at $12 for several years, and it is presumed to be the same for the past year. The parent population can be presumed to have positive skewness. A random sample of 64 vouchers is selected from last year's vouchers to perform a two-tailed test of the hypothesis that the mean is still $160 at the 0.05 level of significance. The mean for the sample is $165.

a. What are the null and the alternative hypotheses? What is the basis for the null hypothesis?

b. What is the standard error of the mean?

c. What is the acceptance region for the null hypothesis in terms of the sample mean? In terms of standard scores?

d. What is your conclusions about the null hypothesis? State your conclusion in terms of the sample mean and in terms of standard scores.

e. Could this test have been performed on the basis of nine observations instead of 64? Why or why not?

9.8 Test of Hypotheses about Population Means—Standard Deviation Unknown   Assume the last federal census (taken 5 years ago) shows the mean age of the residents of Kingston to be 50 years.   We want to determine whether or not the mean age of the present population is the same as it was at the time of the last census.

a. Why is hypothesis testing, rather than interval estimation, appropriate in this case?

b. If the level of significance is to be 0.05, what is the acceptance region for the null hypothesis?

c. On the basis of a random sample of 36 observations, the sample mean is found to be 48 and the population variance is estimated to be 25.   What value of the test statistic is computed from the data?

d. Should the null hypothesis be accepted or rejected?

9.9 Test of Hypothesis about Population Means—Population Standard Deviation Unknown   The same hypothesis is to be tested in this question (at the 0.05 level of significance) as was tested in the last question.   In this case, a random sample produces the following observations: 49, 48, 50, 49.

a. What major assumption would have to be made in order to perform this test?

b. What is the acceptance region for the null hypothesis?

c. What is the computed value of the test statistic?

d. Should the null hypothesis be accepted or rejected?

e. Answer (b), (c), and (d), assuming the null hypothesis that the population mean is greater than or equal to 50.   Assume the same data and level of significance.

9.10 Formula Section   The table below shows the assumptions that are used in several different hypothesis testing situations. For each situation, give the formula needed to compute the test statistic.   If the test should not be performed, write *none* for the formula.

| | Assumptions | | |
Population Distribution	Population Standard Deviation	Sample Size	Formula for Test Statistic
a. Normal	Unknown	5	
b. Unknown	Unknown	100	
c. Skewed	Known	8	
d. Normal	Known	3	
e. Skewed	Unknown	10	

9.11 <u>Finite Population Correction Factor</u> The situation in this is the same as in Question 9.6. In this question, assume the random sample of 225 calls is selected without replacement from a population of 1000 values. Rework Question 9.6 using this assumption.

9.12 <u>Test of a Proportion</u>

    a. In a random sample of 25 housewives, 10 were found to prefer the taste of a modified blend of instant coffee to the current standard blend.

        i. Test the hypothesis that $\pi = 0.5$ using $\alpha = 0.05$.

        ii. Would it be possible to test the hypothesis $\pi = 0.2$ in this situation? Why or why not?

    b. One hundred flips of a coin produced 40 heads. At the 0.05 risk level for rejecting a true hypothesis, test the null hypothesis that the underlying probability of heads for the coin is 0.50.

    c. A geneticist reported on experiments to control the sex of rabbits. Of 169 offspring, the sex was successfully controlled in 113 cases. Test the hypothesis that sex is not controlled at the 0.05 level of significance.

9.13 <u>Power Curve</u> The situation for this exercise is as follows:

$$H_0: \mu \geq 150$$

$$H_A: \mu < 150$$

$$\alpha = 0.10$$

$$n = 25$$

$$\sigma = 5$$

Assume the population is normally distributed

a. On the sketch below, show the critical value of $\overline{X}$ and the acceptance and rejection regions for the null hypothesis.

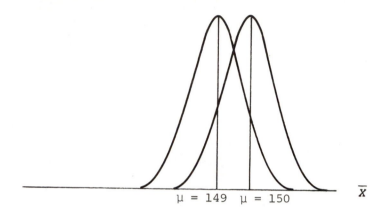

$$\mu = 149 \quad \mu = 150 \qquad \overline{X}$$

b. If μ is actually 149, which hypothesis is actually true? If $\mu = 149$, what type of error is possible? What is the probability of this error? What is the probability of a correct decision? Indicate these probabilities in the sketch. If $\mu = 149$, what is the power of the test?

c. For each possible value of μ listed below, compute the power of the test.

Possible Value of μ	Power
146.0	_____
146.5	_____
147.0	_____
147.5	_____
148.0	_____
148.5	_____
149.0	_____
149.5	_____

d. On the grid provided, plot the values obtained in (c) and make a sketch of the power curve. Explain the influence of the actual value of μ on the probability of making a correct decision.

e. On the grid for (d), sketch the power curve $n = 100$. Assume the same value for α. For values of μ, use 148, 148.5, 149, and 149.5. Explain the influence of n on the probability of a correct decision.

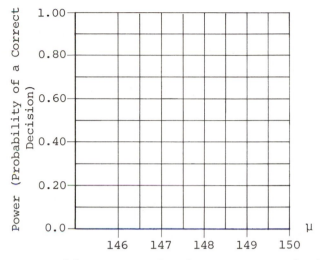

f. Suppose you could use a sample size that would indicate
whether the null or the alternative hypothesis were true
without error. What would the power curve look like for
this sample size? How large would this sample size need
to be?

9.14 Determining Sample Size   The situation for this problem is the
same as in Question 9.4.   Assume $\sigma = 10$ ppm and $\alpha = 0.05$.

a. The plant manager learns that a mean pollutant level of 105
ppm, not detected by the company, will result in a fine of
$10,000 per day. The manager decides that the probability
of not detecting $\mu = 105$ should be 0.10. On the figure
below, indicate the areas corresponding to the probabilities of the type I and type II errors.

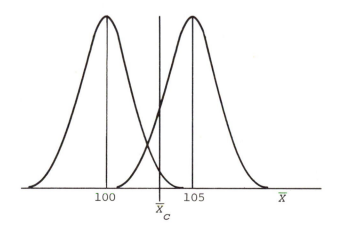

b. If $\mu = 100$, what is the standard score of $\overline{X}_c$? If $\mu = 105$, what is the standard score of $\overline{X}_c$?

c. How many observations will be required to control the probabilities of the type I and type II errors?

d. How would your answer to (c) change if it was desired to detect a mean pollution level of 103 ppm with the same probabilities for type I and type II errors? Compare your answer with that obtained in (c). Explain any difference.

CHAPTER 9.   STUDENT RECORD AND REFERENCE SHEET

Darken the square corresponding to each test item you answered
incorrectly.   References indicate the topics you should study.
See Chapter 1 of this volume for details.

Test Item	Diagnostic Test	Text References	Self-Correcting Exercise References	Program Set References
1	☐	244-250	9.1	9.1
2	☐	244-250	9.1	9.1
3	☐	244-250	9.1	9.1
4	☐	244-250	9.1	9.1
5	☐	244-250	9.2	9.1
6	☐	244-250	9.2-9.4	9.1
7	☐	244-250	9.2-9.4	9.1
8	☐	244-250	9.2-9.4	9.1
9	☐	244-250	9.2-9.4	9.1
10	☐	244-250	9.2-9.4	9.1
11	☐	250-254	9.5-9.6	9.2
12	☐	250-254	9.5-9.6	9.2
13	☐	250-254	9.5-9.6	9.2
14	☐	250-254	9.5-9.6	9.2
15	☐	250-254	9.5-9.6	9.2
16	☐	250-254	9.5-9.6	9.2
17	☐	255-262	9.7-9.11	——
18	☐	255-262	9.7-9.11	——
19	☐	255-262	9.7-9.11	——
20	☐	255-262	9.7-9.11	——
21	☐	255-262	9.7-9.11	——
22	☐	255-262	9.7-9.11	——
23	☐	263-270	9.13	——
24	☐	263-270	9.13	——
25	☐	263-270	9.13	——
26	☐	263-270	9.13	——
27	☐	263-270	9.13	——
28	☐	271-273	9.14	——

10

SIMPLE LINEAR REGRESSION AND CORRELATION

CHAPTER 10.   DIAGNOSTIC TEST

Use these data for questions 1 through 6.

X	Y
2	3
4	2
4	6
6	4
7	7

1. Use the grid below to plot a scattergram.

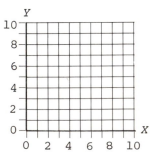

2. Does the scattergram seem to show an exact functional relationship?

3. The least-squares line for these data is Y_c = 1.434 + 0.645X. For X = 6, what is the deviation of the observed value of Y from the least-squares line?

4. What is true about the sum of all the deviations from the regression line?

5. What is true about the sum of the squares of all of the deviations from the regression line?

6. For the given data, find ΣX, ΣY, ΣXY, $(\Sigma X)^2$ and ΣX^2.

7. Use the following information to find the least-squares line: n = 5, ΣX = 22, ΣX^2 = 130, ΣY = 24, ΣY^2 = 166, and ΣXY = 111.

8. For the standard linear regression model, what is assumed about the distribution of Y for any given value X?

9. The equation of a least-squares line is Y_c = 3.2 + 10.0X. What is the point estimate of the dependent variable if the value of the independent variable is 4?

10. For the data shown below, the least-squares line is Y_c = 2.973 + 0.297X. Compute the standard error of estimate *without* finding the deviations from the regression line.

X	Y
2	4
4	2
5	7
6	4
7	5

11. In a regression situation, 15 observations are used to compute the least-squares line. The sample slope is 0.5 and the standard error of the sample slope is 0.25. What is the value of the test statistic that should be computed to test the hypothesis that the population slope is equal to zero?

12. For the situation described in Question 11, what are the critical values of the test statistic if a 0.05 level of significance is used? What is your conclusion about the slope of the population regression line?

13. For a given value of X, what are two types of prediction intervals that are typically used in regression analysis? Which prediction interval half-width is smaller? Why?

14. For the situation shown in Question 10, find the coefficient of determination.

15. In a regression situation, the coefficient of determination is 0.36. What percent of the total variability in the dependent variable is explained by the independent variable? What percent is *not* explained by the independent variable?

16. The least-squares line for the situation in Question 15 is Y_c = 3.0 - 4.1X. What is the correlation coefficient?

17. Is it necessary to find the least-squares line in order to find the correlation coefficient?

PROGRAM SET 10.1 Linear Equations and the Least-Squares Line

1. Since we often work with linear equations, it is important to understand the relationship between an equation and its graph.

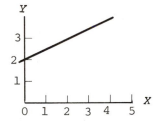

In the graph here, we see that the line crosses the Y-axis at a point where Y = ___ .

2

2. The place where the line crosses the Y-axis is called the *Y-intercept* of the line. In our example, we found that the *Y-intercept* has a numerical value of ___ .

2

3. In the following graph we see that a and b are separated by a horizontal distance and a vertical distance. In fact, we see that the horizontal distance is 2 and the vertical distance is ___

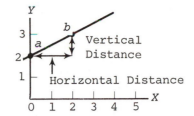

1

4. The ratio of the vertical to the horizontal distance between two
   points on a straight line is called the *slope* of the line. In
   our example, we found the vertical distance to be 1 and the horizontal distance to be 2. The slope of our line must be ____.

1/2

5. Notice that the selection of points makes no difference in determining the slope of a line. For example, suppose we had selected the points *c* and *d*.

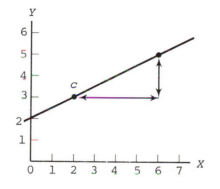

   The graph shows that the horizontal distance between *c* and *d* is
   ___, the vertical distance is ___, and the ratio of vertical to
   horizontal distance is ___.

4, 2, 1/2

6. Once we know the *Y-intercept* and the slope, we can write the
   equation of the line. This equation may be written: $Y =$
   intercept + slope $*$ X. In our example, the Y intercept is 2
   and the slope is 1/2. We can write the equation for the line
   as $Y =$ ___ + _____ $* X$.

2, 1/2

7. In order to write the equation for a line, we need to know the
    numerical values of the Y- _____ and the _____ .

                                                        intercept, slope

8. In statistics, we are faced with a second problem. We still
    need to find the equation of the line, but we usually cannot
    start with a graph of the line. What we usually have is a set
    of observed values of X and Y. The graph here shows the number
    of sales (Y) for a given number of calls (X) for 20 insurance
    salespeople.

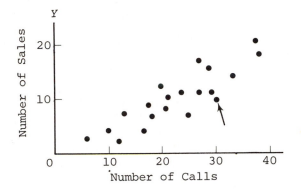

    Notice that the arrow on the diagram refers to a salesperson who
    made _____ calls and ____ sales.

                                                             30, 10

9. The graph in the last frame shows that we cannot draw a single
    straight line through all of the points. Nevertheless, we see
    that there is a tendency for higher values of Y to be associ-
    ated with (higher/lower) values of X.

                                                              higher

10. In cases like this, we would like to fit a single line through
    the points. One way to do this is to place a straightedge on
    the graph, position it in such a way that we guess we have a
    good fit, and draw a line. A difficulty with this procedure is
    that everyone (is/is not) likely to draw exactly the same line.

                                                              is not

11. Therefore we need a method for finding one particular line
    through a set of points. This particular line is called the

least-squares line and it has two important properties. First,
it is the line that best fits a given set of points and, second,
it is determined by a procedure whereby everyone will fit exactly the same line to the points. The line which is the best-
fitting line to a given set of points is called the _____
_____ line.

                                              least-squares

12. For a better understanding of the terms *least squares* and
    best fitting, we turn to an example in which the least-squares
    line has already been graphed. The term *least squares* pertains
    to the amount of dispersion between the points and the line.
    To measure dispersion, we need to calculate the vertical devia-
    tion of each point from the line. These vertical deviations are
    shown by the heavy vertical lines on the graph and the magnitude
    of each deviation is shown beside it. At $X = 1$, the deviation
    is 0.4; at $X = 2$, the deviation is _____; at $X = 3$, the devia-
    tion is _____; and at $X = 4$, the deviation is _____.

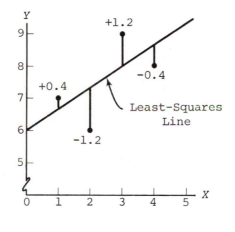

                                              -1.2, 1.2, -0.4

13. In order to measure dispersion, we calculate the sum of the
    squared deviations. Since we found the deviations to be +0.4,
    -1.2, +1.2, and -0.4, the sum of the square deviation is

$$(0.4)^2 + (\underline{\hphantom{xxx}})^2 + (\underline{\hphantom{xxx}})^2 + (\underline{\hphantom{xxx}})^2$$

    or $0.16 + \underline{\hphantom{xxx}} + \underline{\hphantom{xxx}} + \underline{\hphantom{xxx}} = \underline{\hphantom{xxx}}$

                              -1.2, 1.2, -0.4; 1.44, 1.44, 0.16; 3.20

14. The least-squares line is the line that produces the smallest
    possible sum of squared deviations. Since the least-squares

line produces the smallest sum of squared deviations, it must
also produce the smallest dispersion. In other words, any
line that is not the least-squares line must produce a (smaller/
larger) sum of squared deviations and a (smaller/larger) dispersion than the least-squares line.

larger, larger

15. In order to see that the least-squares line produces a sum of
    squared deviations that is smaller than any other line, we will
    look at a line that is not the least-squares line fitted through
    the same points. From the graph below we see that the sum of the
    squared deviations for the line that is not the least-squares
    line is $(-4)^2 + ($ ___ $)^2 + ($ ___ $)^2 + ($ ___ $)^2 = $ ___ .

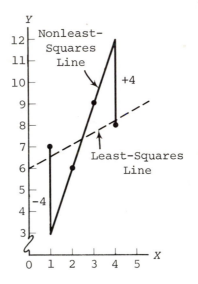

0, 0, 4; 32

16. Recall that we found the sum of the squared deviations for the
    least-squares line to be 3.20. No matter what other line we
    draw through the points, we know that the sum of the squared
    deviations will be (smaller than/equal to/larger than) 3.20.

larger than

17. So far we have discussed the meaning of the least-squares line;
    now we will see how to find it. Recall that in order to write
    the equation for a line we must know its Y- _____ and its
    _____.

intercept, slope

18. What we need is some way to calculate *a* and *b* in terms of the observed values of *X* and *Y*.   By *observed values* of *X* and *Y*, we mean the points on the graph.   Notice that each point on the graph corresponds to one observation consisting of a *pair* of values.   The first value in this pair is a value of *X* and the second is a value of ___ .

Y

20. For our example, the paired *X* and *Y*-values corresponding to each point on the graph in Frame 12 are as shown in the following table.   Notice that there are ___ points on the graph and that there are ___ pairs of observed values.

X	Y
1	7
2	6
3	9
4	8

4, 4

21. We shall use the symbol *n* to indicate the number of pairs of observed values and the number of points on the graph.   In the last frame, we found that for our example *n* = ___ .

4

22. In order to calculate the slope of the least-squares line, we shall use the formula

$$b = \frac{n(\Sigma XY) - (\Sigma X)(\Sigma Y)}{n(\Sigma X^2) - (\Sigma X)^2}$$

All of the quantities on the right-hand side of this equation are calculated from the observed values.   For our example, we have the following table in which $\Sigma X = 10$.   Use the table to find ΣY.

X	Y
1	7
2	6
3	9
4	8
$\Sigma X = 10$	$\Sigma Y =$ ___

30

23. The other quantities we need in order to find the slope of the least-squares line are ΣXY and ΣX^2. The easiest way to find these quantities is to make a table, as follows.

X	Y	X^2	XY
1	7	1	7
2	6	4	12
3	9	____	____
4	8	____	____
$\Sigma X = \overline{10}$	$\Sigma Y = \overline{30}$	$\Sigma X^2 = \overline{\rule{1cm}{0pt}}$	$\Sigma XY = \overline{\rule{1cm}{0pt}}$

9	27
16	32
30	78

24. We have found the following quantities for our example:

$$\Sigma X = 10 \quad \Sigma Y = 30 \quad \Sigma X^2 = 30 \quad \Sigma XY = 78$$

Since we have four pairs of values, we may substitute the above sums and $n = 4$ in the formula for b,

$$b = \frac{n(\Sigma XY) - (\Sigma X)(\Sigma Y)}{n(\Sigma X^2) - (\Sigma X)^2}$$

Thus $b = \dfrac{\overline{\rule{2cm}{0pt}} - \overline{\rule{2cm}{0pt}}}{\rule{1.5cm}{0pt}\ \rule{1.5cm}{0pt}}$. (Substitute the quantities indicated but do not solve. We will perform the arithmetic for you.)

$$\frac{4(78) - (10)(30)}{4(30) - (10)^2} = 0.6$$

25. When using the formula

$$b = \frac{n(\Sigma XY) - (\Sigma X)(\Sigma Y)}{n(\Sigma X^2) - (\Sigma X)^2}$$

for the slope, we must remember that ΣXY is not the same as $\Sigma X * \Sigma Y$, and ΣX^2 is not the same as $(\Sigma X)^2$. In order to find $(\Sigma X * \Sigma Y \text{ or } \Sigma XY)$, we first multiply X times its corresponding Y and then add the results.

ΣXY

26. We add the values of X and square the sum in order to find $(\underline{\Sigma x^2 \text{ or } (\Sigma X)^2})$.

$$(\Sigma X)^2$$

27. To find the slope, b, we used the quantities $\Sigma X = 10$, $\Sigma Y = 30$, $\Sigma X^2 = 30$, $\Sigma XY = 78$, and $n = 4$ to obtain $b = 0.6$. In order to find the Y-intercept, a, we simply substitute into the equation $a = \overline{Y} - b\overline{X}$. Since $\overline{Y} = \Sigma Y/n$, $Y =$ _____, $\overline{X} =$ _____, and $a =$ _____ $-$ _____ (_____) $=$ ___.

$$7.5, \ 2.5, \ 7.5 - 0.6(2.5) = 6$$

28. We now have the slope of the least-squares line, 0.6, and the Y-intercept, 6.0. We substitute these quantities into the equation for the least-squares line, $Y_c = a + bX$. For our example, $Y_c =$ _____ $+$ _____ X.

$$6.0, \ 0.6$$

29. In order to find the equation of the least-squares line, we must calculate several sums and substitute them into the equations:

$$b = \frac{n(\Sigma XY) - (\Sigma X)(\Sigma Y)}{n(\Sigma X^2) - (\Sigma X)^2} \quad \text{and} \quad a = \overline{Y} - b\overline{X}$$

The sums we must calculate to find the slope of the least-squares line are ΣX, _____, _____, and _____.

$$\Sigma Y, \ \Sigma X^2, \ \Sigma XY$$

30. Use the following observations to complete the table and obtain the sums required to find the least-squares line.

X	Y	X^2	XY
1	2	___	___
2	2	___	___
3	1	___	___
4	1	___	___
$\Sigma X =$ ___	$\Sigma Y =$ ___	$\Sigma X^2 =$ ___	$\Sigma XY =$ ___

		1	2
		4	4
		9	3
		16	4

$$\Sigma X = 10, \ \Sigma Y = 6, \ \Sigma X^2 = 30, \ \Sigma XY = 13$$

31. Using the sums developed in the last frame and the equation
    $b = \dfrac{n(\Sigma XY) - (\Sigma X)(\Sigma Y)}{n(\Sigma X^2) - (\Sigma X)^2}$, we find $b =$ ____ .

    $$-0.4 \quad ^{*}_{*} \; b = \frac{4(13) - (10)(6)}{4(30) - (10)^2} = \frac{52 - 60}{120 - 100} = \frac{-8}{20} \; ^{*}_{*}$$

32. We may also use these sums and the equation $a = \overline{Y} - b\overline{X}$ to find
    the Y-intercept for our example: $a =$ ____ .

    $$2.5 \quad ^{*}_{*} \; \frac{6}{4} - (-0.4)\frac{10}{4} \; ^{*}_{*}$$

33. In the foregoing example, we should write the equation for the
    least-squares line as $Y_c =$ _____ .

    $$2.5 - 0.4X$$

PROGRAM SET 10.2   Standard Error of Estimate

1. We have seen that the least-squares line minimizes the sum of
   the squared (horizontal/vertical) deviations of the observed
   points from this line.

   vertical

2. The least-squares line for the data collection

X	Y
1	7
2	6
3	9
4	8

   is $Y_c = 6 + 0.6X$.   At $X = 1$, the value of Y computed from
   the regression equation is $Y_c =$ ____ .

   $$6.6 \quad ^{*}_{*} \; 6 + 0.6(1) \; ^{*}_{*}$$

3. At $X = 1$, the observed value of Y is $Y =$ ___ .

   7

4. Since the observed value of Y (does/does not) equal the value
   of Y computed from the regression equation there is (no/some)
   deviation between the two values.

   does not, some

5. The deviation of a point from the least-squares line is defined by $Y - Y_c$; that is the (computed/observed) minus the
   (computed/observed) value of Y.

   observed, computed

6. For our example, $Y - Y_c =$ ___ − _____ = _____.

   7 − 6.6 = 0.4

7. Since $Y - Y_c$ is positive, it tells us the observed point is
   above the line. If $Y - Y_c$ is negative, we know that the observed point is _____ the line.

   below

8. The least-squares line, $Y_c = 6 + 0.6X$, is based on the data in
   the following table. For each value of X, compute Y_c and $Y -
   Y_c$.

X	Y	Y_c	$Y - Y_c$		
1	7	6.6	7 − 6.6	=	0.4
2	6	____	____	=	____
3	9	____	____	=	____
4	8	____	____	=	____

   7.2 6 − 7.2 = −1.2
   7.8 9 − 7.8 = 1.2
   8.4 8 − 8.4 = −0.4

9. As you will recall, the least-squares line minimizes the sum
   of the squared vertical deviations of the points from the line.
   Since a vertical deviation is denoted by $Y - Y_c$, the sum of the
   squared vertical deviations is represented by _____
   (symbols).

   $$\Sigma (Y - Y_c)^2$$

10. The vertical deviations for our example are repeated here.
    Find the square of each deviation and the sum of the squared
    deviations.

X	Y	$Y - Y_c$	$(Y - Y_c)^2$
1	7	0.4	0.16
2	6	-1.2	_____
3	9	1.2	_____
4	8	-0.4	_____

$$\Sigma(Y - Y_c)^2 = \underline{\qquad}$$

$$
\begin{aligned}
&1.44 \\
&1.44 \\
&\underline{0.16} \\
\Sigma(Y - Y_c)^2 &= 3.20
\end{aligned}
$$

11. The sum of the squared deviations is used to find a special variance. The formula for this is

$$s^2_{Y \cdot X} = \frac{\Sigma(Y - Y_c)^2}{n - 2}$$

This variance measures the dispersion of the observed values from the _____ _____ _____.

least-squares line

12. Use the results of Frame 10 to compute

$$s^2_{Y \cdot X} = \frac{\underline{\qquad}}{\underline{\qquad}} = \underline{\qquad}$$

$$\frac{3.20}{4 - 2} = 1.60$$

13. The *standard error of estimate* is the positive square root of the variance about the regression line. For our example,

$$s_{Y \cdot X} = \sqrt{\underline{\qquad}} \ .$$

1.60

14. Since $s_{Y \cdot X} = \sqrt{1.60} = 1.26$, we know that 1.26 is the numerical value of the _____ _____ ____ _____.

standard error of estimate

15. The standard error of estimate tells us how well the least-squares line fits the observed values. From the formula

$$s_{Y \cdot X} = \sqrt{\frac{\Sigma(Y - Y_C)^2}{n - 2}}$$

we can see that the value of $s_{Y \cdot X}$ (would/would not) equal zero if all of the observed values fell on the line.

would

* * in such a case each value of $Y - Y_C$ would equal zero * *

16. Thus, the smaller the value of $s_{Y \cdot X}$, the closer the observed points are to the _____ _____ _____.

least-squares line

17. There is an alternative method of computing the value of the sum of the squared deviations. (This method is usually easier because we need not calculate each deviation.) The alternative way of calculating $\Sigma(Y - Y_C)^2$ is $\Sigma(Y - Y_C)^2 = \Sigma Y^2 - a(\Sigma Y) - b(\Sigma XY)$. For our example, $\Sigma Y^2 = 230$, $\Sigma Y = 30$, $\Sigma XY = 78$, $a = 6$, and $b = 0.6$. The formula tells us, $\Sigma(Y - Y_C)^2 = $ _____ - _____ - _____ = _____.

230 - 6(30) - 0.6(78) = 3.2

18. In Frame 10, we found $\Sigma(Y - Y_C)^2$ by (the same/a different) method and obtained (the same/a different) numerical value.

a different, the same

PROGRAM SET 10.3   Hypothesis Tests

1. Usually a least-squares line is found on the basis of a random sample. As you might suspect, different random samples taken from the same population are likely to produce (the same/different) least-squares line(s).

different

2. Since one line is distinguished from another by the numerical values assigned to a and to b, we would expect different random samples from the same population to produce different values of a and of b. Thus, we might suppose that a and b (are constant/have sampling distributions).

have sampling distributions

3. In practical situations, we are usually concerned with tests of hypotheses about the slope (B) of the population regression line. As you will recall, B tells us how the population mean value of Y changes with the independent variable (X). Thus B is the slope of the (population/sample) regression line.

> population

4. Suppose repeated random samples of n observations are taken from a population in which the slope of the population regression line is B. For each random sample the quantity $(b - B)/s_b$ is computed. In this relationship, s_b is the standard error of b (which will be discussed shortly), b is the slope of the (population/sample) regression line, and B is the slope of the (population/sample) regression line.

> sample, population

5. Under certain conditions (see text) the quantity $(b - B)/s_b$ has a t-distribution with $n - 2$ degrees of freedom (df). In other words, we can get some idea of the deviation of sample values of b from the population value of B by consulting a t-distribution with _____ (symbol) degrees of freedom.

> $n - 2$

6. Suppose a sample regression line is based on four observations. Then, we would need a t-distribution with ____ (how many?) df.

> 2 ✱ 4 - 2 ✱

7. Turn to Table B-4 in the text. For 2 df, we see that 0.025 of the t-distribution is less than $t =$ _____ and 0.975 of the t-distribution is less than $t =$ _____.

> -4.3027, 4.3027

8. Between $t = -4.3027$ and $t = 4.3027$, we expect to find _____ (what proportion?) of all t-values.

> 0.95 ✱ 0.975 - 0.025 ✱

9. Thus, 95% of the computed values $t = (b - B)/s_b$ will fall between $t =$ _____ and $t =$ _____.

> -4.3027, 4.3027

10. Of course, in practical situations, we are usually limited to a single random sample. Thus we shall compute one value of b, one value of s_b, and one value of ____ (symbol).

t

11. The value of *B* in the computed value $t = (b - B)/s_b$ comes from the statement of the _____ hypothesis.

null

12. If the difference between *b* and *B* is very small, the computed value of *t* will be close to zero. If the difference between *b* and *B* is very large, then the computed value of *t* will be a very large positive value *or* a very large _____ value.

negative

13. It follows that a computed value of *t* near zero will cause us to accept the null hypothesis. A computed value of *t* that differs greatly from zero will cause us to _____ the null hypothesis.

reject

14. For 2 *df* and a 0.05 level of significance, the results of Frame 8 tell us to accept the null hypothesis if the value of *t* computed from the sample is greater than _____ and less than _____.

−4.3027, 4.3027

15. Perhaps the most frequently tested hypothesis about *B* is that it is zero; that is, that the mean value of *Y* in the population does *not* change with *X*. We will illustrate this test with a random sample consisting of four observations:

X	*Y*	X^2	Y^2	*XY*
1	7	1	49	7
2	6	4	36	12
3	9	9	81	27
4	8	16	64	32
	30		230	78

From the table, we see that ΣX = ____ , ΣX^2 = ____ , and $\overline{X}$ = ____ .

10, 30, 2.5

16. In Program Set 10.1 we found the least-squares line for these data is $Y_c = 6 + 0.6X$. Thus, we know that $b = $ _____.

                                                                    0.6

17. To find the computed value of t, we use the equation $t = (b - B)/s_b$. We know that $b = 0.6$ and the null hypothesis states that $B = $ ___. In order to compute t, we must have a numerical value for ___ (symbol).

                                                                    0, s_b

18. The formula for s_b is

$$s_b = \frac{s_{Y \cdot X}}{\sqrt{\Sigma (X - \overline{X})^2}}$$

In Program Set 10.2, we found $s_{Y \cdot X} = 1.26$. As you will recall, $s_{Y \cdot X}$ is called the _____ _____ ____ _____.

                                        standard error of estimate

19. The quantity $\Sigma (X - \overline{X})^2$ is the sum of the squared deviations from the mean of the X-values. Although this quantity may be computed directly, it is usually easier to compute it from the formula

$$\Sigma (X - \overline{X})^2 = \Sigma x^2 - n(\overline{X})^2$$

From the results of Frame 15, we see that

$$\Sigma (X - \overline{X})^2 = \text{\_\_\_\_} - \text{_____} = \text{\_\_\_}$$

                                        $30 - 4(2.5)^2 = 5$

20. Thus, the standard error of b is

$$s_b = \frac{s_{Y \cdot X}}{\sqrt{\Sigma (X - \overline{X})^2}} = \frac{\text{_____}}{\text{_____}} \quad \text{(substitute only)}$$

                                        $1.26/\sqrt{5}$ (or $s_b = 0.56$)

21. Thus the computed value of t is

$$t = (b - B)/s_b = (\text{\_\_\_\_\_} - \text{\_\_\_})/(\text{_____}) \quad \text{(substitute only)}$$

                                        $(0.6 - 0)/0.56$ (or $t = 1.07$)

22. Since the value of t computed from our data (does/does not) fall in the interval $t = -4.3027$ to $t = 4.3027$, we should (accept/reject) the null hypothesis.

does, accept

23. In other words, the chances are good that the true value of B in the population (is/is not) zero.

is

PROGRAM SET 10.4   Prediction

1. A manufacturer concerned with the number of machine malfunctions in the plant wishes to determine whether or not the ages of the machines are related to the frequency of malfunctions. Twenty machines are selected—5 each at the ages of 2, 4, 6, and 8 years. Their monthly malfunctions are as follows:

Age of Machine (X)	Number of Monthly Malfunctions (Y)				
2 years	1	3	3	4	4
4 years	4	5	6	7	3
6 years	6	5	7	9	6
8 years	8	8	10	9	7

An important feature of this particular example is that the values of X were preselected and therefore they (are/are not) free to vary. The Y values (are/are not) free to vary.

are not, are

2. In this example, the age of the machines is the (dependent/independent) variable, denoted by X, and the number of malfunctions is the _____ variable, denoted by Y.

independent, dependent

3. We have one sample set of 20 paired observations (X, Y). Our first objective, then, is to estimate the functional relationship between these variables in the population. To determine if it is reasonable to assume that the functional relationship is linear, plot the scattergram of the sample data below.

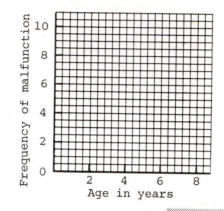

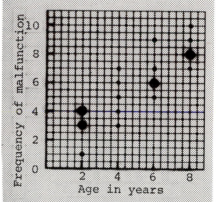

(*Note*: The circles denote two data points that have the same coordinates.)

4. As can be seen in the scattergram, there (is/is no) reason to believe a straight line might be the best-fitting line at this point in the analysis.

is

5. Of course, we must realize that this linear assumption is only meant to apply within the observed range of the data: $2 \leq X \leq$ ___ .

8

6. Now we need to determine the sample least-squares regression line. Recall our earlier formula for a sample regression line, $Y_c = a + bX$.   In this equation for the sample regression line,

the Y-intercept is represented by ___ and the slope is represented by ___.

a, b

7. The least-squares values of the slope and intercept are

$$b = \frac{n(\Sigma XY) - (\Sigma X)(\Sigma X)}{n(\Sigma X^2) - (\Sigma X)^2} \qquad a = \overline{Y} - b\overline{X}$$

Here n is the number of paired observations in the (sample/
population).

sample

Sample Sums for Regression Line

X	Y	X^2	XY	Y^2
2	1	4	2	1
2	3	4	6	9
2	3	4	6	9
2	4	4	8	16
2	4	4	8	16
4	4	16	16	16
4	5	16	20	25
4	6	16	24	36
4	7	16	28	49
4	3	16	12	9
6	6	36	36	36
6	5	36	30	25
6	7	36	42	49
6	9	36	54	81
6	6	36	36	36
8	8	64	64	64
8	8	64	64	64
8	10	64	80	100
8	9	64	72	81
8	7	64	56	49
100	115	600	664	771

8. The preceding table shows the 20 paired observations and other
calculations necessary to find the required sums. From this
table, $\Sigma X =$ _____, $\Sigma Y =$ _____, $\Sigma X^2 =$ _____, $\Sigma XY =$ _____, $\Sigma Y^2 =$
_____.

100, 115, 600, 664, 771

9. The other calculations needed are $(\Sigma X)^2 = ($ ___ $)^2 = $ _____ , and $(\Sigma Y)^2 = ($ _____ $)^2 = $ _____ .

$$(100)^2 = 10{,}000; \quad (115)^2 = 13{,}225$$

10. Using the equation in Frame 7, we can now determine b (substitute but do not solve).

$$b = \frac{\rule{3cm}{0.4pt}}{\rule{2.5cm}{0.4pt}}$$

$$b = \frac{20(664) - (100)(115)}{20(600) - (100)^2} = 0.89$$

11. Once we find $b = 0.89$, then we can find $a = (115/20) - 0.89(100/20)$ = 1.30. Thus the sample regression equation in our example is $Y_c = $ _____ .

$$1.30 + 0.89X$$

12. We know that the Y-intercept is 1.30. We need only determine one other value for Y_c, for example, for $X = 8$, in order to draw the regression line in the scattergram. Substitute and solve for Y_c using $X = 8$: $Y_c = $ _____ $+$ _____ $($ ___ $) = $ _____ .

$$1.30 + 0.89(8) = 8.42$$

13. Plot the sample least-squares regression line in the scattergram you prepared in Frame 3.

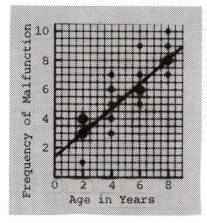

14. It is implicit in the equation $Y_c = a + bX$ that 1.30 and 0.89, being derived from sample data, are estimates of the intercept

and slope for the true underlying relationship in the
statistical _____.

population

15. Recall that in this example the independent variable is not a
random variable. We preselected the ages of the machines.
Thus, because values of X are chosen in advance of making observations, the sample values of X are assumed to be known
(with/without) sampling error.

without

16. However, values of Y (are/are not) conditionally dependent upon
X.

are

17. In order to see the relationship between population and sample,
it is necessary to examine the assumptions about the population. They can be visualized in the mathematical probability
model of Figure 10-1. This figure indicates that, for any
given value of X, Y is _____ distributed around its own
mean ($\mu_{Y \cdot X}$).

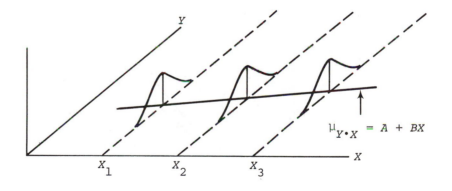

Figure 10-1   Linear Regression Model

normally

18. Thus the expected, or mean, value of Y for any value of X is
$\mu_{Y \cdot X}$ = ___ + ____.

A, BX

19. Associated with any given value of X is a normal distribution
of ___ values.

Y

20. The *Y*-values lying on the population regression line are the means of the *Y*-values for any given *X*. These are symbolized by _____ .

$\mu_{Y \cdot X}$

21. The standard deviation of *Y* for any given value of *X* is $\sigma_{Y \cdot X}$ and is appropriately termed the population standard _____ of estimate.

error

22. In this model, it is assumed that $\sigma_{Y \cdot X}$, the population standard error of estimate, has the same value for every value of *X* within the range of interest. Given this model, it can be shown that *b* is an unbiased estimate of *B* and *a* is an unbiased estimate of ___ .

A

23. Suppose we independently select two more random samples of 20 observations each, with identical specifications regarding age of machines. Figure 10-2 shows our original sample regression line as well as those of the two new samples. It indicates that the sample regression line (does/does not) vary from one sample to the next.

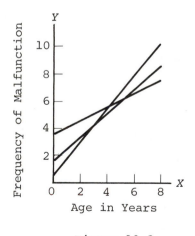

Figure 10-2

does

24. Under sample conditions, the slope (*b*) (does/does not) fluctuate.

does

25. Under sample conditions, the intercept (*a*) (does/does not) fluctuate.

does

26. In fact, any quantity computed from sample data will vary from sample to sample. Since the standard error of estimate ($s_{Y \cdot X}$) and the standard error of b (s_b) are computed from a sample, we (should/should not) anticipate sampling fluctuations for these quantities.

should

27. Let us return to the practical case of predicting *Y* from a sample regression line. Earlier we found the sample regression line to be $Y_C = 1.30 + 0.89X$. In this equation, *X* represents the age of the machine in years and Y_C represents the number of monthly failures. Suppose we wish to make a prediction regarding the number of monthly failures for a machine that is 7 years old. Using the regression equation above, we obtain Y_C = _____ + _____ (___) = _____ .

$1.30 + 0.89(7) = 7.53$

28. From previous experience, we know that we can have no confidence that *Y* will take on the exact value of 7.53. Instead, it will help to have a method for specifying a prediction _____ in which we can have a degree of confidence.

interval

29. As Figure 10-2 suggests, successive sample regression lines are closer together at the (center/extremes) of the range of *X*-values.

center

30. Thus, for a given level of confidence, we are led to expect that the prediction interval at either extreme of the observations of *X* will be (narrower/wider) than at the middle of the range.

wider

31. Since $\overline{X}$ represents the mean of the *X* values, the prediction interval will (widen/narrow) as one moves from $\overline{X}$ in either direction.

widen

32. To account for the above phenomenon the following expression is

used for the prediction interval for a Y-value predicted from
the sample regression line:

$$Y_c \pm ts_{Y \cdot X} \sqrt{1 + \frac{1}{n} + \frac{(X_s - \overline{X})^2}{\Sigma X^2 - n(\overline{X})^2}}$$

In this expression, X_s is the value of X for which we wish to
form a prediction interval estimate of Y.   Although the expression may appear complex, the quantity following the $\pm$ sign
tells within what range above and below the value of Y_c we
might expect to find the predicted value of (X or Y).

Y

33. To compute the prediction interval, we need to find the numerical value of $s_{Y \cdot X}^2$.   In Program Set 10.2, we found the method of
doing this involves computing $\Sigma(Y - Y_C)^2 = \Sigma Y^2 - a(\Sigma Y) - b(\Sigma XY)$.
Use the results of Frames 8, 10, and 11 and substitute the
quantities into this equation:

$$\Sigma(Y - Y_c)^2 = \underline{\hspace{1cm}} - \underline{\hspace{1.5cm}} - \underline{\hspace{1.5cm}}$$

$771 - 1.30(115) - 0.89(664)$

34. Completing the arithmetic, we have $\Sigma(Y - Y_c)^2 = 30.54$.   Since

$$s_{Y \cdot X}^2 = \frac{\Sigma(Y - Y_C)^2}{n - 2}, \quad s_{Y \cdot X}^2 = \underline{\frac{\hspace{1cm}}{\hspace{1cm}}} \quad \text{(substitute only)}$$

$30.54/(20 - 2)$ (or $s_{Y \cdot X}^2 = 1.70$)

35. To find $s_{Y \cdot X}$, we take the square root of this variance.   Thus,
$s_{Y \cdot X} = \sqrt{170} = 1.30$.   To find the last term in the confidence interval formula, we use these results from previous frames:
$X_s = 7$, $\Sigma X^2 = 600$, $\Sigma X = 100$, and $\overline{X} = 5$.   Thus

$$\frac{(X_s - \overline{X})^2}{\Sigma X^2 - n(\overline{X})^2} = \underline{\hspace{1.5cm}}$$

$$\frac{(7 - 5)^2}{600 - 20(5)^2} = \frac{4}{100} = 0.04$$

36. The value of $t_{\alpha/2}$ is from a t-distribution with $n - 2$ degrees
of freedom.   In our example, the confidence is $0.95 = 1 - \alpha$.
Thus we seek a t-value with $\underline{\hspace{0.5cm}}$ degrees of freedom that cuts
off a tail area of $\alpha/2 = \underline{\hspace{0.8cm}}$.

18, 0.025

37. From Table B-4, $t_{0.025}$ =-2.1009 (ignore the sign). At this
point all of the quantities needed to find the prediction interval for X_S = 7 are known. Substitute these quantities into
the prediction interval formula given in Frame 32:

$$\underline{\hspace{1cm}} \pm (\underline{\hspace{1cm}})(\underline{\hspace{1cm}}) \sqrt{\underline{\hspace{1cm}} + \underline{\hspace{1cm}} + \underline{\hspace{1cm}}}$$

$$7.53 \pm (1.30)(2.1009)\sqrt{1 + \frac{1}{20} + 0.04}$$

38. Completing the arithmetic, we have 7.53 ± 2.86. Thus the number
of monthly failures for a machine 7 years old might be expected
to be as low as 7.53 - 2.86 = 4.67 failures per month or as high
as _____ failures per month. (Of course, this statement is
made at the 0.95 confidence level.)

$$10.39 \overset{*}{\underset{*}{*}} 7.53 + 2.86 \overset{*}{\underset{*}{*}}$$

39. Suppose we selected X_S = 12. The 0.95 prediction interval
formula would give 11.98 ± 3.40. For X_S = 7, the 0.95 confidence interval was 7.53 ± 2.86. These examples illustrate the
point that the prediction interval for a fixed level of confidence (lessens/remains the same/widens) as X_S departs from $\overline{X}$.

widens

40. The confidence interval formula we have studied produces an
estimate for a single machine. We may also compute an interval
estimate for the mean failure rate for all machines of a particular age. The formula for doing this is

$$Y_c \pm ts_{Y \cdot X} \sqrt{\frac{1}{n} + \frac{(X_S - \overline{X})^2}{\Sigma x^2 - n(\overline{X})^2}}$$

Compare this formula with the one given in Frame 32. The
quantity under the radical in this formula is always (larger
than/equal to/less than) the corresponding quantity in Frame
32.

less than
(the corresponding quantity in Frame 32 is always greater by 1.0)

41. For a given value of X_S, the confidence interval estimate for
the mean failure rate for all machines will be (wider/narrower)
than the mean failure rate for a single machine.

narrower

42. For X_S = 7, the confidence interval for the mean failure rate
of all machines 7 years old is

$$7.53 \pm (1.3)(2.1009) \sqrt{0.09}, \quad \text{or} \quad 7.53 \pm 0.82$$

The corresponding result from Frame 37 is

7.53 ± _____

2.86

43. Evidently, we are able to predict the mean failure rate
for all machines seven years old with (less/more) accuracy
than the mean failure rate for a single machine 7 years old.

more

CHAPTER 10.   SELF-CORRECTING EXERCISES

10.1 The Scattergram and Linear Equations   The following data
show, for 10 years, the change in production of commercial
onions from the preceding year (in millions of sacks) and
the change in average price received by farmers from the preceding year (in dollars per sack).

Year	Change in Production (X)	Change in Price (Y)
1	−4	2
2	−2	4
3	8	−1
4	−8	7
5	16	−5
6	−10	5
7	13	−8
8	−14	12
9	6	−8
10	−5	2

a. Plot a scattergram of these data on the set of coordinates
on the following page.

b. A straight line fitted to these data by eye passes through
the points (−20, 12) and (20, −10). Find the equation of
this line and plot it as a dashed line on the scattergram below.

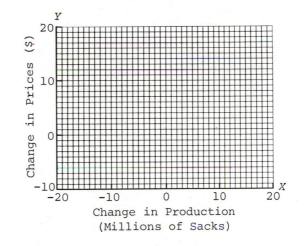

Change in Production
(Millions of Sacks)

10.2 The Least-Squares Line   In the first three parts of this ex-
cise, the least-squares line will be found for the 10 units
of observation in Question 1.

a. Complete the following table to find the values of ΣX,
ΣX^2, ΣY, ΣY^2, and ΣXY.

Year	Production Change (X)	Price Change (Y)	X^2	Y^2	XY
1	−4	2			
2	−2	4			
3	8	−1			
4	−8	7			
5	16	−5			
6	−10	5			
7	13	−8			
8	−14	12			
9	6	−8			
10	−5	2			
Totals					

b. Substitute the totals found in (a) into Equations 10-4 and
10-5 in the text to find the slope and the intercept of
the least-squares regression line. Write the equation of
this line.

c. From the equation found in (b), find the value of Y
when X is −20; also find the value of Y when X is +20.
Plot these two points on the graph in Question 1(a) and
connect them with a solid line to complete the plot of the
least-squares line.

d. On the graph, show the Y-intercept of the least-squares line by drawing an arrow pointing to it.

e. What interpretation can be made about the negative sign for the value of the slope found in (b)?

10.3 The Regression Model   Sales (Y) for a company are related to advertising expenditures (X) by $\mu_{Y \cdot X} = 1000 + 100X$. For this situation the value of the population standard error of estimate is 500.

a. Assume the assumptions for the regression model are met, describe the distribution of sales when $X = 10$ and when $X = 20$.

b. One assumption for the regression model is that Y-values are independent of one another. In your own words, explain what this means.

c. The company observed $Y = 1500$ for a sales figure. They believe this level of sales was produced when $X = 10$, $X = 12$, or $X = 14$, but they cannot identify which value of X is associated with the sales figure $Y = 1500$. For this situation, are any assumptions for the regression model violated? If so, how?

10.4 The Standard Error of Estimate   The data in this exercise are the same as in Question 10.1.

a. Find $\Sigma(Y - Y_c)^2$ by completing the following table.

Year	X	Y	Y_c	$Y - Y_c$	$(Y - Y_c)^2$
1	-4	2	3.32	-1.32	1.7424
2	-2	4	2.16	1.84	3.3856
3	8	-1	-3.64	2.64	6.9696
4	-8	7	5.64	1.36	1.8496
5	16	-5	-8.28	3.28	10.7584
6	-10	5	6.80	-1.80	3.2400
7	13	-8	-6.54	-1.46	2.1316
8	-14	12			
9	6	-8			
10	-5	2			

$$\Sigma(Y - Y_c)^2 = \underline{\hspace{2cm}}$$

b. Use the result of (a) and Equation 10-7 in the text to find the standard error of estimate.

c. Use the results of Question 10.2 and Equation 10-8 in the text to find $\Sigma(Y - Y_c)^2$. Compare this result with the calculation made in (a) of this exercise. Which method of computation is usually easier?

d. Suppose you had used the equation of the line fitted by eye in Question 10.1 as the basis for finding $\Sigma(Y - Y_c)^2$. How would this numerical value compare with the value found in (c) of this question? Explain your answer.

e. For a given data collection, what computational procedure assures us that we obtain the least-squares line?

10.5 Inference about the Slope The data for this question are the same as in Question 10.2. For (a) through (e), you are to test the hypothesis that B is zero against the alternative that B is not zero.

a. Discuss the nature of the null hypothesis in terms of the variables involved. What is the relationship between X and Y if the null hypothesis is true? If it is not true?

b. What is the formula for the test statistic? What quantities in this formula are known?

c. Compute s_b. Use the relationship $\Sigma(X - \bar{X})^2 = \Sigma x^2 - n(\bar{X})^2$ to simplify your computation.

d. What is the value of the test statistic indicated by the data?

e. If the level of significance is 0.05, what is your conclusion?

f. Find the 0.95 confidence interval estimate for B.

10.6 Inferences Based on the Regression Line The data in this question are the same as in Question 10.2.

a. Assume there will be no change in production next year. What is the point estimate of the change in price? What is the 0.95 prediction interval estimate for the change in price?

b. Repeat (a) assuming an increase in production of 10,000,000 sacks.

c. Compare your answers for the two prediction intervals.

d. Find the 0195 confidence interval estimate for the mean change in price for all years in which there is no change in production. Compare your answer with the one obtained in (a). Explain any similarities or differences.

10.7 Correlation   The situation is the same as in Question 10.2.

a. Use Equation 10-23 in the text to compute the sample correlation coefficient.

b. What proportion of the variation in the Y-variable is accounted for by variation in the X-variable?

10.8 Practice Using Regression   The mechanical aptitude scores for 30 employees are known without error. The production rate for these employees is measured and the data are shown below.

a. Plot the scattergram for these data:

Score	Rate
1	11
1	12
2	11
2	12
2	13
2	14
3	13
3	14
3	15
3	16
4	13
4	17
4	19
5	14
5	15
5	16
5	18
6	16
6	18
6	20
7	15
7	17
7	19
7	21
7	22
8	19
8	20
8	21
9	22
10	23

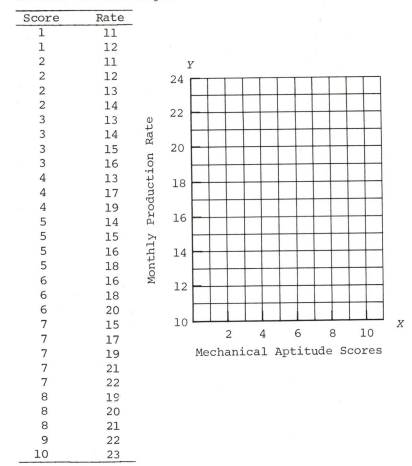

b. Is a linear relationship a plausible one for these variables? If so, find the best linear relationship.

c. Use your knowledge of regression to answer the following questions. Support your answers with appropriate calculations.

   i. The president believes the aptitude test is a complete waste of time because the president feels people's production rates are the same whether they have high or low scores on the test.

   ii. A new employee takes the aptitude test and obtains a score of 6. What production rate might be expected of this individual?

10.9 The Computer and Regression Computer software packages are helpful in assisting with computations in regression analysis. Computer outputs must be interpreted in order to provide useful information. Sometimes more analysis is provided in a printout than you require for your problem. In other instances, you may need to make some calculations based on the printout. This exercise is designed to give you some practice in using and interpreting computer results. The data for this problem consist of 327 observations. The independent variable is the score on an algebra test and the dependent variable is the mathematics portion of the SAT. The data are based on actual observations. A plot of the data is given in Figure 10-3. Computer printouts are given in Figures 10-4 and 10-5.

a. State whether the following estimates are provided by the printouts. If they are, give their values. If they are not, try to compute them from the information that is given.

   i. a and b.

   ii. The equation for the least-squares line.

   iii. $\bar{X}$, ΣX^2, $\bar{Y}$, ΣY^2, s_X^2, s_Y^2.

   iv. The coefficients of determination and correlation.

   v. s_b and $s_{Y \cdot X}$.

b. Use this information given or computed to test the hypothesis that $B = 0$.

c. Use the information given or computed to find the 0.95 confidence interval estimate for B.

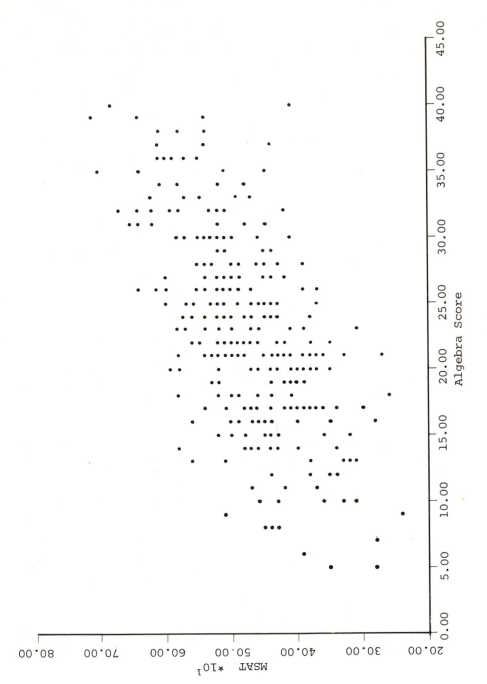

Figure 10-3

Variable	N	Mean	Standard Deviation	Minimum Value	Maximum Value	Std Error of Mean	Sum	Variance	C.V.
ALG	327	22.64220183	7.13307719	5.00000000	40.00000000	0.39446007	7404.00000	50.8807902	31.503
MSAT	327	473.91437309	81.89454543	240.00000000	710.00000000	4.52877871	154970.00000	6706.7165719	17.280

Figure 10-4

DEPENDENT VARIABLE: MSAT

SOURCE	DF	SUM OF SQUARES	MEAN SQUARE	F VALUE	PR > F
Model	1	768560.11065501	768560.11065501	176.17	0.0001
Error	325	1417829.49179147	4362.55228244		
Corrected Total	326	2186389.60244649			

R-SQUARE	C V
0.351520	13.9370

STD DEV	MSAT MEAN
66.04961985	473.91437309

SOURCE	DF	TYPE I SS	F VALUE	PR > F
ALG	1	768560.11065501	176.17	0.0001

SOURCE	DF	TYPE IV SS	F VALUE	PR > F
ALG	1	768560.11065501	176.17	0.0001

Parameter	Estimate	T FOR HO: PARAMETER=0	PR > (T)	STD ERROR OF ESTIMATE
Intercept	319.78981171	26.27	0.0001	12.17281154
ALG	6.80695996	13.27	0.0001	0.51284320

Figure 10-5

CHAPTER 10.   STUDENT RECORD AND REFERENCE SHEET

Darken the square corresponding to each test item you answered *incorrectly*. References indicate the topics you should study. See Chapter 1 of this volume for details.

Test Item	Diagnostic Test	Text References	Self-Correcting Exercise References	Program Set References
1	☐	280-291	10.1, 10.2	10.1
2	☐	280-291	10.1, 10.2	10.1
3	☐	280-291	10.1, 10.2	10.1
4	☐	280-291	10.1, 10.2	10.1
5	☐	280-291	10.1, 10.2	10.1
6	☐	280-291	10.1, 10.2	10.1
7	☐	280-291	10.1, 10.2	10.1
8	☐	293-295	10.3	10.1
9	☐	295-296	10.1, 10.2	10.1
10	☐	295-296	10.4	10.2
11	☐	297-299	10.5	10.3
12	☐	297-299	10.5	10.3
13	☐	302-306	10.6	10.4
14	☐	307-314	10.7	—
15	☐	307-314	10.7	—
16	☐	307-314	10.7	—
17	☐	307-314	10.7	—

11

INFERENCES FROM TWO SAMPLES

CHAPTER 11. SELF-CORRECTING EXERCISES

11.1 Interval Estimation for Differences between Two Means for Normal Populations with Known Standard Deviations Two different mixes of chicken feed are being tested by a grain milling company. Two samples of 15 newborn chicks are selected and each sample is fed one of the mixes. After 3 weeks, only 10 of the chicks fed the first mix are alive. Their mean weight is 14 oz. All 15 of the chicks fed the second mix are alive and their mean weight is 18 oz. Based on past studies, the standard deviation of weights can be assumed to be 3 oz. for both populations, and both are assumed to be normally distributed.

a. What is the standard error of the difference in the two means?

b. What is the 0.95 confidence interval estimate of the difference between the two population means?

c. Assume the standard deviation for the weights associated with the first mix is 3 oz and the standard deviation for the second mix is 5 oz. Will this assumption change your answer to (a) and (b)? If so, how?

d. Refer to Equation 11-4 in the text. If $\overline{X}_1$ is assigned to the second mix and $\overline{X}_2$ is assigned to the first mix, will the answer to (b) change? If so, how?

11.2 Estimation of Differences between Two Means for Normal Populations with Unknown Standard Deviations   Two designs for work stations are under consideration for a certain assembly operation.   Five assemblers selected at random were trained to use design A.   Then their daily mean assembly times in minutes were recorded for a week during which they used that design.   Eight other assemblers went through the same procedure with design B.   From past experience, mean assembly times are known to be normally distributed with equal but unknown standard deviations.   The mean assembly times for the 13 assemblers were

Design A: 1.6, 1.8, 1.3, 1.4, 1.8
Design B: 1.4, 1.3, 1.4, 0.8, 1.4, 1.3, 1.2, 1.2

When the data are processed, they produce the values in the following table.

	Design A	Design B
ΣX	7.9	10.0
s^2	0.052	0.040

a. What is the formula for the estimated standard error of the difference?   What is its numerical value?

b. Find the 0.99 confidence interval estimate of the difference in the population means.

c. Suppose 35 observations were made for design A and 42 were made for design B.   What formula(s), if any, would change?   In this case, must the population standard deviations be equal?

11.3 Testing the Difference between Two Population Means with Known Standard Deviations   The situation for this question is the same as in Question 11.1.   You are to test the hypothesis that the population mean weights for chicks fed with the two mixes are equal.   Assume a 0.05 level of significance.

a. State the null and alternative hypotheses.

b. What is the acceptance region for H_0?

c. What value of the test statistic is computed from the data?

d. What conclusion should be reached concerning the null hypothesis?   Which mix is apparently better?

11.4 <u>Testing the Difference between Two Population Means with Unknown Standard Deviations</u>   The situation for this question is
the same as in Question 11.2.   Test the hypothesis that the
two methods have the same mean assembly times.   Use a 0.05
level of significance.

a. State the null and alternative hypotheses.

b. What is the acceptance region of H_0?

c. What value of the test statistic is computed from the
data?

d. What conclusion should be reached concerning the null
hypothesis?   Which design method would you choose?

11.5 <u>Detection of a Difference in Population Means by Matched
Pairs</u>   Two training methods for sales representatives who
will sell a technical product are being considered.   Four
pairs of sales trainees matched on intelligence and motivation scores were selected.   One member of each pair was assigned randomly to training method A and the other was assigned to method B.   After completing training, all trainees
took a battery of examinations.   Composite scores from the
battery are known to be very nearly normally distributed and
to correlate highly with later sales success.   The composite
scores, classified by trainee pair and training method, are
shown in the following table.

| | Training Method | |
Pair	A	B
1	67	62
2	44	38
3	86	85
4	62	58

a. Express the complete hypothesis statement for a two-tailed
test in symbols and explain it verbally.

b. What is the formula for and the value of the estimated
standard deviation for the population of differences?

c. What is the formula for and value of the standard error of
the mean difference?

d. Test the null hypothesis at the 0.05 level of significance
and state your conclusion.

e. Is the matching described likely to have produced better results than if two independent samples had been used in the test described in conjunction with Equation 11-11 in the text? Discuss.

The responses to the question, "Do you approve or disapprove of the way Carter is handling his job as President?" for 3 months are as follows:

	Approve	Disapprove	No Opinion
February 1-4, 1980	55%	36%	9%
January 4-7, 1980	56%	33%	11%
December 5-6, 1979	61%	30%	9%

These results are based on interviews with 1600 adults each month. Use this information in Questions 11.6 and 11.7.

11.6 Interval Estimate of the Difference in Two Population Proportions In this exercise you are to find the 0.95 confidence interval estimate of the difference in the proportions of persons who approve the way the president is handling his job. Use the difference between February, 1980, and December, 1979.

a. What is the estimated standard error of the difference in these proportions?

b. Find the confidence interval estimate of the difference in proportions and interpret the results.

11.7 Testing a Hypothesis about the Difference in Two Population Proportions Suppose an aide to the president is concerned about the 1% drop in approval rating from January to February. Your help has been requested in analyzing the data.

a. Formulate a suitable two-tailed hypothesis and test it using the given information.

b. What advice would you give the president's assistant?

12

ANALYSIS OF FREQUENCIES

CHAPTER 12. SELF-CORRECTING EXERCISES

12.1 The Chi-Square Distribution Use Table B-5 in the text to answer these problems.

a. What distinguishes one chi-square distribution from another? In Table B-5, what is the meaning of the values in a given row in the table? What is the meaning of the column headings?

b. Consider a chi-square distribution with 5 df. What is the value of $\chi^2_{0.90}$? What is the probability that a value of χ^2 is less than 9.24? What is the probability that a value of χ^2 is greater than 9.24?

12.2 Chi-Square Tests for Multinomial Distributions—Test Rationale A personnel manager for a large federal agency is trying to determine employee preferences among four types of transportation. A sample of 100 employees selected at random will be asked whether they prefer automobile, bus, train, or airplane. The manager wishes to test the hypothesis of equal population proportions for each type of transportation. A 0.05 level of significance is chosen.

a. State the null hypothesis in symbols.

b. Are observed frequencies for the four categories needed in order to calculate the expected frequencies? If not, what information is needed to find expected frequencies?

c. Compute the expected frequencies for the categories *automobile*, *bus*, and *train*. What is the sum of these three expected frequencies? What is the total of the expected frequencies for all four categories? What value of expected frequency must be assigned to *airplane*? How many degrees of freedom are present in this problem?

d. Explain how observed frequencies are obtained. How do they differ from expected frequencies?

e. The tables below show three examples of frequencies that might occur. Before making any calculations, judge which collection of observed frequencies gives the strongest and which gives the weakest support for the null hypothesis. Then compute the value of χ^2 by completing each table.

i.

Type	f_0	f_e	$f_0 - f_e$	$(f_0 - f_e)^2/f_e$
Automobile	25	_____	_____	_____
Bus	25	_____	_____	_____
Train	25	_____	_____	_____
Airplane	25	_____	_____	_____
	100	_____		_____ $= \chi^2$

ii.

Type	f_0	f_e	$f_0 - f_e$	$(f_0 - f_e)^2/f_e$
Automobile	50	_____	_____	_____
Bus	0	_____	_____	_____
Train	0	_____	_____	_____
Airplane	50	_____	_____	_____
	100	_____		_____ $= \chi^2$

iii.

Type	f_0	f_e	$(f_0 - f_e)$	$(f_0 - f_e)^2/f_e$
Automobile	32	___	___	___
Bus	17	___	___	___
Train	19	___	___	___
Airplane	32	___	___	___
	100	___	___	___ $= \chi^2$

f. How do the judgments you made in (e) compare with the computed values of χ^2? Does a large or a small value of χ^2 support the null hypothesis?

g. What is the acceptance region for the null hypothesis? What conclusions would you reach about the null hypothesis for each collection of observed values in (e)?

12.3 Chi-Square Test for a Single Categorial Variable with More Than Two Classifications A service station manager believes that demand for a mechanic's service at his station is evenly distributed by time periods during the day. The following data are immediately available on the number of requests for a mechanic's service for last Wednesday.

Hours	Number of Demands
6 AM - 10 AM	18
10 AM - 2 PM	10
2 PM - 6 PM	24
6 PM - 10 PM	12

a. State the null hypothesis in terms of proportions.

b. Prepare a table of observed and expected frequencies.

c. What is the contribution of each time period to the computed value of χ^2? Display your results in the table for (b). How many degrees of freedom apply?

d. Should the station manager discard his belief that demand is equally distributed among time periods? Use $\alpha = 0.10$.

12.4 Chi-Square Test of Independence—Test Rationale An investigator wishes to determine whether age and income are independent at the 0.05 level of significance. A random sample of 400 persons is selected. All persons contacted are asked to state their ages and incomes. The investigator classifies each response according to the following scheme.

Income	Age		Total
	Under 30	Over 30	
Under $10,000			100
Over $10,000			200
Not Stated	_____	_____	100
Total	200	200	400

(The totals in this table were found from *observed* frequencies, which we will present later in the exercise.)

a. What is the null hypothesis?

b. Convert the observed totals to estimated marginal probabilities. Express these values in fourths.

c. Assume the null hypothesis is true and use the estimated marginal probabilities found in (b) to compute the joint probabilities. Express the joint probabilities in sixteenths. Display the joint and the marginal probabilities in a table.

d. Explain how to use the table of joint probabilities to find expected frequencies. Find the expected frequency for the *under 30 and under $10,000* classification.

e. Explain how the other expected frequencies may be obtained from the computation made in (d). How many degrees of freedom apply to this example? Display all the expected frequencies in a table.

f. What is the acceptance region for this situation?

g. The complete table of observed values is given below. Compute the value of χ^2 for these data and state whether the null hypothesis should be accepted or rejected.

Income	Age Under 30	Over 30	Total
Under $10,000	60	40	100
Over $10,000	60	140	200
Not Stated	80	20	100
Total	200	200	400

h. Suppose the observed frequencies happened to be exactly equal to the expected frequencies. What would you conclude about the null hypothesis? What would be the computed value of X^2? In general, does a large or a small computed value of X^2 cause you to reject the null hypothesis? What determines whether a value of X^2 computed from the data should cause the null hypothesis to be accepted or rejected?

12.5 Chi-Square Test for Independence   A television producer wants to determine whether or not male and female viewers have different opinions of his new program, *The Main Street Gang*. A sample of 174 viewers asks each the question, "Do you like the television program, *The Main Street Gang*?" and obtains the following frequencies.

	Yes	No	Undecided	Total
Male	46	10	30	86
Female	20	18	50	88
Total	66	28	80	174

The null hypothesis is that no association exists between preference and sex in the population. Assume $\alpha = 0.05$.

a. What is the acceptance region? Does the acceptance region depend on the observed frequencies?

b. Prepare a table of expected frequencies.

c. Prepare another table containing the contribution of each cell to the computed chi-square value. What is the computed chi-square value?

d. What is your conclusion about the null hypothesis?

12.6 Multiple Independent Samples—Test Rationale   A manufacturer of automobile parts has learned that 1 of every 4 new cars

sold nationally is an import. Since the parts are sold in
four district markets, the manager wishes to test the hypothesis that 25% of the cars sold in each of the markets are
imports. Assume a 0.10 level of significance.

a. A random sample of 100 new car registrations in the
   northern market is to be selected. If the null hypothesis
   is true, what is the expected number of imports in this
   sample?

b. Use the results from (a) to determine the expected number
   of domestic cars in the sample. How many degrees of
   freedom apply to this sample?

c. This table shows the sample of new car registration that
   is to be observed for each market. Find the expected frequencies for each market.

	Market			
	Northern	Eastern	Southern	Western
Imports	____	____	____	____
Domestics	____	____	____	____
	100	60	80	120

d. Do you need the sample data to make the computations in
   (c)? How many degrees of freedom apply to the table in
   (c)? What is the acceptance region for the null hypothesis?

e. The sample data for this problem are as follows.

	Market			
	Northern	Eastern	Southern	Western
Imports	20	40	40	40
Domestics	80	20	40	80
	100	60	80	120

What value of χ^2 is found from the data? What do you conclude about the null hypothesis?

12.7 Multiple Independent Samples   The responses to the question,
     "Do you approve or disapprove of the way Carter is handling
     his job as president?" for three months are as follows:

	Approve	Disapprove	No Opinion
February 1-4, 1980	55%	36%	9%
January 4-7, 1980	56%	33%	11%
December 5-6, 1979	61%	30%	9%

Each survey used 1600 observations.

a. Construct a new table that has two categories: *Approve* and *Other Opinion*.

b. Convert the percentages to frequencies and display your results in a table.

c. Use the null hypothesis that the true proportion approving is 0.50 to find the expected frequencies. Display your results in a table.

d. Use the frequencies found in (b) and (c) to compute a value of χ^2.

e. How many degrees of freedom are there?

f. If the level of significance is 0.01, what conclusion should be reached about the null hypothesis?

12.8 Goodness of Fit (the Binomial Model) An auditor checks a random sample of 100 billings for five types of errors. The number of errors and the associated frequencies are:

Number of Errors	Frequency
0	47
1	25
2	16
3	6
4	5
5	1
	100

You are to test the hypothesis that the number of errors is a binomial random variable.

a. What is the estimated value of π?

b. What are the binomial probabilities associated with the hypothesis?

c. What are the expected frequencies?

d. What is the computed value of χ^2?   How many degrees of freedom apply?

e. At the 0.05 level of significance, what conclusion is reached about the null hypothesis?

12.9 <u>Goodness of Fit (the Normal Model)</u>   In Question 7.6, we examined the distribution of sample means drawn from a nonnormal population with $\mu = 1$ and $\sigma = 1$.   Three distributions were given for $n = 4$, $n = 16$, and $n = 64$.   In this question, we shall test the hypotheses that the sampling distributions for $n = 4$ and $n = 64$ are normal.

(*Note*:   In many problems involving goodness of fit tests, the mean and standard deviation are unknown and must be computed from the sample data.   A degree of freedom is lost for each estimated parameter.   In this example, the mean and standard deviation are established mathematically and do not have to be estimated from the data.   Thus the corresponding degrees of freedom are not lost.)

a. Refer to the solution for Question 7.6.   Do the distributions for $n = 4$ and $n = 64$ appear to be normally distributed?

b. The data for $n = 4$ are repeated below.   Using Table 12-6 in the text as a guide, compute the value of χ^2 needed to test the hypothesis that the distribution of sample means for $n = 4$ is a normal distribution.

c. How many degrees of freedom are associated with the value found in (b)?

d. If the level of significance is 0.005 what conclusion do you reach about the null hypothesis?

e. The data for $n = 64$ are given below.   Repeat (b) through (d) for these data.

f. Does this example tend to confirm or not confirm the central limit theorem?

$n = 4$ Sample Means $(\overline{X})$	f
0.0195 - 0.215	8
0.215 - 0.455	110
0.455 - 0.695	188
0.695 - 0.935	207
0.935 - 1.175	170
1.175 - 1.415	129
1.415 - 1.655	78
1.655 - 1.895	57
1.895 - 2.135	24
2.135 - 2.275	11
2.275 - 2.615	13
2.615 - 2.855	1
2.855 - 3.095	3
3.095 - 3.335	1
	1000

$n = 64$ Sample Means $(\overline{X})$	f
0.0675 - 0.735	11
0.735 - 0.795	28
0.795 - 0.855	90
0.855 - 0.915	128
0.915 - 0.975	159
0.975 - 1.035	221
1.035 - 1.095	143
1.095 - 1.155	110
1.155 - 1.215	61
1.215 - 1.275	33
1.275 - 1.335	8
1.335 - 1.395	2
1.395 - 1.455	4
1.455 - 1.515	2
	1000

13

ANALYSIS OF VARIANCE

CHAPTER 13. SELF-CORRECTING EXERCISES

13.1 The Family of F-Distributions

a. Make a sketch of the F-distribution with 3 df associated with the numerator and 16 df associated with the denominator. Use Table B-6 to find the value F on this distribution which cuts off 5% of this distribution to its right. Find the value of F on this distribution which cuts off 1% of this distribution to its right. Locate these F-values and the corresponding areas on your sketch.

b. What distinguishes one F-distribution from another?

c. How many F-values does Table B-6 provide for each F-distribution?

d. Consider an F-distribution with $m_1 = 3$ and $m_2 = 16$. Another F-distribution has $m_1 = 16$ and $m_2 = 3$. Are these the same F-distribution? Does the *same* value of F cut off 1% of each distribution to its right? (Use Table B-6 to answer the last question.)

13.2 Notation Four different types of traffic lights are being compared with respect to their average service lives. The service lives (nearest whole year) of 5 lights of each type have been collected and are shown in the following table.

A	B	C	D
1	2	0	4
1	3	3	6
2	5	3	7
3	5	4	8
3	5	5	10

a. What variable is being observed? What distinguishes one column from another? How many rows are there? What do the rows represent?

b. Use Tables 13-1 and 13-2 in the text as models and find all the sums and the means indicated there for the traffic light example.

c. In the table prepared in answer to (b), identify the following values: X_{24}, C_3, $\overline{X}_2$, $\overline{\overline{X}}$ and n.

13.3 Test Based on Two Independent Estimates of σ^2 The numerical example is the same as the one used in Question 2.

a. Using text Equations 13-3 and 13-4, find the estimate (based on column means) of the population variance (σ^2) from which the 20 observations in the example came, under the null hypothesis and the related assumptions. How many degrees of freedom are associated with this estimate?

b. Using text Equation 13-5, find the estimate of σ^2 based on the pooled variances within the columns. How many degrees of freedom are associated with this estimate?

c. Using the procedure explained in conjunction with text Equation 13-6, find the value of F for the example and use it to perform a significance test at the 0.05 level of significance.

d. Explain what null hypothesis is being tested in (c), state the conclusion reached by the test, and present the reasoning which justifies the conclusion.

13.4 Test Rationale

a. What is the null hypothesis in analysis of variance? What is the alternative hypothesis?

b. If the null hypothesis in analysis of variance is true, what would you expect the ratio of variances computed in Equation 13-6 to be on the average?

c. If the alternative hypothesis is true, would you expect the numerator variance to be larger or smaller in comparison with denominator variance? Why? If the alternative hypothesis is true, would you expect the computed F-ratio to be large or small?

13.5 Test Rationale In this question, we shall examine two examples. These are designed to demonstrate the relationship between the null hypothesis and the F ratio. The figure and table below show three random samples of three observations, each with the populations from which they were drawn.

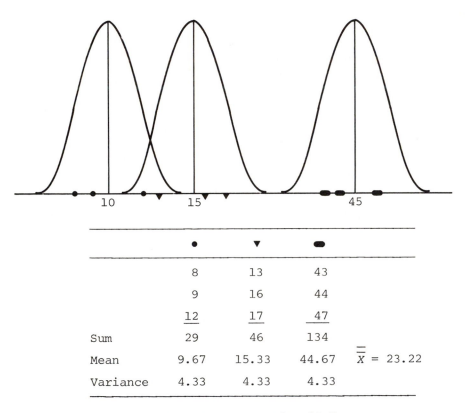

	•	▼	●	
	8	13	43	
	9	16	44	
	12	17	47	
Sum	29	46	134	
Mean	9.67	15.33	44.67	$\overline{\overline{X}} = 23.22$
Variance	4.33	4.33	4.33	

Data A for Question 13.5

a. What is the null hypothesis? According to the sketch, is the hypothesis true or false? In practical problems do you know whether the hypothesis is true or false?

b. Use Equations 13-3 through 13-6 in the text to find the F-ratio. Is the F-ratio large or small? Why?

c. The figure and data below are for the second example. Answer (a) and (b) for these data. The standard deviation for this population is equal to the standard deviation of the population for (a).

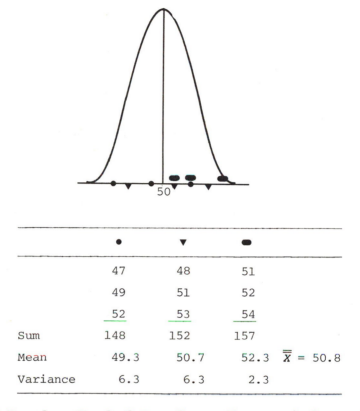

	●	▼	●	
	47	48	51	
	49	51	52	
	52	53	54	
Sum	148	152	157	
Mean	49.3	50.7	52.3	$\overline{\overline{X}} = 50.8$
Variance	6.3	6.3	2.3	

13.6 <u>Test Based on Standard Procedures</u> The numerical example is the same as the one used in Question 13.2.

a. Apply text Equations 13-10, 13-11, and 13-12 to the service life example to find T^2/n, SST, SSA, and SSE.

b. Use Table 13-3 in the text as the model for standard format and fill in the proper numerical values for this example.

c. Compare the results in (b) with those in Question 13.3. Which procedure is usually easier to apply?

13.7 <u>Estimates and Comparisons</u> In order to determine the influence of tire brand on mileage, an analysis of variance is performed on five different brands. Nine tires for each brand are used.   The average mileages for each brand (rounded to the nearest 10,000 miles) are as follows.

Brand	A	B	C	D	E
Average Miles	3	5	7	9	4

The analysis of variance shows that MSE = 1.5.

Parts a-c should be considered as a family of contrasts.

a. Find the 0.95 confidence interval estimate of the difference between the two brands with the lowest mileages. Is this difference significant?

b. Repeat (a) for the two brands with the highest mileages.

c. Find the 0.95 confidence interval estimate for the difference of the average of the two brands with highest mileages and the two brands with the lowest mileages.   Is the difference significant?

d. Repeat (a) assuming it is the only contrast of interest.

13.8 Replication, Randomization, and Cross Classification

a. Briefly explain the purpose of replication, randomization, and cross classification.

b. Define replication, randomization, and cross classification.

c. In which of these processes is a table of random numbers used?

14

MULTIPLE REGRESSION

CHAPTER 14. SELF-CORRECTING EXERCISES

In the first four exercises, use the following data.

Patient	Cost (Y)	Length of Stay (X_1)	Patient Age (X_2)	X_1^2	X_2^2	$X_1 X_2$	$X_1 Y$	$X_2 Y$
1	$ 100	2	20					
2	150	1	20					
3	200	3	40					
4	250	5	60					
5	300	4	60					
6	400	3	40					
	$1400	18	240					

The data give cost in dollars (Y), length of stay in days (X_1), and patient age in years (X_2) for 6 hospital patients. (The number of observations was limited to 6 to keep the computations to a minimum. In actual practice, this number of observations is much too small to give any meaningful results. In Question 14.5, we shall examine a more realistic example.)

14.1 Scattergrams On the grids provided on page 266, draw the scattergrams for each pair of variables.

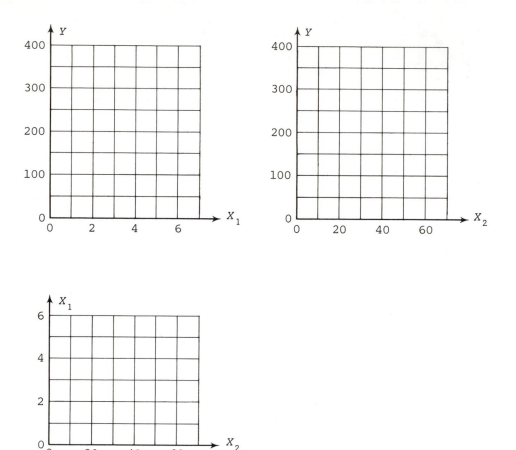

14.2 The Least-Squares Relationship

a. In the space provided in the table, find all the sums needed in order to determine the multiple regression equation.

b. Using these sums, write the normal equations (do not attempt to solve).

c. In your own words, briefly explain what the normal equations mean.

d. Verify that the values $a = 83.33$, $b_1 = -50$, and $b_2 = 7.5$ satisfy the normal equations.

e. Briefly explain how you would solve the normal equations.

f. What is the equation of the least-squares line?

g. If a patient stays 2 days and is 30 years old, what is the expected cost for this patient?

14.3 Standard Error of Estimate and Coefficient of Multiple Determination   In this exercise you are to compute *estimates* of the population parameters from the sample data. You are to use the results of Questions 14.1 and 14.2 in your computations.

a. Find the variance around the regression relationship.

b. Find the coefficient of determination. What does this value tell you?

14.4 Interpreting Computer Output   An investigator is interested in determining the relationship between the mathematics score on the SAT (MSAT), the score on an algebra test (ALG), and the number of years of high school mathematics courses (YHSM). A multiple regression will be performed using MSAT as the dependent variable. Observations for 339 students are available. The computer output is shown in Figure 14-1.

INDIVIDUAL VARIABLES

VARIABLE	COEFFICIENT	STANDARD ERROR	T STAT
CONSTANT	292.84599713	0.50493921	
ALG	6.75237129	0.50493921	13.37
YHSM	13.00213499	5.84669991	2.22

ANALYSIS OF VARIANCE

	SS	DF	MS	F STAT
REGRESSION	845484.38042401	2	422742	102.51
RESIDUAL	1385577.56647866	36	124	
TOTAL	2231061.94690267	338		

STD ERROR OF ESTIMATE   =   64.216374

MULT R SQ (COEFF DETERM)   =   0.378961
MULT R (COEFF CORREL)   =   0.615598

SIMPLE CORRELATION MATRIX

	MSAT	ALG	YHSM
MSAT	1.000	0.609	0.220
ALG		1.000	0.208
YHSM			1.000

ESTIMATED RESPONSE VARIABLE FOR

ALG = 25
YHSM = 3

Figure 14-1   Computer Output for Student Data (Model I)

```
POINT ESTIMATE                      = 500.662
STD ERROR OF MEAN RESPONSE          =   5.607
STD ERROR OF INDIVIDUAL RESPONSE =  64.692
```

RESIDUALS (PARTIAL LISTING)

OBSERVED	ESTIMATED	RESIDUAL
580	513.664	66.34
600	547.426	52.57
370	493.909	-123.91
400	412.378	- 12.38
.	.	.
.	.	.
.	.	.

Figure 14-1
(Continued)

a. Write the equation of the least-squares line. Round the coefficients to two decimal places.

b. On the average, how will the MSAT change for a unit increase on the algebra test? How will the MSAT change for an additional year of high school mathematics?

c. What proportion of the variability of MSAT is explained by ALG and YHSM?

d. What is the mean value of the residuals $\Sigma(Y - Y_c)$? Find a symmetrical interval around this mean within which you would expect to find 95% of the observed residuals if the residuals are normally distributed.

e. The interval found in (d) is shown in Figure 14-2, which is a plot of residuals versus ALG. What proportion of the observed residuals fall outside this interval? Should you suspect the distributions are not normally distributed? Does Figure 14-2 indicate that there is any trend in the residuals versus ALG?

f. What other aspects of the residuals should be investigated for a thorough analysis?

14.5 Statistical Inference   The situation for this question is the same as for Question 14.4. Refer to Figure 14-1 for the information needed to work this exercise.

a. Test the hypothesis that all of the *B*-coefficients in the population model are simultaneously equal to zero. Assume a 0.01 level of significance.

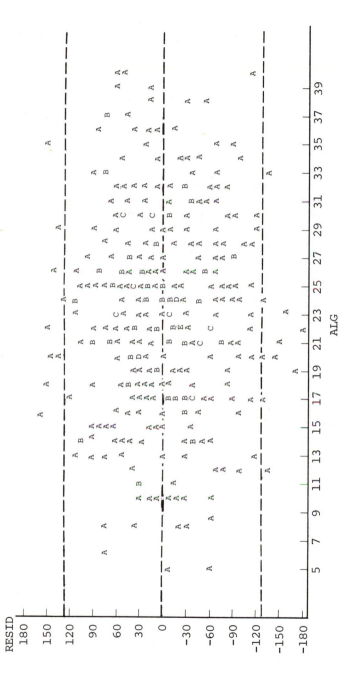

Figure 14-2

b. What is the expected MSAT for an individual with 3 years of high school mathematics and an algebra score of 25? Assume this individual was not in the original data. Find the 0.95 prediction interval for this individual's MSAT.

c. What is the conditional mean MSAT of all persons with 3 years of high school mathematics and an algebra score of 25? Find the 0.95 confidence interval estimate for this mean.

d. Test the hypothesis that the population model regression coefficient for the number of years of high school mathematics is zero. Use a 0.05 level of significance.

e. Find the 0.95 confidence interval estimate for the algebra score coefficient.

14.6 Correlated Independent Variables

a. Refer to the correlation matrix in Figure 14-1. Do the independent variables appear to be related? If so, how?

b. In an attempt to improve the model discussed in Question 14.4 (Model I), the variable SEX was added as a third independent variable. For this variable, males are coded as zero and females as 1. For convenience, we assign the name *Model II* to this. Selected results for Model II are shown in Figure 14-3. Compare the *t*-statistic for the variable YHSM for Model I and for Model II. In Model II, what is the *t*-value of the variables SEX and YHSM? Can you explain the reason for this?

c. Another model is analyzed using MSAT as the independent variable and ALG and SEX as the dependent variables. Selected results for Model III are shown in Figure 14-4. What are the coefficients of determination for the three models? If you had to select one of the models to use for predicting MSAT, which would you choose? Why?

14.7 Indicator Variables

a. How many values does an indicator variable have? For Model III in Question 14.6, is the variable SEX an indicator variable? What equation would you use to predict MSAT for men? For women? Refer to Figure 14-4 in the supplement and Figure 14-4 in the text.

b. In a multiple regression analysis students are to be classified as in-state or out-of-state. In addition, in-state students are to be classified by the population density of their cities of residence. For this purpose, cities with 2600 persons per square mile are high density and those with less than 2600 persons per square mile are low density. There are a total of three classes. How many indicator variables will be required? Devise a coding scheme that will distinguish among the various residency classifications.

c. A linear regression model is proposed in which the dependent variable is MSAT and the independent variables are the score on an algebra test and the residency of the student. The indicator variable X_1 has the value 1 for students from in-state, high-density cities. The indicator variable X_2 has the value 1 for out-of-state students. Both X_1 and X_2 are 0 for in-state low density. Selected results from the computer output are given in Figure 14-5. Use the grid to plot the multiple regression equation. Label the residence groups. How important is the classification *in-state* versus *out-of-state*? The classification *high density* versus *low density*?

INDIVIDUAL VARIABLES

VARIABLE	COEFFICIENTS	STANDARD ERROR	T STAT
CONSTANT	319.35		
ALG	7.31	0.51	14.30
YHSM	5.20	6.20	0.84
SEX	-27.94	7.22	-3.87

MULT R SQ (COEFF DETERM)   = 0.413801

SIMPLE CORRELATION MATRIX

	MSAT	ALG	YHSM	SEX
MSAT	1.000	0.620	0.220	-0.080
ALG		1.000	0.273	0.124
YHSM			1.000	-0.066
SEX				1.000

Figure 14-3 Computer Output For Student Data (Model II)

INDIVIDUAL VARIABLES

VARIABLE	COEFFICIENTS	STANDARD ERROR	T STAT
CONSTANT	335.54		
ALG	7.49	0.49	15.40
SEX	-28.17	7.16	-3.44

MULT R SQ (COEFF DETERM)   = 0.416456

SIMPLE CORRELATION MATRIX

	MSAT	ALG	SEX
MSAT	1.000	0.624	-0.075
ALG		1.000	0.010
SEX			1.000

Figure 14-4   *Computer Data for Student Data (Model III)*

INDIVIDUAL VARIABLES

VARIABLE	COEFFICIENTS	STANDARD ERROR	T STAT
CONSTANT	328.56		
ALG	6.87	0.48	14.17
X_1	10.61	8.42	1.26
X_2	20.94	8.94	2.34

Figure 14-5   *Multiple Regression with Indicator Variables*

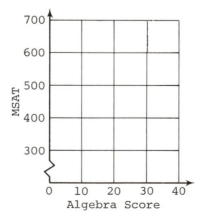

14.8 <u>Nonlinear Regression</u>   These data show the market share for
the Chrysler Corporation for 1963-1977.[*]   (When time is the
independent variable, the inference techniques for regression analysis do not apply.   However, as we shall see in
Chapters 16 and 17, the least-squares regression line is used
for time series data.)   To simplify the computer analysis,
1963 is represented by $X = 3$, 1964 by $X = 4$ and so forth.

[*] *Fortune*, June 19, 1978, p. 58.

Year	X	Market Share (in percent (Y))
1963	3	12.2
1964	4	13.8
1965	5	14.7
1966	6	15.4
1967	7	16.1
1968	8	16.2
1969	9	15.1
1970	10	16.1
1971	11	14.8
1972	12	14.4
1973	13	13.7
1974	14	14.0
1975	15	12.4
1976	16	13.7
1977	17	12.1

a. Plot the data on the grid.

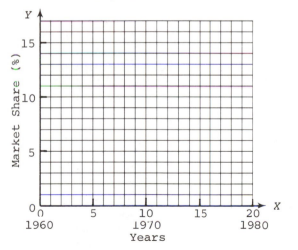

b. Is a linear model for 1963-1968 appropriate?   Would it be
appropriate to obtain a point estimate for market share for
1975 using this model?   Is a linear model appropriate for
1963-1977?   What is the value of making a plot such as the
one in (a)?

c. A simple linear regression analysis produces the following results:

$$Y_c = 15.43 - 0.011X$$

$$r^2 = 0.134$$

$$s_{Y \cdot X} = 1.30$$

When a parabola is used as the model, the following results are produced:

$$Y_c = 10.45 + 1.11X - 0.061X^2$$

$$r^2 = 0.741$$

$$s_{Y \cdot X} = 0.74$$

What is the influence of adding the X^2-term to the model on the standard error of estimate? On the coefficient of determination?

d. Plot the linear equation line on the grid.

e. This table gives the values of Y_c from the parabola. Verify the estimated value for $X = 10$ (1970). Plot the estimated values and sketch the graph of the parabola.

X	Y_c
3	13.242
4	13.928
5	14.491
6	14.931
7	15.250
8	15.445
9	15.519
10	15.469
11	15.298
12	15.004
13	14.587
14	14.048
15	13.387
16	12.603
17	11.697

f. In about what year did Chrysler have its maximum market share? In about what year do you think the decline in market share should have been apparent?

g. Explain how you would use a multiple linear regression computer program to obtain the equation for the parabola.

15

NONPARAMETRIC STATISTICS

CHAPTER 15. SELF-CORRECTING EXERCISES

15.1 Mann–Whitney–Wilcoxon Test Rationale A paint manufacturer
has a new paint that should dry sooner than the present type.
Drying times for two patches of the new type and five patches
of the old type are determined. The drying times are positively skewed. In our Mann–Whitney–Wilcoxon test, the paint
with the fastest drying time will be given the smallest rank.

a. Assume the distributions of drying times are identical
   and that no ties can occur. What is the smallest possible
   value of the test statistic of W? What is the largest
   possible value of W? Find all the values of W and display
   your results in a probability distribution such as Table
   15-1 in the text.

b. Use Equations 15-1 and 15-2 in the text to find the mean
   and standard deviation of this distribution.

c. Suppose a two-tailed test is to be performed. If the acceptance region for the null hypothesis is $4 \leq W \leq 12$, what
   level of significance is being used?

d. Suppose a null hypothesis that the drying time for the old
   paint is faster than the new paint versus the alternative
   that new paint dries faster than the old. What acceptance
   region for the null hypothesis would produce a level of
   significance of approximately 5%?

15.2 Mann–Whitney–Wilcoxon Test for Large Samples   The situation for this question is the same as in Question 15.1 except that 10 patches of the new paint and 11 patches of the old paint are used.   The drying times in minutes are as follows.

New: 61.9   56.6   37.4   49.2   42.8   40.0   38.2   57.8   58.1   60.1

Old: 56.8   74.0   50.2   89.4   45.5   59.9   60.0   63.6   57.9   63.2   65.7

The manufacturer wants to find out if the new paint typically dries faster than does the older type.

a. Are the measurements made on a nominal, ordinal, interval, or ratio scale?   Is the Wilcoxon rank-sum test more appropriate than a two-sample t-test?   Why or why not?

b. Place the data in order by drying time without regard to paint type.   Then underline the drying times that apply to the new paint (because there are fewer of them).   Rank the data from smallest to largest and find the sum of the ranks for the smaller sample.

c. When the values are ranked from smallest to largest, what is the implication of a small value for W?   A large value for W?   When ranking is from smallest to largest, what is the smallest possible value of W that could be observed?   What would be indicated by the latter value if it were observed?

d. Assume that the paint manufacturer will produce the new paint only if it has a shorter drying time than the old type.   State the null and alternative hypotheses verbally.   If $\alpha = 0.005$, what is the critical value of Z?   What is your conclusion?

15.3 Kruskal–Wallis Test Rationale   The following table represents two extreme cases designed to illustrate the rationale of the Kruskal–Wallis test.   In each case, original observations have been assigned ranks shown here.   The null hypothesis for both Case I and Case II is that there is no difference in rankings for A, B, and C.

	Case I			Case II		
	A	B	C	A	B	C
	1	6	11	1	2	3
	2	7	12	4	5	6
	3	8	13	7	8	9
	4	9	14	10	11	12
	5	10	15	13	14	15
T_j	15	40	65	35	40	45
T_j^2	225	1600	4225	1225	1600	2025
T_j^2/n_j	45	320	845	245	320	405

a. By inspecting the ranks, state which case (I or II) appears to support the null hypothesis and which supports the alternative hypothesis.

b. Explain how the quantities T_j, T_j^2, and T_j^2/n_j support your answer to (a).

c. Compute the test statistic H for each case. How do these values of H support your answer to (a)? Explain your answer by reference to Table B-5 in the text.

15.4 Kruskal-Wallis Test Three neighborhoods are to be compared for differences in monthly family incomes. The income distributions are presumed to be heavily skewed. Consequently, a one-way analysis of variance is rejected in favor of a Kruskal-Wallis test. The data are shown in the following table for seven families in each neighborhood.

Mean Monthly Income in Dollars

	Neighborhood	
A	B	C
730	576	263
1211	966	620
455	437	547
766	654	780
962	824	130
948	912	939
531	1031	867

a. Assign rank number 1 to the smallest of the 21 incomes and rank all 21 incomes consecutively.

b. For each column in the table of ranks in (a), find the total (T_j) and the other quantities required to perform the Kruskal-Wallis test as illustrated in Table 15-5 in the text.

c. Calculate the value of the test statistic H, complete the test with a 0.05 level of significance, and state your conclusion with regard to the equality of incomes in the three neighborhoods.

15.5 Matched Pair Signed Rank Test An electronics firm has two booklets to explain the use of one of its complex products to customer engineers. To find out which booklet should be produced in large quantities, the firm's statistician has selected 10 pairs of engineers representative of customers. Each pair is matched on type of education, experience with related equipment, and type of job. One booklet of each type is given to one member of each pair at random. After studying the booklets, the engineers are tested and scored on their ability to operate the equipment. The score for the member of each pair who read the second booklet (B) is subtracted from that of the member who read the first booklet (A). The test scores associated with the two booklets are as follows.

| | Scores | | Absolute | Rank of | Signed |
Pair	A	B	Difference	Absolute Difference	Rank
1	78	62			
2	89	93			
3	65	78			
4	93	72			
5	86	72			
6	79	78			
7	72	63			
8	82	99			
9	70	80			
10	64	84			

At the 0.05 level of significance, perform a two-tailed test of the hypothesis that the booklets are equally effective.

15.6 A Test for Randomness The figure below shows the demand for home attic fans for 30 consecutive days. You are to test the hypothesis that the demands are randomly distributed above and below 50. Use a 0.05 level of significance. To perform the test, use a plus sign for demands over 50 and a minus sign for demands less than fifty. Ignore demands that equal 50.

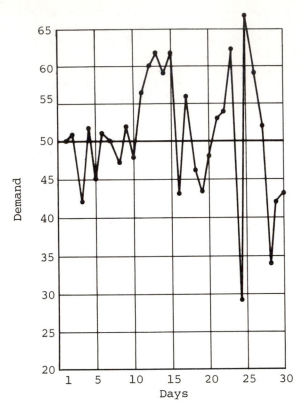

a. Will a large or small number of runs cause you to reject the hypothesis of randomness? Explain.

b. How many runs are there?

c. If the demands are random, what is the mean and standard deviation of the number of runs?

d. What is the observed value of z?

e. What conclusion should be reached?

15.7 Rank-Difference Correlation   Independent of one another, a husband and wife were asked to rank five different sport cars in order of preference with "1" being the most pre- ferred. The result was as follows.

Car	A	B	C	D	E
Husband	5	1	4	2	3
Wife	5	2	4	3	1

Using the difference between the ranks, calculate the Spearman rank-difference correlation coefficient to measure the degree of agreement.

15.8 <u>Test for Significant Correlation as Measured by Spearman Coefficient</u> A district sales manager and assistant have independently ranked the 20 sales trainees in the district on their overall performance.

a. If the manager and assistant are in agreement about performance of the trainees, would you expect the correlation correlation to be positive, negative, or zero? Formulate an appropriate null hypothesis and an appropriate alternative hypothesis.

b. Why is the Spearman rank-difference correlation appropriate in this situation?

c. Suppose that the Spearman rank-difference correlation is computed and is found to be +0.7. Test the null hypothesis of no difference in ranking at the 0.01 level of significance.

d. Suppose that r_s = +0.5. Would your answer to (c) change? Explain.

16

TIME SERIES
AND INDEX NUMBERS

16.1 Determination of Least Squares Linear Trend

a. Determine the least-squares linear trend for the following
   data where Y is annual sales (in ten thousands of dollars)
   of a building materials dealer.

Year	Y
1968	232
1969	201
1970	200
1971	179

b. The following data are the years of life expected at birth
   for white and nonwhite females.* Calculate the least-
   squares linear trend line for each series (carry results
   to one decimal place only).

Year	White	Nonwhite
1920	55.6	45.2
1930	63.5	49.2
1940	66.6	54.9
1950	72.2	62.9
1960	74.1	66.3

*U.S. Bureau of the Census, *Pocket Data Book* (1967), p. 59.

16.2 Exponential Trend

a. Compute the values of $T = 1000(1.1)^x$ for $x = 0$, $x = 1$, $x = 2$, and $x = 3$.   The values of T at $x = 4$, $x = 5$, $x = 6$, $x = 7$, and $x = 8$ are, respectively, $T = 1464$, $T = 1610.5$, $T = 1771.6$, $T = 1948.7$, and $T = 2143.6$.   On the grid provided, make a sketch of the equation $T = 1000(1.1)^x$ by plotting all of these values.   Express this trend equation in logarithmic form.   Under what circumstances might you wish to use an exponential trend?

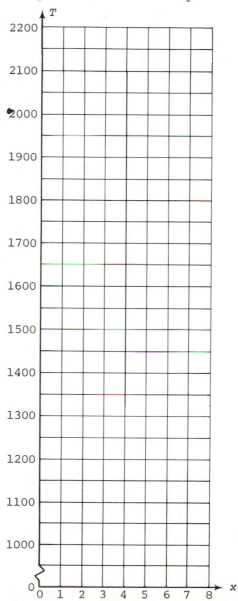

b. The table below shows the annual energy costs for a firm
   in millions of dollars. Complte the table and find the
   exponential trend equation. What is the predicted energy
   cost for 1982?

Year	y	log y	x	x(log y)
1977	420			
1978	480			
1979	630	2.80	0	0
1980	700	2.85	1	2.85
1981	860	2.93	2	5.87

16.3 Nonlinear Trends

a. The per capita income for the United States for 1940-1975
   was as follows:

1940	$ 592
1945	1,234
1950	1,496
1955	1,876
1960	2,222
1965	2,785
1970	4,132
1975	6,403

i. The linear least-squares trend is for these data as
   shown in Figure 16-1. The exponential trend for the
   same data is shown in Figure 16-2. Plot the data on these
   figures. Which model is better? (*Note*: The y-axis in
   Figure 16-2 has a logarithmic scale so that the value of
   log y does not have to be found before plotting.)

ii. The equation for the exponential trend line is $T =
    549.5(1.34)^x$, where $x = 0$ in 1935 and x is in 5-year
    units. Why does this trend appear as a linear function
    in Figure 16-2?

b. In thoroughbred racing, the total handle is the amount of
   money bet through the parimutuel system. The series
   shown in Figure 16-3 is the total handle for New England
   racetracks. The data are in millions of constant 1958
   dollars (that is, the data are adjusted for inflation).[*]

*Eugene M. Johnson and Charles P. Armstrong, "Horse Racing in New
England: Portrait of a Dying Industry." In *Proceedings of the
New England Business and Economics Conference*, November 1980.

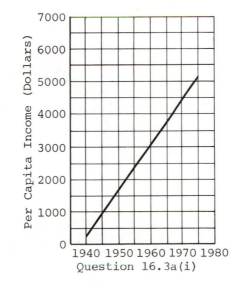

Figure 16-1   Per Capita Income

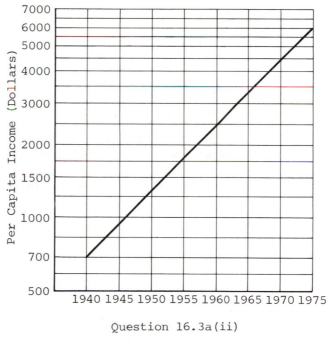

Question 16.3a(ii)

Figure 16-2

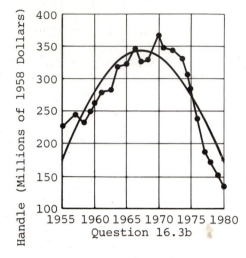

Question 16.3b

Figure 16-3

   i. Is a linear or exponential trend appropriate?

  ii. The linear least-squares trend equation for these data is $T = 279.8 - 0.29x$ where $x = 0$ in 1954 and x is in 1-year units. Plot this trend on Figure 16-3.

 iii. The equation of the smooth curve in Figure 16-3 is

$$T = 145.6 + 20.7x - 1.15x^2$$

where $x = 0$ in 1954 and x is in 1-year units. What is the mathematical form of the trend equation?

  iv. How can one avoid using an inappropriate trend model?

16.4 Percentage of Trend   The following data (y) are the percentage of the total popular vote for Democratic candidates for the U.S. House of Representatives.* These data were used to find the linear least-squares trend line, which is $T = 48.61 + 0.36x$, where $x = 0$ in 1940 and x is in 2-year units.

  a. Use the trend equation to find the computed trend for 1940, 1942, and 1944.

  b. Compute the percentage of trend and record these values in the table below.

---

*U.S. Bureau of the Census, *Statistical Abstract of the United States,* 1975 and 1979.

Year	y	T	Percentage of Trend
1940	51.3		
1942	46.1		
1944	50.6		
1946	44.2	49.7	
1948	51.9	50.0	
1950	49.0	50.4	
1952	49.7	50.8	
1954	52.5	51.1	
1956	51.1	51.5	
1958	56.2	51.8	
1960	54.7	52.2	
1962	52.5	52.6	
1964	57.2	52.9	
1966	50.9	53.3	
1968	50.0	53.6	
1970	53.4	54.0	
1972	51.7	54.3	
1974	57.6	54.7	
1976	56.2	55.1	
1978	53.5	55.4	

c. Plot the original data along with trend line on the grid provided.

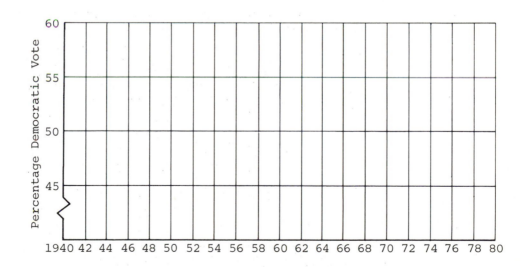

d. Plot the percentage of trend on the grid provided below.

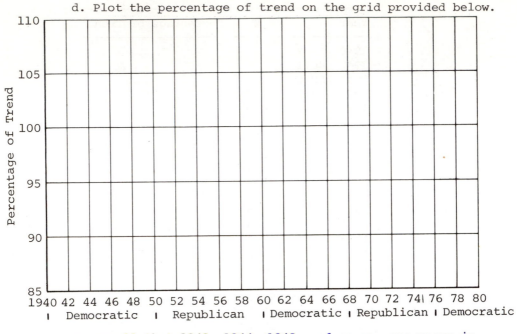

e. Recall that 1940, 1944, 1948, and so on, are years in which presidential elections are held. Over the period considered, a Republican was elected or incumbent in 1952, 1956, 1968, and 1972. Democratic presidents were elected or incumbent in all other years. Comment on any cycles and patterns portrayed by the percentage of trend graphed in (d).

16.5 Moving Averages   The following data represent the weekly demands placed by an airline for a certain part.

Period	y (demand)	Moving Average
1	7	
2	6	
3	10	
4	4	
5	4	3.67
6	3	4.33
7	6	5.33
8	7	7.00
9	8	6.67
10	5	7.00
11	8	6.00
12	5	6.33
13	6	5.67
14	6	6.33
15	7	5.33
16	3	

a. The moving average is a 3-term moving average. What is the first period for which a moving average may be computed? Compute the moving average for all applicable periods that are not given in the table.

b. Compute the first 3 terms of a 5-term moving average.

c. Which moving average has more smoothing power? Under what circumstances would you use a moving average with low smoothing power? With high smoothing power?

16.6 Concepts and Terminology Used in the Study of Index Numbers

a. Explain the meaning of the numerator and denominator of Equation 16-5 in the text. What is the meaning of their ratio?

b. In these formulas, does the summation sign imply adding together values for different years? If not, what is to be summed?

16.7 Index Numbers   The following data represent livestock prices (per 100 lb) and production (millions of pounds) in the United State. Prices are indicated by p and production by q.

Item	1950			1955				1965		
	p_0	q_0	$p_0 q_0$	p_1	q_1	$p_1 q_1$	p_2	q_2	$p_2 q_2$
Cattle	23.3	21.2	493.96	15.6	28.1	438.36	19.9	33.3	662.67
Hogs	18.0	20.2	363.60	15.0	20.2	303.00	20.6	18.2	374.92
Sheep	11.6	1.3	15.08	5.8	1.6	9.28	6.3	1.3	8.19
			872.64			750.64			1045.78

In addition to the tabulated data, the following sums have been calculated.

$$\Sigma p_2 q_1 = 985.39 \quad \Sigma p_1 q_0 = 641.26 \quad \Sigma p_2 q_0 = 846.19$$
$$\Sigma p_1 q_2 = 800.02 \quad \Sigma p_0 q_1 = 1036.89 \quad \Sigma p_0 q_2 = 1118.57$$

a. Calculate an index of livestock prices for 1955 and 1965 on 1950 as a base, using fixed base-year quantity weights.

b. Compute an index of livestock prices for 1965 on 1955 as a base, using fixed base-year (1955) quantity weights.

c. Calculate a livestock production index for 1950 and 1965 using 1955 as a base and fixed base-year prices.

d. Use the index numbers obtained in (a) and convert them so
   that the index number for 1955 is 100. Does the result
   for 1965 agree with that obtained in (b)? Why or why not?

16.8 Index Numbers Based on Price Relatives   The following data
   represent dollar expenditures for U.S. imports of principal
   metals for consumption (including scrap) together with price
   relatives for each principal metal.

	Expenditures (in millions) 1960	(1) Relative Importance (w)	(2) Price Relative (1965)/(1960)	(1) * (2) Price Relative * Relative Importance
Aluminum	77	14.9	0.851	12.7
Copper	113	21.8	1.075	23.4
Lead	62	12.0	0.541	6.5
Nickel	117	22.6	1.036	23.4
Platinum	32	6.2	1.215	7.5
Tin	88	17.0	1.774	30.2
Zinc	30		1.125	6.5
Total	519	100.00		

a. State the formula for price index in terms of price relatives. What is the meaning of w in this formula? What
   is the numerical value of w for zinc?

b. Do the data in the expenditure column reflect price or
   quantity? Discuss.

c. Are the price relatives computed by taking a ratio of expenditures in 1965 to expenditures in 1960? If not, how
   are price relatives determined?

d. What is the meaning of the values in the right-most
   column? Illustrate your answer in terms of aluminum.

e. Find the price index for 1965, using 1960 as the base
   year. What does this value tell you about the change in
   prices between 1960 and 1965? About the change in
   quantities?

16.9 Real Income and Purchasing Power of the Dollar

a. If the consumer price index is 125 in this year, what is
   the percent change in prices from the base to the present

year? What is the purchasing power of the dollar this
year as compared with the base year? Explain the concept
of purchasing power. What is the percent change in purchasing power from the base year to the present year? How
is the percent change in the consumer price index related
to the percent change in purchasing power? (State your
answer in terms of the direction of the percentage
changes.)

b. For the same situation as in (a), consider the incomes of
these individuals.

	Income	
Individual	Base Year	Present Year
A	$10,000	$12,500
B	$10,000	$11,000
C	$10,000	$15,000

i. What is A's present income in terms of the prices
prevailing in the base year? Compute your answers
in two ways by using the consumer price index and by
using purchasing power. Compare these answers.

ii. What is meant by the term *real income*? What is B's
real income? How does B's real income compare with
B's income in the base year?

iii. How much of the change in income for C is due to
inflation of prices and how much is real?

16.10 The Consumer Price Index In the following table are the
consumer price index (1960 = 100) and personal consumption
expenditures ($ billions) for the United States by expendi-
ture categories in 1960 and 1965, along with some calculations based on them.

	CPI-1965	Expenditures		(D)	(E)
		1960	1965		
Expenditure Group	(A)	(B)	(C)	100(C)/(A)	100/(A)
Food	108.4	87.4	106.9	98.6	0.922
Housing	105.2	92.9	124.6	118.4	0.951
Apparel	104.5	33.2	43.5	41.6	0.957
Transportation	107.0	43.2	57.8	54.0	0.934
Medical Care	113.1	19.2	28.0	24.8	0.884
Personal Care	105.6	5.2	7.3	6.9	0.947
Reading & Recreation	109.8	18.2	26.3	24.0	0.911
		299.3	394.4		

a. Given that the weights in the consumer price index are for 1960-1961, interpret the "food" index of 108.4.

b. Give an interpretation of the figure in Column (E) for "medical care"—that is, 0.884.

c. Consumer expenditures increased by $95.1 billion from 1960 to 1965. How much of that dollar increase can be attributed to price changes?
   (*Note*: The sum of the values in Column D is 368.3.)

17

TIME SERIES AND FORECASTING

17.1 Seasonal Variation The following data represent sales (thousands of dollars) of a mercantile establishment over a 4-year period.

Period		y	MA	y/MA (Percent)
1	1	57		
	2	67		
	3	45	57.9	77.7
	4	63	56.1	112.3
2	1	56	53.5	104.7
	2	54	51.4	105.1
	3	37	49.6	74.6
	4	54	49.0	110.2
3	1	51	48.4	105.4
	2	54	48.9	110.4
	3	32	49.4	64.8
	4	63	50.1	125.7
4	1	46	51.5	89.3
	2	65	48.1	135.1
	3	32		
	4	36		

a. Organize the y/MA ratios into the table below and complete the calculation of the seasonal indexes.

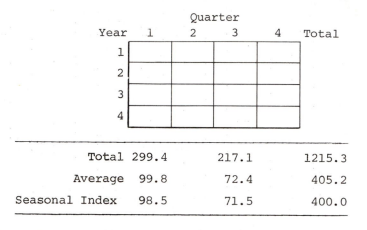

	Quarter				
Year	1	2	3	4	Total
1					
2					
3					
4					

	1	2	3	4	Total
Total	299.4		217.1		1215.3
Average	99.8		72.4		405.2
Seasonal Index	98.5		71.5		400.0

b. The moving average is a centered "two-of-a-four-term" moving average. Check the calculation of the moving average for the second quarter of the fourth year.

17.2 Adjustments for Seasonal Variation and Trend

a. The following table is from a time series analysis of sales (millions of dollars) of a tool company from 1979 to 1981.

		Sales	Seasonal Index (percent)	Trend of Sales
1979	1	5.5	130	4.1
	2	3.5	90	4.2
	3	2.5	70	4.3
	4	5.5	110	4.4
1980	1	5.5	130	4.5
	2	4.0	90	4.6
	3	3.5	70	4.7
	4	6.0	110	4.8
1981	1	7.5	130	4.9
	2	5.0	90	5.0
	3	4.0	70	5.1
	4	6.5	110	5.2

i.   May the first and fourth quarter sales for 1981 be directly compared? What are the sales figures for these quarters after seasonal variation is removed?

What is the magnitude and direction of the change in sales after the seasonal variation is removed? After the seasonal variation is removed, what types of variation are present in the change in sales?

ii. What is the change in trend between the first and fourth quarters of 1981?

iii. What is the difference between the seasonally adjusted change in sales found in (i) and the change in trend found in (ii)? What does the difference found here represent?

b. A long-term trend fitted to sales of an electrical appliance company showed a trend increment of $9,000,000 a year. Actual sales in March of last year were $120,000,000 and in July of last year were $115 million. The season index for March based on the nine previous years was 100, and for July the seasonal index was 90. In the spring of last year, the company shifted its major advertising from television media (which had been its mainstay for over a decade) to print media. No other major change in the company's policies or in general economic conditions took place between March and July of last year. Is the $5,000,000 drop in sales volume a proper measure of the effect of the change in advertising policy? If not, can you suggest a better figure?

17.3 Long-Term Projection of Trend

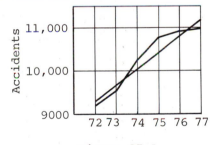

Figure 17-1

Figure 17-1 shows number of hospital admissions due to accidents in Rhode Island for 1972 through 1977. The accidents are due to all causes, that is, automobiles, industrial, violence, and so forth. The trend line equation in Figure 17-1 is

$$T = 8910.5 + 390.6x$$

where $x = 0$ in 1971 and x is in 1-year units.

a. Prepare a forecast for the number of admissions due to accidents for the years 1978 through 1981.

b. How reliable do you believe your forecast for the period 1980-1981 would be in comparison with the period 1978-1979?

c. What are some factors which might make the long-term forecast faulty?

17.4 Short-Term Projections   The data shown in Figure 17-2 are the same as those given in Figure 17-1 but the data have been aggregated by month.   January, 1972, is represented by $x = 1$.

a. Do the data in Figure 17-2 appear to be seasonal?

b. The table below gives the trend and seasonal index for each month in 1978.   Prepare a forecast for each of these months.

Month	Trend	Index	Forecast
1	974	101	
2	977	85	
3	980	95	
4	983	97	
5	987	108	
6	990	107	
7	993	107	
8	996	108	
9	999	105	
10	1002	99	
11	1006	94	
12	1009	96	

c. Do you see any pattern in the seasonal index numbers? What might be a possible explanation for any pattern?

17.5 Time Series Regression—Original Data and First Differences   The table at the bottom of page 297 gives the number of hospital admissions and the number of thousands of gallons of gasoline sold in Rhode Island for 1972-1977.

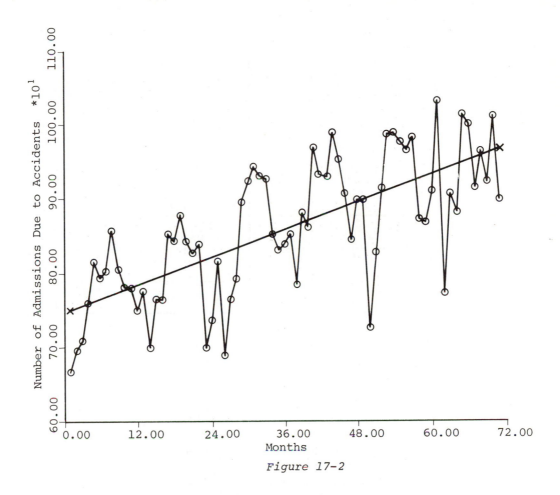

Figure 17-2

| | Original Data | | | |
| | Accidents | Gasoline (thousands of gallons) | First Differences | |
Year	y	x	d_y	d_x
1972	9,221	425,135		
1973	9,528	432,193	307	7058
1974	10,208	435,336		
1975	10,788	456,629		
1976	10,914	448,436		
1977	11,008	422,698		

a. Complete the table by computing the first difference for accident admissions and gasoline sales.

b. On the grids provided plot the original data and the first differences.

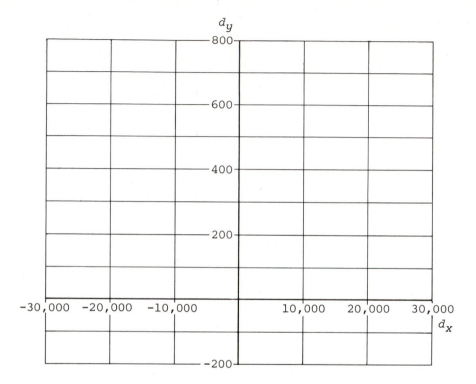

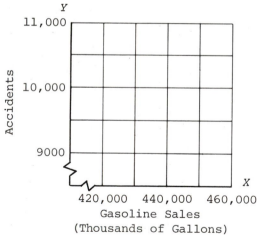

c. The least-squares line for the original data is

$$\hat{y} = -11.00.9 + 0.02605x$$

with $r^2 = 0.209$ and the standard error of estimate equal to 755 admissions. The least-squares line for the first difference is:

$$d_y = 348.4 + 0.01113d_x$$

with $r^2 = 0.572$ and the standard error of estimate equal to 166 admissions. Plot the least-squares lines on the grids.

d. The forecast for gasoline sales in 1978 is 427,396 (thousands of gallons). Forecast the number of accident admissions for 1978 using the least-squares relationships obtained from the hospital data and from the first differences.

e. In general, which of the two methods used in (d) usually gives better results? Why? Illustrate your answer using the results from (d).

17.6 Computing Cyclical Relatives The cyclical relatives for the data given in Question 17.5 are as follows:

	Original Data		Cyclical Relatives	
	Accidents	Gasoline	Accidents	Gasoline
1972	9,221	425,135		
1973	9,528	432,193	0.983	0.995
1974	10,208	435,336	1.012	0.999
1975	10,788	456,629	1.030	1.044
1976	10,914	448,436	1.005	1.021
1977	11,008	422,698	0.978	0.959

The trend equation for accident admissions is $T = 8910.5 + 390.6x$, and the trend equation for gasoline sales is $T = 430,954 + 1652.5x$. For both trends, $x = 0$ in 1971 and x is in one-year units.

a. Compute the cyclical relatives for 1972.

b. Plot the cyclical relatives on the grid provided.

c. Do accident admissions and gasoline sales seem to have the same cycle?

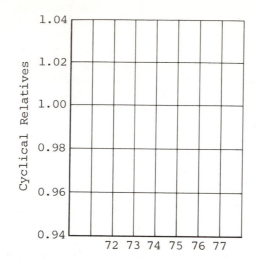

17.7 Using Cyclical Relatives in the Forecast This table gives
the differences in cyclical relatives for the relatives in
Question 17.6.

Year	Differences in Cyclical Relatives	
	Accidents (d_y)	Gasoline (d_x)
1973		
1974	0.029	0.004
1975	0.018	0.045
1976	-0.025	-0.023
1977	-0.027	-0.062

a. Compute the difference in cyclical relatives for 1973.

b. The least-squares relationship for the difference in
cyclical relatives is

$$\hat{d}_y = -0.0003526 + 0.4682126d_x$$

with r^2 = 0.544 and the standard error of estimate of
0.0195. Use this relationship to forecast the difference
in the cyclical relative for accident admissions for 1978.
(Hint: First find the forecasted cyclical relative for
gasoline sales for 1978 and use this result to find the
difference in the cyclical relative for gasoline sales
in 1978.) The forecast for gasoline sales in 1978 is
427,936 (thousands of gallons).

c. Use the result obtained in (b) to find the forecasted
cyclical relative for accident admissions in 1978.

d. Use the result in 17.3(a) and (c) to forecast accident
admissions for 1978.

17.8 Incorporating Seasonal and Cyclical Variation   The forecast developed in Question 17.4 included the trend and seasonal variation for each month of 1978. Modify these results by incorporating the cyclical relative found in Question 17.7.

17.9 Exponential Smoothing   The following data represent the weekly demands placed by an airline for a certain part.

Period	y (demand)	Exponentially Smoothed Series
1	7	
2	6	
3	10	
4	4	
5	4	6.004
6	3	5.253
7	6	5.440
8	7	5.830
9	8	6.372
10	5	6.029
11	8	6.522
12	5	6.141
13	6	6.106
14	6	6.080
15	7	6.310
16	3	5.482

a. The exponentially smoothed series used $w = 0.25$. Compute the values of this series that are not given in the table.

b. Under what circumstances might you use a relatively large value of w to smooth a series? Under what circumstances might you use a relatively small value of w?

17.10 Forecasting by Exponential Smoothing   The situation for this question is the same as Question 17.9. The data and the exponentially smoothed series for $w = 0.25$ are repeated here and have been rounded up to the nearest whole part.

a. Prepare a naive forecast for the airline part series. Start with the first period and continue through the sixteenth period. Find the error and the root mean squared error for this forecast. Record your results in the table.

b. Repeat (a) using the exponentially smoothed series.

c. How do the results obtained in (a) and (b) compare?

d. Forecast the value of the series for the seventeenth period using both methods.

Observed		Naive		Exponential ($w = 0125$)	
Period	Value	Forecast	Error	Forecast	Error
1	7				
2	6	7	1	7	1
3	10	6	-4	7	-3
4	4	10	6	8	4
5	4			7	
6	3			6	
7	6			5	
8	7			5	
9	8			6	
10	5			6	
11	8			6	
12	5			6	
13	6			6	
14	6			6	
15	7			6	
16	3			6	

17.11 Comparison of Forecasting Methods   Compare the forecasting methods used in Question 17.4 with exponential forecasting methods.   Discuss the advantages and disadvantages of each method.   How is the most recent observation used in each method?   Under what circumstances might you use each method?

18

INTRODUCTION TO
DECISION MAKING

18.1 <u>Acts, States, and Payoffs</u> In the evening, a small bakery
prepares an ice cream cake specialty for sale the next day.
The cake sells for $5 and costs $2 to make. Any cake not
sold the following day is given away because the pastry does
not stay fresh.   The bakery may make 0, 1, 2, or 3 cakes.
The number of cakes demanded may be 0, 1, 2, or 3.

a. What acts may the bakery follow? What states may occur?
   Can the bakery exercise control over the states? Can
   they control acts?

b. For each combination of state and act, find the associated profit (or loss). Display your results in the
   table.

	Number of Cakes Made			
Demand	0	1	2	3
0				
1				
2				
3				

18.2 Expected Value of Acts   Consider an insurance company that sells two insurance packages. For each customer contact, there are three possible states: the customer will (1) buy package I, (2) buy package II, or (3) buy neither. The company is trying to decide on a strategy to use in contacting customers. Its alternatives are to contact a customer (1) by mail, (2) by telephone, or (3) by salesperson. The payoff for the company is net profit per customer contact. The net profit for each combination of act and state is given in the following table. The net profit in the body of the table is given in terms of dollars per customer contact.

| | | | | Acts | |
States	S_i	$P(S_i)$	Mail A_1	Telephone A_2	Salesperson A_3
Buy I	S_1	1/4	$20	$ 8	$32
Buy II	S_2	1/4	$16	$24	$ 8
No sale	S_3	1/2	-$ 2	-$ 4	-$ 6

a. Find the expected value of eact act.

b. What is the best (optimal) act?

c. What do the values found in part (a) tell you about a single customer contact? Suppose A_1 is followed for the the next customer contact and a net loss of $2 occurs. What, if anything, is wrong?

d. What do the values found in (a) tell you about the next 1000 customer contacts?

e. Explain the rationale for using expected value to select the optimal act if 1000 customer contacts are to be made. Explain the rationale if only a single contact is to be made.

18.3 Expected Value with Certain Prediction and Expected Value of Perfect Information   The situation for this problem is the same as in Question 18.2.

a. If you knew with complete certainty that the next customer contacted would buy package I, what act would you use to make the contact? Why would you use this act? What would the payoff be for using this act?

b. Answer (a) assuming that you know with complete certainty that the next customer contacted will buy package II.

c. Answer (a) assuming that you know with complete certainty that the next customer contacted will buy neither package.

d. Suppose certain prediction is possible. What proportion of customers will be predicted to be in each state?

e. Suppose a consultant has the ability to predict with complete certainty the state of each customer contacted and that you can select the best act for each customer. What would be the average profit per customer contacted? What is this quantity called?

f. What is the numerical value of the difference between your answer to (e) and the expected value of the optimal act found in Question 18.2(b) above? What is this difference called? How should this difference be interpreted? Would you pay the consultant $4 for perfect prediction? Would you pay $5? Would you pay $6?

g. An analyst for the insurance company makes the following statement: "If we have the ability to make perfect predictions, we should always use A_3 because $32 is the highest possible payoff." Comment.

18.4 Subjective Utility   The table on the left shows the money reward payoffs for a particular situation. The table to the right shows the utility payoffs for the same situation. The utility of the smallest payoff is to be 0 and the utility of the largest payoff is to be 10. Utilities are established by changing the odds in a reference lottery as explained in the text.

S	$P(S)$	Money Reward A_1	A_2	S_i	$P(S)$	Utility A_1	A_2
S_1	0.1	$500	$80	S_1	0.1	___	___
S_2	0.9	$ 10	$20	S_2	0.9	___	4

a. What are the values of $U(500)$ and $U(10)$? Enter these values in the table.

b. In order to determine the value of $U(80)$, the decision maker is offered the following two alternatives.

Alternative 1:   A certain reward for $80.

Alternative 2:   The opportunity to gamble where the outcomes are
either a cash reward of $500 or a cash reward of
$10.   The probability of winning $500 is 0.7 and
the probability of winning $10 is 0.3.

The decision maker states these two alternatives have the
same value to him.   What is the value of $U(80)$?

c. Briefly explain how the probabilities in (b) might be
established.

d. Find the change in utility per change in money reward for
the following changes in money reward.

Change in Money Reward	Change in Utility	Rate of Change
$ 20 - $ 10 = $ 10	4 - 0 = 4	4/$10 = 0.4
$ 80 - $ 20 = $ 60	7 - 4 = 3	_____
$500 - $ 80 = _____	10 - 7 = ____	_____

Does the decision maker have a linear utility function?

e. Find the optimal act based on money reward and based on
utility.   Are the same acts indicated?   Use the results
of (d) to explain your answer.

18.5 Decision Trees   A computer manufacturer has decided to market
a large and a small disk pack to be used with the company's
central processing unit.   If the company buys the disk units
from a wholesaler, the disks can be resold for a profit of
$40,000 for each type of unit.   The company is investigating
the possibility of manufacturing its own disk packs.   If the
large disk pack is to be manufactured, it will be developed
first at a cost of $100,000.   The development cost for the
small pack is $40,000.   If the large pack is developed suc-
cessfully, the company stands to gain $500,000.   A success-
ful small pack will produce a gain of $750,000.   If the
company decides to develop the large pack, there is a 0.20
probability of success.   If the large pack is successful
and the small pack is developed, there is a 0.8 probability
of success.   If the large pack fails, the probability that
the small pack succeeds drops to 0.4.   If the large pack is

not developed, the probability of successfully completing the small pack is 0.5.

a. The partially completed decision tree is shown in Figure 18-1.   Complete the tree. Be sure to include all costs, revenues, and probabilities. Check your solution before going on.

b. Suppose the large pack has been developed successfully. What is the expected profit for developing the small pack? For not developing the small pack? Should the small pack be developed?

c. Answer (b) for the situation in which the large pack is developed and fails.

d. What is the expected profit for developing the large and the small pack?

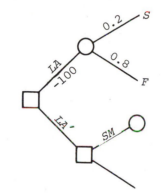

LA = Decide to develop large pack.
LA'= Decide *not* to develop large pack.
SM = Decide to develop small pack.
SM'= Decide *not* to develop small pack.
 S = Development successful.
 F = Development fails.

Figure 18-1

e. What should the company do and what is the expected profit?

18.6 <u>Opportunity Costs (Regrets)</u>   Consider the payoff table in Question 18.2.

a. What is the maximum payoff that can occur if S_1 is the actual state? If you select A_3 when S_1 is the actual

state, what will be the value of your regret? If S_1 is
the true state, what will be the value of your regret if
you select A_2? If you select A_1?

b. Prepare a regrets table for all states and acts. What
is the expected regret for each act? What is the optimal
act? What is the expected regret with certain prediction?
What is the expected regret of the optimal act? What is
the expected value of perfect information?

c. Compare your answers to this exercise with the results
obtained in Questions 18.2 and 18.3. What do you conclude
about using payoffs versus regrets?

18.7 A Marginal Approach

a. Convert the payoff table in Question 18.1 to a regrets
table. Record your answers below.

| Probability | | Acts | | | |
| | | Number of Cakes Made | | | |
States	Demand	0	1	2	3
0.10	0				
0.20	1				
0.40	2				
0.30	3				

b. What is the critical probability?

c. What is the optimal act?

d. Why is a marginal approach appropriate in this exercise?
Is the same approach applicable to Question 18.2? Why or
why not?

19

DECISION MAKING
WITH SAMPLE INFORMATION

CHAPTER 19. SELF-CORRECTING EXERCISES

19.1 <u>Revision of Probabilities Using Bayes Theorem</u> This exercise
is a continuation of Questions 18.2 and 18.6. The insurance
company executives believe that a customer's purchasing
state (S_i) is related to whether or not the customer has
children. By searching the records of past transations, the
company determines 3/4 of those who purchased package I (S_1)
had children while 1/4 of those who purchased this plan had
no children. Of those who purchased package II, 1/4 had
children. Of those who bought neither plan, 1/2 had
children. Let C represent the event *children* and let *NC*
represent the event *no children*.

a. What are the values of $P(S_1)$, $P(S_2)$, and $P(S_3)$? What name
   is given to these quantities?

b. What are the values of $P(C|S_1)$ and $P(NC|S_1)$? What is
   the sum of these values? Explain the last result.

c. What name is given to probabilities such as those given
   in (b)? What type of event is "given" in the probabilities found in (b)? Of what value are these probabilities
   to the decision maker?

d. Suppose it is determined that a potential customer has
   children. Revise the prior probabilities in light of this
   information. Use the table

States	S_i	Prior Probability $P(S_i)$	Likelihood $P(C \mid S_i)$	$P(S_i) * P(C \mid S_i)$	Revised Probability $P(S_i \mid C)$
Buy I	1	1/4	3/4		
Buy II	2	1/4	1/4		
No Sale	3	1/2	1/2		

e. The company analyst states, "There is no reason to compute $P(S_1 \mid C)$ since this is the same as $P(C \mid S_1)$." Comment.

f. Find $P(C)$. What does this value mean?

19.2 Reevaluating a Course of Action In Questions 18.2 and 18.6 we determined that the expected value of perfect information in the insurance example is $5. In the absence of any additional information, the optimal act is A_1 (to contact a customer by mail). The expected regret of this act is $5.

a. Should A_1 be used if it is known that a potential customer has children? Use the results of Question 19.1. The regrets table from Question 18.6 is repeated here for convenience.

	Acts (A_i)		
State (S_i)	A_1	A_2	A_3
S_1	12	24	0
S_2	8	0	16
S_3	0	2	4

b. If the potential customer has children, what is the expected value of perfect information?

19.3 Finding the Expected Value of Sample Information Using Decision Trees A manufacturer of microprocessors has a testing device which can be used to identify defective units for reprocessing. The tester is not perfect, however. When the tester indicates a non-defective, it is correct for 90% of the units. The manufacturing process is currently producing 20% defective microprocessors. When the tester indicates a non-defective, it is also correct for 90% of the units. The costs (excluding testing costs) for the various combinations of states and acts are as follows.

States	Acts	
	Defective (A_D)	Not Defective (A_N)
Defective (D)	0	$1500
Not Defective (N)	$500	0

a. In the absence of any information from the tester, what is the optimal act? What is the expected value of perfect information?

b. Draw the decision tree for this situation.

c. If the tester indicates a defective, what is the best act? If a nondefective is indicated, what is the best act? How often will these situations arise?

d. What is the expected value of the information acts? What is the expected value of the sample information?

e. If it costs $150 to test each unit, is it worthwhile to operate the tester?

19.4 Alternative Calculation of the Expected Value of Sample Information   The joint probabilities for the situation in Question 19.3 are given here.

State	Information Outcome	
	Defective	Not Defective
Defective	0.18	0.08
Not Defective	0.02	0.72

a. Set up the V_{ji} (acts by states) payoff table for the situation in Question 19.3.

b. Carry out the sums of products calculations to find the elements in the V_{ji} (acts by information outcomes) table.

c. Identify the optimal act given such information outcome. Find $EV(IA)$. Compare your result with that obtained in Question 19.3.

19.5 Bayesian Statistics for Population Means—Revision of Probabilities   The manager of a power plant has a prior belief that the probability that a volt meter is giving a faulty reading is 0.10. If the meter is in a faulty state, the manager's expectation (or belief) about readings is a normal distribution with a mean of 116 volts and a standard deviation of 2 volts. If the meter is operating correctly, the expected value of the readings is 120 volts with a standard deviation of 2 volts. Assume normal distributions apply.

a. The value of one reading is 117 volts (stated to the nearest whole number). Revise the manager's prior probabilities based on the single observation. What is the most likely state?

b. A sample of four readings produces the following values: 115, 118, 116, 119, and $\overline{X}$ = 117. Revise the manager's prior probabilities based on the sample information. What is the most likely state? (*Hint*: Find the probability associated with the interval $116.75 \leq X \leq 117.25$.

c. Compare your results from (a) and (b). Explain any similarities or differences.

19.6 Revision of a Normal Prior for a Population Mean A manufacturer of soft drinks is planning to offer a new flavor. The manufacturer's prior belief concerning the average consumption per customer has an expected value of 10 and a standard deviation of 2. Based on a test market consisting of 100 customers, the estimated population mean consumption is 7 bottles per customer. The estimated population standard deviation is 4 bottles per customer. What is the revised mean and variance of the probability distribution for the population mean?

19.7 Decision Making Involving Means A university receives several thousand applicants per year. Students who are admitted have a mean MSAT score of 500. Those who are rejected have a mean MSAT score of 470. A group of 4 students have a mean score of 490. These students were either all accepted or all rejected, but their admission status has been lost and the university must decide whether to admit these applicants. The dean of admissions has determined the revised probability that they are in the rejected group as 0.9433. The dean constructs the following regrets table. The regrets are in terms of utility.

| | Acts | |
State	Admit	Do Not Admit
μ = 500	0	10
μ = 470	1	0

a. What is the decision maker's attitude towards incorrectly rejecting the students versus incorrectly accepting the students? What is the optimal decision?

b. Rework (a) in a hypothesis-testing context. Use $\mu = 500$ as the null hypothesis. What is the cost of a type I error? Of a type II error? What is the critical probability? What decision should be reached?

19.8 <u>Optimal Bayesian Estimates</u> An oil importer has revised his prior distribution concerning the demand for his product. He now believes the mean demand will be 100,000,000 barrels per year with a standard deviation of 10,000,000 barrels per year. The importer must agree to buy a fixed amount of oil at $40 per barrel. If the demand is overestimated, the excess must be sold to a wholesaler for $35 per barrel. If the demand is underestimated, the shortage must be made up by purchases in the spot market at $50 per barrel.

a. What are the opportunity costs of underestimation and overestimation?

b. What is the optimal estimate of the mean demand?

SOLUTIONS

CHAPTER 2: DIAGNOSTIC TEST SOLUTIONS

1. 20

2. 10/30 = 0.33

3. Qualitative

4. 33.6%

5. Admissions are increasing.

6. Time-series.

7. 2

8. 3/15 = 0.20

9.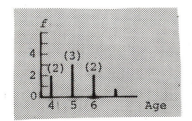

10.   21

11.   The number of observations.

12.   100/7, or about 14 classes.

13.   Right.

14.   25

15.   25 + 25 = 50

16.   25/100 = 0.25

17.   No, a step graph is the correct device.

18.   No, the data are grouped.

CHAPTER 3:   DIAGNOSTIC TEST SOLUTIONS

1. $20/5 = 4$

2. $\overline{X}$

3. $\mu = 4$

4.   15.5

5.   127.5

6. $\overline{X} = 50/10 = 5.0$

7.   The two answers would be nearly, but not necessarily exactly, the same.

8.   4

9.   9

10.   1

11. Y

12.   1/2

13. σ^2

14.   4

15. s

16. $\overline{X} = 18/3 = 6$; $s^2 = [\Sigma x^2 - n(\overline{X})^2]/(n - 1) = [134 - 3(6)^2]/(3 - 1) = 13$

17. $n = 100$; $\overline{X} = [2(10) + 7(50) + 12(40)]/100 = 8.5$

18. $z = (95 - 100)/10 = -0.5$

CHAPTER 4:   DIAGNOSTIC TEST SOLUTIONS

1. Subjective

2. Equally likely outcomes

3. Relative frequency

4. 300/1000

5. 200/1000

6. 150/1000

7. 650/1000

8. 150/1000

9. 50/350

10. 50/200

11. $P(C_2|C_1) = \dfrac{P(C_1 \text{ and } C_2)}{P(C_1)} = \dfrac{0.08}{0.10} = 0.8$

12. Because A, B, and C are mutually exclusive, $P(A \text{ or } C) =$

    $0.20 + 0.10 = 0.30$.

13. $P(A') = 1 - P(A) = 1 - 0.2 = 0.8$

14. $P(A \text{ or } B) = P(A) + P(B) - P(A \text{ and } B) = 0.10 + 0.02 - 0.04 = 0.08$

15. $P(D \text{ and } C) = P(C) \times P(D|C) = 0.2(0.8) = 0.16$

16. Compute the conditional probabilities given males and given females:

	Male	Female		
Above Median	0.75	0.75	=	0.300/0.400
Below Median	0.25	0.25	=	0.100/0.400

Since the conditional probabilities of above or below median are the same for either sex, salary and sex are independent.

17. A_1 and B_2 and A_3; B_1 and A_2 and A_3.

18. $1 - P(A_1 \text{ and } A_2) = 1 - 0.375 = 0.625$

19. $P(A_1$ and B_2 and $A_3) + P(B_1$ and A_2 and $A_3) = 0.0625 + 0.12 = 0.1825$

20. $P(B_1$ and $B_2) = 0.5(1 - 0.4) = 0.3$

21. $P(A$ wins series$|$Lasts 2 games$) = 0.375/0.575 = 15/23 = 0.65$

CHAPTER 5:   DIAGNOSTIC TEST SOLUTIONS

1.   Not a random variable--color does not have a numerical value.

2.   A random variable.

3.   Not a random variable--your age is not uncertain.

4.

X	$P(X)$
1	0.2
2	0.4
4	0.4

5.

X	$P(X)$
1	0.2
2	0.6
4	1.0

6. $X \leq 2$

7. $P(X \leq 2) = 0.6$

8. $P(X = 2) = 0.4$

9. $X_A = 1$ and $X_B = 2$; $X_A = 2$ and $X_B = 1$; $X_A = 3$ and $X_B = 0$

10. $P(T = 2) = P(X_A = 2$ and $X_B = 0) + P(X_A = 1$ and $X_B = 1) =$

0.04 + 0.04 = 0.08

11. $\mu = 10(1/2) + 20(1/4) + 30(1/4) = 17.5$

12. $\mu = E(X) = 17.5$

13. $\sigma^2 = (1 - 2)^2(1/2) + (2 - 2)^2(1/4) + (4 - 2)^2(1/4) = 1.5$

14. $E(X^2) = (1)^2(1/2) + (2)^2(1/4) + (4)^2(1/4) = 5.5$

15. $\sigma^2 = (0.2)(0.8) = 0.16$; $\sigma = 0.4$

16.   *SSF, SFS, FSS*

17. $4! = 4(3)(2)(1) = 24$

18. $_5C_3 = \dfrac{5!}{3!(5-3)!} = \dfrac{120}{6(2)} = 10$

19. $P(2|3, 1/3) = \dfrac{3!}{2!(3-2)!}(1/3)^2(2/3)^1 = 2/9$

20.   0.2503

21. $0.2373 + 0.3955 + 0.2637 = 0.8965$

22. $\mu_r = 20(0.25) = 5$

23. $\sigma_r^2 = 0.5(0.5)(16) = 4; \; \sigma_r = 2$

CHAPTER 6:   DIAGNOSTIC TEST SOLUTIONS

1.   Left graph: discrete;   right graph: continuous

2.   Left graph: $P(X = 2) = 0.1$;   right graph: $P(X = 2) = 0$.   For continuous
     distributions, find the *area* under the density function for the given
     interval; $X = 2$ is an interval with a zero width, so the corresponding
     area is zero.

3.   Left graph: $P(X = 6.5) = 0$, because this discrete random variable has
     integer values only.   Right graph: $P(X = 6.5) = 0$ for the same reason
     given for Question 2.

4.   Left graph: $P(7 \le X \le 9) = 0.3$.   Add the heights of the lines above the
     values 7, 8, and 9.   Right graph: $P(7 \le X \le 9) = 0.2$.   Find the area under
     the density function for the interval $7 \le X \le 9$.   The width of this
     interval is 2 and the height is 0.1.   Since the area is a rectangle, the
     area is the product $(0.1)(2)$, or 0.2.

5. $P(X \le 2) = 0.2$, $P(X \le 3) = 0.3$ and $P(2 \le X \le 3) = 0.1$.   For each, find
     the area under the density function for the given interval.

6.   The numerical answers are the same as in Question 5.   For the first tw
     find the height of the cumulative density function.   Use these results
     to find $P(2 \le X \le 3) = P(X \le 3) - P(X \le 2) = 0.3 - 0.2 = 0.1$.

7. $P(X \le 10) = 1.0$.   Use the same methods as for Questions 5 and 6 or
     observe the total area under any density function is 1.0 by definition.

8.   The values of the mean and of the standard deviation.

9.   0.3413, because the normal distribution is symetric about its mean.

10. The mean is zero ($\mu = 0$) and the standard deviation is one ($\sigma = 1$).

11. There are an infinite number of normal distributions--one for each
     possible value of μ and σ.   The standard normal table is the only
     table needed.

12. Any two normal distributions, when stated in standard deviation units,
     become the standard normal distribution.

13. $z = (x - \mu)/\sigma = (125 - 100)/10 = 2.5$

14. a. $P(Z \le 0.65) = 0.7422$

     b. $P(Z \le 0.6) = 0.7257$

     c. $P(0.6 \le Z \le 0.65) = P(Z \le 0.65) - P(Z \le 0.6) =$

          $0.7422 - 0.7257 = 0.0165$

15. a.   From Table B-2, $P(Z < -2.34) = 0.0096$

     b.   The area under the entire normal distribution is 1.0. Since the area to the left of $Z = -2.34$ is 0.0096, the area to the right is:

$$P(Z < -2.34) = 1.0000 - P(Z < -2.34)$$

$$= 1.000 - 0.0096 = 0.9904$$

16. Very nearly 1.0. The area to the left of the largest value of z given in Table B-2 is 0.9990. Since $z = 6.41$ is larger than $z = 3.09$, the area to the left of $z = 6.41$ will be larger than 0.9990.

17. $Z = (X - \mu)/\sigma = (92 - 100)/10 = -0.8$; $P(X \leq 92) = P(Z \leq -0.8) = 0.2119$.

18. $Z_{lower} = (80 - 100)/10 = -2.0$; $Z_{upper} = (105 - 100)/10 = 0.5$;

$P(80 \leq X \leq 105) = P(-2.0 \leq Z \leq 0.5) = P(Z \leq 0.5) - P(Z \leq -2.0) =$

$0.6915 - 0.0228 = 0.6687$.

19. $z = (75 - 100)/10 = -2.5$; $P(X > 75) = P(Z > -2.5) = 1.0 - 0.0062 = 0.9938$.

20. The 25th percentile of the standard normal is $z_{0.25} = -0.67$ (from Table B-3).

The transform $z = (x - \mu)/\sigma$ when solved for x is $x = \mu + Z(\sigma)$. Thus

$$x_{0.25} = \mu + z_{0.25}(\sigma)$$

$$x_{0.25} = 100 + (-0.67)(10) = 93.3$$

21. First find $z_{0.10} = -1.28$ and $z_{0.90} = 1.28$ from Table B-2. Next find the corresponding values of x from $x = \mu + z(\sigma)$:

$$x_{0.10} = \mu + z_{0.10}(\sigma) = 100 + (-1.28)10 = 87.2$$

$$x_{0.90} = \mu + z_{0.40}(\sigma) = 100 + (1.28)10 = 112.8$$

The interval is $87.2 < x < 112.8$.

22. No because the product $n\pi/(1-\pi)$ is 2.2, which is less than the required value of 9.

23. $\mu = n(\pi) = 10,000(0.5) = 5000$; $\sigma = \sqrt{n\pi(1 - \pi)} = \sqrt{10,000(0.5)(0.5)}$

$= \sqrt{2500} = 50$.

24. $x_{lower} = r - 0.5 = 53 - 0.5 = 52.5$; $x_{upper} = r + 0.5 = 53 + 0.5 = 53.5$. The corresponding interval for the standard normal is

$$z_L = (x_L - \mu)/\sigma = (52.5 - 50)/5 = 0.5$$

$$z_U = (x_U - \mu)/\sigma = (53.5 - 50)/5 = 0.7$$

25. The approximation is found by computing $P(0.5 < Z < 0.7) = P(Z < 7) - P(Z < 5) = 0.7580 - 0.6915 = 0.0665$.

26. First find the 25th percentile of the standard normal from Table B-3. $z_{0.25} = -0.67$; $x_{0.25} = \mu + z_{0.25}\sigma = 50 + (-0.67)5 = 46.65$.

CHAPTER 7:   DIAGNOSTIC TEST SOLUTIONS

1.

Account Number	Balance
7	$150.00
5	$ 40.00
6	$ 35.00
4	$110.00
10	$ 20.00

2. $\bar{X} = \Sigma X/n = 345/5 = \$69$

3.

Account Number	Balance
7	$150.00
5	$ 40.00
7	$150.00
6	$ 35.00
5	$ 40.00

4. $\bar{X} = 415/5 = \$83.00$

5. $\mu = 551/10 = \$55.1$

6. $\mu_{\bar{X}} = \mu = \$55.1$

7. $\sigma_{\bar{X}} = \sigma/\sqrt{n} = 40.88/\sqrt{5} = 18.28$

8. $\sigma_{\bar{X}} = \sqrt{\dfrac{N-n}{N-1}} \times \dfrac{\sigma}{\sqrt{n}} = \sqrt{\dfrac{10-5}{10-1}}\,(18.28) = 0.75\,(18.28) = 13.63$

9. $\sigma_{\bar{X}} = \sigma/\sqrt{n} = 40.88/\sqrt{100} = 4.088$.   The distribution of sample means is approximately normal.

10. $\sigma_{\bar{X}} = 40.88/\sqrt{400} = 40.88/20 = 2.044$.   The distribution of sample means would be approximately normal with a small standard error.   The approximation would be better than the one obtained for Question 9.

11. $z = (106 - 100)/10 = 0.6$; $P(X > 106) = P(Z > 0.6) = 0.2743$

12. $z = (106 - 100)/(10/\sqrt{25}) = 3$; $P(\bar{X} > 106) = P(Z > 3) = 0.0013$.

13. $z_{0.95} = 1.64$; $1.64 = (\bar{X} - 100)/(10/\sqrt{16})$; $X_{0.95} = 100 + 4.1 = 104.1$.

14. $\mu_P = 0.5$; $\sigma_P = \sqrt{0.5(.5)/16} = 0.125$

15. p is used to represent a value of the sample proportion. π is used to represent the mean of a Bernoulli random variable (the mean of a binary population).

16. $P(P \leq 0.20 \mid \pi = 0.4,\ n = 10) = 0.0060 + 0.0403 + 0.1209 = 0.1672$

17. The values of $n\pi/(1-\pi)$ and $n(1-\pi)/\pi$ must be at least 9. For $n = 10$, $n\pi/(1-\pi) = 10(0.4)/(0.6) = 6.7$. The normal approximation cannot be used for $n = 10$. For $n = 20$, $n\pi/(1-\pi) = 20(0.4)/(0.6) = 13.3$ and $n(1-\pi)/\pi = 20(0.6)/(0.4) = 30$. The normal approximation may be used for $n = 20$.

18. $P(P \geq 0.15) = ?$; $\mu_P = 0.10$; $\sigma_P = \sqrt{0.10(.9)}/\sqrt{400} = 0.0015$;

$z = (0.15 - 0.10)/0.0015) = 33.3$;

$P(P \geq 0.5) = P(Z \geq 33.3) = 0$

CHAPTER 8:   DIAGNOSTIC TEST SOLUTIONS

1. The estimator is unbiased.

2. The estimator is biased.

3. $z_{0.10} = 1.28$

4. $\overline{X} = 15$

5. $s^2 = 25$

6. $s = 5$

7. $1.96 \left(\dfrac{20}{\sqrt{100}} \right) = 3.92$

8. $1.96 \sqrt{\dfrac{10,000 - 2500}{10,000 - 1}} \ \dfrac{20}{\sqrt{2500}} = 0.68$

9. Yes, the population is normal.

10. $43 \pm 1.96 \ \dfrac{20}{\sqrt{64}} = 43 \pm 3.9$

11. At least 30 observations are needed for the central limit theorem to produce a reasonable approximation.

12. $-2.9200 \leq t \leq 2.9200$

13. For 20 df: $-1.7247 \leq t \leq 1.7247$; for 200 df: $-1.6525 \leq t \leq 1.6252$; for the standard normal: $-1.645 \leq z \leq 1.645$

14. $s = 2.58$; $s_{\overline{X}} = 2.58/\sqrt{4} = 1.29$

15. $20 \pm 1.8595 \ \dfrac{30}{\sqrt{9}} = 20 \pm 18.595$

16. No.   At least 30 observations would be needed.

17. $p = 80/400 = 0.2$

18. Yes.   For $p = 0.2$ we need at least 300 observations;

    $0.2 \pm 1.645 \ \dfrac{0.2(1 - 0.2)}{400} = 0.2 \pm 0.0329.$

19. $p = 40/400 = 0.1$.   No.   For $p = 0.1$, we need at least 900 observations.

20. $n = \left(\dfrac{1.96\,(20)}{10} \right)^2 = 15.3664$, or 16 observations;

    $n = \left(\dfrac{1.96\,(20)}{1} \right)^2 = 1536.64$, or 1537 observations.

21. $n = \dfrac{(1.96)^2 0.25}{(0.10)^2} = 96.04$, or 97 observations.

22. $n = \dfrac{(1.96)^2 (0.25)}{(0.01)^2} = 9604$ observations.

23. $n = \dfrac{(1.96)^2 (0.09)}{(0.10)^2} = 34.5744$, or 35 observations.

CHAPTER 9:   DIAGNOSTIC TEST SOLUTIONS

1. Form C.

2. Form A.

3. Form B.

4. The hypothesis does not include all possible values of μ.

5. $\sigma_{\bar{x}} = 5\sqrt{9} = 5/3$

6. For two standard errors, 0.9545; for three standard errors, 0.9973.

7. For two standard errors, $-2 \leq Z \leq 2$, $21.67 \leq \bar{X} \leq 28.3$;
    for three standard errors, $-3 \leq Z \leq 3$, $20 \leq \bar{X} \leq 30$

8. $-1.96 \leq Z \leq 1.96$,
    $21.73 \leq \bar{X} \leq 28.27$

9. $\bar{X} = 21.89$; accept the null hypothesis.

10. It may be true or false. Without knowing μ we cannot tell which is
    the case.

11. The probability of a correct decision is 0.95 and the probability of
    an error is 0.05.

12. The probability of a correct decision is 0.6406 and the probability of
    an error is 0.3594.

13. H_0: $\mu \leq \$10,000$; H_A: $\mu > \$10,000$

14. Accept H_0 if $Z \leq 1.28$.

15. Accept H_0 if $\bar{X} \leq \$10,640$.

16. $\bar{X} = \$10,250$; accept H_0.

17. $\mu_0 \pm t*(s/\sqrt{n})$

18. Not permissible.

19. $\mu_0 \pm Z*(\sigma/\sqrt{n})$

20. $\mu_0 \pm Z*(\sigma/\sqrt{n})$

21. $\mu_0 \pm Z*(\sigma/\sqrt{\ }) \ \dfrac{N-n}{N-1}$

22. $z = \sqrt{\dfrac{P - \dfrac{1}{2n} - \pi_0}{\sqrt{\dfrac{\pi_0(1 - \pi_0)}{n}}\sqrt{\dfrac{N - n}{N - 1}}}} = \dfrac{0.250 - 0.0005 - 0.10}{0.0095\,(0.949)} = 16.6$

23. The power of the test is 0.6406. This is the probability of $\overline{X} < 11.59$ when $\mu = 11.5$.

24. The symmetry of the curves indicates a two-tailed test.

25. B, because the probability of accepting H_A when $\mu_0 = 100$ is 0.05. The corresponding value for A and C is 0.10.

26. C, because the power is greater for every value of μ. Plan C must use a larger sample size than Plan B.

27. 0.4, the height of the power curve at $\mu = 115$.

28. $n = \left[\dfrac{\sigma(z_\alpha + z_\beta)}{\delta}\right]^2 = \left[\dfrac{50(0.84 + 1.645)}{10}\right]^2 = 155.$

CHAPTER 10:   DIAGNOSTIC TEST SOLUTIONS

1.

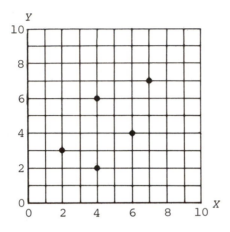

2.   The relationship is not an exact functional relationship.

3.   4 - 5.304 = -1.304

4.   The sum of the deviations equals zero.

5.   The sum of the squared deviation from the least-square line is smaller than for any other line.

$$\Sigma X = 23, \quad \Sigma Y = 22, \quad \Sigma XY = 111, \quad (\Sigma X)^2 = 529; \quad \Sigma X^2 = 121$$

7. $Y_c = 4.08 + 0.16X$

8.   The Y values are normally distributed with a mean equal to the corresponding Y-value on the population regression line.   Each normal distribution has the same variance.

9. $Y_c = 3.2 + 10.0(4) = 43.2.$

10. $\Sigma(Y - Y_c)^2 = 110 - 2.973(22) - 0.297(110) = 11.924;$

$$s_{Y \cdot X} = \sqrt{11.924/3} = 1.99$$

11. $t = (0.5 - 0)/0.25 = 2$

12.   The critical value from Appendix B, Table B-4, is $t_{0.025} = 2.1448$. Since the computed value is less than 2.1498, accept $B = 0$.

13. Confidence interval of Y for an individual value of X and a confidence interval for the mean value of Y for a given value of X. The latter has the smaller half-width.

14. 0.047

15. Here 36% is explained by the independent variable and 64% is *not* explained.

16. $-\sqrt{0.76} = -0.6$

17. No, the value of r may be computed directly from the formula.

CHAPTER 2.   SOLUTIONS TO SELF-CORRECTING EXERCISES

2.1   Absolute scale.

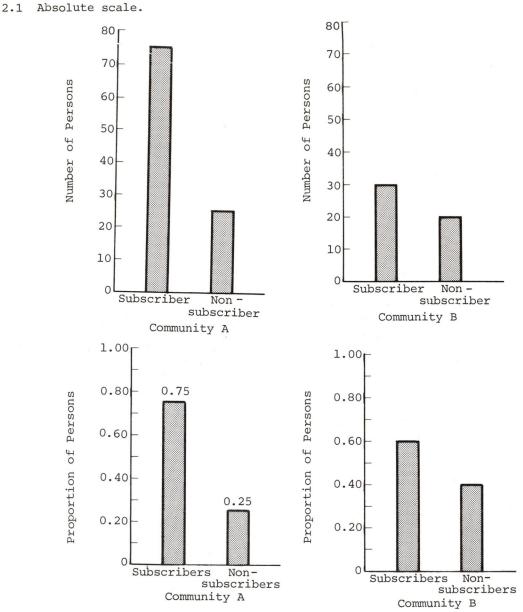

c. The relative scale is better for comparing two or more data collections in which the total number of observations differs for each collection.

2.2 Convert dollar amounts to percents:

Commercial	$2.9 billion	40%
Government	$2.6 billion	36%
Homeowners	$1.7 billion	24%
	$7.2 billion	

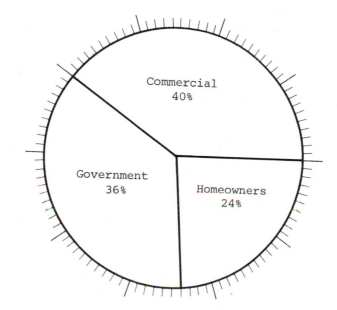

2.3.a.

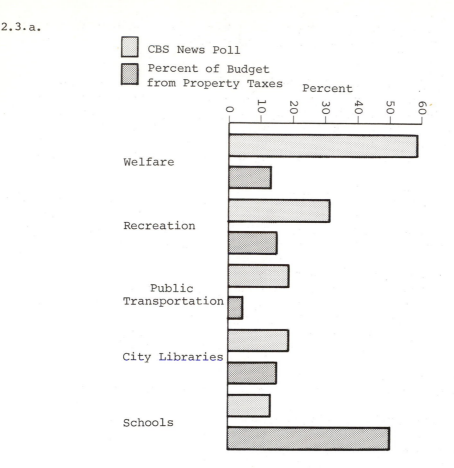

b. No. The services the voters were most willing to have cut are the least influenced by property tax revenues and vice versa.

2.4.a. City A has more accident hospitalizations than city B, and city B has more accident hospitalizations than city C. Accidents for all three cities fluctuate from month to month, which reflects the random nature of accidents. Hospitalizations for accidents in city B appear to be increasing over time. Rates of increase (or decrease) for the other two cities are less clear from the graphs. In a later chapter, we shall learn how to make more precise statements about time-series data.

b. We could make no statements about rates of change of accident-related hospitalizations over time. For the month in question, city A had an exceptionally low number of accident admissions.

2.5.a.

Radios per Home	Number of Homes
0	///
1	//// ///// //
2	//// ////
3	//// ///
4	////
5	//
6	
7	/

b.

Radios per Home	Number of homes
0	3
1	12
2	10
3	8
4	4
5	2
6	0
7	1
	40

c.

Radios per Home	Relative Frequency
0	0.075
1	0.300
2	0.250
3	0.200
4	0.100
5	0.050
6	0.000
7	0.025
	1.000

The relative frequencies in Exercise 2.5c are calculated by dividing the frequencies in Exercise 2.5b by 40, the number of observations.

d.

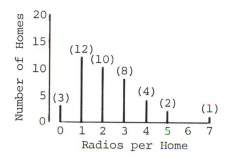

2.6.a.   Families are being observed and the characteristic observed is the number of automobiles per family. A total of 200 families were observed. This is the sum of the families with 0, 1, 2, and 3 automobiles read from the diagram (30 + 100 + 50 + 20 = 200 families). There were 100 families with one car per family.

b.   The proportion of families with no auto is 0.15, the height of the vertical above 0 autos. The proportion of families with 3 autos is 0.10.

c.

Number of Automobiles	Number of Families
0	30
1	100
2	50
3	20
	200

d.

Number of Automobiles	Relative Frequency
0	0.15
1	0.50
2	0.25
3	0.10
	1.00

The frequencies in Exercise 2.6c are the heights of the verticals above the four values of the variable read from the graph on the left. The relative frequencies in Exercise 2.6d are the heights from the right-hand graph.

2.7.a.   The total numbers of observations from both groups are vastly different, so the absolute frequencies cannot be compared directly.

b.

New Employees		Experienced Employees	
Error Rate	Relative Frequency	Error Rate	Relative Frequency
0	0.07	0	0.30
1	0.08	1	0.25
2	0.09	2	0.22
3	0.15	3	0.10
4	0.25	4	0.07
5	0.28	5	0.04
6	0.08	6	0.02
	1.00		1.00

Each relative frequency is found by dividing the frequency by the total number of observations. For an error rate of 0 in the table to the left, the relative frequency is 35/500 = 0.07.

c. Since the number of observations is different for the two groups, we cannot compare frequencies directly. By converting frequencies to relative frequencies, the occurrence of each value of the variable for both groups is shown on the same scale (that is, from 0 to 1). Thus we may make a meaningful comparison between the two groups on the basis of relative frequency. Now we see, for example, that 7% of the new employees have a zero error rate compared with 30% for experienced operators.

d. The relative frequency distribution for new employees shows that low error rates such as 0, 1, 2 occur less frequently than high rates such as 3, 4, 5, and 6. The opposite trend is true for the experienced employees. As one would expect, the more experienced employees produce work of better quality.

2.8.a. The number of classes needed to maintain an average number of values per class is the number of observations divided by 7: in this case, 50/7 or about 7 classes.

b. The smallest observation is 0 and 25 is the largest. The number of different values of x between and including these two values is 26. Note that the range is not the difference between the largest and smallest value, but is (25 - 0) + 1.

c. Class length is found by dividing the range by the number of classes, which is 26/7 = 3.7. The latter is rounded to 4, the next higher whole number, to reflect that the data are whole numbers.

d. The first value class starts with the smallest observation (0) as the lower limit. The lower limits of all other classes are found by successively adding the class interval length (4) to the first lower limit. Thus the lower limits of each class are: 0, 4, 8, 12, 16, 20, 24. The class length is 4, which implies four values of the variable are to be accommodated in each class. For the first class, the four values to be accommodated are 0, 1, 2, 3. Thus, the upper limit of the first class is 3. Next, all other upper limits are found by adding the class interval length (4) to the upper limits of the value classes. Thus the upper limits of each class are 3, 7, 11, 15, 19, 23, and 27. The class length reflects the number of values in the class, which is not the same as the upper minus the lower limit. For the first class, 3 - 0 = 3. The number of possible values of the variable in the class is always one more than this difference, provided we have integer data.

e.

Number of Outpatient Visits per Year	Number of Patients
0-3	15
4-7	12
8-11	8
12-15	6
16-19	4
20-23	3
24-27	2
	50

f. When values are grouped into many-value classes, the identity of
   the individual observations within the class is lost. Thus we do
   not know how many patients had 0 visits. The first value class
   tells us that 15 patients had between 0 and 3 visits per year.

2.9.a.

	New Employees				Experienced Employees		
Error Rate	Number of Occurrences	Cumulative Frequency	Cumulative Relative Frequency	Error Rate	Number of Occurrences	Cumulative Frequency	Cumulative Relative Frequency
0	35	35	0.07	0	30	30	0.30
1	40	75	0.15	1	25	55	0.55
2	45	120	0.24	2	22	77	0.77
3	75	195	0.39	3	10	87	0.87
4	125	320	0.64	4	7	94	0.94
5	140	460	0.92	5	4	98	0.98
6	40	500	1.00	6	2	100	1.00
	500				100		

The cumulative frequencies are found by adding the frequencies for
the given and smaller values of the error rate. For the left-hand
distribution and an error rate of 2 the cumulative frequency is
35 + 40 + 45 = 120. The cumulative relative frequencies are
found by dividing the cumulative frequency by the total number of
observations. For the situation just mentioned, the cumulative
relative frequency is 120/500 = 0.24.

b. Since we are concerned with an error rate that is less than or
   equal to a given number, some type of cumulative distribution is
   required. Since the number of observations for the two groups is
   different, a cumulative relative frequency is needed.

c.

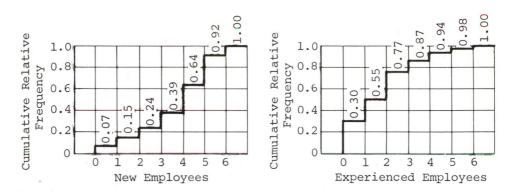

d. For the new operators, the step graph rises slowly at low error
   rates and more steeply at higher error rates. This indicates that
   most of the observations are accumulated at the higher error rate.
   The opposite trend occurs for experienced operators indicating that
   most of the observations are accumulated at lower error rates.

e. For discrete variables in single-value classes, frequency describes
   the number of observations having a particular value of the variable; relative frequency describes the proportion of observations
   having a particular value of the variable; cumulative frequency describes the number of observations less than or equal to a given
   value of the variable; cumulative relative frequency describes the
   proportion of observations less than or equal to a given value of
   the variable. In this example, supervisors may well be concerned
   with low error rates. It is unlikely that interest will center on
   a particular error rate such as 2. It is more likely that interest
   will be focused on low error rates such as 0, 1, or 2; in other
   words, interest will be directed toward the proportion of observations less than or equal to a particular value. Selection of a
   particular type of distribution depends on what is to be emphasized
   in a given application.

2.10.a.

Age	Cumulative Frequency
4–13	7
14–23	13
24–33	20
34–43	32
44–53	37
54–63	39
64–73	40

b.

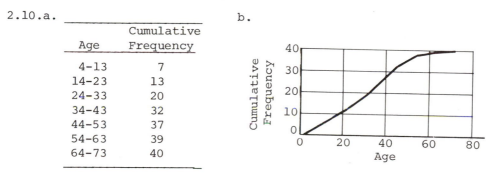

c. The upper class limit is 23, so we know that exactly 13 people are less than or equal to 23 years of age.

d. Here 20 is not an upper class limit, so we cannot tell exactly how many of the original people are younger than or equal to this value by examining the cumulative frequency distribution. From the graph of the distribution in (b), we may estimate the number of people that are less than 20 to be 11. This approximation is based on the assumption that observations are uniformly distributed throughout the class.

e. By inspecting the original observations, we see that exactly 13 people are less than or equal to the upper class limit of 23 years. This agrees with the result in 5c, as it should. Exactly 10 people are younger than 20. In (d), we estimated this number to be 11. The error is introduced because the latter estimation is based on grouped data in which the identity of the individual values in a class is lost.

CHAPTER 3: SOLUTIONS TO SELF-CORRECTING EXERCISES

3.1.a. $\mu = \Sigma x/N = 250/7 = 35.7$ ($\Sigma x = 10 + 60 + 60 + 40 + 20 + 30 + 30$
$= 250$)

b. $\mu = 130/4 = 32.5$ ($\Sigma x = 10 + 60 + 30 + 30 = 130$, $N = 4$)

c. $\mu = 120/3 = 40$ ($\Sigma x = 60 + 40 + 20 = 120$, $N = 3$)

d. $\overline{X} = \Sigma X/n = (60 + 20 + 30)/3 = 36.67$

e. The population mean age is $\mu = 35.7$; the sample mean age is
$\overline{X} = 36.67$. Note the two values are different. The population
mean is based on all seven values in the population. The sample
mean is based on a portion of the values in the population.

3.2.a. $\mu = \Sigma fm/N$, where m is the class midvalue, f is the frequency of
the class, and N is the number of observations.

b.

Age	Class Midvalue (m)	f	fm
4–13	8.5	7	59.5
14–23	18.5	6	111.0
24–33	28.5	7	199.5
34–43	38.5	12	462.0
44–53	48.5	5	242.5
54–63	58.5	2	117.0
64–73	68.5	1	68.5
		40	1260.0

$\mu = 1260/40 = 31.5$

c. $\mu = 1302/40 = 32.55$

d. The answers differ slightly. The value 32.55 is computed from the
original observations. All of the observations are actually
summed. When the mean is computed from the frequency distribution, the class midvalue is used as an approximation for all
values in the class. For example, the actual sum of the seven
observations in the first class is $4 + 7 + 10 + 10 + 12 + 13 + 13$
or 69. This is approximated in the grouped data by $(8.5)(7)$, or
59.5. The saving in computational effort is usually greater for
grouped data if a large number of observations are present.

e. Grouping data in value classes helps to develop a pattern in the
data. For large data collections, it is virtually impossible to
comprehend the pattern of the data unless grouping is used. It
is true that grouping causes the loss of identity of values
within a class. If you consider the ages of persons in the

United States, there may be several million observations in one class. It should be clear that trying to preserve the identity of these observations will lead to confusion. It is true that grouping leads to inaccuracies in computing such measures as the mean and that high-speed computers are capable of handling original observations. Often, however, the results of a statistical study are published in the form of a frequency distribution. In such cases, the desired measure may be computed directly from the frequency distribution with little effort or expense. In many cases, the original observations are not available or are prohibitively expensive.

f. The error is ignoring frequency. There are 98 ones, 1 two, and 1 three for a total of $(98)(1) + (1)(2) + (1)(3) = 103$. The mean is $103/100 = 1.03$.

3.3.a. The population of ages, arranged from smallest to largest, is 10, 20, 30, 30, 40, 60, 60. Since there are seven values, the fourth value is the middle value. Thus $Md = 30$.

b. The mean and median of a population are not necessarily the same. This result is natural because different procedures are used to find the mean and median. For the mean, every value in the population is added to find ΣX. For the median, only the relative magnitudes of the values are considered. If the largest age were 90 instead of 60, the median would be the same but the mean would change.

c. The ages of females arranged from the smallest to largest are 10, 30, 30, 60. Since there is an even number of values, the median is the average of the two middle values. Thus $Md = (30 + 30)/2 = 30$.

d. The ordered values are 20, 40, 60 and the median is $Md = 40$.

e. The ordered values are 20, 30, 40, 60. The average of the two middle values is the median. Thus $Md = (30 + 40)/2 = 35$.

3.4.a. The body temperature 98.6° appears three times, which is more frequent than any other value. Thus the mode is 98.6°.

b. The value 30 appears twice and the value 60 appears twice. All other values appear once. Thus there are two modes, 30 and 60.

3.5.a. The mean (μ) must be computed first.

b. $\sigma^2 = \Sigma(X - \mu)^2/N = [(60 - 40)^2 + (40 - 40)^2 + (20 - 40)^2]/3$
$= [(20)^2 + 0^2 + (-20)^2]/3 = 800/3 = 266.7$

c. ΣX^2 and μ

d. $\Sigma X^2 = (60)^2 + (40)^2 + (20)^2 = 5600$
$\Sigma X = 60 + 40 + 20 = 120$ $\mu = \Sigma X/N = 120/3 = 40$
$\sigma^2 = \Sigma X^2/N - (\mu)^2 = 5600/3 - 40^2 = 1866.7 - 1600 = 266.7$

e.   Both formulas produce the same result.

f.   The second formula is usually easier to use if the deviations are not whole numbers.

3.6.a. $\overline{X} = (64 + 72 + 61)/3 = 197/3 = 65.67$; $s^2 = \Sigma(X - \overline{X})^2/(n - 1)$
$= [(64 - 65.67)^2 + (72 - 65.67)^2 + (61 - 65.67)^2]/(3 - 1)$
$= [(-1.67)^2 + (6.33)^2 + (-4.67)^2]/2$
$= (2.7889 + 40.0689 + 21.8089)/2 = 64.6667/2 = 32.33335$

b. $\overline{X} = 65.67$; $\Sigma X^2 = (64)^2 + (72)^2 + (61)^2$
$= 4096 + 5184 + 3721 = 13{,}001$
$s^2 = [\Sigma X^2 - n(\overline{X})^2]/(n - 1) = [(13{,}001 - 3(65.67)^2]/(3 - 1)$
$= (13{,}001 - 12{,}937.647)/2 = 63.3533/2 = 31.67665$

c.   The two formulas are logically equivalent. The numerical answers differ because of rounding errors.

d.   If we use values correct to one decimal place, then
$s^2 = (\Sigma X^2 - n(\overline{X})^2)/(n - 1) = (13{,}001 - 3(65.7)^2)/(3 - 1)$
$= (13{,}001 - 12949.47)/2 = 51.53/2 = 25.765.$
The formula for the sample variance is sensitive to the accuracy maintained in computing the mean. If this formula were used with $\overline{X} = 65.667$, then we would find $s^2 = 32.268$.

e.   The variance of all values in the population is $\sigma^2 = 266.7$. This value never changes for this fixed population. The sample variance is $s^2 = 32$ (to the nearest whole number). Note that the sample variance could have a different value if a different sample had been selected.

3.7.a.   Since 4 has fewer than three significant digits, we find it under N. Because 4 is already in the range from 1 to 100, we do not need to move the decimal point. Since 4 is less than 10, we find the square root under $\sqrt{N}$. The result is 2.00000. These first two statements also apply to 36. But since 36 is greater than 10 (36 > 10), we must look under $\sqrt{10N}$ for its square root, which is 6.00000.

To find $\sqrt{144}$, we find 1.44 under N, move the decimal point in 144 two places left, find 1.2 under $\sqrt{N}$, and move the decimal one place right to get 12 as the square root of 144.

To find $\sqrt{3600}$, we begin by locating 3.60 under N. Then we move the decimal point in 3600 two places left to produce a number between 1 and 100. We cannot move it three places left, because the rule restricts us to an even number of places. Since 36 > 10, we find 6 under $\sqrt{10N}$ and move the decimal point one place to the right to get 60 as the square root of 3600.

To find $\sqrt{0.0144}$, move the decimal point two places to the right and find 1.2 under $\sqrt{N}$ opposite 1.44 under N. Move the decimal point in 1.2 one place left to get 0.12 as the square root of 0.0144.

To find $\sqrt{0.0036}$, move the decimal point four places to the right and find 6 under $\sqrt{10N}$ opposite 3.60 under N. Move the decimal point in 6 two places to the left to get 0.06 as the square root of 0.0036.

b.   Round 3,159,531.4 to 3,160,000 and move the decimal six places left to get 3.16. Find this under N and find 1.77764 under $\sqrt{N}$. Move the decimal three places right to get 1777.64.

755,500 becomes 75.6 after rounding and moving the decimal four places left. Opposite 7.56 under N, find 8.69483 under $\sqrt{10N}$. Move the decimal two places right to get 869.483 as the square root of 755,500.

After rounding and moving the decimal point six places right, 0.00000456501 becomes 4.57. Find 4.57 under N. Because 4.57 < 10, find 2.13776 under $\sqrt{N}$. Move the decimal three places left to get 0.00213776 as the square root of the original number.

3.8.a.   The computation of the variance must precede the computation of the standard deviation.

b.   From Exercise 3.5, σ^2 = 266.7. Thus $\sigma = \sqrt{267}$. From the table of square roots, σ = 16.3401.

3.9.a.   For temperature, $z = (x - \mu)/\sigma = (99.5 - 98.6)/(1/3) = 2.7$. For weight, $z = (200 - 175)/25 = 1$. Since the hospital staff considers anything over $z = 2$ to be abnormal, this patient would be classified as having an abnormal temperature and a normal weight.

b.   The standard score for a weight of 150 pounds is $z = (X - \mu)/\sigma$ = (150 - 175)/25 = -1. The standard score for a weight of 200 pounds is $z = (200 - 175)/25 = 1$. Thus a weight of 200 lb is one standard deviation above the mean and a weight of 175 lb is one standard deviation below the mean. From normal curve theory (see Figure 3-5 on page 74 in the text), 68.3% of the values in a normal population lie within plus or minus one standard deviation of the mean. The range of 125 to 225 corresponds to a standard score range of $z = (125 - 175)/25 = -2$ to $z = (225 - 175)/25 = 2$. For normal populations, 95.5% of the population lies in this range.

3.10.a. The range is $(7 - 1) + 1 = 7$ for both populations.

b. Population A is clustered more tightly.

c. For population A, $\Sigma X^2 = 222$, $\mu = 4$, and $\sigma^2 = \Sigma X^2/N - \mu^2$ $= 222/12 - 4^2 = 18.5 - 16 = 2.5$.
For population B, $\Sigma X^2 = 250$, $\mu = 4$, and $\sigma^2 = 250/12 - 4^2$ $= 20.8 - 16 = 4.8$.

d. The variance is usually the better measure of dispersion. In this example, both populations have the same range. From the graphs we can see that population A clusters more tightly around the mean. The smaller variance for population A correctly reflects this, but the range does not. In computing the variance, each value in a population is included. In the range, only the largest and smallest observations are considered.

CHAPTER 4:   SOLUTIONS TO SELF-CORRECTING EXERCISES

4.1.a. The elements in the sample space are the 6 sides of the die and their relationship to the experiment is that they represent all possible outcomes of the experiment *roll the die.*

   b. The probability of each sample point is 1/6.   Thus *P(A)* = 1/6.

   c. By relative frequency, *P(A)* is approximately 140/1000.   In order to find the "true" value of *P(A)* by relative frequency, we would need to repeat the experiment an indefinite number of times. Since 1000 trials is a finite number, saying *P(A)* = 0.140 is an approximation.

   d. The observer is assigning the probability according to personal belief (degree-of-belief method).

   e. Three different approaches have been used to assign probabilities, so different numerical values may result for each method.   The assignments made by all three methods must obey the rules for assigning probabilities.   For example, the observer could not say that he or she believed the probability of rolling a one is 0.75 and the probability of rolling a two is 0.50 since this would imply that the probability assigned to the entire sample space would exceed 1.0.   The equally likely method rests with the assumption that the die is in fact "fair."   If in fact the die is fair, a large number of trials would eventually produce an assignment close to 0.1666....   The fact that 1000 trials assigned the probability of 0.140 to *P(A)* may indicate that an insufficient number of trials was conducted or that the die is not exactly "fair."   The degree of belief assignment incorporates subjective factors not included in the other two methods.   If the observer is skilled at incorporating these factors, the assignment of *P(A)* = 0.75 may well be sound.

   f. The equally likely method is really an assumption one might make if there were no reason to cause one to believe it is invalid. This assumption is often made when no empirical evidence is available.   The relative-frequency method requires actual observations of an experiment.   In order to use it, one must have a collection of observations or the resources to obtain the observations.   In addition, the collection of outcomes of interest must be compatible with the concept of a repetitive experiment.   For example, the events *winning or losing tomorrow's golf match* cannot be determined from an experiment.   In such cases, a degree-of-belief probability assignment may be made.   The accuracy of probability assignments made in this way rests with the soundness of an individual's judgment.

4.2.a-b.

	B_1	B_2	Total
A_1	0.344	0.456	0.800
A_2	0.056	0.144	0.200
Total	0.400	0.600	1.000

Each entry in the table is found by dividing the number of individuals in a given classification by the total number of individuals. For example, $P(A_1$ and $B_1) = 172/500 = 0.344$ and $P(B_1) = 200/500 = 0.4$.

c. The event A_2 and B_2 means unemployed and unskilled. The events A_2 and B_2 ... B_2 and A_2 are identical. $P(A_2$ and $B_2) = 72/500 = 0.144$.

d. A_2 and B_2 is the event *unemployed and unskilled*. The probability of this event is $P(A_2$ and $B_2)$.

e. The event $A_2 | B_2$ is *unemployed given unskilled*. The event $B_2 | A_2$ is *unskilled given unemployed*. The two events are totally different. The probabilities of these events are found from the frequencies as

$$P(A_2 | B_2) = 72/300 = 0.24$$

$$P(B_2 | A_2) = 72/100 = 0.72$$

f.

	Given skilled (B_1)		Given unskilled (B_2)
Employed (A_1)	0.86	= 172/200	0.76
Unemployed (A_2)	0.14		0.24
	1.00		1.00

The probability of unemployment depends on whether the worker is skilled or unskilled. Skilled workers have a lower probability of unemployment.

4.3.a. $P(S) = 0.30 + 0.10 = 0.40$; $P(S') = 0.20 + 0.40 = 0.6$ (or $1 - 0.4$); $P(R) = 0.5$; $P(R') = 0.5$. These are marginal probabilities.

b. $P(R'$ and $S') = 0.4$

c-d. $P(R|S) = \dfrac{P(R \text{ and } S)}{P(S)} = \dfrac{0.3}{0.4} = 0.75$;

$P(R'|S) = \dfrac{P(R' \text{ and } S)}{P(S)} = \dfrac{0.1}{0.4} = 0.25$;

$$P(R \mid S') = \frac{P(R \text{ and } S')}{P(S')} = \frac{0.2}{0.6} = 0.33;$$

$$P(R' \mid S') = \frac{P(R' \text{ and } S')}{P(S')} = \frac{0.4}{0.6} = 0.67;$$

$$P(S \mid R) = \frac{P(S \text{ and } R)}{P(R)} = \frac{0.3}{0.5} = 0.6;$$

$$P(S' \mid R) = \frac{P(S' \text{ and } R)}{P(R)} = \frac{0.2}{0.5} = 0.4;$$

$$P(S \mid R') = \frac{P(S \text{ and } R')}{P(R')} = \frac{0.1}{0.5} = 0.2;$$

$$P(S' \mid R') = \frac{P(S' \text{ and } R')}{P(R')} = \frac{0.4}{0.5} = 0.8.$$

e. The conditional probabilities $P(S \mid R) = 0.6$ and $P(S' \mid R) = 0.4$ indicate more favorable chances of subscription than nonsubscription when the brochure was received. The conditional probabilities $P(S \mid R') = 0.2$ and $P(S' \mid R') = 0.8$ indicate the chances of nonsubscription are greater when the brochure was *not* received. This seems to indicate the effectiveness of the brochure. Since the largest joint probability is $P(S' \text{ and } R') = 0.4$, the publisher may wish to expand the distribution of the brochure. Cost and revenue, as well as probability considerations, would have to be used to reach a comprehensive solution.—

4.4.a. $P(A \text{ or } S) = P(A) + P(S) - P(A \text{ and } S) = 4/52 + 13/52 - 1/52$
= 16/52 = 0.31

b. $P(H \text{ and } S) = 0$ because hearts and spades are mutually exclusive.

c. $P(H \text{ or } S) = P(H) + P(S) - P(H \text{ and } S) = 13/52 + 13/52 - 0$
= 26/52 = 0.5

d. No, $P(A \text{ and } S) = 1/52$.

e. Yes, $P(H \text{ and } S) = 0$.

4.5.a. P(Female or graduate) = P(Female) + P(Graduate) - P(Female and graduate) = 0.25 + 0.15 - 0.10 = 0.30

b. *Female* and *college graduate* are not mutually exclusive because P(Female and graduate) is not zero.

4.6.a. $P(S \text{ and } M) = P(M)P(S \mid M); P(M) = 0.6$ and $P(S \mid M) = 1/3$;
$P(S \text{ and } M) = 0.6(1/3) = 0.2$

b. $P(S \text{ and } F) = P(F)P(S \mid F); P(F) = 1 - P(M) = 1 - 0.6 = 0.4;$
$P(S \mid F) = 1/4; P(S \text{ and } F) = 0.4(1/4) = 0.1$

4.7.a.

	R	R'	
S	0.5(0.4)	0.5(0.4)	0.4
S'	0.5(0.6)	0.5(0.6)	0.6
	0.5	0.5	

	R	R'	
S	0.2	0.2	0.4
S'	0.3	0.3	0.6
	0.5	0.5	

b. None of the values computed in (a) are equal to the true joint
   probabilities. The assumption of independence is not correct.

4.8.a. $P(M)$ = 0.225 + 0.075 = 0.3;

$$P(A|M) = \frac{P(A \text{ and } M)}{P(M)} = \frac{0.225}{0.3} = 0.75;$$

$$P(D|M) = \frac{P(D \text{ and } M)}{P(M)} = \frac{0.075}{0.3} = 0.25;$$

$P(F)$ = 0.175 + 0.525 = 0.70;

$$P(A|F) = \frac{P(A \text{ and } F)}{P(F)} = \frac{0.525}{0.70} = 0.75;$$

$$P(D|F) = \frac{P(D \text{ and } F)}{P(F)} = \frac{0.175}{0.70} = 0.25;$$

$P(A)$ = 0.225 + 0.525 = 0.75;

$P(D)$ = 0.075 + 0.175 = 0.25.

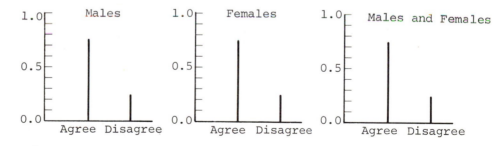

b. $P(M)$ = 0.225 + 0.075 = 0.3

$$P(A|M) = \frac{P(A \text{ and } M)}{P(M)} = \frac{0.225}{0.3} = 0.75$$

$$P(D|M) = \frac{P(D \text{ and } M)}{P(M)} = \frac{0.075}{0.3} = 0.25$$

$P(F)$ = 0.175 + 0.525 = 0.7

$$P(A|F) = \frac{P(A \text{ and } F)}{P(F)} = \frac{0.175}{0.7} = 0.25$$

$$P(D|F) = \frac{P(D \text{ and } F)}{P(F)} = \frac{0.525}{0.7} = 0.75$$

$$P(A) = 0.225 + 0.175 = 0.4$$

$$P(D) = 0.075 + 0.525 = 0.6$$

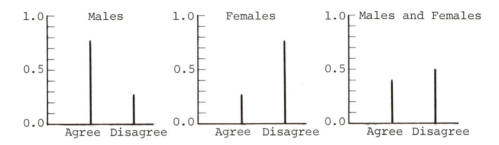

c. Sex and opinion are independent for the first question. For the second question, opinion depends on sex.

d. If two variables are independent, the marginal probabilities are equal to the corresponding conditional probabilities. For example, the probability of agreement for the first question (see (a)) is $P(A) = 0.75$, $P(A|M) = 0.75$, $P(A|F) = 0.75$.

4.9.a. $P(D \text{ and } S_2) = P(D|S_2) \cdot P(S_2) = 0.15(0.40) = 0.06$

b.

	S_1	S_2	S_3	
D	0.04	0.06		0.11
N	0.30	0.40		

c. $P(N) = 1 - P(D) = 1 - 0.11 = 0.89$;
$P(S_3) = 1 - [P(S_1) + P(S_2)] = 1 - (0.3 + 0.4) = 0.3$;

$P(S_1 \text{ and } N) = 0.3 - 0.04 = 0.26$;
$P(S_2 \text{ and } N) = 0.4 - 0.06 = 0.34$;

$P(D \text{ and } S_3) = 0.11 - (0.04 + 0.06) = 0.01$;
$P(N \text{ and } S_3) = P(S_3) - P(D \text{ and } S_3) = 0.3 - 0.01 = 0.29$.

Other solutions are possible. They all produce the following table:

	S_1	S_2	S_3	
D	0.04	0.06	0.01	0.11
N	0.26	0.34	0.29	0.89
	0.30	0.40	0.30	1.00

The sum of the marginal probabilities must equal 1.0 and the sum of the joint probabilities in a given row (or column) must equal the corresponding marginal probability for the given row (or column).

d. This formula for the joint probability is correct but cannot be used in this case because $P(S_2|D)$ is not known.

4.10.a.

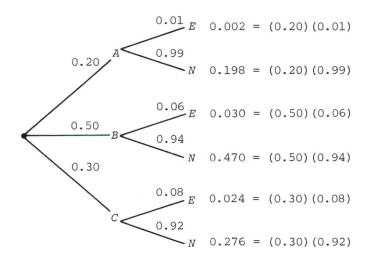

$$0.01 \quad E \quad 0.002 = (0.20)(0.01)$$

$$0.99 \quad N \quad 0.198 = (0.20)(0.99)$$

$$0.06 \quad E \quad 0.030 = (0.50)(0.06)$$

$$0.94 \quad N \quad 0.470 = (0.50)(0.94)$$

$$0.08 \quad E \quad 0.024 = (0.30)(0.08)$$

$$0.92 \quad N \quad 0.276 = (0.30)(0.92)$$

b. A and E, B and E, C and E.

c. $P(A \text{ and } N) = P(N|A) \, P(A)$. $P(A) = 0.20$ is given in the problem statement. $P(N|A)$ is computed from $P(N|A) = 1 - P(E|A) = 1 - 0.01 = 0.99$; $P(A \text{ and } N) = 0.99(0.2) = 0.198$.

d. See the probability tree. All joint probabilities are found in (c).

e. $P(E) = P(A \text{ and } E) + P(B \text{ and } E) + P(C \text{ and } E) = 0.002 + 0.03 + 0.024 = 0.056$
$P(N) = 1 - P(E) = 1 - 0.056 = 0.944$

f. $P(A|E) = \dfrac{P(A \text{ and } E)}{P(E)} = \dfrac{0.002}{0.056} = 0.036$

$P(B|E) = \dfrac{P(B \text{ and } E)}{P(E)} = \dfrac{0.03}{0.056} = 0.536$

$P(C|E) = \dfrac{P(C \text{ and } E)}{P(E)} = \dfrac{0.024}{0.056} = 0.429$

g.

	Supplier			
	A	B	C	
Error	0.002	0.030	0.024	0.056
No error	0.198	0.470	0.276	0.944
	0.200	0.500	0.300	

One set of marginal probabilities is displayed on the first set
of branches. The conditional probabilities are placed on the
second set of branches. The product of the marginal and conditional probabilities produces the joint probabilities which
appear at the end of each sequence in the tree. These joint
probabilities appear in the body of the frequency table.

CHAPTER 5:   SOLUTIONS TO SELF-CORRECTING EXERCISES

5.1.a.

Value of Random Variable	1	1	1	5	5	5
	↓	↓	↓	↓	↓	↓
	•	•	•	•	•	•
Sample Space	P_1	P_2	P_3	N_1	N_2	N_3
Probability	$\frac{1}{6}$	$\frac{1}{6}$	$\frac{1}{6}$	$\frac{1}{6}$	$\frac{1}{6}$	$\frac{1}{6}$

b.

x	$P(x)$
1	3/6 = 1/6 + 1/6 + 1/6
5	3/6 = 1/6 + 1/6 + 1/6

The elements in the sample space are mutually exclusive. $P(X = 1)$ = $P(P_1$ or P_2 or $P_3) = P(P_1) + P(P_2) + P(P_3)$.

c. The event P_1 is the same as the event *draw P_1 from the box*.   The event $X = 1$ is the same as *draw P_1 or P_2 or P_3 from the box*.

d. Weight, diameter, and date of issue may be random variables because they assign numerical values to the elements in the sample space. Color, type of metal, and city where minted do not assign numerical values.

e. A very large number of random variables might be defined on this sample space. The probability assigned to each element in the sample space is not influenced by the choice of a random variable. If each element is equally likely, then the probability of each element is 1/6. The probability distributions are likely to be different. For example, $P(Y = 1975) = 1/6$ and $P(Y = 1976) = 5/6$. In general, different random variables will "collect" the elements in the sample space in different ways and this results in dif‐ ferent probability distributions.

f. The choice of a random variable should reflect the objectives of the study.

5.2.a.

	J	Q	K	A
S	1/16	1/16	1/16	1/16
H	1/16	1/16	1/16	1/16
D	1/16	1/16	1/16	1/16
C	1/16	1/16	1/16	1/16

	J	Q	K	A
S	2	3	4	5
H	2	3	4	5
D	1	2	3	4
C	1	2	3	4

b.

x	$P(x)$
1	2/16
2	4/16
3	4/16
4	4/16
5	2/16

c.

x	$P(X \leq x)$
1	2/16
2	6/16
3	10/16
4	14/16
5	16/16

5.3.a.

Probability
Demand for A

Demand for B	x_B	x_A 1	2
	1	6/16	2/16
	2	3/16	1/16
	3	2/16	2/16

Total Demands
Demand for A

Demand for B	x_B	x_A 1	2
	1	2	3
	2	3	4
	3	4	5

b. The events $X_A = 1$, $X_B = 2$ and $X_A = 2$, $X_B = 1$ both produce $T = 3$. The value of $P(T = 3)$ is found by adding the probabilities of these events. Thus $P(T = 3) = P(X_A = 1, X_B = 2) + P(X_A = 2, X_B = 1) = 3/16 + 2/16 = 5/16$.

c.

t	$P(t)$
2	6/16
3	5/16 = 3/16 + 2/16
4	3/16 = 2/16 + 1/16
5	2/16

5.4.a.

x	$P(x)$	$x * P(x)$	$(x - \mu)$	$(x - \mu)^2$	$(x - \mu)^2 P(x)$
1	1/2	1/2	-2	4	2
5	1/2	5/2	2	4	2
		$\mu = 6/2 = 3$			$\sigma^2 = 4$

x	$P(x)$	$x * P(x)$	$(x - \mu)$	$(x - \mu)^2$	$(x - \mu)^2 P(x)$
1	1/8	1/8	-2	4	4/8
2	2/8	4/8	-1	1	2/8
3	2/8	6/8	0	0	0/8
4	2/8	8/8	1	1	2/8
5	1/8	5/8	2	4	4/8
		$\mu = 24/8 = 3$			$\sigma^2 = 12/8 = 3/2$

b. For Question 5.2, $E(X) = \mu = 3$ and $[E(X)]^2 = (3)^2 = 9$.   For Question 5.3, $E(X) = \mu = 3$ and $[E(X)]^2 = (3)^2 = 9$.

x	x^2	$P(x)$	$(x^2) * P(x)$	x	x^2	$P(x)$	$(x^2) * P(x)$
1	1	1/2	1/2	1	1	1/8	1/8
5	25	1/2	25/2	2	4	2/8	8/8
		$E(x^2) = $	$\overline{26/2} = 13$	3	9	2/8	18/8
				4	16	2/8	32/8
				5	25	1/8	25/8
						$E(x^2) = $	$\overline{84/8}$

The value of $[E(x)]^2$ *does not* equal the value of $E(x^2)$.   Such equality would occur only if $\sigma^2 = 0$.

c. For Question 5.2, $\sigma^2 = E(X^2) - [E(X)]^2 = 13 - 9 = 4$.
   For Question 5.3, $\sigma^2 = 84/8 - 9 = 10.5 - 9 = 1.5$.
   Note that the procedure used in (a) produced the same result.

5.5.a. $X:x = 10, 12, 14, 16, 19, 20$

   b. (i) $P(X = 10)$ (ii) $P(X > 10)$

   c. (i) The probability that the random variable equals 16.
     (ii) The probability that the random variable equals or exceeds 14.

5.6.a. Sex, (d) (Whether or not the patient has health insurance), and
   (f) (Normal or abnormal weight) are all suitable for defining a
   Bernoulli process because they involve two classifications.
   Although (e) has three classifications, it may be converted to
   two classifications as shown in (f).

5.7.a.

x	$P(x)$
0	2/3
1	1/3 = π

Notice that the condition we are interested in counting is coded
as $x = 1$.   In this case, we are interested in the event *succeeds*
so it is coded as $x = 1$.   Also, π is the probability that $x = 1$.
The mean and variance of this distribution are $\mu = \pi = 1/3$ and
$\sigma^2 = \pi(1 - \pi) = 1/3(1 - 1/3) = 2/9$.

b.

$$2/3 \quad B \quad P(B, B, B) = 8/27$$

$$2/3 \quad B$$

$$B$$

$$1/3 \quad S \quad P(B, B, S) = 4/27$$

$$2/3 \quad B \quad P(B, S, B) = 4/27$$

$$2/3$$

$$1/3 \quad S$$

$$1/3 \quad S \quad P(B, S, S) = 2/27$$

$$2/3 \quad B \quad P(S, B, B) = 4/27$$

$$2/3 \quad B$$

$$1/3$$

$$1/3 \quad S \quad P(S, B, S) = 2/27$$

$$S \qquad 2/3 \quad B \quad P(S, S, B) = 2/27$$

$$1/3 \quad S$$

$$1/3 \quad S \quad P(S, S, S) = 1/27$$

c.

Number of Successful Calls r	Probability $P(r)$	
0	8/27	$_3C_0 (1/3)^0 (2/3)^3 = 1(1)(8/27) = 8/27$
1	12/27	$_3C_1 (1/3)^1 (2/3)^2 = 3(1/3)(4/9) = 12/27$
2	6/27	$_3C_2 (1/3)^2 (2/3)^1 = 3(1/9)(2/3) = 6/27$
3	1/27	$_3C_3 (1/3)^3 (2/3)^0 = 1(1/27)(1) = 1/27$

d. The distributions in (a) and (c) are different, but they are related. The distribution in (a) shows the probability of *succeeds* on any call and it represents the Bernoulli process. The distribution in (c) represents the probability of 0, 1, 2, or 3 successful calls in three attempts from the Bernoulli process in (a).

e. See calculations at the right of the table in Part c.

f. $P(r \geq 2) = P(r = 2) + P(r = 3) = 6/27 + 1/27 = 7/27$
   $P(r \leq 1) = P(r = 0) + P(r = 1) = 8/27 + 12/27 = 20/27$

g. We code busy calls as $x = 1$ and $\pi = 2/3$. Notice that in (c) $r = 0$ means *no successful calls in three attempts*, which is the same as *3 busys in three attempts*. Following such reasoning, we could write:

Number of Busy Calls	Probability
0	1/27
1	6/27
2	12/27
3	8/27

The two methods convey the same information. It is important, however, to be consistent and the entire problem should be discussed in terms of *busy calls* or in terms of *successful calls*.

5.8.a. i. $P(R = 2 | n = 3, \pi = 0.6) = {}_3C_2(0.6)^2(0.4)^1$

$$= \frac{3!}{(3 - 2)!2!}(0.36)(0.4)$$

$$= 3(0.36)(0.4) = 0.432$$

ii. $P(R = 0 | n = 4, \pi = 0.2) = {}_4C_0(0.2)^0(0.8)^4$

$$= \frac{4!}{(4 - 0)!0!}(1)(0.4096)$$

$$= (1)(1)(0.4096) = 0.4096$$

iii. $P(R = 3 | n = 3, \pi = 0.3) = {}_3C_3(0.3)^3(0.7)^0$

$$= \frac{3!}{(3 - 3)!3!}(0.027)(1)$$

$$= (1)(0.027)(1) = 0.027$$

b. i. $P(R \geq 2 | n = 3, \pi = 0.6) = P(R = 2 | n = 3, \pi = 0.6)$
$+ P(R = 3 | n = 3, \pi = 0.6) = 0.4320 + 0.2160 = 0.6480$

ii. $P(R < 2 | n = 3, \pi = 0.6) = P(R = 0 | n = 3, \pi = 0.6)$
$+ P(R = 1 | n = 3, \pi = 0.6) = 0.0640 + 0.2880 = 0.3520$

iii. $P(R \leq 3 | n = 9, \pi = 0.3) = 0.0404 + 0.1556 + 0.2668$
$+ 0.2668 = 0.7296$

iv. $P(R > 12 | n = 15, \pi = 0.50) = 0.0032 + 0.0005 + 0.0000 = 0.0037$

5.9.a. $P(R = 2 | n = 4, \pi = 0.20) = {}_4C_2(0.20)^2(0.80)^2$

$$= \frac{4!}{(4 - 2)!2!}(0.04)(0.64)$$

$$= 6(0.04)(0.64) = 0.1536$$

b. $P(R = 2 | n = 4, \pi = 0.10) = {}_4C_2(0.10)^2(0.90)^2$

$$= \frac{4!}{(4 - 2)!2!}(0.01)(0.81)$$

$$= 6(0.01)(0.81) = 0.0486$$

5.10.a. The Bernoulli random variable represents what will happen on any one trial. The binomial probability distribution describes the possible results of a fixed number of trials from a given Bernoulli random variable. Bernoulli random variables may be distinguished from each other by the numerical values of π.

b. For a given Bernoulli random variable, there are an infinite number of binomial distributions--one binomial distribution for each value of n.

c. The statement is false. $P(X = 1) = \pi = 0.5$ is a term in the probability distribution for the Bernoulli random variable and $P(R = 1 | n = 3, \pi = 0.5)$ is a term in the binomial distribution and it equals

$$\frac{3!}{1!2!}(0.5)^1(0.5)^2 = 0.375$$

d. i. True, the complement of $R \geq 1$ is $R < 1$ (or $R = 0$).

   ii. False, $R \geq 1$, means $R = 1$ or $R = 2$.

  iii. True, $R \geq 2$, means any value of R that is 2 or more; $R > 1$, means R must be a value that exceeds 1--that is, R must be 2 or more.

   iv. False, these are terms from two different binomial distributions. One is associated with the Bernoulli random variable having $\pi = 0.5$ and the other with a Bernoulli random variable having $\pi = 0.1$.

    v. False, these are terms from two different binomial disbributions--one for $n = 2$ and the other for $n = 10$.

   vi. False, Table B-1 lists the probability as 0.0000, but this result has been rounded to four decimal places. The binomial formula gives $P(R = 0 | n = 8, \pi = 0.75) = 1(0.75)^0(0.25)^8 = (0.25)^8$, which is approximately 0.00001526. Thus 0.0000 in Table B-1 means a number smaller than 0.0001.

5.11.a. i. $P(R \geq 1 | n = 5, \pi = 0.05) = 0.2036 + 0.0214 + 0.0011 + 0.0000$
          $= 0.2261$

    ii. $P(R = 0 | n = 5, \pi = 0.15) = 0.4437$

b. If the tasters were making identifications at random, or simply by guessing, each taster would have a 0.25 probability (one-in-four chance) of correctly identifying brand X. (This is a good criterion for no ability to distinguish.) Therefore we want $P(R \geq 6 | n = 10, \pi = 0.25)$, and this probability is $0.0162 + 0.0031 + 0.0004 = 0.0197$.

c. An equal number of customers preferring either alternative implies $\pi = 0.50$. For a result as uneven as 9 out of 12, $R \geq 9$ or $R \leq 3$.

$P(R \geq 9 | n = 12, \pi = 0.50) = 0.0537 + 0.0161 + 0.0029 + 0.0002 = 0.0729$

$P(R \leq 3 | n = 12, \pi = 0.50) = 0.0002 + 0.0029 + 0.0161 + 0.0537 = \underline{0.0729}$

$P(\text{result as uneven as 9 out of 12}) = 0.1458$

d. i. $P(R \geq 3 | n = 10, \pi = 0.05) = 0.0105 + 0.0010 + 0.0001 = 0.0116$

  ii. $P(R \leq 2 | n = 10, \pi = 0.40) = 0.0060 + 0.0403 + 0.1209 = 0.1672$

5.12.a. The mean and variance of a Bernoulli random variable are given by $\mu = \pi$ and $\sigma^2 = \pi(1 - \pi)$. For (i) of Question 5.11d, $\mu = 0.05$, and $\sigma^2 = 0.05(0.95) = 0.0475$. For (ii) of Question 5.11d, $\pi = 0.40$, $\mu = 0.40$, and $\sigma^2 = 0.40(0.60) = 0.24$. The mean and variance of a Bernoulli random variable are determined by the value of π.

  b. The mean and variance of a binomial distribution are given by $\mu_r = n\pi$ and $\sigma^2 = n\pi(1 - \pi)$. For (i) of Exercise 5.11d, $\pi = 0.05$, and $n = 10$. $\mu_r = 10(0.05) = 0.5$ and $\sigma^2 = 10(0.05)(0.95) = 0.475$. For (ii) of Exercise 5.11d, $\pi = 0.40$ and $n = 10$, $\mu_r = 4$, $\sigma^2 = 2.4$. The mean and variance of a binomial distribution are determined by values of π and n.

  c. Doubling the value of n will not influence the parameters of the Bernoulli random variable, Part a, but will double the mean and variance of the binomial distributions, Part b.

5.13.a-b. $\pi = 0.1$ $\pi = 0.5$ $\pi = 0.9$

r	$P(r)$		r	$P(r)$		r	$P(r)$
0	0.6561		0	0.0625		0	0.0001
1	0.2916		1	0.2500		1	0.0036
2	0.0486		2	0.3750		2	0.0486
3	0.0036		3	0.2500		3	0.2916
4	0.0001		4	0.0625		4	0.6561

$\mu = \pi = 0.10$ $\mu = 0.5$ $\mu = 0.9$

$\sigma^2 = \pi(1 - \pi) = 0.1(0.9) = 0.09$ $\sigma^2 = 0.25$ $\sigma^2 = 0.09$

$\sigma = \sqrt{0.09} = 0.3$ $\sigma = 0.5$ $\sigma = 0.3$

$\mu_r = n\pi = 4(0.1) = 0.4$ $\mu_r = 2$ $\mu_r = 3.6$

$\sigma_r^2 = n\pi(1 - \pi) = 4(0.1)(0.9)$ $\sigma_r^2 = 1$ $\sigma_r^2 = 0.36$

$= 0.36$

$\sigma_r = 0.6$ $\sigma_r = 1$ $\sigma_r = 0.6$

c.

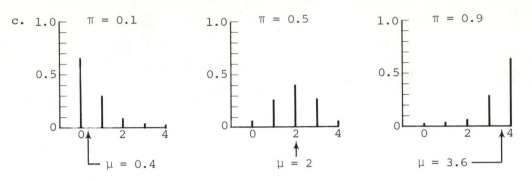

d. The mean of binomial distribution increases with larger values of
π. The largest standard deviation occurs when π = 0.5. Binomial
distributions with π smaller or larger than 0.5 have smaller
standard deviations. A binomial distribution with π = 0.5 is symmetric. Binomial distributions with π less than 0.5 have positive
skewness. Binomial distributions with values of π greater than
0.5 have negative skewness.

e. For $n = 4$, $\mu_r = n\pi = 4(0.1) = \underline{0.4}$, $\sigma_r^2 = n\pi(1 - \pi) =$
   $4(0.1)(0.9) = 0.36$, and $\sigma_r = \sqrt{0.36} = 0.6$.

   For $n = 16$, $\mu_r = 16(0.1) = 1.6$, $\sigma_r^2 = 16(0.1)(0.9) = 1.44$, and
   $\sigma_r = 1.2$.

   For $n = 64$, $\mu_r = 6.4$ and $\sigma_r = 2.4$.

f.

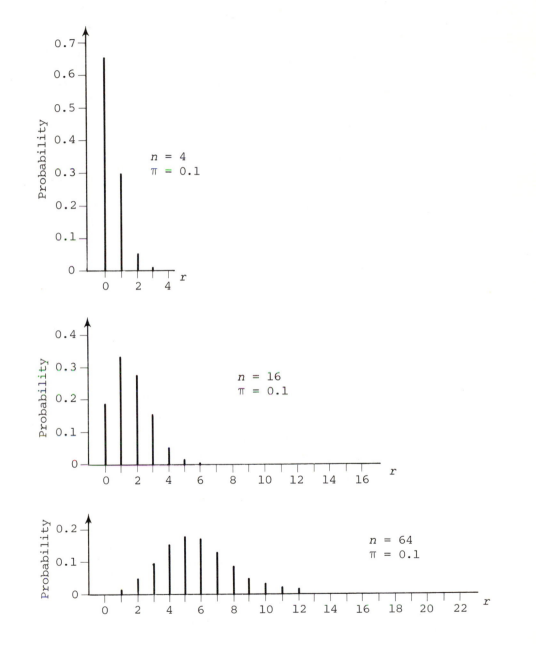

CHAPTER 6:   SOLUTIONS TO SELF-CORRECTING EXERCISES

6.1.a. Probability that X lies in a specified interval is the area under the density function within the specified interval.

   b. The area between 0 and 10 is $(1/10)(10 - 0) = 1$.   The total area under any density function must be 1.   This is equivalent to saying that if an experiment is performed, it must have some outcome.

   c. Each probability is found by computing the corresponding area. Since this density function has a rectangular shape, we may find the area by multiplying the height of the density function by the width of the interval.

   i. $P(1 \leq X \quad 4) = (1/10)(4 - 1) = 0.3$

   ii. $P(X \leq 4) = (1/10)(4 - 0) = 0.4$

   iii. $P(X \leq 1) = (1/10)(1 - 0) = 0.1$

   iv. $P(X \geq 4) = (1/10)(10 - 4) = 0.6$

   v. $P(0 \leq X \leq 10) = (1/10)(10 - 0) = 1$

   vi. $P(X \leq 10) = (1/10)(10 - 0) = 1$

   vii. $P(X \leq 0) = 0$

   d.   i. $P(1 \leq X \leq 4) \overset{?}{=} P(X \leq 4) - P(X \leq 1)$
   $$0.3 \overset{?}{=} 0.4 - 0.1, \text{ or } 0.3 = 0.3$$
   ii. $P(0 \leq X \leq 10) \overset{?}{=} P(X \leq 10) - P(X \leq 0)$
   $$1 \overset{?}{=} 1 - 0, \text{ or } 1 = 1$$
   iii. $P(X \geq 4) \overset{?}{=} 1 - P(X \leq 4)$
   $$0.6 \overset{?}{=} 1 - 0.4, \text{ or } 0.6 = 0.6$$

   Probabilities such as $P(X \leq 4)$ are known as cumulative probabilities and they may be used to compute probabilities such as the ones shown here.   The first two problems illustrate how to find the probability that X lies within an interval from the difference between cumulative probabilities at the end points of the interval. The third problem illustrates how a cumulative probability may be used to find the probability of a complement.

   e.   i. $P(3 \leq X \leq 4) = (1/10)(4 - 3) = 0.1$

   ii. $P(3.25 \leq X \leq 3.75) = (1/10)(3.75 - 3.25) = 0.05$

iii. $P(3.375 \leq X \leq 3.625) = (1/10)(3.625 - 3.375) = 0.025$

iv. $P(3.4375 \leq X \leq 3.5625) = (1/10)(3.5625 - 3.4375) = 0.0125$

f. As the interval around 3.5 is reduced, the area under the density function and the probability are both reduced. If the interval is reduced to zero width, the area and the probability become zero. Thus $P(X = 3.5) = 0$. For a continuous variable, the probability that X equals any given value must be zero because there is no area under the density function.

6.2.a. $P(Z \leq -1.5) = 0.0668$

b. $P(Z > 1.80) = 1 - P(Z \leq 1.80)$
$= 1 - 0.9641 = 0.0359$

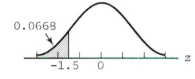

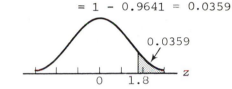

c. $P(1.2 \leq Z \leq 2.5) = P(Z \leq 2.5) - P(Z \leq 1.2)$
$= 0.9938 - 0.8849 = 0.1089$

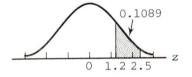

d. $P(Z \leq 1.28) = 0.8997$, or about 90th percentile

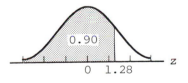

e. $P(Z \leq -1.64) = 0.0505$, or about 5th percentile

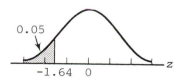

6.3. $\mu = 55$, $\sigma = 6$, normal distribution.

a. 1. $P(X < 52) = ?$

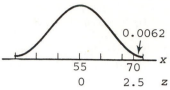

2. $z = \dfrac{52 - 55}{6} = -0.5$

3. $P(z < -0.5) = 0.3085$

   $P(X < 52) = 0.3085$

b. 1. $P(X > 70) = ?$

2. $z = \dfrac{70 - 55}{6} = 2.5$

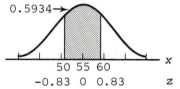

3. $P(z > 2.5) = 1 - P(z \leqq 2.5)$

   $\qquad\qquad = 1 - 0.9938$

   $\qquad\qquad = 0.062$

   $P(X > 70) = 0.0062$

c. 1. $P(50 \leqq X \leqq 60) = ?$

2. $z = \dfrac{50 - 55}{6} = -0.83$

   $z = \dfrac{60 - 55}{6} = 0.83$

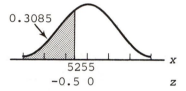

3. $P(-0.83 \leqq z \leqq 0.83)$

   $\qquad = P(z \leqq 0.83) - P(z \leqq -0.83)$

   $\qquad = 0.7967 - 0.2033$

   $\qquad = 0.5934$

   $P(50 \leqq X \leqq 60) = 0.5934$

d. 1. $P(X > 62.68)$

2. $z = \dfrac{62.68 - 55}{6} = 1.28$

3. $P(Z > 1.28) = 1 - P(Z < 1.28)$

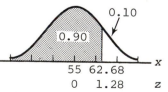

   $\qquad\qquad = 1 - 0.8997$

   $\qquad\qquad = 0.1003$

   $P(X > 62.68) = 0.1003,$

   or about the 10th percentile

6.4.a. The most direct approach is to read the values directly from Table B-3 in Appendix B-3. Table B-2 may also be used with the following results:

$z_{0.005}$ = -2.58 (or -2.57), $z_{0.010}$ = - 2.33, $z_{0.025}$ = -1.96, $z_{0.05}$ = -1.65, $z_{0.10}$ = -1.28, $z_{0.90}$ = 1.28, $z_{0.95}$ = 1.64, $z_{0.975}$ = 1.96, $z_{0.99}$ = 2.33, $z_{0.995}$ = 2.58 (or 2.57). When finding percentiles of the standard normal distribution, we use the z-value corresponding to the closest area. If the required area is one which falls exactly between two z values, then either z-value may be used. For example, $z_{0.0049}$ = -2.58 and $z_{0.0051}$ = -2.57. For $z_{0.0050}$, we could use either -2.58 or -2.57 and introduce very little error. In such cases, we shall use the first of the two values (2.58 and 1.64) as a matter of convenience.

The two approaches may give slightly different results due to rounding. In general, Table B-3 is more convenient for finding percentiles.

b.i.-ii. $z_{0.025}$ = -1.96 cuts off an area of 0.025 to its left and 0.975 to its right.

iii. $z_{0.975}$ = 1.96 cuts off an area of 0.975 to its left.

iv. $P(z_{0.01} \leq Z \leq z_{0.99})$ = 0.99 - 0.01 = 0.98

v. The area outside $z_{0.01} \leq z \leq z_{0.99}$ is 1 - 0.98 or 0.02.

vi. Note the area *outside* of the interval is 1 - 0.90 = 0.10. Because the interval is symmetric, 1/2 of the area outside of the required interval must be to the *right* and 1/2 must be to the *left*.   Thus, the required interval is $z_{0.05} \leq z \leq z_{0.95}$ or -1.64 $\leq z \leq$ 1.64.   We may verify that $P(z_{0.05} \leq Z \leq z_{0.95})$ = 0.95 - 0.05 = 0.90 as required. In problems of this type, we divide the area outside the interval into two equal parts and find the corresponding values of z. Thus, 0.10/2 = 0.05 and the corresponding values of z are $z_{0.05}$ =-1.645 and $z_{0.95}$ (which has 0.05 to its right) = +1.645.

vii. Using the same reasoning as in (vi), 0.01/2 = 0.005. The interval is $z_{0.005} \leq z \leq z_{0.995}$ or -2.58 $\leq z \leq$ 2.58.

viii. 0.05/2 = 0.025, $z_{0.025} \leq z \leq z_{0.975}$, or -1.96 $\leq z \leq$ 1.96

c. i. The area outside the interval is $1 - 0.4514 = 0.5486$, half of which is to be in each tail. Thus, we seek $x_{0.2743}$ and $x_{0.7257}$.

1. $x_{0.2743} = ?$

   $x_{0.7257} = ?$

   $z_{0.2743} = ?$

   $z_{0.7257} = ?$

2. $z_{0.2743} = -0.61$

   $z_{0.7257} = 0.61$

   (from Table B-3).

3. $x_{0.2743} = \mu + z_{0.2753}\ (\sigma)$

   $\phantom{x_{0.2743}} = 40 + (-0.6)(5) = 37$ thousand miles

   $x_{0.7257} = 40 + (0.6)(5) = 43$ thousand miles

ii. 1. $x_{0.25} = ?$

   $z_{0.25} = ?$

   2. $z_{0.25} = -0.67$

   3. $x_{0.25} = \mu + z_{0.25}(\sigma)$

   $\phantom{x_{0.25}} = 40 + (-0.67)(5)$

   $\phantom{x_{0.25}} = 36.65$ thousand miles

iii. 1. $x_{0.80} = ?$

   $z_{0.80} = ?$

   2. $z_{0.80} = 0.84$

   3. $z_{0.80} = \mu + z_{0.80}(\sigma)$

   $\phantom{z_{0.80}} = 40 + 0.84(5)$

   $\phantom{z_{0.80}} = 44.2$ thousand miles

iv. 1. $x_{0.008} = ?$

   $z_{0.008} = ?$

   $z_{0.008} = -2.4$

   $x_{0.008} = \mu + z_{0.008}(\sigma)$

   $\phantom{x_{0.008}} = 40 + (-2.41)(5)$

   $\phantom{x_{0.008}} = 28$ thousand miles

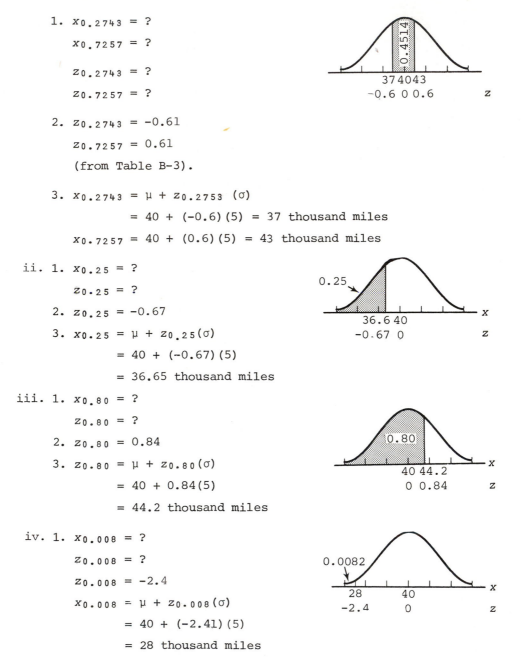

6.5.a. For $\pi = 0.5$ and $n - 16$, $\mu_r = n\pi = 16(0.05) = 8$. $\sigma_r = \sqrt{n\pi(1 - \pi)}$
$= \sqrt{16(0.5)(1 - 0.5)} = \sqrt{4} = 2$.

  i. For the probability of an individual value of r, find
     z-values corresponding to $r + 0.5$ and $r - 0.5$.   Then find

$$z_U = \frac{(r + 0.5) - \mu r}{\sigma_r}$$

$$z_L = \frac{(r - 0.5) - \mu r}{\sigma_r}$$

For $r = 9$, $z_U = \dfrac{[(9 + 0.5) - 8]}{2} = 0.75$ and $z_L =$

$\dfrac{[(9 - 0.5) - 8]}{2} = 0.25$. $P(R = 9) = P(Z \leq 0.75) - P(Z \leq 0.25)$
$= 0.7734 - 0.5987 = 0.1747$. $P(R = 9) = 0.1747$.   Thus, the
exact binomial probability is approximately equal to the
probability "slice" centered at $r = 9$ and extending from
$9 - 0.5$ to $9 + 0.5$ on the normal distribution having
$\mu_r = 8$ and $\sigma_r = 2$.

  ii. For $r = 4$, $z_U = \dfrac{[(4 + 0.5) - 8]}{2} = -1.75$ and

$z_L = \dfrac{[(4 - 0.5) - 8]}{2} = -2.25$. $P(R = 4) = P(Z \leq -1.75)$
$- P(Z \leq -2.25) = 0.0401 - 0.0122 = 0.0279$.

  iii. $P(R \leq 6) = P\left(Z \leq \dfrac{(6 + 0.5) - 8}{2}\right) = P(Z \leq -0.75) = 0.2266$

  iv. $P(R \geq 4) = 1 - P(R \leq 3)$

$P(R \leq 3) = P\left(Z \leq \dfrac{(3 + 0.5) - 8}{2}\right) = P(Z \leq -2.25) = 0.0122$

$P(R \geq 4) = 1 - 0.0122 = 0.9878$

 b. $P(R = 9 | n = 16, \pi = 0.5) = 0.1746$ (binomial table)
    $P(R = 4 | n = 16, \pi = 0.5) = 0.0278$ (bimonial table)

CHAPTER 7:   SOLUTIONS TO SELF-CORRECTING EXERCISES

7.1.a. All units in the population are numbered from 1 to N where N is the number of units in the population. A collection of n numbers in the interval 1 to N is taken from the table of random numbers. The numbers selected from the table are the numbers that identify the units of observation which are to be included in the sample.

b.

Random Number	Apartment Number Selected	Income (x)	Random Number	Apartment Number Selected	Income (x)
10	(10)	5	09	(9)	8
37	*		91	*	
08	(8)	8	80	*	
99	*		44	*	
12	(12)	14	12	+	
66	*		63	*	
31	*		61	*	
85	*		15	(15)	5
63	*		94	*	
73	*		42	*	
98	*		23	*	
11	(11)	12	04	(4)	4
83	*		00	*	
88	*		35	*	
99	*		59	*	
65	*		46	*	
80	*		32	*	
74	*		69	*	
69	*		19	(19)	12

* Random number outside the interval of 1 to 20.
+ Random number used before.

Note that the process stops after 8 observations are taken.

c. The sampling is done without replacement. Notice the random number 12 appears twice in (b). By disregarding the random number 12 the second time it appears, we assure that apartment 12 will not appear twice in the sample. Thus sampling is without replacement.

d. $\bar{x}$ = (5 + 8 + 14 + 12 + 8 + 5 + 4 + 12)/8 = 68/8 = 8.5

e. Almost anything except going back to the original starting point. You could read up the second column, or down the second column, or down the twelfth column, and so on. The idea is to maintain the randomness of the selection process.

f. i. False. Two persons acting independently would, with high probability, select different random numbers from the table.

   ii. False. The idea of a random number table is to be random. Starting in the same place and counting in the same way will always produce the same sample, which cannot be random.

7.2.a. Without replacement.

b. $\mu = 9.1$, $\sigma = 3.0$

c. $\mu_{\overline{x}} = 9.1$; $\sigma_{\overline{x}} = \sqrt{\dfrac{N - n}{N - 1}}\ \dfrac{\sigma}{\sqrt{n}} = \sqrt{\dfrac{20 - 8}{20 - 1}}\ \dfrac{3.0}{\sqrt{8}}\quad \sqrt{0.631}\ \dfrac{3.0}{\sqrt{8}}$

$= 0.795\,(1.061)$; $\sigma_{\overline{x}} = 0.843$

d. For $n = 16$, $\mu_{\overline{x}} = 9.1$ and $\sigma_{\overline{x}} = 0.459(0.75) = 0.344$.

For $n = 4$, $\mu_{\overline{x}} = 9.1$ and $\sigma_{\overline{x}} = 0.918(1.5) = 1.376$.

e. For sampling with replacement, the finite population correction factor is not needed. Thus for $n = 4$, $\mu_{\overline{x}} = 9.1$ and $\sigma_{\overline{x}} = \sigma/\sqrt{n}$ $= 3.0/\sqrt{4} = 1.5$; for $n = 8$, $\mu_{\overline{x}} = 9.1$ and $\sigma_{\overline{x}} = 3.0/\sqrt{8} = 1.061$; for $n = 16$, $\mu_{\overline{x}} = 9.1$ and $\sigma_{\overline{x}} = 3.00/\sqrt{16} = 0.75$.

f. Part e shows the influence of n in the computation of the standard error. As n increases, the standard error becomes smaller. This result holds whether the sampling is with or without replacement. Sampling without replacement always produces a smaller standard error than sampling with replacement for any fixed value of n. Notice $\sigma_{\overline{x}} = 0$ if $n = N$ and sampling is without replacement. Regardless of the sampling method, the mean of the sampling distribution $(\mu_{\overline{x}})$ is always equal to the mean of the population (μ).

g. The two are not equal. We would expect them to be equal very rarely.

7.3.a.

x	$P(x)$
2	1/4
4	1/4
6	1/4
8	1/4

$\mu = \Sigma[x * P(x)] = \dfrac{2 + 4 + 6 + 8}{4} = 5$

$\sigma^2 = \Sigma[(x - \mu)^2 * P(x)]$

$= \dfrac{(2 - 5)^2 + (4 - 5)^2 + (6 - 5)^2 + (8 - 5)^2}{4} = 5$

b.

Sample	$\bar{x}$	Sample	$\bar{x}$
6,2	(6+2)/2 = 4	8,2	5
6,4	5	8,4	6
6,6	6	8,6	7
6,8	7	8,8	8

c.-d.

$\bar{x}$	$f(\bar{x})$	$\bar{x}$	$P(\bar{x})$	$\bar{x}*P(\bar{x})$	$(\bar{x})^2 P(\bar{x})$
2	1	2	1/16	2/16	4/16
3	2	3	2/16	6/16	18/16
4	3	4	3/16	12/16	48/16
5	4	5	4/16	20/16	100/16
6	3	6	3/16	18/16	108/16
7	2	7	2/16	14/16	98/16
8	1	8	1/16	8/16	64/16
	16			$E(\bar{x})$ = 80/16	$E(\bar{x}^2)$ = 440/16

$$\mu_{\bar{x}} = E(\bar{x}) = 80/16 = 5; \quad \sigma_{\bar{x}}^2 = E(\bar{x}^2) - (\mu_{\bar{x}})^2 = 440/16 - (5)^2$$

$$= 27.5 - 25 = 2.5; \quad \sigma_{\bar{x}} = \sqrt{2.5} = 1.58.$$

e. $\mu_{\bar{x}} = \mu$ and $\sigma_{\bar{x}}^2 = \sigma^2/n$. From (a), $\mu = 5$ and $\sigma^2 = 5$. Thus

$\mu_{\bar{x}} = 5$, $\sigma_{\bar{x}}^2 = 5/2 = 2.5$, and $\sigma_{\bar{x}} = 1.58$. These are the same

results obtained in the computations based on the probability
distribution of the sample means in (d).

f. If sampling is without replacement, the samples (2, 2), (4, 4),
   (6, 6), and (8, 8) are not possible. The distribution of sample
   means is as follows.

$\bar{x}$	$f(\bar{x})$	$\bar{X}$	$P(\bar{x})$
3	2	3	2/12
4	2	4	2/12
5	4	5	4/12
6	2	6	2/12
7	2	7	2/12
	12		

g. $\mu_{\bar{x}} = \Sigma[\bar{x} * P(\bar{x})]$; $\sigma_{\bar{x}}^2 = E(\bar{X})^2 - (\mu_{\bar{x}})^2$.

$\bar{x}$	$P(\bar{x})$	$\bar{x} * P(\bar{x})$	$(\bar{x})^2 P(\bar{x})$
3	2/12	6/12	18/12
4	2/12	8/12	32/12
5	4/12	20/12	100/12
6	2/12	12/12	72/12
7	2/12	14/12	98/12
		60/12	320/12

$\mu_{\overline{x}} = 60/12 = 5$; $\sigma_{\overline{x}}^2 = E(\overline{X})^2 - (\mu_{\overline{x}})^2 = 320/12 - (5)^2 = 26.67 - 25$
= 1.67; $\sigma_{\overline{x}} = 1.29$.

Sampling with replacement (see Part d) produces the same value of $\mu_{\overline{x}}$ but a larger value for $\sigma_{\overline{x}}$.

h. $\mu_{\overline{x}} = \mu = 5$; $\sigma_{\overline{x}} = \sqrt{\dfrac{N-n}{N-1}} \ \dfrac{\sigma}{\sqrt{n}} = \sqrt{\dfrac{4-2}{4-1}} \ \dfrac{\sqrt{5}}{\sqrt{2}} = (0.816)\ (1.58) = 1.29$.

The results are the same as those obtained directly from the distribution of sample means in (g).

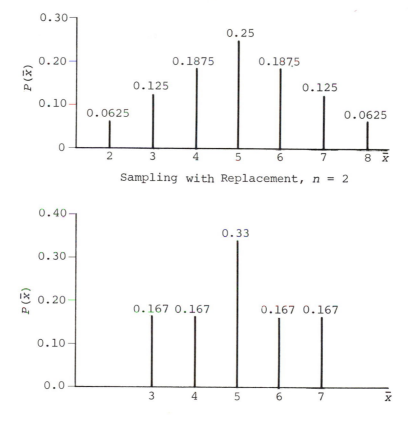

Sampling with Replacement, $n = 2$

Sampling without Replacement, $n = 2$

7.4. a.

$\bar{x}$	$P(\bar{x})$
2.00	1/64
2.67	3/64
3.33	6/64
4.00	10/64
4.67	12/64
5.33	12/64
6.00	10/64
6.67	6/64
7.33	3/64
8.00	1/64

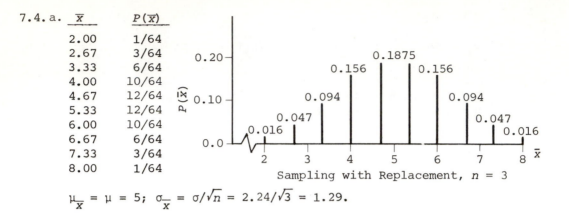

$$\mu_{\bar{x}} = \mu = 5; \quad \sigma_{\bar{x}} = \sigma/\sqrt{n} = 2.24/\sqrt{3} = 1.29.$$

b. The samples that are possible if sampling is without replacement are listed here:

$\bar{x}$	$P(\bar{x})$
4.00	6/24
4.67	6/24
5.33	6/24
6.00	6/24

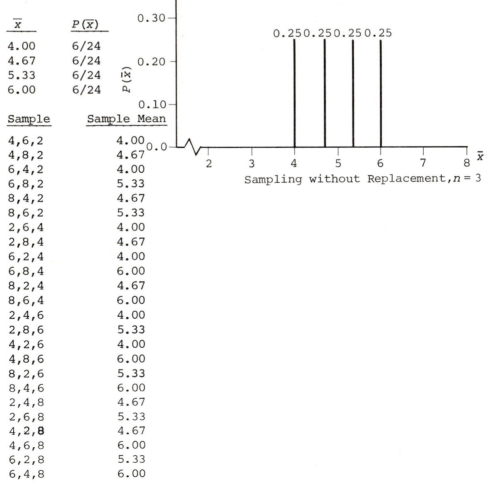

Sample	Sample Mean
4,6,2	4.00
4,8,2	4.67
6,4,2	4.00
6,8,2	5.33
8,4,2	4.67
8,6,2	5.33
2,6,4	4.00
2,8,4	4.67
6,2,4	4.00
6,8,4	6.00
8,2,4	4.67
8,6,4	6.00
2,4,6	4.00
2,8,6	5.33
4,2,6	4.00
4,8,6	6.00
8,2,6	5.33
8,4,6	6.00
2,4,8	4.67
2,6,8	5.33
4,2,8	4.67
4,6,8	6.00
6,2,8	5.33
6,4,8	6.00

$$\mu_{\overline{X}} = \mu = 5; \quad \sigma_{\overline{X}} = \sqrt{\frac{N-n}{N-1}} \ \frac{\sigma}{\sqrt{n}} = \sqrt{\frac{4-3}{4-1}} \ \frac{\sqrt{5}}{\sqrt{3}} \doteq 0.577 \ (1.29) = 0.744.$$

c. For a fixed sample size, sampling without replacement reduces the standard error (from 1.29 to 0.74 in our example). The graphs for (a) and (b) show the wider dispersion for sampling with replacement.

d. For a sample of four observations without replacement, only one sample is possible: 2,4,6,8, with mean $\overline{X} = 5$. Since the entire population is exhausted in 4 draws, there is only one sample mean and the standard error is zero. Note the finite population correction factor is zero. If the sampling were done with replacement, several sample means would be possible and the standard error would be $\sigma_{\overline{X}} = \sigma/\sqrt{n} = \sqrt{5}/\sqrt{4} = 1.12$.

e. A larger sample size always produces a smaller standard error. This results whether sampling is with or without replacement. If sampling is without replacement, a given sample size will produce a value for the finite population correction factor which is less than 1.0. This causes the standard error for sampling without replacement to be smaller than the corresponding standard error for sampling with replacement.

f. The sample size has no influence on the mean of the sampling distribution.

7.5.a. $\overline{X} = 2130/4 = 532.5$. An infinite number of sample means are possible.

b. $\mu_{\overline{X}} = \mu = 500; \quad \sigma_{\overline{X}} = \sigma/\sqrt{n} = 100/\sqrt{4} = 50$

c.

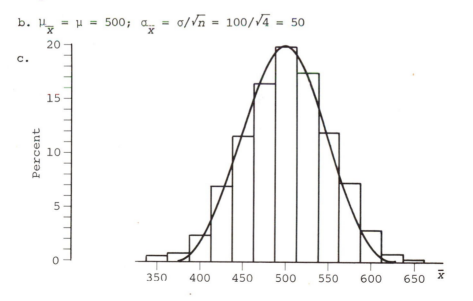

    d. The distribution appears to be normal. Sampling theory says that
the distribution of sample means will be exactly normal if the
population is normally distributed. (Since the histogram is based
on 1000 samples rather than an infinite number of samples, the
histogram is only an approximation to the sampling distribution.)
Sampling theory tells us the sampling distribution of the mean for
a normal population will always be normally distributed regardless
of sample size.

7.6.a. $\overline{X}$ = (0.90 + 1.10 + 1.21 + 0.86)/4 = 4.07/4 = 1.02; this is one of
an infinite number of possible sample means.

    b. $\mu_{\overline{X}} = \mu = 1$, $\sigma_{\overline{X}} = \sigma/\sqrt{n} = 1/\sqrt{4} = 0.5$

    c. The sample means do not seem to be normally distributed. The
distribution is more nearly like the parent population.

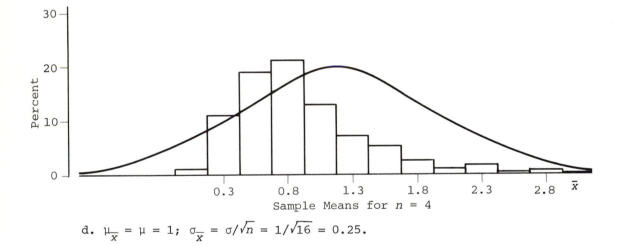

Sample Means for n = 4

    d. $\mu_{\overline{X}} = \mu = 1$; $\sigma_{\overline{X}} = \sigma/\sqrt{n} = 1/\sqrt{16} = 0.25$.

e. The distribution is still positively skewed but is closer to a normal distribution than the distribution of $\bar{X}$ for $n = 4$.

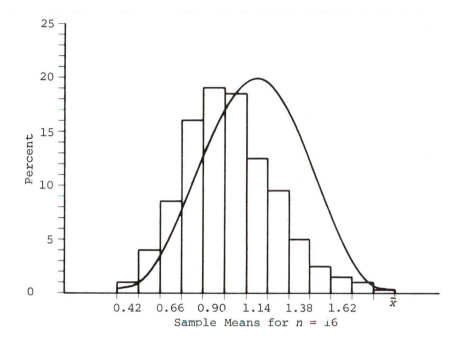

f. $\mu_{\bar{x}} = \mu = 1$; $\sigma_{\bar{x}} = \sigma/\sqrt{n} = 1/\sqrt{64} = 0.125$; the distribution is very nearly normal.

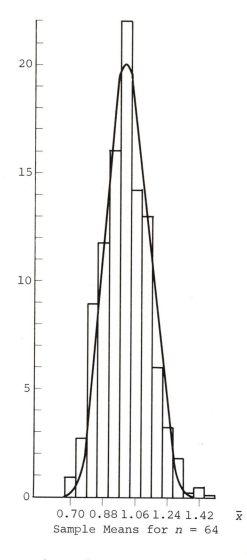

Sample Means for $n = 64$

g. The samples were drawn from a nonnormal population with heavy positive skewness. As the sample size is increased, the distribution of sample means becomes more nearly normally distributed. This is because of the central limit theorem.

7.7.a-c. For $n = 9$, $\mu_{\bar{X}} = 15$, $\sigma_{\bar{X}} = 2/3$; for $n = 36$, $\mu_{\bar{X}} = 15$, $\sigma_{\bar{X}} = 1/3$; for the population, $\mu = 15$ and $\sigma = 2$.

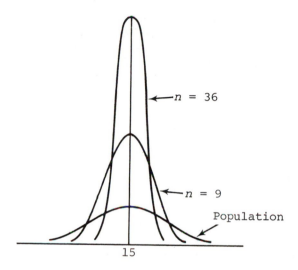

7.8.a. $P(X > 16) = P(Z > \dfrac{16 - 15}{2}) = P(Z > 0.5) = 1 - 0.6915$;

$P(X > 16) = 0.3085$

b. For $n = 9$, $\mu_{\bar{X}} = 15$, $\sigma_{\bar{X}} = 2/3$;

$P(\bar{X} > 16) = P(X > \dfrac{16 - 15}{2/3}) = P(Z > 1.5) = 1 - 0.9332$;

$P(\bar{X} > 16) = 0.0668$.

c. For $n = 36$, $\mu_{\bar{X}} = 15$, $\sigma_{\bar{X}} = 1/3$;

$P(\bar{X} > 16) = P(Z > \dfrac{16 - 15}{1/3}) = P(Z > 3.0) = 1 - 0.9987$;

$P(\bar{X} > 16) = 0.0013$.

d. The problem requires us to find two values of Z that correspond to points on the $\bar{X}$-axis which are \$0.50 below and \$0.50 above the mean. For the lower Z-value,

$$z_L = \frac{\bar{X} - \mu_X}{\sigma_X} = \frac{-0.5}{2/3} = -0.75$$

For the upper Z-value,

$$z_U = \frac{\bar{X} - \mu_{\bar{X}}}{\sigma_{\bar{X}}} = \frac{0.5}{2/3} = 0.75$$

Thus we seek $P(-0.75 \leq Z \leq 0.75) = 0.7734 - 0.2266 = 0.5468$.

e. For z_L, $z_L = \dfrac{-0.5}{1/3} = -1.5$.   For z_U, $z_U = \dfrac{0.5}{1/3} = 1.5$.

Thus, we evaluate $(-1.5 \le Z \le 1.5) = 0.9332 - 0.0668 = 0.8664$.

Note: Table B-3 rounds z-values to two decimal places. For some situations such as $z_{0.95}$ a third decimal place is justified. In this case, $z_{0.95} = 1.645$. Using the value 1.65 from Table B-3 may change the numerical results slightly in the second decimal place. Such differences are not serious.

7.9.a. $\mu_{\bar{x}} = 15$, $\sigma_{\bar{x}} = 2/3$; $z_{0.95} = 1.64$; $\bar{x}_{0.95} = \mu_{\bar{x}} + z_{0.95}\,\sigma_{\bar{x}}$

$= 15 + 1.645(2/3) = 15 + 1.10$

$\bar{x}_{0.95} = \$16.10$

$z_{0.99} = 2.33$

$\bar{x}_{0.99} = 15 + 2.33\,(2/3) = 15 + 1.55 = \$16.55$

b. $\bar{x}_{0.95} = 15 + 1.645(1/3) = 15 + 0.55 = \$15.55$

$\bar{x}_{0.99} = 15 + 2.33(1/3) = 15 + 0.78 = \$15.78$

7.10.a. $\mu_{\bar{x}} = \mu = 100$, $\sigma_{\bar{x}}^2 = \sigma^2/n = (10)^2/25 = 4$, $\sigma_{\bar{x}} = \sqrt{4} = 2$

b. In these exercises, it is necessary to solve the relationship $z = (x - \mu_{\bar{x}})/\sigma_{\bar{x}}$ for $\bar{x}$. Thus $z\sigma_{\bar{x}} = \bar{x} - \mu_{\bar{x}}$ and $\bar{x} = \mu_{\bar{x}} + z\sigma_{\bar{x}}$.

i. $\bar{x}_{0.025} = \mu_{\bar{x}} + z_{0.025}\sigma_{\bar{x}} = 100 + (-1.96)(2) = 96.08$

ii. $\bar{x} = 96.08$ also cuts off an area of 01975 to its right.

iii. $\bar{x}_{0.975} = \mu_{\bar{x}} + z_{0.975}\sigma_{\bar{x}} = 100 + (1.96)(2) = 103.92$

iv. $P(\bar{x}_{0.01} \le \bar{X} \le \bar{x}_{0.99}) = 0.99 - 0.01 = 0.98$

v. The area outside this interval is $1 - 0.98 = 0.02$.

vi. $\bar{x}_{0.95} = \mu_{\bar{x}} + z_{0.95}\sigma_{\bar{x}} = 100 + (1.645)(2) = 103.29$.

$x_{0.05} = \mu_{\bar{x}} + z_{0.05}\sigma_{\bar{x}} = 100 + (-1.645)(2) = 96.71$

Thus the interval $\bar{x}_{0.05} \le \bar{x} \le \bar{x}_{0.95}$, or $96.71 \le \bar{x} \le 103.29$ is a symmetric interval around $\mu_{\bar{x}} = 100$, which contains 90% of all sample means.

vii. $\bar{x}_{0.995} = \mu_{\bar{x}} + z_{0\ 995}(\sigma_{\bar{x}}) = 100 + (2.58)(2) = 105.16$

$\bar{x}_{0.005} = \mu_{\bar{x}} + z_{0\ 005}(\sigma_{\bar{x}}) = 100 + (-2.58)(2) = 94.84$

viii. $\bar{x}_{0.975} = \mu_{\bar{x}} + z_{0\ 975}(\sigma_{\bar{x}}) = 100 + (1.96)(2) = 103.92$

$\bar{x}_{0.025} = \mu_{\bar{x}} + z_{0\ 025}(\sigma_{\bar{x}}) = 100 + (-1.96)(2) = 96.08$

c. The first statement has very little chance of being true. The second statement is always true. If you were to take 25 observations from the given population and compute $\bar{x}$ from these observations, the result is likely to be some value near, but not equal to, $\mu_{\bar{x}} = 100$. For example, Part vi of Exercise 4.10b shows we should find 90% of all sample means in the interval $96.72 \leq \bar{x} \leq 103.28$. If, on the other hand, you took a very large number of samples, each with 25 observations, and averaged all of the $\bar{x}$'s, you would find this average to be 100 (that is, $\mu_{\bar{x}}$).

7.11.a. In a given binomial distribution, n is the largest possible value of r. In this case, $n = 3$.

b.

p	$P(p)$
0	8/27
1/3	12/27
2/3	6/27
1	1/27

Each value of p is found by dividing the corresponding value of r by n. For $r = 2$, $p = 2/3$. The largest value of p is 1 and the smallest is 0. This will always be the case for every binomial distribution of the proportion.

c. Both are binomial distributions from a Bernoulli random variable having $\pi = 1/3$ and based on $n = 3$. The probabilities of corresponding values of p and r are the same. For example, $P(R = 2) = P(P = 2/3) = 6/27$. The major difference is the random variable. For the binomial distribution, the variable is the *total number* of successes. For the sampling distribution of the proportion, the variable is the *proportion* of successes.

d. The two distributions have different means and variances because the variables are different.

e.

r	Binomial $P(r)$	$r * P(r)$	p	Proportion $P(p)$	$p * P(p)$
0	8/27	0/27	0	8/27	0/81
1	12/27	12/27	1/3	12/27	12/81
2	6/27	12/27	2/3	6/27	12/81
3	1/27	3/27	3/3	1/27	3/81
		$\mu = 27/27 = 1$			$\mu_p = 27/81 = 1/3$

f. $\mu = n\pi = 3(1/3) = 1$, $\mu_p = \pi = 1/3$

g. $\sigma^2 = n\pi(1 - \pi) = 3(1/3)(2/3) = 2/3; \ \sigma = \sqrt{2/3} = 0.816;$

$\sigma_P^2 = \dfrac{\pi(1 - \pi)}{n} = \dfrac{(1/3)(2/3)}{3} = \dfrac{2}{27}; \ \sigma_P = \sqrt{\dfrac{2}{27}} = 0.272$

h. For $n = 49$, the binomial parameters are $\mu = n\pi = (49)(1/3) = 16.33$, $\sigma^2 = n\pi(1 - \pi) = 49(1/3)(2/3) = 10.89, \ \sigma = \sqrt{10.89} = 3.3.$ For proportions, $\mu_P = \pi = 1/3, \ \sigma_P^2 = \dfrac{\pi(1 - \pi)}{n} = \dfrac{(1/3)(2/3)}{49} = 0.00454,$
$\sigma_P = \sqrt{0.00454} = 0.0674.$ Note that all parameters are influenced
by the value of n except μ_P.

i. $P(R = 1) = P(P = 1/3) = 12/27.$ The probabilities are equal
because the events are the same.   Thus $r = 1$ is assigned when
one call is successful and $p = 1/3$ is assigned when one call
is successful.

7.12.a. $\mu_p = \pi = 1/4;$

$\sigma_p^2 = \dfrac{\pi(1 - \pi)}{n} = \dfrac{(1/4)(3/4)}{300} = 0.000625; \ \sigma_p = 0.025.$

b. Yes. $n\pi/(1 - \pi) = 300(0.25)/0.75 = 100$ and $n(1 - \pi)/\pi$
$= 300(0.75)/0.25 = 900.$ Both quantities exceed 9, which is a
requirement for using the normal approximation.

c. $z = \dfrac{p + 0.5/n - \mu_p}{\sigma_P} = \dfrac{0.20 + 0.5/300 - 0.25}{0.025} = -1.93.$

$P(P \le 0.2) = P(Z \le -1.93) = 0.0268.$

d. $z = \dfrac{p - \mu_p}{\sigma_p} = \dfrac{0.20 - 0.25}{0.025} = -2.00; \ P(P \le 0.2) = P(Z \le -2.00)$
$= 0.0228.$ The two answers differ slightly.   For small values
of n, it is wise to include the correction factor.

e. $\mu = n\pi = 300(0.25) = 75; \ \sigma^2 = n\pi(1 - \pi) = 300(0.25)(0.75) = 56.25;$
$\sigma = 7.5$

f. $P(R \le 60) = P(Z \le \dfrac{60.5 - 75}{7.5}) = P(Z \le -1.93) = 0.0268$

g. The answers are the same because the events are the same.   For
$n = 300$, the event $r \le 60$ is the same as the event $p \le 60/300$ or
$p \le 0.20.$ Thus the probabilities must be equal.

CHAPTER 8:   SOLUTIONS TO SELF-CORRECTING EXERCISES

8.1.a. i. The sample mean because its sampling distribution has the smaller standard deviation; thus, the sample mean is more efficient than the sample median.

ii. Unbiasedness because $E(\overline{X}) = \mu$ and $E(Md) = \mu$.

8.2.a. $\mu = 1$, $\sigma^2 = [(0 - 1)^2 + (1 - 1)^2 + (2 - 1)^2]/3 = 2/3$

b.

Sample values			Values of $\overline{X}$			Values of s^2		
1,0	1,1	1,2	0.5	1	1.5	0.5*	0	0.5

c.

$\overline{x}$	$P(\overline{x})$
0	1/9
0.5	2/9
1.0	3/9
1.5	2/9
2.0	1/9

$E(\overline{X}) = 0(1/9) + 0.5(2/9) + 1.0(3/9) + 1.5(2/9) + 2.0(1/9) = 1$

s^2	$P(s^2)$
0	3/9
0.5	4/9
2	2/9

$E(s^2) = 0(3/9) + 0.5(4/9) + 2/(/9) = 2/3$

d. Since $E(\overline{X}) = \mu$ and $E(s^2) = \sigma^2$, both estimators are unbiased.

e. $S^2 = [(2 - 1.5)^2 + (1 - 1.5)^2]/2 = 0.25$

f. $E(S^2) = 0(3/9) + 0.25(4/9) + 1(2/9) = 1/3$

g. Bias $= E(S^2) - \sigma^2 = 1/3 - 2/3 = -1/3$

h. Using $s^2 = \Sigma(X - \overline{X})^2/(n - 1)$ produces an unbiased estimate of σ^2.

---

*for the values 1,0, $s^2 = [(1 - 0.5)^2 + (0 - 0.5)^2]/(2 - 1) = 0.5$.

8.3.a. $\overline{X}$ = (100 + 150 + 50)/3 = 300/3 = 100;

s^2 = [(100 - 100)^2 + (150 - 100)^2 + (50 - 100)^2]/(3 - 1)

= 5000/2 = 2500

b. p = 75/250 = 0.3

8.4.a. The unbiased point estimate of the population mean is $\overline{x}$. From the data, $\overline{x}$ = $\Sigma x/n$ = 40.3/4 = 10.075 ft.

b. $\sigma_{\overline{x}}$ = $\sigma/\sqrt{n}$ = 0.6/$\sqrt{4}$ = 0.3 ft.

c. 1 - α = 0.95, α = 0.05, $\alpha/2$ = 0.025, $z_{0.025}$ = 1.96 (see Appendix B-3); $\overline{X} \pm Z * \sigma_{\overline{X}}$ = 10.075 $\pm$ 1.96(0.3) = 10.075 $\pm$ 0.588;

The 0.95 confidence interval estimate of the population mean is 9.487 to 10.663 ft.

d. The population mean (μ) is unknown and it is unlikely that its value is 10.075. The confidence interval estimate found in (c) gives an interval within which we have a high degree of confidence (0.95) of finding the true population mean. By measuring the length of every bar cut by this machine, the inspector could find the actual population mean; however, it is likely that such a procedure would be too expensive (or time consuming) in practice.

e. The point estimate of the population mean (10.075) gives us only a single numerical estimate for which we have no measurable confidence. The confidence interval removes this deficiency and is generally more useful.

f. The mistake is in using the standard deviation of the population (σ) rather than the standard error of the mean ($\sigma_{\overline{x}}$). The standard error gives information regarding the dispersion of sample means   the distribution of sample means is the basis of confidence interval estimates.

g. $z\sigma_{\overline{x}}$ = 1.96(0.3) = 0.588. For n = 16, $\sigma_{\overline{x}}$ = 0.6/$\sqrt{16}$ = 0.15 and $z\sigma_{\overline{x}}$ = 1.96(0.15) = 0.294.

h. For a 0.90 confidence coefficient and n = 4, z = 1.645 and $z\sigma_{\overline{x}}$ = 1.645(0.3) = 0.4935.

i. For a fixed confidence coefficient, the interval decreases as n increases. For a fixed n, increasing the confidence coefficient increases the interval width.

8.5.a. 1 − α = 0.9545. α = 0.0455, α/2 = 0.0228, $z_{0.0228}$ = 2. $\sigma_{\overline{X}} = \sigma/\sqrt{n}$

= 3/$\sqrt{144}$ = 3/12 = $0.25. From the 144 observations, $\overline{x}$ = $7.50.

$\overline{X} \pm z\sigma_{\overline{X}}$ = 7.50 ± 2(0.25) = 7.50 ± 0.50. The 0.9545 confidence

interval is $7.00 to $8.00.

b. Although the population is skewed, a large sample size allows us
to say (because of the central limit theorem) that the distribution of the sample mean is essentially normal.

c. For populations that are not normally distributed, we usually
need at least 30 observations before the normal distribution is
a good approximation for the distribution of sample means. Thus,
10 observations would not be enough to make the procedure valid.
The auditor would have to increase the number of observations to
at least 30.

8.6.a. Since 144/1000 = 0.144 is more than 10% of the population, we
should adjust the standard error by the finite population correction factor. The correct formula is

$$\overline{X} \pm z\,\frac{\sigma}{\sqrt{n}}\,\sqrt{\frac{N-n}{N-1}}$$

Because $\overline{X}$ = 7.50, z = 2, $\sigma_{\overline{X}}$ = 3/$\sqrt{144}$ = 0.25, and $\sqrt{\dfrac{1000-144}{1000-1}}$

= 0.9257, we have 7.50 ± 2(0.25)(0.9257) or 7.50 ± 0.46.

b. The confidence interval in this exercise is narrower than the one
found in Part a of Question 8.5. In this question, we assume a
relatively large sample from a small population. In Question 8.5,
we assumed a relatively small sample from a large population.
As more of the population is drawn into the sample, more is known
about the population, the finite population correction factor
becomes smaller, and the confidence interval width decreases.

8.7.a. Sample 1: $\overline{X}$ = 546.7; Sample 2: $\overline{X}$ = 483.3; an infinite number of
sample means are possible.

b. Sample 1: z = (546.7 − 500)/(100/$\sqrt{3}$) = 46.7/57.7 = 0.81;
Sample 2: z = (483.3 − 500)/57.7 = −0.29; an infinite number
of standard scores are possible.

c.

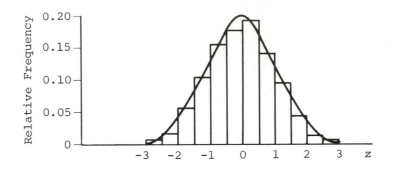

d. The data appear to be normally distributed. (If more sample means were used along with a smaller class interval width, the normality of the sample means would become clear.) The result is in accordance with sampling theory which indicates the distribution of sample means from a normal population with a known value of σ will be normally distributed.

e. For sample 1: $\overline{X} = 546.7$; $s^2 = [(480 - 546.7)^2 + (610 - 546.7)^2 + (550 - 546.7)^2]/(3 - 1) = 4233.3$; $s = 65.1$; $t = (546.7 - 500)/(65.1/\sqrt{3}) = 1.24$. For sample 2: $\overline{X} = 483.3$, $s^2 = 3033.3$, $s = 55.1$, $t = -0.52$.

f. The standardized scores are not the same because we estimate the population standard deviation (s) from the sample when σ is unknown. Each standard score has two sources of variability that arise from the values in the sample--the sample mean and the sample standard deviation.

g. The distribution of sample means becomes more dispersed when the population mean is unknown and must be estimated from the sample data.

h. The curve is more dispersed than the standard normal. The distribution is a t-distribution with 2 df.

i. The standardized distribution will be a t-distribution under these circumstances.

j. For $n = 4$, a t-distribution with 3 df would result and for $n = 100$, a t-distribution with 99 df would result. As the sample size and degrees of freedom are increased, more accurate estimates of σ are obtained; consequently, the dispersion in the t-distribution decreases.

8.8.a. From **the** fifth line of Table B-4:

$$
\begin{aligned}
t_{0.005} &= -4.0322 \\
t_{0.01} &= -3.3649 \\
t_{0.025} &= -2.5706 \\
t_{0.05} &= -2.0150 \\
t_{0.10} &= -1.4759 \\
t_{0.90} &= 1.4759 \\
t_{0.95} &= 2.0150 \\
t_{0.975} &= 2.5706 \\
t_{0.99} &= 3.3649 \\
t_{0.995} &= 4.0322
\end{aligned}
$$

b. This value for a t-distribution with 6 degrees of freedom is 1.9432. This is slightly smaller than the corresponding value (2.0150) for a t-distribution with 5 degrees of freedom. The reason for the decrease is that the variance of the t-distribution decreases as the degrees of freedom increase.

c. The subscript refers to the proportion of the t-distribution which is to the *left* of the given value. Thus $t_{0.01} = -3.3649$ means the area to the left of -3.3649 is 0.01. The area to the left of 3.3649 is 0.99. One value is the negative of the other because the t-distribution is symmetric.

d. For 10 df, $t_{0.005} = -3.1693$. Since $t_{0.995} = 3.1693$ has an area of 0.995 to its left, the area to its right must be $1 - 0.995 = 0.005$. The area between -3.1693 and 3.1693 is $0.995 - 0.005 = 0.990$.

e. Zero.

f. $t_{0.025} = -2.2010$ to $t_{0.975} = 2.2010$. Note that $0.975 - 0.025 = 0.950$, as required.

g. The standard normal distribution has a standard deviation of 1. All t-distributions have more dispersion than the standard normal distribution, so their standard deviations are greater than 1.

h. For confidence intervals with a confidence coefficient of 0.90 the required t-value cuts off 0.05. At 20 df, $t_{0.05} = -1.7247$. (In confidence interval computations, we ignore the sign of the t-value.)

i. For 40 df, $t_{0.95} = 1.6839$; for 132 df, $t_{0.95} = 1.6565$.

j. For 0.95 confidence interval with 20 df, $t_{0.975} = 2.0860$.   For the 0.99 interval with 20 df, $t_{0.995} = 2.8453$.

8.9.a. Unbiased point estimates of μ are obtained from $\overline{x} = \Sigma x/n$.   Unbiased estimates of σ^2 are obtained from $s^2 = \Sigma(x - \overline{x})^2/(n - 1)$.   For the first student, $x = 196/4 = 49$. $s^2 = [(49 - 49)^2 + (48 - 49)^2 + (50 - 49)^2 + (49 - 49)^2]/(4 - 1) = 2/3$, or 0.67.   For the second student, $\overline{x} = 184/4 = 46$. $s^2 = 392/3 = 130.7$.

b. No.   The estimates are obtained from samples.   In general, we expect one random sample to differ from another; consequently, the values of $\overline{x}$ and s^2 computed from samples will differ.

c. $s = \sqrt{s^2}$.   For the first student, $s = \sqrt{0.67} = 0.82$.   For the second, $s = \sqrt{130.7} = 11.4$.

d. $s_{\overline{x}} = s/\sqrt{n}$.   For the first student, $s_{\overline{x}} = 0.82/\sqrt{4} = 0.41$.   For the second, $s_{\overline{x}} = 11.4/\sqrt{4} = 5.7$.

e. On the average, s^2 will underestimate the population variance. Note the slight difference between the average of all of the values of s^2 (10,706) and the true variance (10,000).   This difference would tend to disappear if the number of samples in the experiment were increased.   The relatively large bias for s^2 estimated as (7134 – 10,000) would persist even if more samples were included.

8.10.a. The population must be normal if a small sample is used.   Usually a sample of 30 or more will be required if normality is not present.

b. From Question 8.9, $\overline{X} = 46$, $s^2 = 130.7$, $s = 11.2$, and $s_{\overline{x}} = 5.7$. The t-value from Table B-4 at 3 df is $t_{0.975} = 3.1824$ for 0.95 confidence coefficient. $X \pm t s_{\overline{x}} = 46 \pm 3.1824 (5.7) = 46 \pm 18.13968$, or about 46 ± 18.14.

8.11.a. Degrees of freedom $= n - 1 = 36 - 1 = 35$.

b. $s = \sqrt{s^2} = \sqrt{25} = 5$; $s_{\overline{x}} = s/\sqrt{n} = 5/\sqrt{36} = 5/6$, or 0.83.

c. $t_{0.975} = 2.0301$ for 35 df; $\overline{X} \pm t s_{\overline{x}} = 48 \pm (2.0301)(0.83) = 48 \pm 1.684983$, or about 48 ± 1.68.

d. The confidence interval estimate in (c) gives us a 0.95 confidence that the true population mean is in the interval 46.32 to 49.68. that is, within ± 1.68 years of the point estimate of the population mean, $\overline{x} = 48$.   The point estimate by itself gives us no assurance of how close it might be to the true mean.   Thus, the confidence interval estimate is usually preferred.

e. Yes, usually more than 30 observations are sufficient if the population is not normal.

8.12.a. $p = r/n = 40/100 = 0.4$; $z_{0.025} = -1.96$ (ignore the sign of z for confidence intervals). The confidence interval formula is

$$p \pm z \sqrt{\frac{p(1-p)}{n}} = 0.4 \pm (1.96) \sqrt{\frac{(0.4)(1-0.4)}{100}} = 0.4 \pm 1.96(0.049)$$

$= 0.4 \pm 0.096$. Thus the confidence interval goes from 0.304 to 0.496.

b. $p = 170/300 = 0.567$, $z_{0.01} = 2.33$.

$$p \pm z_{\alpha/2} \sqrt{\frac{p(1-p)}{n}} = 0.567 \pm 2.33 \sqrt{\frac{0.567(1-0.567)}{300}} = 0.567 \pm$$

$2.33\sqrt{0.000818} = 0.567 \pm 2.33(0.0286) = 0.567 \pm 0.067$. The confidence interval extends from 0.500 to 0.634.

c. In (a), $p = 0.40$ and the minimum sample size for the normal approximation is 60. In (b), $p = 0.567$, $1 - p = 0.433$. The lesser of the two is 0.433 and the minimum sample size is between 30 and 60. In both cases, the minimum sample size is met.

8.13.a. $p = 8/20 = 0.4$.

b. From Figure 8-6 in the text, locate $p = 0.4$ on the horizontal axis. Follow vertical line above 0.4 and locate the points where this line crosses the two curves labeled $n = 20$. The two points are $\pi = 0.19$ and $\pi = 0.64$. The confidence interval is $0.19 < \pi < 0.64$.

8.14.a. If the half-length of the confidence interval (e) is to be fixed at 0.5 feet, then the required sample size is given by Equation 8-4 in the text as

$$n = \left(\frac{z_{\alpha/2}\sigma}{e}\right)^2 = \left(\frac{1.96(0.6)}{0.5}\right)^2 = (2.352)^2 = 5.53$$

which would be rounded to the next highest integer, or $n = 6$. If the half-length of the interval were to be maintained at

$e = 0.1$ ft, then $n = \left(\dfrac{1.96(0.6)}{0.1}\right)^2 = (11.76)^2 = 138.3$, or $n = 139$.

For $e = 0.01$ ft, $n = \left(\dfrac{1.96(0.6)}{0.01}\right)^2 = (117.6)^2 = 13{,}829.76$, or $n = 13{,}830$.

b. For a fixed confidence coefficient, the length of the confidence interval *decreases* as the sample size *increases*. In other words, as we use more observations to determine the sample mean, we narrow the interval within which we have a given level of confidence of finding μ.

8.15.   From Question 8.5, $\sigma = 3$ and $Z = 2$; $N = 1000$ and $e = 0.25$.

$$n = \frac{N\, z^2 \sigma^2}{(N-1)e^2 + z^2 \sigma^2}$$

$$= \frac{1000\,(1.96)^2\,(3)^2}{(1000-1)(0.25)^2 + (1.96)^2\,(3)^2}$$

$$= 356.4,\text{ or } 357 \text{ observations}$$

8.16.a.i.   The conservative formula, $n = \dfrac{(z_{\alpha/2})^2\,(0.25)}{e^2}$, should be used.

In this case, $z_{\alpha/2} = z_{0.025} = 1.96$, $e = 0.01$ and

$$n = \frac{(1.96)^2\,(0.25)}{(0.01)^2} = 9604.$$

ii.   Replace 0.25 in the last formula with the maximum value of $\pi(1-\pi)$, which is thought to be $0.8(1-0.8) = 0.16$. (This will decrease the required sample size.) $n = \dfrac{(1.96)^2\,(0.16)}{(0.01)^2} = 6146.56$, or 6147.

b. If $1 - p = 1 - 0.90 = 0.10$, the minimum sample size is $n = 900$. Thus both sample sizes satisfy the requirements for the normal approximation.

8.17.a. $\overline{X} \pm t(s/\sqrt{n}\,)$

b. $p \pm z\,\sqrt{\dfrac{p(1-p)}{n}}\,\sqrt{\dfrac{N-n}{N-1}}$.   In addition, the measured value of p would have to be in the range $0.2 \leq p \leq 0.8$ in order to have a valid confidence interval.

c. $p \pm z\,\sqrt{\dfrac{p(1-p)}{n}}$ provided the actual measured value of p is in the range $0.40 < p < 0.60$.

d. There are too few observations to make the computation. The sample size should be increased to 30 or more. Then we can use $\overline{X} \pm t(s/\sqrt{n}\,)$

e. For n greater than 30 and σ known, we have $\overline{X} \pm z(\sigma/\sqrt{n})$.

CHAPTER 9:   SOLUTIONS TO SELF-CORRECTING EXERCISES

9.1.a. H_0: $\mu \leq 478$; H_A: $\mu > 478$

b. H_0: $\mu \geq 478$; H_A: $\mu < 478$

c. H_0: $\mu = 478$; H_A: $\mu \neq 478$

9.2.a. H_0: $\mu = 10$; H_A: $\mu \neq 10$

b. $\sigma_{\bar{X}} = 0.5/\sqrt{16} = 0.125$

c. $\mu_{\bar{X}} \pm 2\sigma_{\bar{X}} = 10 \pm 2(0.125)$, or $9.75 \leq \bar{X} \leq 10.25$

d. $10 \pm 3(0.125)$, or $9.625 \leq \bar{X} \leq 10.375$

e. For $\alpha = 0.05$, the acceptance region in terms of Z is $-1.96 \leq Z \leq 1.96$. The acceptance region in terms of $\bar{X}$ is $\mu_{\bar{X}} \pm 1.96(\sigma_{\bar{X}})$ = $10 \pm 1.96(0.125) = 10 \pm 0.245$, or $9.755 \leq \bar{X} \leq 10.245$.

f. For $\alpha = 0.10$, the acceptance region in terms of Z is $-1.645 \leq Z \leq 1.645$. The acceptance region in terms of $\bar{X}$ is $\mu_{\bar{X}} \pm 1.645(\sigma_{\bar{X}})$ = $10 \pm 1.645(0.125) = 10 \pm 0.21$, or $9.79 \leq \bar{X} \leq 10.21$.

g. For a two-tailed test with $\alpha = 0.05$ the correct acceptance region is $-1.96 \leq Z \leq 1.96$. The total area outside the acceptance region must sum to 0.05. For the inspector's proposed acceptance region, this area is 0.10 and not 0.05 as it should be.

9.3.a. H_0: $\mu = 112$, H_A: $\mu \neq 112$

b. $\alpha = 0.0456$

c. $\sigma_{\bar{X}} = \sigma/\sqrt{n} = 6/\sqrt{9} = 2$

d. These values are determined by finding a symmetric interval about $\mu_0 = 112$ on the sampling distribution of the sample mean for $n = 9$. Since the population is normally distributed with $\sigma = 6$, the sampling distribution will be normally distributed with $\sigma_{\bar{X}} = 2$. Since this is a two-tailed test, α must be divided into two parts with $\alpha/2$ placed in each tail. Since $\alpha = 0.0456$, $\alpha/2$ is 0.0228. The value of z that cuts off 0.0228 in the lower tail is found from Table B-3 to be $z_{0.0228} = -2$. The value of z that cuts off 0.0228 in the upper tail is $z_{0.9772} = 2$. The required interval is $\mu_0 \pm z_{\alpha/2} * \sigma_{\bar{X}} = 112 \pm 2(2)$. The upper critical value is 116 oz. The lower is 108 oz. The decision rule is to accept the null hypothesis if the sample mean falls within this interval and reject the null hypothesis if the sample mean falls outside this interval.

e. We do not need a random sample to determine any of these. The null hypothesis is based on the anticipated performance of the machine. The level of significance is based on the decision maker's attitude toward the risk of rejecting the null hypothesis if it is actually true. The acceptance region is based on the level of significance and sampling theory. To find the acceptance region we need to know that there will be $n = 9$ observations in the random sample but we do *not* need to know the specific values of the observations. Thus the null hypothesis, level of significance, and acceptance region are established without reference to the data.

f. $\Sigma x = 999$, and $x = 999/9 = 111$. This sample mean falls in the acceptance region and we accept the null hypothesis that the population mean is 112; that is, we act as though the machine is operating with a mean fill rate of 112 ounces.

g. $\bar{x} = 963/9 = 107$. We reject the null hypothesis because this sample mean falls outside the acceptance region. We conclude the mean fill rate for the machine is not 112 ounces.

h. Nothing is wrong with the procedure. The level of significance is 0.0456. This implies that when the mean fill rate *is* 112 ounces, we expect to find 4.56% of the sample means outside the acceptance region. In such cases we make unavoidable incorrect decisions about the null hypothesis.

i. The acceptance region for the null hypothesis for this two-tailed test is

$$z_{\alpha/2} \leqq z \leqq z_{1-\alpha/2}$$
$$z_{0.0228} \leqq z \leqq z_{0.9772}$$
$$-2 \leqq z \leqq 2$$

If a value of z computed from the observed sample mean falls in this interval, we accept the null hypothesis. The computed value of z is found from $z = (\bar{x} - \mu_0)/\sigma_{\bar{x}}$. For (f), $\bar{x} = 111$ and $z = (111 - 112)/2 = -0.5$, which falls within the interval; we accept the null hypothesis. For (g), $\bar{x} = 107$ and $z = (107 - 112)/2 = -2.5$, and we reject the null hypothesis. The two procedures produce the same conclusions about the null hypothesis. Since the procedures are logically equivalent, either method may be used and we will always reach the same conclusion.

9.4.a. The manufacturer is concerned with detecting a mean level that is too high. Thus H_0: $\mu \leqq 100$, and H_A: $\mu > 100$.

b. $\sigma_{\bar{x}} = 10/\sqrt{16} = 2.5$. Since $\alpha = 0.05$, $Z = 1.645$. The action limit is $100 + 1.645(2.5) = 104.1125$ and the acceptance region for the null hypothesis is $\bar{X} \leqq 104$.

c. If the process mean is actually 100, the null hypothesis is true. The only type of error that can occur is if the null hypothesis is rejected. This will occur if the sample mean is more than 104.1 and the probability of this is 0.05. Rejecting the null hypothesis when it is true is a type I error.

d. The manufacturer will reject the null hypothesis and will believe the mean pollutant level is too high. No cause for a high pollutant level will be found. Notice that such errors occur due to sampling fluctuations and cannot be avoided.

e. If μ = 105, the alternative hypothesis is true. Only type II errors are possible. When μ = 105, this will happen if the sample mean is less than the critical value of 104.1. For μ = 105, $z = (104.1 - 105)/2.5 = -0.36$ and $P(\overline{X} \leq 104.1) = P(Z \leq -0.36) = 0.3594$.

f. $z = (104.1 - 110)/2.5 = -2.36$; $P(\overline{X} \leq 104.1) = P(Z \leq - 2.36) = 0.0091$

g. The manufacturer believes the mean pollutant level is 100 or less, so fails to detect the higher pollutant level.

h. For a fixed level of significance, reducing the sample size increases the probability of a type II error because the standard error of the mean is increased. For a fixed level of significance, an increased sample size will decrease this probability. Increasing the sample size is one way of decreasing the risks discussed in (g). (For a fixed sample size, the probability of a type II error may be reduced at the expense of increasing the probability of a type I error.)

9.5.a.

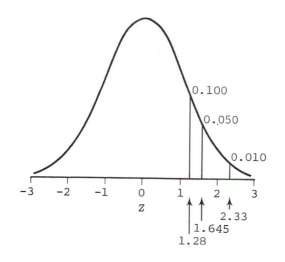

b.

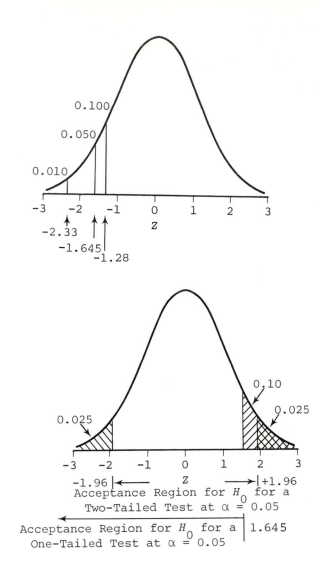

c.

The acceptance regions for the two tests are different. For the two-tailed test with $\alpha = 0.05$, the acceptance region is centered about the mean. Notice that each tail area is 0.025, so that the total area outside the acceptance region is 0.05. For the one-tail test with $\alpha = 0.05$, this area is in one tail of the distribution. Thus the action limits for the two tests are different even though the level of significance is the same.

d. $\mu_0 = 80$, $\sigma_{\bar{x}} = 5/\sqrt{16} = 1.25$, and $z_{0.95} = 1.645$; we may use the formula $z = (\bar{X} - \mu_0)/\sigma_{\bar{x}}$ and solve for $\bar{X}$, which is the action limit. Thus $1.645 = (\bar{X} - 80)/1.25$ and $\bar{X} = 80 + 1.645(1.25) = 82.05625$. The acceptance region for the null hypothesis in this test is $\bar{X} \leq 82.06$.

9.6.a. H_0: $\mu \geq 5$, H_A: $\mu < 5$

b. $\sigma = 1.5$, $n = 225$, $\sigma_{\bar{x}} = 1.5/\sqrt{225} = 0.1$

c. $\alpha = 0.025$ and $z_{0.025} = -1.96$; if the sample mean is greater than $\mu_0 + z_\alpha \sigma_{\bar{x}} = 5 - 1.96(0.1) = 4.804$ min, we accept the null hypothesis. If the value z computed from the data is greater than -1.96, we accept the null hypothesis.

d. $\bar{x} = 1080/225 = 4.8$, which is less than 4.804. We conclude that the population mean is less than 5 min. The value of z computed from the data is $z = (4.8 - 5)/0.1 = -2$, which is less than -1.96.

e. A two-tailed test is not appropriate. The management wishes to know if calls are being kept to less than 5 min. A two-tailed test would be appropriate if we were asking whether or not the mean length of calls is greater *or* less than 5 min.

9.7.a. H_0: $\mu = 160$ and H_A: $\mu \neq 160$; the basis of the null hypothesis is the mean expenditure two years ago.

b. $\sigma = 12$, $n = 64$, $\sigma_{\bar{x}} = 12/\sqrt{64} = 1.5$

c. $\alpha = 0.05$, $\alpha/2 = 0.025$, $z_{0.025} = -1.96$, $z_{0.975} = 1.96$; the acceptance region in terms of the sample mean is $\mu_0 \pm z_{\alpha/2}\sigma_{\bar{x}}$ or $160 \pm 1.96(1.5)$. The acceptance region is 157.06 to 162.94. In terms of standard scores, the acceptance region is $-1.96 \leq z \leq 1.96$.

d. The sample mean is $\bar{x} = 165$ which is greater than 162.94 and is outside the acceptance region. The value of z computed from the data is $z = (165 - 160)/1.5 = 3.33$ which is greater than 1.96. We conclude the population mean from which the sample was drawn is not 160.

e. No, the population is skewed. At least 30 observations are needed before the central limit theorem gives us reasonable assurance that the normal distribution is an adequate approximation to the sampling distribution.

9.8.a. The question to be answered in this case is not "What is the estimated mean?" The question is, "Is the population mean 50, or is it some other value? This is a two-tailed test. In symbols, H_0: $\mu = 50$ and H_A: $\mu \neq 50$.

b. In terms of standard scores, the computed value of z from the data must fall in the interval of -1.96 to $+1.96$ in order for us to accept H_0.

c. $z = \dfrac{(\bar{x} - \mu)}{s/\sqrt{n}} = \dfrac{(48 - 50)}{5/\sqrt{36}} = \dfrac{48 - 50}{5/6} = -2.4$

d. The computed test statistic falls outside the acceptance region. We reject H_0.

9.9.a. The population would have to be normally distributed.

b. $\alpha = 0.05$, $\alpha/2 = 0.025$, and $1 - \alpha/2 = 0.975$; at $n - 1 = 4 - 1 = 3$ df, $t_{0.025} = -3.182$ and $t_{0.975} = 3.182$. A value of t computed from the data which falls in the interval -3.182 to $+3.182$ will cause the null hypothesis to be accepted.

c. $s^2 = 0.67$, $s = 0.82$, $s_{\bar{x}} = 0.41$, and $\bar{x} = 49$; notice that these values are computed from the random sample. The value of t computed from the sample is $t = (\bar{x} - \mu)/(s/\sqrt{n}) = (49 - 50)/0.41 = -2.44$.

d. Since $t = -2.44$ falls in the interval -3.182 to 3.182, we accept the null hypothesis.

e. For this test the null hypothesis will be accepted if the computed value of t is greater than $t_{0.05} = -2.353$. The computed value is $t = -2.44$. (This value is not influenced by the type of hypothesis.) Since $-2.44 < t_{0.05}$, we would reject the null hypothesis.

9.10.a. $t = (\bar{X} - \mu_0)/s_{\bar{x}}$

b. $t = (\bar{X} - \mu_0)/s_{\bar{x}}$

c. None.

d. $z = (\bar{X} - \mu_0)/\sigma_{\bar{x}}$

e. None.

9.11. For sampling without replacement, we use $\sigma_{\bar{x}} = \sqrt{\dfrac{N - n}{N - 1}} * \dfrac{\sigma}{\sqrt{n}}$ for the standard error. In this case, $\sigma_{\bar{x}} = \sqrt{\dfrac{1000 - 225}{1000 - 1}} * \dfrac{1.5}{\sqrt{225}} = 0.881(0.1)$ = 0.0881. The test statistic is $z = (4.8 - 5)/0.0881 = -2.27$. Since $z = -2.27$ is less than the critical value of -1.95, we reject the null hypothesis. Notice that sampling without replacement produces a smaller standard error (0.0881 instead of 0.1) and thus makes the test more sensitive.

9.12.a.i. H_0: $\pi = 0.5$ and H_A: $\pi \neq 0.5$; since $\frac{n\pi}{1 - \pi}$ and $\frac{n(1 - \pi)}{\pi}$ are both 25, we may use the normal approximation.   For $\alpha = 0.05$, the acceptance region for the null hypothesis is $-1.96 \leq z \leq 1.96$.

The test statistic is

$$z = \frac{(p + \frac{1}{2n} - \pi_0)}{\sqrt{\frac{\pi_0(1 - \pi_0)}{n}}} = \frac{\frac{10}{25} + \frac{1}{2(25)} - 0.5}{\sqrt{\frac{0.5(0.5)}{25}}} = \frac{(0.42 - 0.5)}{0.1} = -0.8.$$

The value $z = -0.8$ is in the acceptance region for the null hypothesis, so we accept the hypothesis that $\pi = 0.5$.

ii. Since $\frac{n\pi}{1 - \pi} = \frac{25(0.2)}{(0.8)} = 6.25$ and this value is less than the required minimum of 9, we cannot use the normal approximation. In more advanced treatments, it is shown that the hypothesis may be tested by using a more extensive binomial table than the one given in the appendix or by using the binomial formula.

b. H_0: $\pi = 0.5$, and H_A: $\pi \neq 0.5$; for $\alpha = 0.05$, the acceptance region is $-1.96 \leq z \leq 1.96$.   (Since $\frac{n\pi}{1 - \pi}$ and $\frac{n(1 - \pi)}{\pi}$ both equal 100, the normal approximation is appropriate.   The test statistic is

$$z = \frac{(p + \frac{1}{2n} - \pi_0)}{\sqrt{\frac{\pi_0(1 - \pi_0)}{n}}} = \frac{(\frac{40}{100} + \frac{1}{2(100)} - 0.5)}{\sqrt{\frac{0.5(0.5)}{100}}} = \frac{(0.405 - 0.5)}{0.05} = -1.9$$

which is within the acceptance region for the null hypothesis.

c. H_0: $\pi = 0.5$, and H_A: $\pi \neq 0.5$; the normal approximation is appropriate and the acceptance region for the null hypothesis is $-1.96 \leq z \leq 1.96$.   The test statistic is

$$z = \frac{(p - \frac{1}{2n} - \pi_0)}{\sqrt{\frac{\pi_0(1 - \pi_0)}{n}}} = \frac{(\frac{113}{169} - \frac{1}{2(169)} - 0.5)}{\sqrt{\frac{0.5(0.5)}{169}}}$$

$$= \frac{(0.669 - 0.003 - 0.5)}{0.038} = 4.31$$

and we reject the null hypothesis and conclude that the geneticist can control sex.   Notice that the factor $1/2n$ is small and could have been neglected in this case.

9.13.a. The critical value is $\mu_0 - z\sigma_{\bar{x}} = 150 - 1.28(5/\sqrt{25}) = 148.72.$

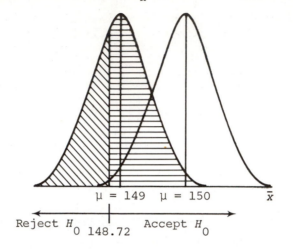

$\mu = 149$ $\mu = 150$ $\bar{x}$

Reject H_0 148.72   Accept H_0

b. If $\mu = 149$, the alternative hypothesis is true and a type II
error is possible. A type II error will occur in this case if
a sample mean is greater than the critical value of $\bar{X} = 148.72$.
The horizontally shaded area on the sketch shows the probability
of a type II error. The value of this probability is found from
$z = (148.72 - 149)/(5/\sqrt{25}) = -0.28.$ The probability of this
type II error is $P(Z \geq -0.28) = 0.6103.$ The probability of a
correct decision is $1 - 0.6103 = 0.3897$, which is also the power
of the test when $\mu = 149$. This is shown by the cross-hatched
portion of the figure.

c-f. Each point on the power curve is found by computing the standardized score of the critical value $\bar{X} = 148.72$ from the assumed value
of μ and finding the area to the left of the critical value of $\bar{X}$.
Notice this area indicates the probability of rejecting the null
hypothesis when it is not true. This probability is the power of
the test for the assumed value of μ.

For $n = 25$:

Possible value of μ	$z = (\bar{X} - \mu)/\sigma_{\bar{x}}$		Power
146.0	$(148.72 - 146)/1$	$= 2.72$	0.9967
146.5	$(148.72 - 146.5)/1 =$	2.22	0.9868
147.0	$(148.72 - 147)/1$	$= 1.72$	0.9573
147.5	$(148.72 - 147.5)/1 =$	1.22	0.8888
148.0	$(148.72 - 148)/1$	$= 0.72$	0.7642
148.5	$(148.72 - 148.5)/1 =$	0.22	0.5871
149.0	$(148.72 - 149)/1$	$= -0.28$	0.3897
149.5	$(148.72 - 149.5)/1 =$	-0.78	0.2177

For $n = 100$, the critical value of $\overline{X}$ is $\overline{X} = 150 - 1.28 \quad (5/\sqrt{100})$
$= 149.36$.

μ	z		Power
148	$(149.36 - 148)/0.5$	$= 2.72$	0.9967
148.5	$(149.36 - 148.5)/0.05$	$= 1.72$	0.9573
149	$(149.36 - 149)/0.5$	$= 0.72$	0.7642
149.5	$(149.36 - 149.5)/0.5$	$= -0.28$	0.3897

For a given value of α and n, the probability of a correct decision increases as μ departs from μ_0.   In this case, values of μ
much smaller than 150 are associated with large probabilities of
correctly rejecting the null hypothesis rather than values of μ
closer to 150.

A larger value of n will increase the probability of a correct
decision for all values of μ.   The dashed line in the solution
grid shows an idealized power curve, which would cause the null
hypothesis to be correctly rejected with probability 1.0.   Such
a plan would require an infinite sample size.

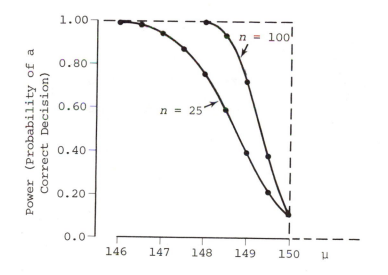

9.14.a.

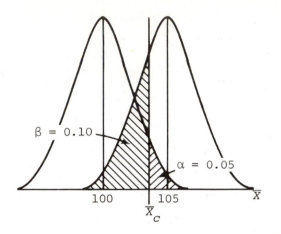

$\beta = 0.10$

$\alpha = 0.05$

100   105 $\overline{X}$

$\overline{X}_c$

b. $z_{0.95} = 1.645$ and $z_{0.10} = -1.28$;   be sure to notice that the probabilities of error are given in problems involving sample size determination.

c. $n = \left[\dfrac{\sigma(z_\beta + z_\alpha)}{\delta}\right]^2$; in this formula δ is $105 - 100 = 5$, $z_\alpha = 1.645$, and $z_\beta = 1.28$ (we ignore the sign in problems of sample-size determination).

$n = \left[\dfrac{10(1.645 + 1.282)}{5}\right]^2 = 34.22$, or about 35 observations.

d. A plan for detecting $\mu = 103$ would require

$n = \left[\dfrac{10(1.645 + 1.28)}{3}\right]^2 = 95.06$, or about 96 observations.

This is a larger sample size than that given in (c).   In this case, we are attempting to detect a value of μ closer to μ_0 with the sample probabilities of error and more information is required to do so.

CHAPTER 10:   SOLUTIONS TO SELF-CORRECTING EXERCISES

10.1.a.

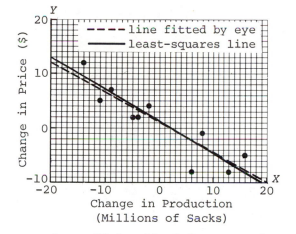

b. As X increases from −20 to +20, Y decreases from 12 to −10, a
total decrease of 22 units. The slope (b) is the ratio of the
change in Y to the *increase* in X:

$$b = \frac{-10 - (12)}{20 - (-20)} = \frac{-22}{40} = -0.55$$

The other value needed is a, the value of Y when $X = 0$. For
every unit X increases, Y changes by −0.55 unit. When X is
−20, Y is 12. If we let X increase to 0, it will have increased
by 20 units. Accompanying a 20-unit increase in X will be a
change in Y of −0.55(20) = −11. Since X was 12 when Y was −20,
Y will be 12 − 11 = 1 when $X = 0$. The equation is

$$Y = 1.0 - 0.55X.$$

The equation of $Y = 1.0 - 0.55X$ is plotted by connecting the
points (−20,12) and (20,−10) with a dashed straight line.

10.2.a.

X	Y	X^2	Y^2	XY
-4	2	16	4	-8
-2	4	4	16	-8
8	-1	64	1	-8
-8	7	64	49	-56
16	-5	256	25	-80
-10	5	100	25	-50
13	-8	169	64	-104
-14	12	196	144	-168
6	-8	36	64	-48
-5	2	25	4	-10
Totals 0	10	930	396	-540

$$\Sigma X = 0 \quad \Sigma Y = 10 \quad \Sigma X^2 = 930 \quad \Sigma Y^2 = 396 \quad \Sigma XY = -540$$

b. To two decimal places,

$$b = \frac{n(\Sigma XY) - (\Sigma X)(\Sigma Y)}{n(\Sigma X^2) - (\Sigma X)^2} = \frac{10(-540) - 0(10)}{10(930) - (0)^2} = -0.58$$

$$a = \bar{Y} - b\bar{X} \quad \bar{Y} = \frac{\Sigma Y}{n} \quad \bar{X} = \frac{\Sigma X}{n}$$

$$a = \frac{10}{10} - (-0.58)\frac{0}{10} = 1.0$$

The least-squares line is $Y_C = 1.0 - 0.58X$.

c. When X is -20, $Y_C = 1.0 - 0.58(-20) = 1.0 + 11.6$, or 12.6.
   When X is +20, $Y_C = 1.0 - 0.58(20) = 1.0 - 11.6$, or -10.6.

The two points (-20,12.6) and (20,-10.6) are shown on the
graph in the solution to Question 1(a). They are connected
by a solid line, which is the least-squares line.

d. The Y-intercept is the value of Y_C when X is 0:

$$Y_C = 1.0 - 0.58(0) \quad \text{or } 1.0$$

This is of course the same as $a = 1.0$ found in (b). The point
(0,1) is the *same* for both the least-squares line and the
dashed line found in Question 1(b). The point (0,1) is shown
by an arrow in the solution to Question 1(a).

e. The negative sign indicates that as the values of X grow larger,
   the values of Y that lie along the least-squares line *decrease*.

10.3.a. At $X = 10$, $\mu_{Y \cdot 10} = 1000 + 100(10) = 2000$, so the Y-values are normally distributed with a mean of 2000 and a standard deviation of $\sigma_{Y \cdot X} = 500$. At $X = 20$, $\mu_{Y \cdot 20} = 1000 + 100(20) = 3000$ and the Y-values are normally distributed with a mean of 3000 and a standard deviation of 500.

b. Individual observations of Y cannot be related to each other in any way.

c. In a regression analysis, the values of X must be known without error. This is not the case here since there is uncertainty about the value of X which produces the sales figure of 1500.

10.4.a.

Year	X	Y	Y_C	$Y - Y_C$	$(Y - Y_C)^2$
:	:	:	:	:	:
8	-14	12	9.12	2.88	8.2944
9	6	-8	-2.48	-5.52	30.4704
10	-5	2	3.90	-1.90	3.6100
				$\Sigma (Y - Y_C)^2$	72.4520

For year 8:

$$Y_C = 1.0 - 0.58(-14) = 9.12$$
$$Y - Y_C = 12 - 9.12 = 2.88$$
$$(Y - Y_C)^2 = (2.88)^2 = 8.2944$$

The values of $(Y - Y_C)^2$ for all other years are found in the same way.

b. Substitute in Equation 10-7 to find, to two decimal places,

$$s_{Y \cdot X} = \sqrt{\frac{\Sigma (Y - Y_C)^2}{n - 2}} = \sqrt{\frac{72.452}{10 - 2}} = \sqrt{9.0565} = 3.01$$

c. From Equation 10-8,

$$\Sigma (Y - Y_C)^2 = \Sigma (Y^2) - a(\Sigma Y) - b(\Sigma XY)$$
$$= 396 - 1.0(10) - (-0.58)(-540)$$
$$= 72.8.$$

The result from Part a (72.452) is very nearly the same as the value obtained here. The difference is due to rounding errors in the computation of the slope (b). If the latter computation had been carried to more decimal places, the two methods would produce values that are very nearly the same. Unless the values of $(Y - Y_C)$ are whole numbers, it is easier to use Equation 10-8.

d. The line fitted by eye is *not* the least-squares line. It follows that the value of $\Sigma(Y - Y_c)^2$ for a line that is not a least-squares line would have to be larger than the value of $\Sigma(Y - Y_c)^2$ for the least-squares line. The least-squares line has the property of minimizing the value of $\Sigma(Y - Y_c)^2$ for any given data collection.

e. Formulas 10-4 and 10-5 in the text are for the slope (*b*) and intercept (*a*) of the least-squares line. By using these formulas, we are assured of obtaining the least-squares line and obtaining the smallest possible value of $\Sigma(Y - Y_c)^2$.

10.5.a. If the null hypothesis is true, Y is a constant which is not influenced by X; that is, if the null hypothesis is true, the population regression line is horizontal. If this is so, changes in production (X) will not influence changes in price. If the alternative is true, the population regression line will have a nonzero slope.

b. $t = (b - B)/s_b$ (Equation 10-9 in the text). From Question 10.2, $b = -0.58$. By the null hypothesis, $B = 0$. The value of s_b needs to be computed (see (c)).

c. $s_b = \dfrac{s_{Y \cdot X}}{\sqrt{\Sigma X^2 - n\overline{X}^2}}$ From Question 10.2, $\Sigma X^2 = 930$ and $\overline{X} = 0/10 = 0$,

and $s_{Y \cdot X} = 3.01$ from Question 10.4. Thus $s_b = \dfrac{3.01}{\sqrt{930 - 10(0)^2}} = $ 0.10 (to two decimal places).

d. $t = (-0.58 - 0)/0.10 = -5.8$

e. From Appendix B Table B-4 for a two-tailed test at the 0.05 level of significance and for 8 degrees of freedom, the acceptance region is the interval -2.306 to +2.306. The computed value of t is -5.8 which falls outside the acceptance region of the null hypothesis. Thus we reject the null hypothesis and conclude that changes in production have a significant impact on changes in price.

f. From Equation 10-11, the confidence interval is given by

$$b - ts_b < B < b + ts_b$$

For the 0.95 confidence coefficient at 8 *df*, $t = 2.306$. Thus the confidence interval for B is:

$$(-0.58) - (2.306)(0.10) < B < (-0.58) + (2.306)(0.10)$$

$$-0.81 < B < -0.35$$

10.6.a. For $X = 0$ (no change in production), $Y_C = 1.0 - 0.58(0) = 1.0$, which is the point estimate at $X = 0$. Equation 10-18 in the text gives the formula for finding the interval estimate:

$$Y_C \pm ts_{Y \cdot X} \sqrt{1 + \frac{1}{n} + \frac{(X_S - \bar{X})^2}{\Sigma X^2 - n\bar{X}^2}}$$

From Appendix B Table B-4, $t = 2.306$. From Question 10.2, $\Sigma X^2 = 930$ and $\bar{X} = 0/10 = 0$. From Question 10.4, $s_{Y \cdot X} = 3.01$. Thus

$$1.0 \pm (2.306)(3.01) \sqrt{1 + \frac{1}{10} + \frac{(0 - 0)^2}{930 - 10(0)^2}}$$

$$= 1.0 \pm 6.941 \sqrt{1.1}$$

$$= 1.0 \pm 6.941(1.049)$$

$$= 1.0 \pm 7.280$$

For $X = 0$, the prediction interval runs from -6.28 to 8.28; that is, if no change is made in production, the change in price may be expected to be in the range of $-\$6.28$ per sack to $\$8.28$ per sack with 0.95 confidence.

b. For $X_S = 10$, $Y_C = 1.0 - 0.58(10) = -4.8$. Substituting into Equation 10-18 in the text, we find:

$$-4.8 \pm (2.306)(3.01) \sqrt{1 + \frac{1}{10} + \frac{(10 - 0)^2}{930 - 10(0)^2}}$$

$$= -4.8 \pm 6.941 \sqrt{1 + 0.1 + 0.108}$$

$$= -4.8 \pm 6.941 \sqrt{1.208}$$

$$= -4.8 \pm 7.63$$

or -12.43 to 2.83.

c. The prediction interval in (b) is wider. As prediction intervals are found at values of X that are farther from $\bar{X}$, the intervals widen.

d. The confidence interval estimate for the mean of *all* years is given by Equation 10-16 in the text

$$\bar{Y}_C \pm ts_{Y \cdot X} \sqrt{\frac{1}{n} + \frac{(X_S - \bar{X})^2}{\Sigma X^2 - n\bar{X}^2}}$$

Notice that the quantity under the square root in Equation 10-16 is one less than the corresponding quantity in Equation 10-18. Thus we should expect a narrower confidence interval in this case. Substituting, we have

$$1.0 \pm (2.306)(3.01)\sqrt{\frac{1}{10} + \frac{(0-0)^2}{930-10(0)}}$$

$$= 1.0 \pm 6.941 \sqrt{0.1}$$

$$= 1.0 \pm 2.195$$

or -1.19 to 3.19. The confidence interval is narrower than in (a). The formula and the computations correctly reflect our ability to determine the mean price for all years in which $X = 0$ more precisely than the mean price for any single years in which $X = 0$.

10.7.a. To two decimal places,

$$r = \frac{n(\Sigma XY) - (\Sigma X)(\Sigma Y)}{\sqrt{[n\Sigma X^2 - (\Sigma X)^2][n\Sigma Y^2 - (\Sigma Y)^2]}}$$

$$= \frac{10(-540) - 0(10)}{\sqrt{[10(930) - (0)^2][10(396) - (10)^2]}}$$

$$= \frac{-5400}{\sqrt{(9300)(3860)}} = \frac{-5400}{\sqrt{35,898,000}} = -\frac{5400}{5991}$$

$$= -0.90$$

b. $r^2 = (0.90)^2 = 0.81$, or 81% of the variation in Y is accounted for by the variation in X. This proportion (r^2) is called the *coefficient of determination*.

10.8.a.

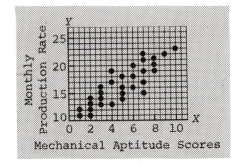

b. From the scattergram, the data seem to be increasing in a linear fashion. The best linear relationship is the least-squares line. From the data we compute $n = 30$, $\Sigma X = 150$, $\Sigma X^2 = 928$, $\Sigma Y = 496$, $\Sigma Y^2 = 8556$, and $\Sigma XY = 2698$. The equation for the slope and intercept are given in the text in Equations 10-4 and 10-5. Substituting, we have

$$b = \frac{n\Sigma XY - \Sigma X(\Sigma Y)}{n\Sigma X^2 - (\Sigma X)^2}$$

$$= \frac{30(2698) - (150)(496)}{30(928) - (150)^2} = \frac{6540}{5340}$$

$$= 1.22$$

and

$$a = \bar{Y} - b(\bar{X})$$

$$= \frac{496}{30} - 1.22 \left(\frac{150}{30}\right) = 10.4$$

Thus the least squares line is $Y_C = 10.4 + 1.22X$.

c.i.   Test the hypothesis that $B = 0$. To do so, compute the test statistic $t = \dfrac{(1.22 - 0)}{s_b}$. First find $s_{Y \cdot X} = \sqrt{\dfrac{\Sigma Y^2 - a\Sigma Y - b\Sigma XY}{n - 2}}$.

$$s_{Y \cdot X} = \sqrt{\frac{8556 - 10.4(496) - 1.22(2698)}{30 - 2}} = \sqrt{\frac{106.04}{28}} = 1.95$$

Next find

$$s_b = \frac{s_{Y \cdot X}}{\sqrt{\Sigma X^2 - n(\bar{X})^2}} = \frac{1.95}{\sqrt{928 - 30(5)^2}} = 0.15$$

Thus, $t = \dfrac{1.22 - 0}{0.15} = 8.35$. This would cause us to reject the hypothesis that $B = 0$ at any reasonable level of significance. Notice that the hypothesis $B = 0$ corresponds to the president's belief.

ii.   The mean production rate for this worker would be $Y_C = 10.4 + 1.22(6) = 17.72$. A 0.95 confidence interval estimate for this individual would be

$$Y_C \pm t s_{Y \cdot X} \sqrt{1 + \frac{1}{n} + \frac{(X_S - \bar{X})^2}{\Sigma X^2 - n\bar{X}^2}}$$

$$= 17.72 \pm (2.0484)(1.95) \sqrt{1 + \frac{1}{30} + \frac{(6 - 5)^2}{928 - 30(5)^2}}$$

$$= 17.72 \pm 4.0 \sqrt{1.03}$$

$$= 17.7 \pm 4.1$$

It would be reasonable for this individual's production rate to be between 13.6 and 21.8.

10.9.a.i. $a = 319.8$, $b = 6.8$ (Figure 10-5)

ii. $Y_C = 319.8 + 6.8X$

iii. $\bar{X}$ = 22.6   (Figure 10-4)
$\bar{Y}$ = 473.9   (Figure 10-4)
s_x^2 = 50.8   (Figure 10-4)
s_y^2 = 6706.7   (Figure 10-4)

ΣX^2 and ΣY^2 are not given, nor are they easily computed from the printout.

iv. r^2 = 0.351520 (Figure 10-5), from which we can compute $r = \sqrt{0.351520}$ = 0.593.

v. s_b = 0.513, which is listed as the standard error of estimate for the slope due to the independent variable (ALG) in Figure 10-5; $s_{Y \cdot X}$ = 66.0, which is listed as "STD DEV" on Figure 10-5.

b. The computed t-value is given in Figure 10-5 as 13.27.   The printout also indicates that we would accept the null hypothesis *only* if our level of significance were less than 0.0001.

c. $b - ts_b < B < b + ts_b$

$6.8 - 1.9679(0.513) < B < 6.8 + 1.9679(0.513)$

$5.8 < B < 7.8$

CHAPTER 11:   SOLUTIONS TO SELF-CORRECTING EXERCISES

11.1.a.   Since the standard deviation is known and is the same for both populations.

$$\sigma_{\bar{X}_1 - \bar{X}_2} = \sigma \sqrt{\frac{1}{n_1} + \frac{1}{n_2}} = 3 \sqrt{\frac{1}{10} + \frac{1}{15}} = 1.22$$

b. $(\bar{X}_1 - \bar{X}_2) - z\,\sigma_{\bar{X}_1 - \bar{X}_2} \leqq \mu_1 - \mu_2 \leqq (\bar{X}_1 - \bar{X}_2) + z\,\sigma_{\bar{X}_1 - \bar{X}_2}$

$\bar{X}_1 = 14, \bar{X}_2 = 18, z = 1.96, (\bar{X}_1 - \bar{X}_2) = (14 - 18) = -4$

$-4 - 1.96(1.22) \leqq \mu_1 - \mu_2 \leqq (-4) + 1.96(1.22)$

$-4 - 2.39 \leqq \mu_1 - \mu_2 \leqq -4 + 2.39$

$-6.39 \leqq \mu_1 - \mu_2 \leqq -1.61$

c.   The formula for the standard error of the difference is

$$\sigma_{\bar{X}_1 - \bar{X}_2} = \sqrt{\frac{\sigma_1^2}{n_1} + \frac{\sigma_2^2}{n_2}} = \sqrt{\frac{3^2}{10} + \frac{5^2}{15}} = 1.60$$

The confidence interval estimate becomes

$-4 - 1.96(1.6) \leqq \mu_1 - \mu_2 \leqq -4 + 1.96(1.6)$

$-7.14 \leqq \mu_1 - \mu_2 \leqq -0.86$

d.   The confidence interval becomes

$4 \pm 1.96(1.22)$ or $1.6 \leqq \mu_1 - \mu_2 \leqq 6.40$

The two confidence intervals are logically equivalent. They both correctly convey the impression that the mean weight for the checks fed with mix 1 is *less* than the mean weight produced by mix 2.   The assignment of a particular mix to the subscript 1 or 2 is arbitrary.   Once the subscripts have been assigned, these definitions must not be changed.

11.2.   Let the subscript 1 refer to design A and 2 refer to design B.

a. $s_{\bar{X}_1 - \bar{X}_2} = \sqrt{\left[\frac{(n_1 - 1)s_1^2 + (n_2 - 1)s_2^2}{n_1 + n_2 - 2}\right]\left(\frac{1}{n_1} + \frac{1}{n_2}\right)}$

$= \sqrt{\left[\frac{4(0.052) + 7(0.040)}{5 + 8 - 2}\right]\left(\frac{1}{5} + \frac{1}{8}\right)}$

$= 0.120$

b. $(\bar{X}_1 - \bar{X}_2) \pm ts_{\overline{X}_1-\overline{X}_2}$, $\bar{X}_1 = \dfrac{7.9}{5} = 1.58$, $\bar{X}_2 = \dfrac{10}{8} = 1.25$,

$(\bar{X}_1 - \bar{X}_2) = 0.33$.

The required t-value is for the 0.995 percentile with $5 + 8 - 2 = 11$ df. From the t-table (Table B-4), $t = 3.1058$. The confidence interval is $0.33 \pm 3.1058(0.120)$ or 0.33 ± 0.37. Thus the confidence interval estimate is $-0.04 \leq \mu_2 - \mu_1 \leq 0.70$.

c. The formula for the standard error of the difference would be

$$s_{\overline{X}_1-\overline{X}_2} = \sqrt{\dfrac{s_1^2}{n_1} + \dfrac{s_2^2}{n_2}}$$

The standard deviations for the populations need not be equal. In addition, the populations would not have to be normally distributed.

11.3.a. H_0: $\mu_1 - \mu_2 = 0$; H_A: $\mu_1 - \mu_2 \neq 0$. An equivalent statement is

H_0: $\mu_1 = \mu_2$; H_A: $\mu_1 \neq \mu_2$.

b. At the 0.05 level of significance, the acceptance region for H_0 is $-1.96 \leq Z \leq 1.96$.

c. From Question 11.1, $\bar{X}_1 - \bar{X}_2 = -4$ and $\sigma_{\overline{X}_1-\overline{X}_2} = 1.22$

$$z = \dfrac{(\bar{X}_1 - \bar{X}_2) - (\mu_1 - \mu_2)}{\sigma_{\overline{X}_1-\overline{X}_2}} = \dfrac{-4 - 0}{1.22} = -3.28$$

d. Accept H_A. Apparently mix 2 is better than mix 1.

11.4.   Let the subscript 1 refer to design A and 2 refer to design B.

a. H_0: $\mu_1 - \mu_2 = 0$, H_A: $\mu_1 - \mu_2 \neq 0$

b. Use the 0.975 percentile of the t-distribution with $5 + 8 - 2 = 11$ df. Thus, the acceptance region is $-2.2010 \leq t \leq 2.2010$.

c. The formula for the test statistics is

$$t = \dfrac{(\bar{X}_1 - \bar{X}_2) - (\mu_1 - \mu_2)}{s_{\overline{X}_1-\overline{X}_2}}$$

From Question 11.2, $s_{\overline{X}_1-\overline{X}_2} = 0.120$ and $\bar{X}_1 - \bar{X}_2 = 0.33$. Thus

$$t = \dfrac{0.33 - 0}{0.120} = 2.75$$

d. Reject the null hypothesis. Design B apparently has a shorter assembly time.

11.5.a. Null hypothesis (H_0): $\mu_d = 0$.
Alternative hypothesis (H_A): $\mu_d \neq 0$

The population mean difference between the scores of matched pairs of salespeople, one of whom is assigned to each of the two training methods, is zero under the null hypothesis. Alternatively, either method is considerably better.

b. $s_d \sqrt{\dfrac{\Sigma(d - \bar{d})^2}{n - 1}}$ (text Equation 11-14a. First find s_d^2:

Scores				
A	B	d	$d - \bar{d}$	$(d - \bar{d})^2$
67	62	5	1	1
44	38	6	2	4
86	85	1	-3	9
62	58	4	0	0
		Total 16		14

$$\bar{d} = 4$$

$n = 4$ pairs

$s_d^2 = \Sigma(d - \bar{d})^2/(n - 1) = 14/3$, or 4.67

$s_d = 2.16$

c. $s_{\bar{d}} = s_d/\sqrt{n} = 2.16/\sqrt{4} = 1.08$ (text Equation 11-5).

d. From text Equation 11-17 $t = (\bar{d} - \mu_d)/s_{\bar{d}} = (4 - 0)/1.08$, or 3.70. From Appendix Table B-4, $t_{0.975} = 3.1824$ for 3 df. The null hypothesis must be rejected. Method A appears to be considerably better.

e. Yes, the matching described probably is the better procedure. Sales results with a technical product are likely to be influenced by differences in intelligence and motivation of salesmen. By matching on the basis of intelligence and motivation we remove the influence of these variables and have more assurance that the difference in composite scores is due to the training method. The procedures associated with text Equation 11-11, on the other hand, do not account for motivation and intelligence.

11.6.a. Let the subscript 1 refer to February and 2 refer to December.

$$p_1 = 0.55, \; p_2 = 0.61$$

$$s_{p_1 - p_2} = \sqrt{s^2_{p_1} + s^2_{p_2}}$$

$$s^2_{p_1} = \frac{p_1(1 - p)}{n_1 - 1} = \frac{0.55(1 - 0.55)}{1599} = 0.0001548$$

$$s^2_{p_2} = \frac{0.61(1 - 0.61)}{1599} = 0.0001488$$

$$s_{p_1 - p_2} = \sqrt{0.0001548 + 0.000148} = 0.0174241$$

b. $(p_1 - p_2) \leq zs_{p_1 - p_2} \leq \pi_1 - \pi_2 \leq p_1 - p_2 + zs_{p_1 - p_2}$.   For a
0.95 confidence coefficient, $z = 1.96$. From the data,
$(p_1 - p_2) = 0.06$.   The confidence interval is: (-0.06)
$- 1.96(0.0174241) \leq \pi_1 - \pi_2 \leq (-0.06) + 1.96(0.0174241)$ or
$-0.06 - 0.034 \leq \pi_1 - \pi_2 \leq -0.06 + 0.034$; $-0.094 \leq \pi_1 - \pi_2 \leq -0.026$.

11.7.a. H_0: $\pi_1 - \pi_2 = 0$; H_A: $\pi_1 - \pi_2 \neq 0$

$$p_c = \frac{n_1 p_1 + n_2 p_2}{n_1 + n_2} = \frac{1600(0.55) + 1600(0.56)}{1600 + 1600} = 0.555$$

$$s_{p_c} = \sqrt{p_c\left(1 - p_c\right)\left(\frac{1}{n_1} + \frac{1}{n_2}\right)}$$

$$= \sqrt{0.555(1 - 0.555)\left(\frac{1}{1600} + \frac{1}{1600}\right)} = 0.0175703$$

$$z = \frac{(p_1 - p_2) - (\pi_1 - \pi_2)}{s_{p_c}} = \frac{(0.55 - 0.56) - 0}{0.0175703} = -0.57$$

For any reasonable level of significance, we would accept the
null hypothesis.

b. The observed difference of -1.0% is only about a half of a
standard error ($z = -0.57$) from the hypothesized value of no
difference. This is well within the sampling fluctuations
that would occur if the true difference were zero. Thus there
is little evidence to support anything other than the hypothesis
of no difference.

CHAPTER 12:   SOLUTIONS TO SELF-CORRECTING EXERCISES

12.1.a. One chi-square distribution is distinguished from another by
the numerical value of degrees of freedom. In Table B-5, each
row pertains to a given chi-square distribution. The column
headings refer to the area to the *left* of the value of χ^2 that
appears in the body of the table (see (b)).

b. To find $\chi^2_{0.90}$, locate the row for *df* = 5 in the left-hand
column and find the column headed $\chi^2_{0.90}$. The value at the
intersection of this row and column is 9.24. For a chi-square
distribution with 5 *df*, $\chi^2_{0.90}$ = 9.24. This value cuts off
an area of 0.90 to its left and 0.10 to its right. (See the
figure in Table B-5 in the text.)

12.2.a. Let π_1 refer to the proportion of the population that prefers
automobile transportation, π_2 refer to the proportion of the
population that prefers bus transportation, and so forth. The
null hypothesis is that all of these proportions are equal.
Since there are four categories, each proportion is hypothesized to equal one-fourth. In symbols, (H_0): $\pi_1 = \pi_2 = \pi_3$
$= \pi_4 = 1/4$.

b. The observed frequencies for each category are not needed to
compute the expected frequencies. We need to know the total
number of observations and the null hypothesis in order to
compute expected frequencies.

c. The expected frequency for each classification represents the
number of observations we would expect to find on the average
in each category *if the null hypothesis is true*. Since there
will be 100 observations and the null hypothesis states that
the proportion of the population in each category is 1/4, the
expected frequency for each category is 1/4(100) = 25. The
sum of the expected frequencies for the first three categories
is 75. The total of the expected frequencies for all four categories must equal the total number of observations, which is 100.
Since the total number of observations *must* be 100 and the sum
of the first three expected frequencies is 75, we have no choice
except to assign an expected frequency of 25 to the fourth
category in order to assure that the sum of the observations
is 100. This line of reasoning is the basis of saying there
are three degrees of freedom in the problem. The expected
frequency in the fourth category is constrained by the expected
frequencies assigned to the other three and by the total number
of observations.

d. The observed frequencies are simply the observations which
result from the random sample.   Expected frequencies are *not*
related to the observed result (except for the total). Expected frequencies are related to the null hypothesis.

e. The observed frequencies in (i) are exactly equal to the expected frequencies and give the strongest possible evidence supporting the null hypothesis. The observed frequencies in (ii) are far different than the expected frequencies and do not support the null hypothesis. Note that both (i) and (ii) are extreme cases that are not likely to occur in practice. The observed frequencies in (iii) are more realistic. In this case, there is no obvious support for or against the null hypothesis.

i.

Type	f_0	f_e	$f_0 - f_e$	$(f_0 - f_e)^2/f_e$
Automobile	25	25	0	0
Bus	25	25	0	0
Train	25	25	0	0
Airplane	25	25	0	0
Total	100	100		$0 = \chi^2$

ii.

Type	f_0	f_e	$f_0 - f_e$	$(f_0 - f_e)^2/f_e$
Automobile	50	25	25	$25 = (25)^2/25$
Bus	0	25	-25	25
Train	0	25	-25	25
Airplane	50	25	25	25
Total	100	100		$100 = \chi^2$

iii.

Type	f_0	f_e	$f_0 - f_e$	$(f_0 - f_e)^2/f_e$
Automobile	32	25	7	$1.96 = (7)^2/25$
Bus	17	25	-8	2.56
Train	19	25	-6	1.44
Airplane	32	25	7	1.96
Total	100	100		$7.92 = \chi^2$

f. A small value of χ^2 tends to support the null hypothesis. A large value of χ^2 tends to refute the null hypothesis. For (i), where the observed and expected frequencies matched exactly, the computed value of chi-square is zero. For (ii), where there is wide disagreement between observed and expected frequencies, the computed chi-square value (100) is large and this correctly reflects the magnitude of the disagreement. For (iii), the computed value of χ^2 is 7.92, which is an intermediate value (see (g)).

g. For $\alpha = 0.05$ and 3 df,   Table B-5 in the text gives $\chi^2_{0.95} = 7.81$. The acceptance region for the null hypothesis includes all values of chi-square that are less than 7.81.   If the null hypothesis is true, 95 percent of all sample values of chi square will be less than 7.81.   According to this criterion, we would accept the null hypothesis for (i) and reject it for (ii) and (iii).

12.3.a. H_0: $\pi_1 = \pi_2 = \pi_3 = \pi_4 = 1/4$

b,c.

Hours	f_0	f_e	$f_0 - f_e$	$(f_0 - f_e)^2/f_e$
6 AM - 10 AM	18	16 = (1/4)64	2	0.25 = $(2)^2/16$
10 AM - 2 PM	10	16	-6	2.25
2 PM - 6 PM	24	16	8	4.00
6 PM - 10 PM	12	16	-4	1.00
Totals	64	64		7.50 = χ^2

Three degrees of freedom apply.

d. For $\alpha = 0.10$ and 3 df, Table B-5 gives $\chi^2_{0.90} = 6.25$.   If the null hypothesis is true, 90% of all sample values of χ^2 will be less than 6.25.   For this sample, the computed value of χ^2 is 7.50, which is larger than 6.25.   At the 0.10 level of significance, the notion of equally distributed demands should be rejected.

12.4.a. The null hypothesis is that age and income are independent.

b,c.

Income	AGE			
	Under 30		Over 30	
Under $10,000	2/16 = (2/4)(1/4)		2/16	1/4 = (100/400)
Over $10,000	4/16		4/16	2/4
Not stated	2/16		2/16	1/4
	2/4 = (200/400)		2/4	

Each marginal probability is estimated by dividing each row or column total by the total number of observations (400).   Each joint probability is the product of the corresponding marginal probabilities.   Be careful to notice that the computation of joint probabilities in this way is based on the assumption that age and income are *independent*; that is, the computation is based on the assumption that the *null hypothesis is true*.

d. The expected frequencies present the average frequency for each cell that we expect to find if repeated samples were taken and the null hypothesis were true.   The expected frequencies for this situation are found by multiplying the total number of observations by the estimated joint probability. For the *under 30 and under $10,000* classification, the estimated joint probability is 2/16 and the expected frequency is (2/16)(400) = 50.

e. Note that the expected frequencies must have the same row and column totals as the observed frequencies. These totals and the expected frequency from (d) are shown in the following table.

Income	Age Under 30	Over 30	Total
Under $10,000	50	___	100
Over $10,000	100	___	200
Not stated		___	100
Total	200	200	400

The expected frequencies not given in this table may be determined by subtractions from the row and column totals. Once one of the expected frequencies is found, the other three are determined. Thus, for this table, there are only two degrees of freedom. The complete table of expected frequencies is shown here.

Expected (f_e)

Income	Age Under 30	Over 30	Total
Under $10,000	50	50	100
Over $10,000	100	100	200
Not stated	50	50	100
Totals	200	200	400

f. For $\alpha = 0.05$ and 2 *df*, Table B-5 in the text gives $\chi^2_{0.95} = 5.99$. A computed value of χ^2 less than 5.99 will indicate acceptance of the null hypothesis.

g. The table shows the observed and expected frequencies along with the computed value of χ^2.

f_0	f_e	$f_0 - f_e$	$(f_0 - f_e)^2/f_e$
60	50	10	$2.0 = (10^2)/50$
40	50	−10	2.0
60	100	−40	16.0
140	100	40	16.0
80	50	30	18.0
20	50	−30	18.0
			$\overline{72.0} = \chi^2$

Since the computed value of χ^2 (72.0) exceeds the critical value (5.99), we reject the null hypothesis. We conclude age and income are related.

h. If all the observed frequencies happened to be equal to the expected frequencies, one would certainly accept the null hypothesis. The computed value of χ^2 would be zero. In general, the larger the difference between observed and expected frequencies, the larger the computed value of χ^2. Thus a large value of χ^2 is required to reject the null hypothesis. For a fixed number of degrees of freedom, the level of significance determines the critical value of χ^2.

12.5.a. Notice that this is a 2-row by 3-column table. The degrees of freedom are $(r - 1)(c - 1) = (2 - 1)(3 - 1) = 2$. From Table B-5 for $\alpha = 0.05$ and 2 df, $\chi^2_{0.95} = 5.99$. The acceptance region consists of all values of χ^2 that are less than 5.99. The acceptance region does *not* depend on the observed frequencies. It does depend on the level of significance and on the degrees of freedom.

b.

Expected Frequencies (f_e)

	Yes	No	Undecided	Total
Male	$(86/174)*(66/174)*$ $(174) = 32.6$	$(86/174)*(28/174)*$ $(174) = 13.8$	$(86/174)*(80/174)*$ $(174) = 39.5$	86
Female	$(88/174)*(66/174)*$ $(174) = 33.4$	$(88/174)*(28/174)*$ $(174) = 14.2$	$(88/174)*(80/174)*$ $(174) = 40.5$	88
Totals	66	28	80	174

c.

f_0	f_e	$(f_0 - f_e)$	$(f_0 - f_e)^2/f_e$
46	32.6	13.4	$5.51 = (13.4)^2/32.6$
20	33.4	-13.4	5.38
10	13.8	-3.8	1.05
18	14.2	3.8	1.02
30	39.5	-9.5	2.28
50	40.5	9.5	2.23

$$17.47 = \chi^2$$

d. The computed value (17.47) exceeds the critical value (5.99). We reject the null hypothesis and conclude sex and preference *are* related.

12.6.a. The null hypothesis is that 25% of the new cars in each region are imports. For a random sample of 100 cars in the northern market, the expected number of imports is 0.25(100) = 25.

b. The expected number of domestic cars may be found by subtraction. Thus 100 - 25 = 75. Hence, 1 *df* applies to this sample.

c.

	MARKET			
	Northern	Eastern	Southern	Western
Imports	25	15 = 0.25(60)	20	30
Domestics	75	45	60	90
	100	60	80	120

d. No. We need to know the sample sizes and the null hypothesis. Notice that the null hypothesis does *not* come from the data. There is 1 *df* for each sample. Since there are four independent samples, there are 4 *df*. From Table B-5, the critical value of χ^2 at the 0.10 level of significance with 4 *df* is 11.4. Any sample value less than or equal to this value will cause us to accept the null hypothesis.

e. $\chi^2 = \dfrac{(20 - 25)^2}{25} + \dfrac{(15 - 40)^2}{40} + \dfrac{(40 - 20)^2}{20} + \dfrac{(40 - 30)^2}{30}$

$+ \dfrac{(80 - 75)^2}{75} + \dfrac{(20 - 45)^2}{45} + \dfrac{(40 - 60)^2}{60} + \dfrac{(80 - 90)^2}{90}$

$= 1.0 + 15.6 + 20.0 + 3.3 + 0.3 + 13.9 + 6.7 + 1.1$

$= 61.9$

Since this value is in the rejection region, we conclude that the proportion of imports is not 25% in all markets.

12.7.a.

	February	January	December
Approve	55	56	61
Other opinion	45	44	39
	100	100	100

b. Observed frequencies:

	February	January	December
Approve	880	896	976
Other opinion	720	704	624
	1600	1600	1600

c. Expected frequencies:

	February	January	December
Approve	800	800	800
Other opinion	800	800	800
	1600	1600	1600

d. $\chi^2 = \sum \dfrac{(f_0 - f_e)^2}{f_e} = \dfrac{(880 - 800)^2}{800} + \dfrac{(896 - 800)^2}{800} + \dfrac{(976 - 800)^2}{800}$

$$+ \dfrac{(720 - 800)^2}{800} + \dfrac{(704 - 800)^2}{800} + \dfrac{(624 - 800)^2}{800}$$

$$= 8.00 + 11.52 + 38.72 + 8.00 + 11.52 + 38.72$$

$$= 116.48$$

e. There are 3 df--one for each independent sample.

f. The null hypothesis should be rejected. It is very unlikely that the true proportion is 0.50 for all months.

12.8.a. The mean number of errors in the sample is:

$$\frac{0(47) + 1(25) + 2(16) + 3(6) + 4(5) + 5(1)}{100} = \frac{100}{100} = 1$$

Thus, $n\pi = 1$ and $\pi = 1/5 = 0.2$.

b. From Appendix B, Table B-1, for $n = 5$ and $\pi = 0.2$.

x	$P(x)$
0	0.3277
1	0.4096
2	0.2048
3	0.0512
4	0.0064
5	0.0003

c,d. To obtain the expected frequencies, multiply each binomial probability by the sample size (100):

x	f_0	f_e	$(f_0 - f_e)^2/f_e$
0	47	32.77	6.18
1	25	40.96	6.22
2	16	20.48	0.98
3	6 ⎫	5.12 ⎫	
4	5 ⎬ 12	0.64 ⎬ 5.79	6.66
5	1 ⎭	0.03 ⎭	

$$\chi^2 = 20.04$$

Notice that the expected frequencies for $x = 4$ and $x = 5$ are less than 5 so these frequencies are combined with the frequency for $x = 3$. Thus there are 4 categories and $df = 4 - 2 = 2$. (One df is lost because we estimated π from the data.)

e. At the 0.05 level of significance, $\chi^2_{0.95}(2) = 5.99$. Since the computed value exceeds the critical value, we reject the hypothesis of a binomial random variable.

12.9.a. The distribution for $n = 4$ does not seem to be normally distributed. The distribution for $n = 64$ does not appear to be normally distributed.

b. From sampling theory the mean and standard deviation of this distribution are $\mu_{\bar{x}} = 1$ and $\sigma_{\bar{x}} = \sigma/\sqrt{n} = 1/\sqrt{4} = 0.5$. (Sample calculations are given beneath the table.)

			NORMAL PROBABILITY			
Interval	f_0	z(upper)	Cumula-tive	Interval	f_e	$\dfrac{(f_0 - f_e)^2}{f_e}$
0.0195–0.215	8	−1.57	0.0582	0.0582	58.2	43.3
0.215–0.455	110	−1.09	0.1379	0.0797	79.7	11.5
0.455–0.695	188	−0.61	0.2709	0.1330	133.0	22.7
0.695–0.935	207	−0.13	0.4483	0.1774	177.4	4.9
0.935–1.175	170	0.35	0.6368	0.1885	188.5	1.8
1.175–1.415	129	0.83	0.7967	0.1599	159.9	6.0
1.415–1.655	78	1.31	0.9049	0.1082	108.2	8.4
1.655–1.895	57	1.79	0.9633	0.0584	58.4	0.0
1.895–2.135	24	2.26	0.9881	0.0248	24.8	0.0
2.135–2.275	11	2.54	0.9945	0.0065	6.5	3.3
2.275–2.615	13 ⎫					
2.615–2.855	1 ⎬ 18	3.71	1.0000	0.0055	5.5	28.4
2.855–3.095	3					
3.095–3.335	1 ⎭					
	1000			1.0001		$\chi^2 = 130.3$

For the interval 0.0195–0.215, $z = \dfrac{0.215 - 1}{0.5} = 1.57$ and $P(z \le -1.57) = 0.0582$, which is also the probability for the interval. The expected frequency for this interval is $(100)0.0582 = 58.2$. The value of $\dfrac{(f_0 - f_e)^2}{f_e}$ is $\dfrac{(8 - 58.2)^2}{58.2} = 43.3$.

For the interval 0.215–0.455, $z = \dfrac{0.455 - 1}{0.5} = -1.09$; $P(z \le 1.09) = 0.1379$, $P(-1.57 \le z \le -1.09) = 0.1379 - 0.0582 = 0.0797$, and the expected frequency is $1000(0.0797) = 79.7$.

c. Since the mean and standard deviation are known in this situation, the degrees of freedom is equal to the number of classes minus 1, or 10. (In many problems encountered in practice, a degree of freedom is lost when the mean or standard deviation is computed from the data.)

d. At the 0.005 level of significance and 10 df, $\chi^2 = 25.19$. Since the value of χ^2 computed from the data is 130.3, we reject the hypothesis of normality.

e. For $n = 64$, $\mu_{\bar{x}} = 1$ and $\sigma_{\bar{x}} = 1/\sqrt{64} = 0.125$.

NORMAL PROBABILITY

Interval	f_0	z (upper)	Cumulative	Interval	f_e	$\dfrac{(f_0 - f_e)^2}{f_e}$
0.675-0.735	11	-2.12	0.0170	0.0170	7.0	2.12
0.735-0.795	28	-.164	0.0505	0.0335	33.5	0.90
0.795-0.855	90	-1.16	0.1230	0.0725	72.5	4.33
0.855-0.915	128	-0.68	0.2483	0.1253	125.3	0.06
0.915-0.975	159	-0.20	0.4207	0.1724	172.4	1.04
0.975-1.035	221	0.28	0.6103	0.1896	189.6	5.20
1.035-1.095	143	0.76	0.7764	0.1661	166.1	3.21
1.095-1.155	110	1.24	0.8925	0.1161	116.1	0.32
1.155-1.215	61	1.72	0.9573	0.0648	64.8	0.22
1.215-1.275	33	2.20	0.9861	0.0288	28.8	0.61
1.275-1.335	8	2.68	0.9963	0.0102	10.2	0.47
1.335-1.395	2 ⎫					
1.395-1.455	4 ⎬ 8	3.64	1.0000	0.0037	3.7	5.00
1.455-1.515	2 ⎭					
	1000			1.000		23.48

At the 0.005 level of significance with 11 df, $\chi^2 = 26.76$. We cannot reject the hypothesis of normality.

f. The example tends to confirm the central limit theorem and is in line with the graphical analysis in part a. Notice the computed values of χ^2 are 130.3 for $n = 4$ and 23.48 for $n = 64$. If these values are used as a measure of discrepancy between a normal distribution and the observed data, the smaller value of χ^2 indicates the normal distribution is a better fit for $n = 64$ than for $n = 4$.

CHAPTER 13:   SOLUTIONS TO SELF-CORRECTING EXERCISES

13.1.a.

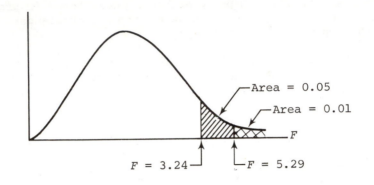

Area = 0.05
Area = 0.01
F
$F = 3.24$ $F = 5.29$

In Table B-6, find the column labeled m_1 = 3 and the rows labeled m_2 = 16. In the body of the table at the intersection of this column and these rows, find F = 3.24 in lightface type and F = 5.29 in boldface type. The larger value (5.29) is rightmost on the F-axis in the sketch and has 1% of the area under the distribution to its right. The F-value 3.24 cuts off 5% of the area to its right.

b. Each F-distribution has two parameters called *degrees of freedom for the numerator* (m_1) and *degrees of freedom for the denominator* (m_2). Different F-distributions are distinguished from each other by the pair of numerical values assigned to m_1 and m_2.

c. Table B-6 gives only the 1% and 5% F-values for a given distribution. (Although more extensive tables are available in statistical handbooks, the abbreviated tables in Table B-6 will be adequate to illustrate analysis of variance problems.)

d. The F-distributions are different because the values assigned to the parameters are different. (Note m_1 and m_2 are different parameters.) From Table B-6, the 1% F-value for the distribution with m_1 = 3 and m_2 = 16 is F = 5.29. For m_1 = 16 and m_2 = 3, the 1% F-value is F = 26.83. Thus the 1% F-values are different as we would expect since the distributions are different.

13.2.a. Service life is the variable observed. Each column refers to a different type of light. There are 5 rows. Each row represents a different observation for the 4 lights. In this problem, there is an equal number of observations for each light. Other problems may have unequal numbers of observations.

b.

	Level			
	A	B	C	D
	1	2	0	4
	1	3	3	6
	2	5	3	7
	3	5	4	8
	3	5	5	10
Level totals	10	20	15	35
Grand total	= 80			
Level means	2	4	3	7
Grand mean	= 4			
Number of observations	5	5	5	5	20

c. $X_{24} = 6$, the value in the second row and fourth column.
$C_3 = 15$, the sum of the third column.
$\overline{X}_2 = 4$, the mean of the second column.
$\overline{\overline{X}} = 4$, the grand mean of all 20 values.
$n = 20$, the number of values in the table.

13.3.a. From Equation 13-3, the estimate of the variance of the sampling distribution of means of five observation samples is

$$s_{\overline{X}}^2 = \frac{\Sigma(\overline{X} - \overline{\overline{X}})^2}{c - 1} = \frac{(2 - 4)^2 + (4 - 4)^2 + (3 - 4)^2 + (7 - 4)^2}{4 - 1},$$

or $\frac{14}{3}$.

Then, from Equation 13-4, the estimate of σ^2 based on the four sample means is $r(s_{\overline{X}}^2) = 5(14/3)$, or 70/3 with $c - 1$, or 3, degrees of freedom.

b. Equation 13-5 states that we are to find the variance in each column measured from the column mean and average these variances to get a "within columns" estimate of σ^2. For the first column,

$$s_1^2 = \frac{\Sigma(X - \overline{X})^2}{r - 1}$$

$$= \frac{(1 - 2)^2 + (1 - 2)^2 + (2 - 2)^2 + (3 - 2)^2 + (3 - 2)^2}{5 - 1} = \frac{4}{4}, \text{ or } 1$$

Similarly,

$$s_2^2 = \frac{8}{4} = 2 \quad s_3^2 = \frac{14}{4} \quad s_4^2 = \frac{20}{4} = 5$$

Finally, the within-columns estimate of σ^2 is:

$$\frac{1}{4}\left(\frac{4}{4}+\frac{8}{4}+\frac{14}{4}+\frac{20}{4}\right)=\frac{46}{16}=\frac{23}{8}$$

with 16 df (4 from each column).

c. Equation 13-6 instructs us to find the ratio of the among columns estimate of σ^2 to the within-columns estimate of σ^2. For this example, $F=\frac{70/3}{23/8}$, or 8.12, with 3 df in the numerator and 16 in the denominator. From Table B-6, $F_{0.95,3,16}=3.24$ so there is evidence of significant differences in mean service lives at the 0.05 level.

d. The null hypothesis states that the four population level means are equal--that is, all four types of lights have the same mean service life. If, in fact, the means are different, we can expect the four sample means to be widely dispersed relative to the within-columns variability. The resulting F-ration will be much larger than can be explained by sampling fluctuation.

13.4.a. The null hypothesis is that *all* of the population means are equal: H_0: $\mu_1=\mu_2=\ldots=\mu_k$. The alternative is that at least one population mean is not equal to the others.

b. If the null hypothesis is true, both the numerator and denominator variances should be approximately equal so their ratio will, on the average, be close to 1.

c. If the alternative hypothesis is true, at least one of the population means will not be equal to the others. This can be expected to cause greater than usual dispersion among the sample means. This dispersion will be reflected in the value of the among-column estimate of σ^2 which, in turn, will cause the numerator variance to be large in comparison with the denominator variance. As a result, the entire F-ratio will have a tendency to be large when the alternative hypothesis is true.

13.5.a. The null hypothesis is that the three populations have equal means. From the figure, we can see that the null hypothesis is false. In practical problems, we do not know when the null hypothesis is true or false. (In this example, we are illustrating the relationship between the true state of the hypothesis and the resulting F-ratio.)

b. From Equation 13-4 the among-columns estimate of σ^2 is

$$\sigma = \frac{r\Sigma(\overline{X} - \overline{\overline{X}})^2}{c - 1}$$

$$= \frac{3[(9.67 - 23.22)^2 + (15.33 - 23.22)^2 + (44.67 - 23.22)^2]}{3 - 1}$$

$$= \frac{3(706)}{2} = 1059$$

The within-columns estimate of σ^2 is the average of the column estimates, or $\frac{1}{3}(4.33 + 4.33 + 4.33) = 4.33$. The F-ratio is large because of the dispersion of the sample means. correctly reflects the inequality of the population means.

c. In this case the null hypothesis is true. Using the same procedure as in (b), the among-columns estimate of σ^2 is 6.76. The within-columns estimate of $\sigma^2 = 4.97$. The F-ratio is $F = 6.76/4.97 = 1.36$. This F-ratio is small due to the small dispersion among sample means. This correctly reflects the equality of population means. Notice that the denominators for each F-ratio are roughly equal because σ^2 is the same for both examples. The difference in the F-ratios is due primarily to the dispersion of sample means—the greater the dispersion, the larger the F-ratio. A large F-ratio tends to refute the null hypothesis of equality of population means.

13.6.a. The correction term is $T^2/n = (80)^2/20 = 320$. SST is found by adding the squares of all of the observations and subtracting T^2/n. Thus

$$SST = 1^2 + 1^2 + 2^2 + 3^2 + 3^2 + \ldots 4^2 + 6^2$$

$$+ 7^2 + 8^2 + 10^2 - 320$$

$$= 24 + 88 + 59 + 265 - 320, \text{ or } 116$$

SSA is found by squaring each column total and dividing by the number of observations in the column. The resulting quantities are added and T^2/n is subtracted from this sum. Thus

$$SSA = \frac{10^2}{5} + \frac{20^2}{5} + \frac{15^2}{5} + \frac{35^2}{5} - 320$$

$$= 20 + 80 + 45 + 245 - 320, \text{ or } 70$$

Finally, SSE = SST − SSA = 116 − 70, or 46.

b.

Source of Variation	Sums of Squares	Degrees of Freedom	Mean Squares	F
Type of light	70	3	70/3	8.12
Residual	46	16	23/8	
Total	116	19		

c. The values of MSA and MSE are the same as the numerator and denominator of F as found in Question 13.3. The procedures in Questions 13.3 and 13.6 are equivalent. The latter is computationally easier when the observations do not produce small integers for deviations.

13.7.a. $K = (1)\bar{X}_E + (-1)\bar{X}_A = 4 - 3 = 1$

$$s^2(K) = b_1{}^2 \frac{MSE}{n_1} + b_2{}^2 \frac{MSE}{n_2}$$

$$s^2(K) = (1)^2 \frac{1.5}{9} + (-1)^2 \frac{1.5}{9} = 0.33$$

$s(K) = 0.58$

$$T = \sqrt{(c - 1)\ F_{df_1,\ df_2}}$$

$c = 5,\ F_{0.95,4,40} = 3.23$

$T = \sqrt{4(3.23)} = 3.59$

The confidence interval is:

$K \pm Ts(K) = 1 \pm 3.59(0.58) = 1 \pm 2.08$ or -1.08 to 3.08

Since the confidence interval includes zero, the difference between $\bar{X}_E$ and $\bar{X}_A$ is not significant.

b. $K = \bar{X}_D - \bar{X}_C = 9 - 7 = 2$; since two means are compared,

$s(K) = 0.58$ as in (a) and $T = 3.59$.

$K \pm Ts(K) = 2 \pm -2.08$ or -0.08 to 4.08

Since this interval includes zero, the difference between $\bar{X}_D$ and $\bar{X}_C$ is not significant.

c. $K = \frac{1}{2} X_D + \frac{1}{2} X_C - \left(\frac{1}{2} X_E + \frac{1}{2} X_A\right)$

$K = \frac{1}{2}\left(9\right) + \left(+\frac{1}{2}\right)\left(7\right) - \left[\left(\frac{1}{2}\right)\left(4\right) + \left(\frac{1}{2}\right)\left(3\right)\right] = 4.5$

$S^2(K) = b_1{}^2 \frac{MSE}{n_2} + b_2{}^2 \frac{MSE}{n_2} + b_3{}^2 \frac{MSE}{n_3} + b_4{}^2 \frac{MSE}{n_4}$

$= \left(\frac{1}{2}\right)^2 \frac{1.5}{9} + \left(+\frac{1}{2}\right)^2 \frac{1.5}{9} + \left(\frac{-1}{2}\right)^2 \frac{1.5}{9} + \left(\frac{-1}{2}\right)^2 \frac{1.5}{9}$

$S^2(K) = 0.167, \quad S(K) = 0.41$

$K \pm Ts(K) = 4.5 \pm 3.59(0.41) \quad 4.5 \pm 1.47 \quad \text{or} \quad 3.03 \text{ to } 5.97$

Since the confidence interval does not include zero, the difference is significant.

d. As in (a), $K = 1$, $s(K) = 0.58$. The formula for a single comparison is $K \pm ts(K)$. The t-value is from Table B-4 with $9 - 1 = 8$ df. For a 0.95 confidence coefficient, $t = 2.3060$. Thus the confidence interval is

$$1 \pm 2.3060(0.58) \quad \text{or } 1 \pm 1.34$$

or −0.34 to 2.34. The interval includes zero so there is no significant difference. Note the confidence interval is narrower than the one found in (a), but no other confidence intervals can be found.

13.8.a. The purpose of replication and randomization is to minimize the influence of factors not specifically controlled in the experiment on the response variable. The purpose of cross classification is to include a factor in an experiment in such a way that the factor's influence on the response variable can be determined.

b. Replication means selecting a random sample of *several* units of observation and subjecting each to the same conditions. Randomization is the (random) process by which units of observation are assigned to the various experimental conditions. Cross classification is a technique in which every possible combination of factors included in the design is actually incorporated into the experiment.

c. Replication and randomization require random selection and placement. Cross classification is not a random process since it is purposely planned.

CHAPTER 14:   SOLUTIONS TO SELF-CORRECTING EXERCISES

14.1.

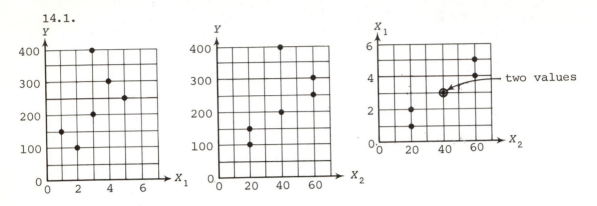

Notice that the number of observations is not large enough to draw any realistic conclusion about the assumptions of linearity or general trends in the data.

14.2.a.

Patient	X_1^2	X_2^2	X_1X_2	X_1Y	X_2Y
1	4	400	40	200	2000
2	1	400	20	150	3000
3	9	1600	120	600	8000
4	25	3600	300	1250	15,000
5	16	3600	240	1200	18,000
6	9	1600	120	1200	16,000
	64	11,200	840	4600	62,000

b. Substituting the appropriate sums in text Equations 14-3, the normal equations are

$$1400 = 6a + 18b_1 + 240b_2$$
$$4600 = 18a + 64b_1 + 840b_2$$
$$62,000 = 240a + 840b_1 + 11,200b_2$$

c. The normal equations are a system of linear equations in which the variables are the regression coefficients. When the system of equations is solved simultaneously, the values obtained in the solution are the least-squares regression coefficients; that is, they are the coefficients that cause the sum of the squared deviations to be minimized.

d. Substituting $a = 83.33$ $b_1 = -50$, and $b_1 = 7.5$ into the right-hand side of the normal equations in (b), we obtain

$$6(83.33) + 18(-50) + 240(7.5) = 1399.98$$
$$18(83.33) + 64(-50) + 840(7.5) = 4599.94$$
$$240(83.33) + 840(-50) + 11,200(7.5) = 61,999.2$$

These results are very nearly equal to the left-hand side of the normal equations. This verifies that these values are a solution to the normal equations; consequently, they are the least-squares estimates in the regression equation.

e. There are several ways to solve these equations. Although some methods involve knowledge of mathematics that we do not presume the reader to have, the elimination technique involves only ordinary algebra. One way to apply this technique is as follows. Multiply the first equation by 3 and subtract the resulting equation from the second equation. The result is $400 = 10b_1 + 120b_2$. Multiply the first equation by 40 and subtract the result from the third equation. The result is $6000 = 120b_1 + 1600b_2$. (These steps were taken to eliminate the variable a from the system.) The resulting equations are a system of two equations in two variables. This system may be solved in a similar fashion giving $b_1 = -50$ and $b_2 = 7.5$. These values may now be substituted into any one of the original equations, which in turn is solved to obtain $a = 83.33$.

f. $Y_c = 83.33 - 50X_1 + 7.5X_2$

g. Substituting $X_1 = 2$ and $X_2 = 30$ into the least-squares equation, we have $Y_c = 83.33 - 50(2) + 7.5(30) = \$208.33$.

14.3.a. $s_{Y \cdot 12}^2 = \Sigma(Y - Y_c)^2/(n - 3)$. The numerator is most easily calculated from the relationship

$$\Sigma(Y - Y_c)^2 = \Sigma Y^2 - a\Sigma Y - b_1 \Sigma X_1 Y - b_2 \Sigma X_2 Y$$

From the original data, $\Sigma Y^2 = 100^2 + 150^2 + \ldots + 400^2 = 385,000$. (All other sums and quantities needed are found in Questions 14.1 and 14.2.)

$$\Sigma(Y - Y_c)^2 = 385,000 - (83.33)(1400) - (-50)(4600)$$
$$- (7.5)(62,000)$$
$$= 33,338$$

$$s_{Y \cdot 12}^2 = 33,338/(6 - 3) = 11,113 \text{ (to the nearest whole number)}$$
$$s_{Y \cdot 12} = \sqrt{11,113} = 105.4$$

b. Text equation 14-8 is applicable:

$$r^2{}_{Y \cdot 12} = \frac{a\Sigma Y + b_1 \Sigma X_1 Y + b_2 \Sigma X_2 Y - n\overline{Y}^2}{\Sigma Y^2 - n\,\overline{Y}^2}$$

To the nearest whole number,

$$\Sigma(Y - \overline{Y})^2 = \Sigma Y^2 - n(\overline{Y})^2 = 385,000 - 6\left(\frac{1400}{6}\right)^2 = 58,333$$

$$r^2{}_{Y \cdot 12} = \frac{83.33(1400) + (-50)(4600) + 7.5(62,000) - 6(1400/6)^2}{58,333}$$

$$= \frac{24,995}{58,333}$$

$$= 0.43$$

The coefficient of determination tells us the estimated proportion of the population variance of Y that is accounted for by the independent variables X_1 and X_2.

14.4.a. $Y_C = 292.85 + 6.75X_1 + 13.00X_2$

or $MSAT_C = 292.85 + 6.75*ALG + 13.00*YHSM$

b. The MSAT will increase an average of 6.75 points for a unit increase on the algebra score with YHSM held constant and 13.0 points for an additional year of high school mathematics with ALG held constant.

c. Since the coefficient of determination is 0.378961, about 38% of the variabilility in MSAT is explained by ALG and YHSM.

d. The mean value of the residuals is always zero. If the residuals are normally distributed, 95% of the residuals will be within the interval $0 \pm s_{Y \cdot 12}$ $(t_{0.975})$, where the t-value has $n - 3$ degrees of freedom. this case the interval is

$0 \pm 64.22(1.96)$ or 0 ± 125.9

e. There are 15 observations outside this interval. In terms of a proportion, this is 15/339 or 0.044. In (d), we found that this proportion would be 0.05 if the residuals are normally distributed. There is no reason to believe the assumption of normality is incorrect. In addition, Figure 14-2 shows no tendency for the residuals to be related to ALG.

f. Plots of the residuals versus each variable in the model should be constructed. These plots should be analyzed to see if the assumption of normality is violated or if there appears to be any relationship between the residuals and any of the variables in the model. Most computer packages have provisions that make it easy to generate plots such as the one shown in Figure 14-2. In addition, it is usually easy to perform simple regressions using the residuals as the dependent variable and using each variable in the model as the independent variable.

14.5.a. From the analysis of variance portion of the computer output, the computed F-ratio is 102.51. This value should be compared with the F-value from Table B-6 at the 0.01 level of significance with $m_1 = 2$ and $m_2 = 36$. Table B-6 gives the value as 7.39. Since the computed F-value (102.51) is much larger than the critical value, we can safely reject the null hypothesis.

b. From the estimated response portion of the computer printout, the expected value of MSAT is 500.662. The 0.95 confidence interval for this individual is 500.662 ± 1.96(64.69) or 500.662 ± 126.8, where 1.96 is $t_{0.975}$ with 338 df.

c. The conditional mean is 500.662, as read from the computer printout. The confidence interval for the mean MSAT for all persons with ALG = 25 and YHSM = 3 is 500.662 + 1.96(5.607) or 500.662 ± 10.99. Note that confidence interval for the mean will always be narrower than the prediction interval for an individual.

d. The computer printout gives a computed t-statistic of 2.22 for this hypothesis. From Table B-4, the critical value is approximately 1.96. We reject the hypothesis that the regression coefficient is zero in the model population.

e. The confidence interval is

$$b_1 \pm t\left(s_{b_1}\right)$$

For this problem, we have

6.76 ± 1.96(0.50)   or   6.76 ± 0.98.

Thus we have 0.95 confidence that $5.77 \leqq B_1 \leqq 7.73$.

14.6.a. There is a modest positive correlation of 0.208 between ALG and YHSM.

b. In model I, the computed t-statistic for YHSM is 2.22.   In
   Question 14.5(d), we concluded that the regression coefficient
   differed significantly from zero.   In model II, the t-statistic
   for this regression coefficient is only 0.84, which is not
   significantly different than zero.   In other words with the
   variable SEX in the model, the variable YHSM is no longer very
   useful in predicting MSAT.

c.

Model	Independent Variables	Coefficient of Determination
I	ALG, YHSM	0.378961
II	ALG, YHSM, SEX	0.413801
III	ALG, SEX	0.416456

In terms of the coefficient of determination, models II and III
both explain about the same proportion of the variability of
MSAT.   Generally it is best to use the model that achieves a
high value of R^2 with the fewest variables.   Notice that there
are other criteria for selecting a model such as the availability of data, the cost of data, and meeting the assumptions
of the population model.   Model III still has correlation between the independent variables.   The researcher might look
at other candidates for independent variables before selecting
the final model.

14.7.a. An indicator variable has two values (0 and 1).   In model III,
   SEX is an indicator variable.   Men are coded as zero and women
   as 1.   The equation for men is

$$\text{MSAT}_C = 335.54 + 7.48(\text{ALG})$$

For women, the equation is

$$\text{MSAT}_C = (335.54 - 28.17) + 7.48(\text{ALG}) \quad \text{or}$$

$$\text{MSAT}_C = 307.37 + 7.48(\text{ALG})$$

Notice that these two equations are equations that are equivalent
to

$$\text{MSAT}_C = 335.54 + 7.48(\text{ALG}) - 28.17 \, (\text{SEX})$$

b. The number of indicator variables is $c - 1$, where c is the number
   of classifications.   In this case, $3 - 1 = 2$.   One scheme for
   the indicator variables is as follows.

Classification	X_1	X_2
In-state, high-density	0	0
In-state, low-density	1	0
Out-of-state	0	1

Other arrangements are possible. The point is to make the combination of values of the indicator assigned to each classification unique.

c.

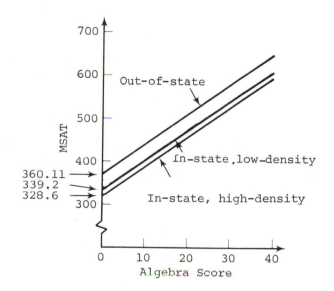

The t-statistic for the coefficient of X_1 is 1.26 and for the coefficient of X_2 is 2.34. For any reasonable level of significance, we can conclude that the coefficient of X_1 does not differ significantly from zero and the coefficient of X_2 does not differ significantly from zero. In other words, the classification of within state students by population density is not important. The classification of out-of-state is important.

14.8.a,d,e.

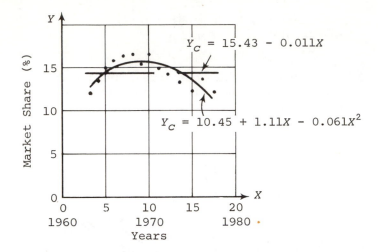

$$Y_C = 15.43 - 0.011X$$

$$Y_C = 10.45 + 1.11X - 0.061X^2$$

b. A linear model would have been appropriate for the years 1963 through 1968. Projections for beyond the range of the data are not appropriate. When all of the values for 1963–1977 are examined, a nonlinear model is required. A simple plot of the data will frequently reveal nonlinearities in the data.

c. The standard error for the parabola is about half that of the linear equation. The parabola explains about six times more of the variability of market share than the linear model.

f. The maximum value of market share was reached in about 1969. Since the data were collected over time, it would be difficult to say exactly when the decline should have been recognized. By the early 1970s, the decline in market share was probably clear.

g. Use the multiple regression model $Y_C = a + b_1X_1 + b_2X_2$ with $X_1 = X$ and $X_2 = X^2$

CHAPTER 15:   SOLUTIONS TO SELF-CORRECTING EXERCISES

15.1.a. The test statistic W is the sum of the ranks assigned to the smaller sample $n_1 = 2$.   The smallest possible value of W is $W = 1 + 2 = 3$ and the largest is $W = 6 + 7 = 13$.   The complete test of the possible ranks and corresponding values of W are as follows.

Ranks	W
1 + 2	3
1 + 3	4
1 + 4	5
1 + 5	6
1 + 6	7
1 + 7	8
2 + 3	5
2 + 4	6
2 + 5	7
2 + 6	8
2 + 7	9
3 + 4	7
3 + 5	8
3 + 6	9
3 + 7	10
4 + 5	9
4 + 6	10
4 + 7	11
5 + 6	11
5 + 7	12
6 + 7	13

The probability distribution is the following:

W	f	Probability
3	1	0.048
4	1	0.048
5	2	0.095
6	2	0.095
7	3	0.143
8	3	0.143
9	3	0.143
10	2	0.095
11	2	0.095
12	1	0.048
13	1	0.048
	21	

b. $\mu_W = \dfrac{n_1(n + 1)}{2}$

$\sigma_W = \sqrt{\dfrac{n_1 n_2(n + 1)}{12}}$

$n_1 = 2$

$n_2 = 5$

$n = 2 + 5 = 7$

$\mu_W = \dfrac{2(7 + 1)}{2} = 8$

$\sigma_W = \sqrt{\dfrac{2(5)(7 + 1)}{12}} = 2.58$

c. $\alpha = 0.048 + 0.048 = 0.096$

d. $W \geq 4$

15.2.a. The time measurements are made on a ratio scale. The two-sample
t-test not only requires data measured on an interval or ratio
scale, it also requires the population to be normally distributed.
Since the latter requirement is violated, the Wilcoxon test is
appropriate.

b. Data ranked from smallest to largest:

Rank	Drying Time	Rank	Drying Time
1	37.4	11	57.9
2	38.2	12	58.1
3	40.0	13	59.9
4	42.8	14	60.0
5	45.5	15	60.1
6	49.2	16	61.9
7	50.2	17	63.2
8	56.6	18	63.6
9	56.8	19	65.7
10	57.8	20	74.0
		21	89.4

The drying times for the smaller sample are underlined in the table.

The test statistic is the sum of the ranks for the smaller sample:

$$W = 1 + 2 + 3 + 4 + 6 + 8 + 10 + 12 + 15 + 16 = 77$$

c. A small value of W implies that the new paint dries faster than the old; a large value indicates the opposite. The smallest possible value of W would occur if the ranks one through eight were assigned to the new paint. In this case $W = 36$. This value would occur if all of the new paint drying times were faster than all of the old paint drying times. This would be the clearest possible evidence that the new paint dries faster. In practice such clear-cut sample evidence occurs infrequently.

d. H_0: The old paint dries at least as fast or faster
   H_A: The new paint dries faster.

$$n_1 = 10, \quad n_2 = 11, \quad n = 10 + 11 = 21$$

$$\mu_W = \frac{10(21+1)}{2} = 110$$

$$\sigma_W = \sqrt{\frac{10(11)(21+1)}{12}} = 14.2$$

$$z = \frac{77 - 110}{14.2} = -2.32$$

$$z_{0.005} = -2.58$$

Since the observed value of   is greater than the critical value, we accept the null hypothesis. The new paint apparently does not dry faster.

15.3.a. For case I, A, B, and C have different central locations, which supports H_A. The ranks 1-5 are associated with A, 6-10 with B, and 11-15 with C; thus, all low ranks are associated with A, middle ranks with B, and high ranks with C. For case II, there is no clear separation of ranks; some low, middle, and high ranks are associated with A, B, and C. Case II supports H_0.

b. For case II, T_j T_j^2 and T_j^2/n_j are about the same order of magnitude which indicates the ranks are mixed between A, B, and C. For case I, there is more variability in these quantities indicating a separation of ranks.

c. $H = \dfrac{12}{n(n+1)} S - 3(n+1), \quad S = \sum \dfrac{T_j^2}{n_j}$

Case I: $H = \dfrac{12}{15(15 + 1)}(45 + 320 + 845) - 3(15 + 1)$

$= 0.05(45 + 320 + 845) - 48$

$= 60.5 - 48 = 12.5$

Case II: $H = 0.05(245 + 320 + 405) - 48$

$= 48.5 - 48 = 0.5$

The higher variability in T_j^2/n_j mentioned in (c) is reflected in a higher value of H. If there are at least five observations per treatment level, H is approximately distributed as chi-square with $k - 1$ degrees of freedom. Here, $k - 1 = 2$. (Note this is an upper-tail test.) Table B-5 shows that H for case I is too large to support anything other than the alternative hypothesis and that H for case II is too small to support anything other than the null hypothesis.

15.4.a,b.   Ranked Incomes

	Neighborhood		
	A	B	C
	10	7	2
	21	19	8
	4	3	6
	11	9	12
	18	13	1
	17	15	16
	5	20	14
$T_j =$	86	86	59
$T_j^2 =$	7396	7396	3481
$T_j^2/n_j =$	1056.6	1056.6	497.3

c. From text Equation 15-4, $H = \dfrac{12}{21(22)}(1056.6 + 1056.6 + 497.3)$

$- 3(22)$, or 1.805. Since there are 3 neighborhoods, a chi-square distribution with 2 df applies. From Table B-5, $\chi_{0.95,2}^2 = 5.99$. Consequently, we cannot reject the null hypothesis that all three income distributions have the same central location.

15.5.

Pair	Scores A	Scores B	Absolute Difference	Rank of Absolute Difference	Signed Rank
1	78	62	16	7	7
2	89	93	4	2	-2
3	65	78	13	5	-5
4	93	72	21	10	10
5	86	72	14	6	16
6	79	78	1	1	1
7	72	63	9	3	3
8	82	99	17	8	-8
9	70	80	10	4	-4
10	64	84	20	9	-9

$$V = 9$$

$$\mu_V = 0$$

$$\sigma_V = \sqrt{\frac{n(n + 1)(2n + 1)}{6}} = \sqrt{\frac{10(10 + 1)[2(10) + 1]}{6}} = 19.6$$

$$Z_{observed} = \frac{V - \mu_V}{\sigma_V} = \frac{9 - 0}{19.6} = 0.46$$

For a level of significance of 0.05, the acceptance region is $-1.96 \leq z \leq 1.96$. Since the observed value falls within the acceptance region, we accept the null hypothesis. There is no significant difference between the booklets.

15.6.a. Either a large or a small number of runs will cause us to reject the null hypothesis of randomness. A large number of runs might indicate a too thorough mixing of the signs and a small number of runs might indicate too much grouping of the signs.

b.
```
   _ _ _ _   _ _ _   _____ _ _   _____ _ _____  _____
 0 + - + - + 0 - + -  + + + + + - +  - - - + + + - + + + - - -
```

There are $R = 16$ runs.

c. There are $n_1 = 16$ plus signs and $n_2 = 12$ minus signs; $n = 12 + 16 = 28$.

$$\mu_R \quad \frac{n + 2n_1 n_2}{n} = \frac{28 + 2(16)(12)}{28} = 14.7$$

$$\sigma_R = \sqrt{\frac{2n_1n_2(2n_1n_2 - n)}{n^2(n-1)}} = \sqrt{\frac{2(16)(12)\,[2(16)(12) - 28]}{28^2(28-1)}}$$

$$= 2.5$$

d. $z_{observed} = \dfrac{R - \mu_R}{\sigma_R} = \dfrac{16 - 14.7}{2.5} = -0.51$

e. The acceptance region for H_0 at the 0.05 level is $-1.96 \le z \le 1.96$. Since the observed value of $z = -0.51$ falls within the acceptance region, we accept the null hypothesis and conclude the demands are randomly distributed around 50.

Car	A	B	C	D	E	
Husband	5	1	4	2	3	
Wife	5	2	4	3	1	
d	0	-1	0	-1	2	
d^2	0	1	0	1	4	$\Sigma d^2 = 6$

From text Equation 15-11, $r_s = 1 - \dfrac{6\Sigma d^2}{n(n^2 - 1)} = 1 - \dfrac{6(6)}{5(25 - 1)}$, or $+0.7$.

15.8.a *Agreement* means positive correlation because both the manager and assistant would have to assign higher ranks to essentially the same trainees and to assign lower ranks to essentially the same trainees. Thus an appropriate set of hypotheses is $H_0: \rho_s \le 0$ (disagreement) and $H_A: \rho_s > 0$ (agreement).

b. Because the data are ordinal.

c. The *t*-statistic defined in text Equation 15-12 for this test is

$$t = r_s \sqrt{\frac{n - 2}{1 - r_s^2}} = 0.7\sqrt{\frac{18}{0.51}}, \quad \text{or} \quad 4.16$$

Table B-4 shows that $t_{0.99} = 2.25524$ at $n - 2 = 18$ *df*. We accept the hypothesis of agreement.

d. If $r_s = 0.5$, then Equation 15-12 gives

$$t = 0.5\sqrt{\frac{20 - 2}{1 - (0.5)^2}} = 2.449$$

Since this is less than the critical value $t_{0.99} = 2.5524$, we accept H_0 (disagreement). Although the sample value of $r_s = 0.5$ is positive, it is not sufficiently large to be statistically significant (that is, to support H_A) at the 0.01 level of significance.

CHAPTER 16:   SOLUTIONS TO SELF-CORRECTING EXERCISES

16.1.a.

Year	X	Y	XY	X^2
1968	-3	232	-696	9
1969	-1	201	-201	1
1970	1	200	200	1
1971	3	179	537	9
		812	-160	20

$$a = \frac{\Sigma Y}{n} = \frac{812}{4} = 203$$

$$b = \frac{\Sigma XY}{\Sigma X^2} = \frac{-160}{20} = -8.0$$

$$\left.\begin{array}{l} T = a + bx \\ T = 203 - 8.0x \end{array}\right\} \quad x = 0 \text{ in } 1969\frac{1}{2} \text{ (that is, January 1, 1970)}$$
x is in 6-month units.

b.

Year	X	X^2	White		Nonwhite	
			Y	XY	Y	XY
1920	-2	4	55.6	-111.2	45.2	-90.4
1930	-1	1	63.5	-63.5	49.2	-49.2
1940	0	0	66.6	00.0	54.9	00.0
1950	1	1	72.2	72.2	62.9	62.9
1960	2	4	74.1	148.2	66.3	132.6
		10	332.0	45.7	278.5	55.9

$$a = \frac{\Sigma Y}{n} = \frac{332.0}{5} = 66.4 \qquad\qquad a = \frac{278.5}{5} = 55.7$$

$$b = \frac{\Sigma XY}{\Sigma X^2} = \frac{45.7}{10} = 4.6 \qquad\qquad b = \frac{55.9}{10} = 5.6$$

White: $T = 66.4 + 4.6x$ $x = 0$ in 1940.
Nonwhite: $T = 55.7 + 5.6x$ x is in 10-year units.

16.2.a.

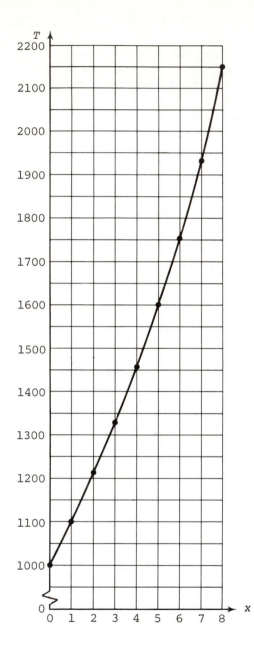

The table below shows the exponential trend for the given equation.

x	T	=	$1000(1.1)^x$
0	$1000(1.1)^0$	=	1000
1	$1000(1.1)^1$	=	1100
2	$1000(1.1)^2$	= $1000(1.21)$ =	1210
3	$1000(1.1)^3$	= $1000(1.331)$ =	1331

Notice that each successive value is a constant percentage (110%) of the previous value. For example, at $x = 2$, $T = 1210$. At $x = 3$, $T = 1210(1.1) = 1331$. This property is a principal motivation for using the exponential trend. The logarithmic form of this equation is found by taking logarithms of both sides of the equation and applying the rules for logarithms to the result.

$$T = 1000(1.1)^x$$

$$\log(T) = \log[1000(1.1)^x]$$

$$= \log 1000 + \log(1.1)^x$$

$$= \log 1000 + x(\log 1.1)$$

By using a table of common logarithms, we may write $\log(T) = 3 + 0.0414x$. In its logarithmic form, the exponential is a linear equation in x.

b.

Year	y	$\log(y)$	x	$x\log(y)$
1977	420	2.62	−2	−5.25
1978	480	2.68	−1	−2.68
1979	630	2.80	0	0
1980	700	2.85	1	2.85
1981	860	2.93	2	5.87
				0.79

$$\log(a) = \frac{\Sigma \log(y)}{n} = \frac{13.88}{5} = 2.78$$

$$\log(b) = \frac{\Sigma \log(y)}{\Sigma x^2} = \frac{0.79}{10} = 0.079$$

$$\log T = \log a + (\log b)X$$

$$\log T = 2.78 + 0.079X$$

Using a table of common logarithms or a calculator, $10^{2.78} =$ 602.56 and $10^{0.079} = 1.2$.   The trend equation in exponential form is

$$T = 602.56(1.2)^X$$

where 602.56 is the trend in 1979 and X is in 1-year units. The predicted trend for 1982 is

$$T(1982) = 602.56(1.2)^3 = 1041.22$$

16.3.a.i.   The exponential trend is better.

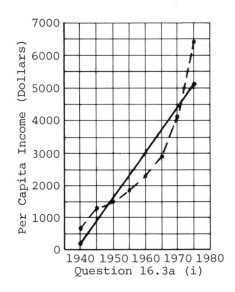

Question 16.3a (i)

ii.   The *Y*-axis in Figure 16-2 has a logarithmic scale. Thus,
the logarithms of the *Y*-values rather than the *Y*-values
are plotted. In logarithmic form, the trend equation is

$$\log(T) = \log(549.5) + [\log(1.34)]x$$

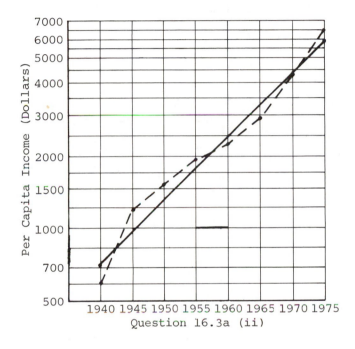

Question 16.3a (ii)

16.3.b.i.   Neither is appropriate. The linear least-squares line is
plotted in the solution graph. The linear model presumes
a constant rate of change is in effect. The exponential
model presumes a constant percentage rate of change.

ii.

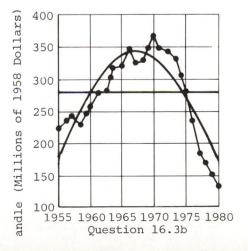

Question 16.3b

iii. The equation is a parabola.

iv. Inappropriate models can often by avoided by plotting the data before attempting to fit a trend equation. In this example it would be obvious that the linear and exponential models are not appropriate.

16.4.a. $T(1940) = 48.61 + 0.36(0) = 48.6$

$T(1942) = 48.61 + 0.36(1) = 49.0$

$T(1944) = 48.61 + 0.36(2) = 49.3$

b. | Year | Percentage of Trend | |
|------|---------------------|--|
| 1940 | 105.5 | = (51.3/48.6)(100) |
| 1942 | 94.1 | |
| 1944 | 102.6 | |
| 1946 | 89.0 | |
| 1948 | 103.7 | |
| 1950 | 97.2 | |
| 1952 | 97.9 | |
| 1954 | 102.7 | |
| 1956 | 99.3 | |
| 1958 | 108.4 | |
| 1960 | 104.8 | |
| 1962 | 99.4 | |
| 1964 | 108.1 | |
| 1966 | 95.6 | |
| 1968 | 93.2 | |
| 1970 | 98.9 | |
| 1972 | 95.1 | |
| 1974 | 105.3 | |
| 1976 | 102.1 | |
| 1978 | 96.6 | |

c.

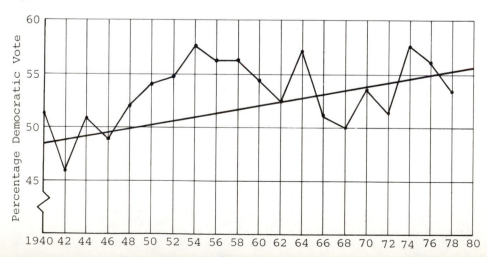

d.

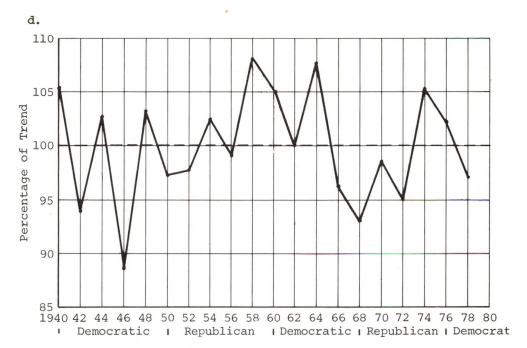

e. In the period of 1940 to 1950, Democratic presidents were
either elected or incumbent. In presidential elections during
this period, the Democratic percentage of the popular vote
is above the trend [$(y/T) > 1$]. In off-year elections during
the same period, the popular vote percentage is below trend.
In the period between 1952 and 1958, when a Republican was in
the White House, the pattern reverses itself--the Democratic
percentage of the popular vote is below trend in the presidential election years and above trend in the off-year elections. The pattern reverses itself once again in 1960 when
a Democrat was elected president, and again in 1968 when a
Republican was elected.

16.5.a. A 3-term moving average must start with the second period.
Thus

$$MA_2 = (7 + 6 + 10)/3 = 7.67$$

$$MA_3 = (6 + 10 + 4)/3 = 6.67$$

$$MA_4 = (10 + 4 + 4)/3 = 6.00$$

b. Total$_3$ = 7 + 6 + 10 + 4 + 4 = 31

$$MA_3 = 31/5 = 6.2$$

$$Total_4 = 31 - 7 + 3 = 27$$

$$MA_4 = 27/5 = 5.4$$

$$Total_5 = 27 - 6 + 6 = 27$$

$$MA_5 = 27/5 = 5.4$$

c. A moving average with more terms has more smoothing power than one with fewer terms. A moving average with fewer terms is more responsive to changes in the series.

16.6.a. The numerator expresses the total expenditures for fixed quantities (q) using prices (p_n) prevailing in the year of interest. The denominator expresses the total expenditure for the same fixed quantities (q) in terms of prices (p_0) prevailing in the base year. The ratio reflects the influence of price changes on the fixed quantities from the base year to the year of interest.

b. No, the summation is performed over some fixed "market basket" of goods.

16.7.   (*Note*: In Equations 16.5 and 16.6 the subscript zero is used to identify the base year. In the following solutions, the subscripts are always the same as in the problem statement to facilitate identification of sums. For example, in (b), the base year is 1955 and the appropriate sum for the denominator is $\Sigma p_1 q_1$.)

a. $PI(1955) = \dfrac{\Sigma(p_1 q_0)}{\Sigma(p_0 q_0)} * 100 = \dfrac{641.26}{872.64} * 100 = 73.5$

$PI(1965) = \dfrac{\Sigma(p_2 q_0)}{\Sigma(p_0 q_0)} * 100 = \dfrac{846.19}{872.64} * 100 = 97.0$

b. $PI(1965) = \dfrac{\Sigma(p_2 q_1)}{\Sigma(p_1 q_1)} * 100 = \dfrac{985.39}{750.64} * 100 = 131.3$

c. $QI(1950) = \dfrac{\Sigma(p_1 q_0)}{\Sigma(p_1 q_1)} * 100 = \dfrac{641.26}{750.64} * 100 = 85.4$

$QI(1950) = \dfrac{\Sigma(p_1 q_2)}{\Sigma(p_1 q_1)} * 100 = \dfrac{800.02}{750.64} * 100 = 106.6$

d. Divide each result from (a) by 73.5 (the index number for 1955) and multiply by 100. Thus the new values are

$PI(1950) = \dfrac{100}{73.5} * 100 = 136.1$

$$PI(1955) = \frac{73.5}{73.5} * 100 = 100.0$$

$$PI(1965) = \frac{97.0}{73.5} * 100 = 132.0$$

In (b), $PI(1965) = 131.3$. This result used quantity weights from 1955. In (a), 1950 quantity weights were used that are still present in the calculations of (d). The only change made in (d) is to change the point of reference to 1955.

16.8.a. The formula is $\Sigma[w(p_n/p_0)]$, where w is the relative importance of a commodity in the index expressed as a percentage of the total expenditures. For zinc, $w = (30/519)(100) = 5.78$.

b. The data in the expenditure column reflect *both* price and quantity. For example in 1960, 77 million was expended on aluminum. This value does not tell us the price per pound or the number of pounds but rather reflects the product of these quantities.

c. No, price relatives are not determined from expenditures. They are determined by separate pricing surveys. The price relative is simply the ratio of the price in 1965 to the price in 1960. (These individual prices are not shown in the problem statement because only their ratio, or price relative, is needed for computations.

d. These values are the product $w(p_n/p_0)$. For aluminum, this is $(0.851)(14.9) = 12.7$. This is the amount which would have been spent for 1960's quantity of aluminum in terms of 1965 prices.

e. The sum of the values in the right-most column is 110.2. This value is the index number. This value tells us that prices are 10.2% higher in 1965 than they were in 1960. Since this is a price index, it tells us nothing about quantity changes.

16.9.a. If CPI = 125, then current prices are 25% higher than the base year. The purchasing power of the dollar is found by dividing 100 by the CPI. Thus $100/125 = 0.8$. This means that $1 in the present year will buy only 0.8 as much as $1 in the base year, or a 20% decrease. The changes are opposite in direction.

b.i.   Either $(12,500)100/125 = 10,000$ or $(12,500)(0.8) = 10,000$.

Both methods are identical since purchasing power is 100/CPI. Notice that there is no change in A's income after the price increase has been taken into account.

ii. Real income is the present income evaluated in terms of what it would buy in the base year. For B, real income is 11,000(0.8) = 8800. This reflects a net drop in income of 10,000 - 8800 = 1200 in terms of buying power.

iii. C's real income is 15,000(0.8) = 12,000. Of the 5000 increase in actual wages, 12,000 - 10,000 = 2000 is real and the rest (3000) is due to inflation of prices.

16.10.a. It cost 8.4% more in 1965 to purchase the 1960 market basket of food products than it would have cost in 1960 to purchase the same basket of food products.

b. 0.884 is the reciprocal of the price index expressed as a relative. It is the purchasing power index expressed as a relative. One dollar spent on the "market basket" of medical care goods and services in 1965 would buy 11.6% less goods and services than $1 bought of those services in 1960. Or, the 1965 dollar is worth only 0.884 as much as the 1960 dollar in buying medical care.

c. In column (D) the 1965 expenditures in each category are divided by the price index for the category. The result for each category is 1965 expenditures in terms of 1960 prices. The total, $368.3 billion, then represents the quantity of 1965 consumption at 1960 prices. The change 368.3 - 299.3 = 69 billion (1960) dollars represents a change in quantity of goods and services. The remainder, 394.4 - 368.3 = 26.1 billion, is the result of changes in prices of the goods and services in the CPI market basket.

CHAPTER 17:   SOLUTIONS TO SELF-CORRECTING EXERCISES

17.1.a.

Year	Quarter 1	2	3	4
1			77.7	112.3
2	104.7	105.1	74.6	110.2
3	105.4	110.4	64.8	125.7
4	89.3	135.1		
Total	299.4	350.6	217.1	348.2	1215.3
Average	99.8	116.9	72.4	116.1	405.2
Seasonal Index	98.5	115.4	71.5	114.6	400.0

Seasonal index = (average) (400.0/405.2) = (average)(0.98716)

b. MA(1 April, Year 4) = (63 + 46 + 65 + 32)/4 = 206/4
   MA(1 July, Year 4) = (46 + 65 + 32 + 36)/4 = 179/4
   MA(15 May, Year 4) = ([(206/4) + (179/4)]/2 = 385/8 = 48.125

17.2.a.i.   Notice that we cannot directly compare first and fourth
             quarter observations. The seasonal index tells us that
             first-quarter sales are likely to be 110% of the trend-
             cycle value. By dividing the observed values by the
             seasonal index we discount or remove the seasonal influ-
             ence. The adjusted figures may then be compared.

Quarter	Actual		Seasonal Relative		Adjusted for Seasonal
1	7.5	÷	1.30	=	5.769
4	6.5	÷	1.10	=	5.909
					+ 0.140

Notice that the change in sales, after the adjustment for
seasonal variation has been made, is a 0.140 increase. We
conclude that the seasonal influence in the observed figures
is the reason for the decrease in sales. The seasonally
adjusted data indicate that, in the absence of seasonal
variation sales would have increased. Thus, the nonseasonal
change is positive. Trend, cycle, and irregular variation
remain.

ii.   Notice that the change in trend values in this period is
      5.2 - 4.9, or a 0.300 increase.

iii. The change in the actual sales which are seasonally adjusted is only +0.140. We conclude the difference between the adjusted actual figures and the expected change in trend (0.140 − 0.300 = −0.160) must be attributable to a combination of cyclical and irregular changes. The change associated with these factors is thus a decrease of 0.160.

b. No, because the actual change, 115 − 120 = −5 includes normal effects of trend and seasonal variation. To adjust for seasonal variation, we divide each observed figure by the seasonal relative and find the difference: (115/0.90) − (120/1.0) = 127.8 − 120.0 = 7.8. This difference (7.8) reflects an adjustment for seasonal variation but includes the trend. Since there is a 4-month difference between March and July, there will be a 4/12, or 1/3, year trend change between the two months. Since the trend change for 1 year is 9, we expect a (1/3)(9) = 3.0 change due to trend. The difference between the seasonally adjusted observed value (7.8) and the change in trend (3.0) gives a difference of 4.8. This latter figure reflects the difference due to all other factors except seasonal and trend. These other factors include the change in advertising policy, cyclical variation, and several other irregular components such as actions taken by competitors. Certainly the $4.8 million figure is a better assessment of the change due to advertising providing the other factors can be ruled out.

17.3.a. $T(1978) = 8910.5 + 390.6(7)\ = 11,645$
$T(1979) = 8910.5 + 390.6(8)\ = 12,036$
$T(1980) = 8910.5 + 390.6(9)\ = 12,426$
$T(1981) = 8910.5 + 390.6(10) = 12,817$

b. In general, forecasts become less reliable for more distant time periods.

c. The forecasting model presumes that the causes of accidents in the past will continue in the future. Changes in factors such as the availability of fuel, driving habits, safety programs, or industrial activity may influence the number of accidents and thus necessitate changes in the model.

17.4.a. Yes. Some months seem to be consistently above or below the trend. Also, see (b) and (c).

b.

Month	Forecast	
1	984	= 974(101/100)
2	830	
3	931	
4	954	
5	1066	
6	1059	
7	1063	
8	1076	
9	1049	
10	992	
11	946	
12	969	

c. The months May through September have seasonal index numbers which are greater than 100. This suggests a higher number of accidents associated with the mild weather for these months. It may be that people have increased participation in accident causing activities such as driving, boating, and so forth during these months.

17.5.a.

Year	d_y	d_x
1972		
1973	307	7,058
1974	680	3,143
1975	580	21,293
1976	126	-8,193
1977	94	-25,738

For example, d_y for 1974 is $d_y = 10{,}208 - 9528 = 680$.

b.

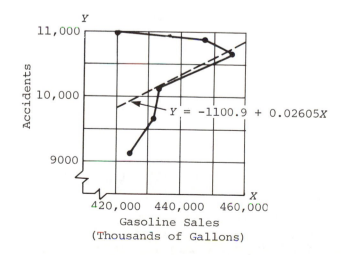

$Y = -1100.9 + 0.02605X$

Accidents

Gasoline Sales
(Thousands of Gallons)

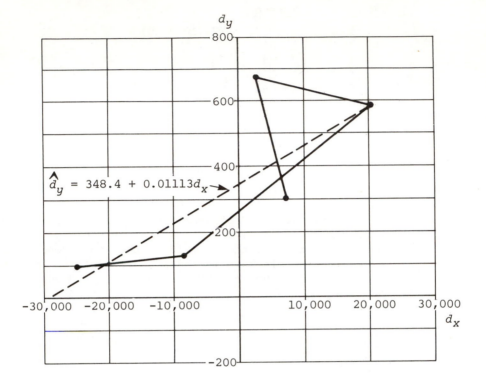

d. Using the relationship for the original data, the forecasted value is

$$\hat{y}(1978) = -1100.9 + 0.02605(427,396)$$
$$= 10,033$$

To use the difference, find the first difference for 1978.

$$\hat{d}(1978) = 427,396 - 422,698 = 4698$$

The forecasted first difference for accident admissions is

$$\hat{d}(1978) = 348.4 + 0.01113(4698)$$
$$= 401$$

The forecast for 1978 is

$$\hat{y}(1978) = 11,008 + 401 = 11,409$$

e. Usually the method of first differences works better, as was the case in this example. The method of first differences produced a much smaller standard error of estimate (166 compared to 755). Using the original data may involve using a value for *x* which is outside the range of the original data.   In addition, there may be serial correlation of the residuals.

17.6.a. The cyclical relative is the ratio of the observed value to the trend for accidents:

$$T(1972) = 8910.5 + 390.6(1) = 9301$$

The relative is 9221/9301 = 0.991.

For gasoline sales

$$T(1972) = 430,954 + 1652.5(1) = 432,606$$

and the cyclical relative is 425,135/432,606 = 0.983.

b.

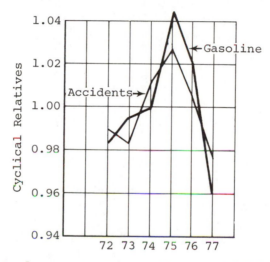

c. The cyclicals do move together.   Also see 17.7(b).

17.7.a. For accident admissions:

$$d_y(1973) = 0.983 - 0.991 = -0.008$$

For gasoline sales:

$$d_y(1973) = 0.995 - 0.983 = 0.012$$

b. The trend value for gasoline sales for 1978 is

$$T(1978) = 430,954 + 1652.5(7) = 442,522$$

and the cyclical relative is 427,396/442,522 = 0.966.   The difference in cyclical relatives for 1978 is 0.966 - 0.959 = 0.007.

c. The difference in cyclical relatives for accident admissions is:

$$\hat{a}_y(1978) = -0.0003526 + 0.4682126(0.007) = 0.003$$

Thus the cyclical relative for 1978 is $0.978 + 0.003 = 0.981$. Note that the least-squares relationship predicts an increase of 0.003 in the cyclical relative for 1978 as compared with 1977.

d. In 17.3(a), we forecasted 11,645 accident admissions for 1978. Applying the cyclical relative from (c), this figure should be $11,645(0.981) = 11,424$. Thus the forecasted accident admissions are 11,424.

17.8.   Multiply each trend-seasonal product in Question 17.4 by 0.981:

Month	Forecast
1	965
2	814
3	913
4	936
5	1046
6	1039
7	1043
8	1056
9	1029
10	973
11	928
12	951

17.9.a. The general formula (text Equation 17-3) for exponential smoothing is

$$\hat{y}_t = (1 - w)\hat{y}_{t-1} + wy_t,$$

where y_{t-1} is the exponentially smoothed value for the immediately preceding period and y_t is the observed value for the current period. The first smoothed value must be for the second time period. To initiate the process, we set $\hat{y}_{2-1} = y_{2-1} = 7$, which is the first observed value. Since $y_2 = 6$, $\hat{y}_2 = (1 - 0.25)(7) + (0.25)(6) = 6.75$. The formula for the smoothed value for the third period is $\hat{y}_3 = (1 - w)\hat{y}_2 + wy_3 = (1 - 0.25)(6.75) + (0.25)(10) = 7.5625$; $\hat{y}_4 = (1 - 0.25)7.5625 + 0.25(4) = 6.672$. In other words, the smoothed value for the present period is $(1 - w)$ times the smoothed value for the previous period plus w times the observed value of the present period.

b. Since w is the weight applied to the current observed value, the numberical value of w indicates how much emphasis is to be placed on the most recent value in the series. A large value of w emphasizes the present and, consequently, does not smooth the series as much as a small value of w, which places less weight on the most recent value. The choice of w depends on what is desired for a particular problem. An element of judgment is present and no "exact" answer can be given regarding the selection of w. Since computer routines are available for exponential smoothing, you can often try several values of w in order to select one that suits your purpose.

17.10.a. A naive forecast is obtained by using the observed value in the present period as the forecasted value for the next period. Actual demand in the first period was 7. The naive forecast for the second period would be 7. The actual value for the second period was 6 and the naive forecast for the third period would be 6. The results are shown in the following table.

Period	Observed	Forecasted	Error (Forecasted - Observed)
1	7	--	
2	6	7	1
3	10	6	-4
4	4	10	6
5	4	4	0
6	3	4	1
7	6	3	-3
8	7	6	-1
9	8	7	-1
10	5	8	3
11	8	5	-3
12	5	8	3
13	6	5	-1
14	6	6	0
15	7	6	-1
16	3	7	4
17	--	3	--

The sum of the squared errors is 110. Thus RMSE = $\sqrt{110/15}$ = 2.71.

b.

Period	Observed	Forecasted ($w = 0.25$)	Error
1	7	--	--
2	6	7	1
3	10	7	-3
4	4	8	4
5	4	7	3
6	3	6	3
7	6	5	-1
8	7	5	-2
9	8	6	-2
10	5	6	1
11	8	6	-2
12	5	6	1
13	6	6	0
14	6	6	0
15	7	6	-1
16	3	6	3
17	--	5	--

The sum of the squared errors is 69. Thus RMSE = $\sqrt{69/15}$ = 2.14.

c. The forecast from the exponential smoothing method produces a smaller root mean squared error and is therefore superior to naive forecasting in this example.

d. See solution to (a) and (b) for the seventeenth period.

17.11.   The forecast prepared for Question 17.4 takes trend and seasonal variation into account. The trend and seasonal factors were found by using 72 observations (12 mo times 6 years). The most recent observation (the last month of 1977) has relatively little influence on the forecasted values because that observation is only one of 72 values used to compute the trend and seasonal relative. This method might be used when strong trend and seasonal forces are in fact at work and the influence of the most recent observation on the future observations is small in comparison with seasonal and trend forces. Forecasting for several periods is possible with this method provided past trend and seasonal variations may be expected to continue in the future

Forecasting by exponential smoothing places no emphasis on trend or seasonal variation. This is an advantage when these forces are not at work. Higher emphasis is given to the most recent observation unless an exceptionally small value is used for w. Emphasis is placed on "next period" forecasting. The analyst

is able to control the degree to which the last observation in-
fluences the forecast by selecting a value for w.   For any given
series, several values of w may be used and the value having a
low root mean squared error may be used for the actual forecasting.
Exponential smoothing is very easy to use since the only information needed is the most recent observation and the most recent
forecast.   The forecasted value is a simple weighted average of
these two values.

CHAPTER 18:   SOLUTIONS TO SELF-CORRECTING EXERCISES

18.1.a. The bakery's acts are to make 0, 1, 2, or 3 cakes. The possible states are that 0, 1, 2, or 3 cakes will be demanded. The bakery can exercise control over the number of cakes made (acts). They cannot control the number demanded (states).

b. The payoff is (5 - 2)(cakes sold) - (2)(cakes not sold), in dollars. For example, if 2 cakes are made and the demand is zero, payoff = 3(0) - 2(2) = -4; if 2 cakes are made and the demand is 3, payoff = 3(2) - 2(0) = 6. The payoff table is as follows.

Demand	Number of Cakes Made			
	0	1	2	3
0	0	-2	-4	-6
1	0	3	1	-1
2	0	3	6	4
3	0	3	6	9

18.2.a. $EV(A_1)$ = (1/4)($20) + (1/4)($16) + (1/2)(-$2) = $8
$EV(A_2)$ = (1/4)($8) + (1/4)($24) + (1/2)(-$4) = $6
$EV(A_3)$ = (1/4)($32) + (1/4)($8) + (1/2)(-$6) = $7

b. A_1 is best because it has the highest expected payoff.

c. The expected value of each strategy tells us what we might expect to happen *on the average* when the state occurs with the given probabilities. If strategy 1 is used, the payoff will be either $20, $16, or -$2 depending on what state actually occurs. In this case, the payoff of -$2 means that state 3 occurred.

d. If A_1 is followed for a large number of contacts, $EV(A_1)$ = $8 tells us that the average payoff per contact should be very close to $8.

e. If a large number of contacts is made the actual average payoff per contact will be very close to the expected value of the act. If a single contact is to be made, the actual payoff is unlikely to equal the expected value. The rationale for using the expected value criterion when a single contact is to be made is that the expected value of each act produces a single numerical value for each act. These may be thought of as values of merit that allow us to see the relative value of one act versus the alternatives.

18.3.a. If we knew state 1--buy package I--were going to occur, we would use A_3 because the payoff ($32) for using A_3 when S_1 is going to occur is higher than the payoff for using A_2 ($8) or for using A_1 ($20).

b. Select A_2 because the payoff is $24, which is higher than the payoffs for A_1 ($16) and A_3 ($8) when S_2 occurs.

c. Select A_1 because it has the highest payoff (in this case the smallest loss) when S_3 occurs.

d. If certain prediction is available, the state probabilities tell us that 1/4 of the customers will be found in state 1, 1/4 in state 2, and 1/2 in state 3.

e. The expected value of certain prediction is $EV(CP)$ = (1/4)($32) + (1/4)($24) + (1/2)(-$2) = $13.

f. The expected value of perfect information is $EV(PI)$ = $EV(CP)$ - $EV(A_1)$ = $13 - $8 = $5. This value represents the average improvement in payoff per customer contact we could obtain if we could have perfect prediction. The improvement is measured in terms of the expected value of the optimal act, which is A_1. $EV(A_1)$ is the best we can do in the absence of the ability to predict the state and it represents the expected value of the most rational action in the absence of a certain prediction. Thus $EV(PI)$ represents the maximum improvement we can obtain by completely removing uncertainty from the problem. If the cost of certain prediction were $4, we would choose to pay the fee because the net improvement would be $5 - $4 = $1. If the fee were $5 for certain prediction we would not care whether we had used A_1 and did not pay the fee or whether we used perfect prediction and paid $5 for the privilege. We would not pay $6 for certain prediction since our net profit would be $13 - $6 = $7, which is less than $EV(A_1)$ = $8. In other words, $EV(PI)$ is the maximum we would pay for certain prediction.

g. The analyst is wrong. We would use A_3 only if state 1 were predicted. Even when S_1 is predicted with certainty, it will occur in only 1/4 of the cases predicted. You should be careful to note that certain prediction implies the ability to predict the state of the next customer contact. Certain prediction does *not* imply the ability to control or to change the state. Even with perfect prediction, 1/4 of the customers will be in state 1, 1/4 in state 2, and 1/2 in state 3.

18.4.a. The largest money reward is assigned a utility of 10 and the smallest money reward is assigned a utility of 0. Thus $U(500)$ = 10 and $U(10)$ = 0.

b. According to the decision maker, the utility of both alternatives is the same. Thus, the utility of the first alternative, $U(80)$, equals the utility of the second alternative, $0.7*U(500) + 0.3*U(10)$, or $U(80) = 0.7(10) + 0.3(0) = 7.0$.

c. The probabilities are determined by asking the decision maker a series of questions about his attitude toward the two alternatives. The probabilities are changed in each question until the decision maker concludes the alternatives have the same value. The probabilities that cause the utility of both alternatives to be equal are the ones needed to determine the values of utilities such as $U(80)$.

d.

Change in Money Reward	Change in Utility	Rate of Change
$20 - $10 = $10	4	0.4
$80 - $20 = $60	3	3/60 = 0.05
$500 - $80 = $420	3	3/420 = 0.007

Since the rate of change of utility with respect to money reward is not constant, the relationship between utility and money reward is not linear. Notice that the decision maker's increase in utility per dollar increase in money reward is 0.4 per dollar in the interval of $10 to $20. In the interval of $80 to $500 the increase in utility is only 0.007 per dollar. In other words, changes in money reward in the interval of $10 to $20 are more valuable to the decision maker than changes in money reward in the interval of $80 to $500.

e. For money reward:

S_i	$P(S_i)$	A_1	A_2
S_1	0.1	$500	$80
S_2	0.9	$ 10	$20
Expected value		$ 59	$26

The optimal act is A_1 for money reward.

For utility:

S_i	$P(S_i)$	A_1	A_2
S_1	0.1	10	7
S_2	0.9	0	4
Expected utility		1	4.3

The optimal act is A_2 for utility. If utility is considered, A_2 is the optimal act instead of A_1. Since the utility curve is rising more rapidly at \$20 than it is at \$500, the decision maker is risk adverse; that is, a sure return will be preferred to a gamble with expected gain equal to the sure return.

18.5.a.

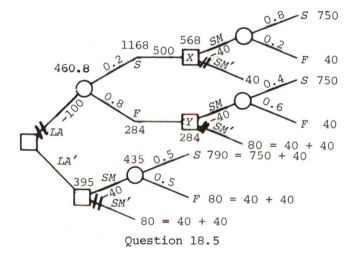

Question 18.5

b. Refer to the terminus labeled X. The expected profit for developing the small pack is

$$750(0.8) + 40(0.2) - 40 = 568$$

Since the expected profit from not developing the small pack is only 40, this decision is ruled out.

c. Refer to the terminus labeled Y. The expected cost of not developing the small pack under this set of circumstances (that is, failed development of large pack) is 80 because both packs will be purchased from a wholesaler at a net profit (when resold to the company's customers) at \$40,000 each. The expected profit from developing the small pack is

750(0.4) + 40(0.6) - 40 = 284

Since the expected profit for developing the small pack is greater than the profit for not developing it, the latter decision is ruled out.

d. If the large pack is developed successfully, the expected gain is 568 + 500 or 1168. The probability of this outcome is 0.2. If the large pack is developed and fails, the expected gain is 284 with a probability of 0.8. Since the development cost is 100, the expected profit is

1168(0.2) + 284(0.8) - 100 = 360.8.

e. The expected profit for not developing the large pack and developing the small pack is

790(0.5) + 80(0.5) - 40 = 395

Notice this value is larger than the expected profit developed in (d). Thus the company should decide not to develop the large pack and they should decide to develop the small pack for an expected profit of $395,000.

18.6.a. Given S_1, the maximum payoff is $32. Thus $(V_{max}|S_1) = 32$. If you select A_3 when S_1 is true, your regret will be zero. If you select A_2 when S_1 is true, your regret will be the maximum you could have received, less the amount actually received or $32 - $8 = $24. The regret for using A_1 when S_1 is true is $32 - $20 = $12.

b.

S_1	A_1	A_2	A_3
S_1	12	24	0
S_2	24 - 16 = 8	24 - 24 = 0	24 - 8 = 16
S_3	-2 - (-2) = 0	-2 - (-4) = 2	-2 - (-6) = 4

The expected regrets for each act are found by using the state probabilities $P(S_1) = 1/4$, $P(S_2) = 1/4$, and $P(S_3) = 1/2$. The expected regrets are

$ER(A_1) = 12(1/4) + 8(1/4) + 0(1/2) = 5$
$ER(A_2) = 24(1/4) + 0(1/4) + 2(1/2) = 7$
$ER(A_3) = 0(1/4) + 16(1/4) + 4(1/2) = 6$

The optimal act is A_1 because it has the smallest expected regret. The expected regret with certain prediction is zero because we would always choose the strategy having zero regrets in the face of perfect prediction. This causes $EV(PI) = ER(S_{opt})$ = \$5.

c. Using expected payoff and using expected regrets both lead to the same choice of A_1 as the optimal act and the same $EV(PI)$. The two methods are logically equivalent.

18.7.a. Regrets table (see 18.6 for procedure):

	ACTS			
	Number of Cakes Made			
Demand	0	1	2	3
0	0	2	4	6
1	3	0	2	4
2	6	3	0	2
3	9	6	3	0

b. The cost of overestimating demand by 1 unit is $C_o = 2$. The opportunity cost of underestimating demand by 1 unit is $C_u = 3$. The critical probability is

$$P* = \frac{C_O}{C_u + C_O} = \frac{2}{3 + 2} = 0.4$$

c. Compute the cumulative probabilities $P(X < x)$ and their complements, $P(X \geq x)$:

x = demand	0	1	2	3
$P(X = x)$	0.10	0.20	0.40	0.30
$P(X < x)$	--	0.10	0.30	0.70
$P(X \geq x)$	1.00	0.90	0.70	0.30

The largest demand for which $P(X \geq x)$ equals or exceeds $P*$ is optimal order quantity. Since $P(X \geq 2) = 0.70$, which is greater than $P* = 0.40$, and $P(X \geq 3) = 0.30$, the optimal order quantity is 2 cakes.

d. Since the regrets are a linear function, the marginal method can be used. In Question 18.2, there is no "decision variable." There are only discrete acts. Thus cumulative probabilities are meaningless.

CHAPTER 19:   SOLUTIONS TO SELF-CORRECTING EXERCISES

19.1.a. $P(S_1) = 1/4$, $P(S_2) = 1/4$, $P(S_3) = 1/2$.   These are called the
prior probabilities of the states.

b. According to the problem statement $P(C|S_1) = 3/4$ and $P(NC|S_1)$
$= 1/4$.   The sum of these probabilities is 1.0, because customers
in S_1 either do or do not have children--there are no other
possiblities.

c. These probabilities are called likelihoods.   The state is the
given event.   Since the given events are the states, which are
not known before a customer contact is made, these probabilities
are not directly useful to the decision maker.   They are needed
for the revision process.

d.

State	S_i	Prior Probability $P(S_i)$	Likelihood $P(C|S_i)$	$P(S_i)*P(C|S_i)$	Revised Probability $P(S_i|C)$
Buy I	1	1/4	3/4	3/16	3/8 = (3/16)/(8/16)
Buy II	2	1/4	1/4	1/16	1/8 = (1/16)/(8/16)
No sale	3	1/2	1/2	4/16	4/8 = (4/16)/(8/16)
				8/16	

e. The events S_1 given C and C given S_1 are not the same.   Since
the events are different, we would in general expect the probabilities of the events to be different.

f. This is the marginal probability and tells us the unconditional
probability of the event C.   The value of $P(C)$ is 8/16 and it
may be found by summing the values in the $P(S_i)*P(C|S_i)$ column
in the table.

19.2.a.

S_i	$P(S_i|C)$	A_1	A_2	A_3
S_1	3/8	12(3/8)	24(3/8)	0(3/8)
S_2	1/8	8(1/8)	0(1/8)	16(1/8)
S_3	4/8	0(4/8)	2(4/8)	4(4/8)
	$ER(A_i)$	5.5	10	4

When it is known that the potential customer has children, the expected regrets are computed using the revised probabilities. The computations are shown in the table. When the information C is given, A_3 is the optimal act because it has the smallest expected regret.

b. $EV(PI) = ER(A_{opt}) = ER(A_3) = 4$

19.3.a. $EV(A_D) = 0.2(0) + 0.8(500) = \$400$

$EV(A_N) = 0.2(1500) + 0.8(0) = 300$

The optimal act is A_N that is, act as if the part is not defective. Note the optimal act is the one with the smallest expected cost. Thus, $EV(PI) = \$300$.

b. The first figure shows the decision tree. The first set of branches (E_D and E_N) shows the types of evidence indicated by the tester. The next set of branches (A_D and A_N) indicates the possible acts. The last set of branches indicates the possible states.

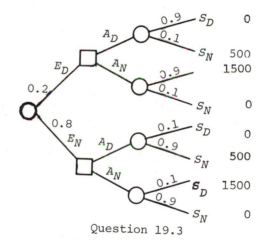

Question 19.3

The second figure shows the solved decision tree. The solution is obtained by working from right to left, finding expected values based on the conditional information. For example, the expected value of the acts when E_D is given are:

$E(A_D | E_D) = (0)(0.9) + (500)(0.1) = 50$

$E(A_N | E_D) = (1500)(0.9) + (0)(0.1) = 1350$

When a defective is indicated by the tester, we choose A_D because the act has a lower expected cost.   Thus we rule out A_N as shown on the figure.

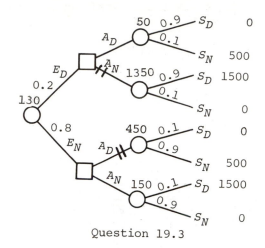

Question 19.3

c. As shown in the second figure, A_D is the best act when a defective is indicated by the tester and A_N is the best act when a nondefective is indicated.   Defectives are indicated in 20% of the cases and nondefectives are indicated in 80% of the cases.

d. As shown in the second figure,

$$EV(IA) = (50)(0.2) + (150)(0.8) = 130$$

$$EV(SI) = EV(IA) - EV(A_N) = 130 - 300 = -170.$$

Thus a cost savings of \$170 is achieved by using the tester.

19.4.a.

$$V_{ji} = \begin{pmatrix} 0 & 500 \\ 1500 & 0 \end{pmatrix}$$

Note the rows refer to acts and the columns to states.   The expected values of V_{jk} are

$$V_{11} = (0)(0.18) + (500)(0.02) = 10$$

$$V_{12} = (0)(0.08) + (500)(0.72) = 360$$

$$V_{21} = (1500)(0.18) + (0)(0.02) = 270$$

$$V_{22} = (1500)(0.08) + (0)(0.72) = 120$$

The V_{jk} table is, therefore, as follows.

Acts	Information E_D	E_N
A_D	<u>10</u>	360
A_N	270	<u>120</u>

c. The optimal act is indicated by the maximum value (that is, the smallest cost) in each column. These values have been underlined in the table. Thus the optimal acts are A_D if E_D is indicated and A_N if E_N is indicated. The expected value of the information acts is

$$EV(IA) = (10) + (120) = 130$$

Note these are the same results as obtained in 19.3.

19.5.a. For both states, find the probability that reading is in the interval $116.5 \leq X \leq 117.5$. For $\mu = 116$,

$$Z = \frac{116.5 - 116}{2} = 0.25$$

$$Z = \frac{117.5 - 116}{2} = 0.75$$

$$P(116.5 \leq X \leq 117.5) = P(0.25 \leq Z \leq 0.75) = 0.7734 - 0.5987$$

$$= 0.1747$$

For $\mu = 120$,

$$Z = \frac{116.5 - 120}{2} = -1.75$$

$$Z = \frac{117.5 - 120}{2} = -1.25$$

$$P(116.5 \leq X \leq 117.5) = P(-1.75 \leq Z \leq -1.25) = 0.1057 - 0.0401$$

$$= 0.0656.$$

The prior probabilities need to be revised incorporating the evidence that $X = 117$. This is shown in the following:

State (S)	$P(S)$	$P(E\|S)$	$P(S)*P(E\|S)$	$P(S\|E)$
$\mu = 116$	0.1	0.1747	0.01747	0.2283
$\mu = 120$	0.9	0.0656	0.05904	0.7717
			0.07651	1.0000

The most likely state is $\mu = 120$; that is, the meter is reading correctly.

b. The sample mean is $\bar{x} = 117$. For both states, find the probability that $116.75 \leqq \bar{X} \leqq 117.25$. Notice that we must use the standard error of the mean $\sigma_{\bar{x}}$ $\sigma/\sqrt{n} = 2/\sqrt{4} = 1$.

For $\mu = 116$,

$$Z = \frac{116.75 - 116}{1} = 0.75$$

$$Z = \frac{117.25 - 116}{1} = 1.25$$

$$P(116.75 \leqq \bar{X} \leqq 117.25) = 0.8943 - 0.7734 = 0.1209$$

For $\mu = 120$,

$$Z = \frac{117.75 - 120}{1} = -2.25$$

$$Z = \frac{116.25 - 120}{1} = -3.75$$

$$P(-2.25 \leqq \bar{X} \leqq -3.75) = 0.0122 - 0.0000 = 0.0122$$

The revised probabilities are as follows.

State (S)	$P(S)$	$P(E\|S)$	$P(S)*P(E\|S)$	$P(S\|E)$
$\mu = 116$	0.1	0.1209	0.01209	0.5241
$\mu = 120$	0.9	0.0122	0.01098	0.4759
			0.02307	1.0000

For a sample mean of $\bar{x} = 117$, the faulty state is a bit more likely.

c. In conjunction with the prior distribution, a single observation, $x = 117$, causes a balance of belief that the meter is not faulty, while a sample mean of $\bar{x} = 117$ based on $n = 4$ causes a balance of belief that the meter is faulty. The evidence favors 116 in both cases, 1747 to 656 and 1209 to 122.

19.6. Before the data are collected, the estimates of the mean and standard deviation are $E(\mu) = 10$ and $\sigma_\mu = 2$. The formulas for the mean standard deviation of the revised distribution are:

$$E'(\mu) = \frac{I_p * E(\mu) + I_s * \bar{x}}{I_p + I_s}$$

$$\sigma'^2_\mu = \frac{1}{I_p + I_s}$$

The quantities I_p and I_s are the information content of the prior and of the sample, respectively. Thus

$$I_p = \frac{1}{(\sigma_\mu)^2} = \frac{1}{(2)^2} = 0.25$$

$$I_s = \frac{1}{s_{\bar{x}}^{-2}} = \frac{1}{4^2/100} = 6.25$$

The revised estimates are therefore

$$E'(\mu) = \frac{0.25(10) + 6.25(7)}{0.25 + 6.25} = 7.1 \quad \text{and}$$

$$(\sigma_\mu')^2 = \frac{1}{0.25 + 6.25} = 0.15$$

19.7.a. The admissions officer considers the cost of incorrectly rejecting the students to be ten times the cost of incorrectly accepting the students. The probabilities of each state are:

$$P(\mu = 470) = 0.9433$$
$$P(\mu = 500) = 0.0567$$

The expected regret from admitting the students is $0(0.0567) + 1(0.9433)$ or 0.9433. The expected regret for not admitting the students is $10(0.0567) + 0(0.0567)$ or 0.567. The optimal act is not to admit the students because this act has minimum expected regret.

b.

	Decision	
True State	Accept H_0 (Admit)	Accept H_A (Do not admit)
H_0 True (μ = 500)		Type I error C_I = 10
H_A True (μ = 470)	Type II error C_{II} = 1	

The critical probability is:

$$P* = \frac{c_{II}}{c_I + c_{II}} = \frac{1}{1 + 10} = 0.0909$$

The probability that the null hypothesis is true is 0.0567. Since this value does not exceed the critical probability, we accept H_A. Note this is the same decision reached in (a).

19.8.a. c_u = 50 - 40 = 10; c_o = 40 - 35 = 5

b. Compute the level of the normal distribution by using

$$\frac{c_u}{c_o + c_u} = \frac{10}{5 + 10} = 0.67. \quad \text{The value of } z_{0.67} \text{ is } 0.44.$$

Thus the optimal estimate of the mean is

$$\hat{\mu}_{opt} = E'(\mu) + 0.44\sigma'_\mu$$

$$= 100 + 0.44(10) = 104.4$$

or 104.4 million barrels per year.

CHAPTER 2:   ACHIEVEMENT TEST SOLUTIONS

1.   90

2. $1 - 0.9 = 0.1$

3.   Qualitative.

4. $44,000

5.   Accidents tend to occur at random.

6.   Time.

7.   4

8. $3/12 = 0.25$

9.

Value	Frequency	Relative Frequencies
1	5	$1/6 = 0.17$
2	10	$1/3 = 0.33$
3	10	$1/3 = 0.33$
4	5	$1/6 = 0.17$
	30	

10.   10 years

11.   There are too few observations to make a table.

12.   Because 10,000/10 gives 1000 classes, which exceeds a practical limit of 20, try 20 classes.

13.   It has no skewness.

14. $0.25(100) = 25$

15. $0.70(100) = 70$

16.   0.25

17.   1.00

18. $(15 - 10)/15 = 5/15 = 0.33$

CHAPTER 3:   ACHIEVEMENT TEST SOLUTIONS

1.   29/4 = 7.25

2.   μ

3. $\overline{X}$

4.   3

5.   24

6.   14.5

7.   No.

8.   4

9.   10

10.   1

11. X

12.   2.8

13.   σ

14.   13

15. s

16.   340

17.   5

18.   2.2

CHAPTER 4:   ACHIEVEMENT TEST SOLUTIONS

1-3.   A subjective assignment may be made in all three cases. For Question 1, only subjective assignments can be made. For Question 2, a relative frequency assignment could be used. For Question 3, an equally likely assignment could be used.

4. $P(F \text{ and } H) = 0.40 - 0.32 = 0.08$

5. $P(M) = 0.16 + 0.04 = 0.20$

6. $P(W \text{ and } F) = 0.60 - 0.16 - 0.08 = 0.36$

7. $P(O) = 1 - 0.60 = 0.40$

8. $P(W \text{ and } O) = 0.40 - 0.36 = 0.04$

9. $P(F|M) = \dfrac{P(F \text{ and } M)}{P(M)} = \dfrac{0.16}{0.20} = 0.8$

10. $P(M|F) = \dfrac{P(M \text{ and } F)}{P(F)} = \dfrac{0.16}{0.60} = 0.27$

11. $P(C_2|C_1) = \dfrac{P(C_1 \text{ and } C_2)}{P(C_1)} = \dfrac{0.06}{0.30} = 0.20$

12. $P(A \text{ or } C) = P(A) + P(C); \ P(C) = P(C \text{ or } B) - P(B) = 0.8 - 0.5 = 0.3;$

   $P(A) = 0.2; \ P(A \text{ or } C) = 0.2 + 0.3 = 0.5$

13. $P(A') = 1 - P(A) = 1 - 0.2 = 0.8$

14. $P(X \text{ or } Y) = P(X) + P(Y) - P(X \text{ and } Y) = 0.25 + 0.15 - 0.20 = 0.20$

15. $P(R \text{ and } S) = P(R) \times P(S|R) = 0.8(0.2) = 0.16$

16.

	Given Males	Given Females		
Below	0.33	0.40	=	0.25/0.625
Above	0.67	0.60	=	0.375/0.625
		1.00		

Since the conditional probability distributions are not equal, age depends on sex.

17. $M_1 \text{ and } N_2 \text{ and } M_3; \ N_1 \text{ and } M_2 \text{ and } M_3.$

18. $P(N_1 \text{ and } N_2) = P(N_1) \times P(N_2|N_1) = 0.4(0.9) = 0.36$

19. $P(N_1) = 0.4$

20. $P(M_1 \text{ and } M_2) = P(M_1) \times P(M_2 | M_1) = 0.6(0.9) = 0.54$

21. $P(\text{Match} | \text{Two variables}) = 0.54/0.90 = 0.6$

CHAPTER 5:   ACHIEVEMENT TEST SOLUTIONS

1. Not a random variable--middle initial is not numerical.

2. A random variable

3. Not a random variable--event is not numerical.

4.

h	$P(h)$
15	0.2
30	0.4
45	0.4

5.

h	$P(H \leq h)$
15	0.2
30	0.6
45	1.0

6   $H \leq 30$

7. 0.6

8. 0.2

9. $X_E = 2$ and $X_W = 1$; $X_E = 1$ and $X_W = 2$

10. $0.05 + 0.20 + 0.05 = 0.30$

11. 5.5

12. 5.5

13. 6.0

14. 31.0

15. 0.4

16. $S\ S\ S\ F$
    $S\ S\ F\ S$
    $S\ F\ S\ S$
    $F\ S\ S\ S$

17. 120

18. 20

19. $3(1/6)^2(5/6) = 0.069$

20. 0.0001

21.   0.5931

22.   6

23.   3

CHAPTER 6: ACHIEVEMENT TEST SOLUTIONS

1. Left: continuous; right: discrete

2. Left: 0; right: 0.05

3. Left: 0; right: 0

4. Left: 0.35; right: 0.40

5-6.a. 0.3
   b. 0.7
   c. 0.4

7. 0

8. No, their standard deviations may differ.

9. 0.1587

10. $\mu = 0$, $\sigma = 1$

11. All normal distributions may be transformed to the standard normal.

12. By expressing each in standard units.

13. 5.2

14.a. 0.8023
   b. 0.2743
   c. 0.5280

15.a. 0.9904
   b. 0.0096

16. Very nearly zero.

17. 0.0359

18. 0.9318

19. 0.9332

20. 106.7

21. $83.5 \leq X \leq 116.5$

22. Yes, $n\pi/(1-\pi) > 9$

23. $\mu = 800$; $\sigma = 20$

24. $46.5 \leqq X \leqq 47.5$; $-0.7 \leqq Z \leqq -0.5$

25.   0.0665

26.   53

CHAPTER 7: ACHIEVEMENT TEST SOLUTIONS

1.
Account	Amount
6	$ 890
4	550
3	875
5	1210

2. $\overline{X} = 881.25$

3.
Account	Amount
6	$890
4	550
3	875
4	550

4. $\overline{X} = 716.25$

5. $\mu = 885$, which is rarely equal to any sample mean

6. $\mu_{\overline{X}} = \mu = 885$

7. $\sigma_{\overline{X}} = \sigma/\sqrt{n} = 177/\sqrt{4} = 88.5$

8. $\sigma_{\overline{X}} = \sqrt{\dfrac{N-n}{N-1}} * \dfrac{\sigma}{\sqrt{n}} = \dfrac{0}{9}$; $\dfrac{177}{\sqrt{10}} = 0$

9. $\sigma_{\overline{X}} = 177/\sqrt{144} = 14.8$; the distribution of sample means is approximately normal.

10. $\sigma_{\overline{X}} = 177/\sqrt{9} = 59.0$; the sample size is too small to make the normal distribution a reasonable approximation for the distribution of sample means.

11. $z = (19,000 - 20,000)/1000 = -1$; $P(X < 19000) = 0.1587$

12. $\sigma_{\overline{X}} = 1000/\sqrt{25} = 200$; $z = (19,000 - 20,000)/200 = -5$;

   $P(\overline{X} < 19,000) = P(z < -5) = 0$

13. $z_{0.90} = 1.64$; $x_{0.90} = 20,000 + 1.64(1000) = \$21,640$

14. $\mu_P = 0.50$; $\mu_P{}^2 = \dfrac{0.5(0.5)}{64}$; $\sigma_P = 0.0625$

15. μ_P

16. 0.9165

17. The normal approximation may be used for $n = 20$, but not for $n = 10$.

18. $z = -5.21$; $P(p \le 0.30) = 0.0$

CHAPTER 8:   ACHIEVEMENT TEST SOLUTIONS

1.   Unbiased.

2.   Unbiased.

3. $z_{0.075} = 1.44$

4. $\overline{X} = 10$

5. $s^2 = 4$

6. $s = 2$

7.   1.645

8.   1.163

9.   Yes

10. 40 ± 3.29

11.   For $n = 10$, no; for $n = 32$, yes

12. $-2.7764 \leqq t \leqq 2.7764$

13.   For 10 df: $-2.2281 \leqq t \leqq 2.2281$; for 300 df: $-1.9679 \leqq t \leqq 1.9679$;
      for the standard normal: $-1.96 \leqq Z \leqq 1.96$

14. $s = 2.58$; $s_{\overline{X}} = 1.29$

15. 20 ± 0.21315

16.   No

17.   0.4

18.   Yes.   For $p = 0.4$, $n \geqq 60$.

19.   No

20.   3; 271

21.   68

22.   17

23.   57

SQUARES AND SQUARE ROOTS

HOW TO FIND SQUARE ROOTS

1. If the number contains more than three significant digits, round it to just three significant digits. Find the significant digits under column *N*.

2. Move the decimal point either left or right an *even* number of places until a number from 1 to 100 is found. If the result is less than 10, use the column under $\sqrt{N}$. If the result is greater than 10, use the column under $\sqrt{10N}$.

3. For the appropriate entry under either $\sqrt{N}$ or $\sqrt{10N}$, move the decimal point *half* as many places in the *opposite* direction as you moved it in step 2.

Example A Find $\sqrt{12345}$.

Step 1: Change 12345 to 12300.

Step 2: Change 12300 to 1.23 by moving the decimal point four places left. For the row with digits 1.23 under *N* in the table, use the entry under $\sqrt{N}$, which is 1.10905.

Step 3: Move the decimal two places *right* in 1.10905 to get 110.905, the square root of 12345 as accurately as is possible from the table.

Example B Find $\sqrt{0.0093}$

Step 2: Change 0.0093 to 93 by moving the decimal point four places right. For the row with digits 9.30 under *N* in the table, use the entry under $\sqrt{10N}$, which is 9.64365.

Step 3: Move the decimal two places *left* in 9.64365 to get 0.0964365, the square root of 0.0093 to seven decimal places.

481

N	N^2	$\sqrt{N}$	$\sqrt{10N}$	N	N^2	$\sqrt{N}$	$\sqrt{10N}$
1.00	1.0000	1.00000	3.16228	1.50	2.2500	1.22474	3.87298
1.01	1.0201	1.00499	3.17805	1.51	2.2801	1.22882	3.88587
1.02	1.0404	1.00995	3.19374	1.52	2.3104	1.23288	3.89872
1.03	1.0609	1.01489	3.20936	1.53	2.3409	1.23693	3.91152
1.04	1.0816	1.01980	3.22490	1.54	2.3716	1.24097	3.92428
1.05	1.1025	1.02470	3.24037	1.55	2.4025	1.24499	3.93700
1.06	1.1236	1.02956	3.25576	1.56	2.4336	1.24900	3.94968
1.07	1.1449	1.03441	3.27109	1.57	2.4649	1.25300	3.96232
1.08	1.1664	1.03923	3.28634	1.58	2.4964	1.25698	3.97492
1.09	1.1881	1.04403	3.30151	1.59	2.5281	1.26095	3.98748
1.10	1.2100	1.04881	3.31662	1.60	2.5600	1.26491	4.00000
1.11	1.2321	1.05357	3.33167	1.61	2.5921	1.26886	4.01248
1.12	1.2544	1.05830	3.34664	1.62	2.6244	1.27279	4.02492
1.13	1.2769	1.06301	3.36155	1.63	2.6569	1.27671	4.03733
1.14	1.2996	1.06771	3.37639	1.64	2.6896	1.28062	4.04969
1.15	1.3225	1.07238	3.39116	1.65	2.7225	1.28452	4.06202
1.16	1.3456	1.07703	3.40588	1.66	2.7556	1.28841	4.07431
1.17	1.3689	1.08167	3.42053	1.67	2.7889	1.29228	4.08656
1.18	1.3924	1.08628	3.43511	1.68	2.8224	1.29615	4.09878
1.19	1.4161	1.09087	3.44964	1.69	2.8561	1.30000	4.11096
1.20	1.4400	1.09545	3.46410	1.70	2.8900	1.30384	4.12311
1.21	1.4641	1.10000	3.47851	1.71	2.9241	1.30767	4.13521
1.22	1.4884	1.10454	3.49285	1.72	2.9584	1.31149	4.14729
1.23	1.5129	1.10905	3.50714	1.73	2.9929	1.31529	4.15933
1.24	1.5376	1.11355	3.52136	1.74	3.0276	1.31909	4.17133
1.25	1.5625	1.11803	3.53553	1.75	3.0625	1.32288	4.18330
1.26	1.5876	1.12250	3.54965	1.76	3.0976	1.32665	4.19524
1.27	1.6129	1.12694	3.56371	1.77	3.1329	1.33041	4.20714
1.28	1.6384	1.13137	3.57771	1.78	3.1684	1.33417	4.21900
1.29	1.6641	1.13578	3.59166	1.79	3.2041	1.33791	4.23084
1.30	1.6900	1.14018	3.60555	1.80	3.2400	1.34164	4.24264
1.31	1.7161	1.14455	3.61939	1.81	3.2761	1.34536	4.25441
1.32	1.7424	1.14891	3.63318	1.82	3.3124	1.34907	4.26615
1.33	1.7689	1.15326	3.64692	1.83	3.3489	1.35277	4.27785
1.34	1.7956	1.15758	3.66060	1.84	3.3856	1.35647	4.28952
1.35	1.8225	1.16190	3.67423	1.85	3.4225	1.36015	4.30116
1.36	1.8496	1.16619	3.68782	1.86	3.4596	1.36382	4.31277
1.37	1.8769	1.17047	3.70135	1.87	3.4969	1.36748	4.32435
1.38	1.9044	1.17473	3.71484	1.88	3.5344	1.37113	4.33590
1.39	1.9321	1.17898	3.72827	1.89	3.5721	1.37477	4.34741
1.40	1.9600	1.18322	3.74166	1.90	3.6100	1.37840	4.35890
1.41	1.9881	1.18743	3.75500	1.91	3.6481	1.38203	4.37035
1.42	2.0164	1.19164	3.76829	1.92	3.6864	1.38564	4.38178
1.43	2.0449	1.19583	3.78153	1.93	3.7249	1.38924	4.39318
1.44	2.0736	1.20000	3.79473	1.94	3.7636	1.39284	4.40454
1.45	2.1025	1.20416	3.80789	1.95	3.8025	1.39642	4.41588
1.46	2.1316	1.20830	3.82099	1.96	3.8416	1.40000	4.42719
1.47	2.1609	1.21244	3.83406	1.97	3.8809	1.40357	4.43847
1.48	2.1904	1.21655	3.84708	1.98	3.9204	1.40712	4.44972
1.49	2.2201	1.22066	3.86005	1.99	3.9601	1.41067	4.46094

N	N²	√N	√10N	N	N²	√N	√10N
2.00	4.0000	1.41421	4.47214	2.50	6.2500	1.58114	5.00000
2.01	4.0401	1.41774	4.48330	2.51	6.3001	1.58430	5.00999
2.02	4.0804	1.42127	4.49444	2.52	6.3504	1.58745	5.01996
2.03	4.1209	1.42478	4.50555	2.53	6.4009	1.59060	5.02991
2.04	4.1616	1.42829	4.51664	2.54	6.4516	1.59374	5.03984
2.05	4.2025	1.43178	4.52769	2.55	6.5025	1.59687	5.04975
2.06	4.2436	1.43527	4.53872	2.56	6.5536	1.60000	5.05964
2.07	4.2849	1.43875	4.54973	2.57	6.6049	1.60312	5.06952
2.08	4.3264	1.44222	4.56070	2.58	6.6564	1.60624	5.07937
2.09	4.3681	1.44568	4.57165	2.59	6.7081	1.60935	5.08920
2.10	4.4100	1.44914	4.58258	2.60	6.7600	1.61245	5.09902
2.11	4.4521	1.45258	4.59347	2.61	6.8121	1.61555	5.10882
2.12	4.4944	1.45602	4.60435	2.62	6.8644	1.61864	5.11859
2.13	4.5369	1.45945	4.61519	2.63	6.9169	1.62173	5.12835
2.14	4.5796	1.46287	4.62601	2.64	6.9696	1.62481	5.13809
2.15	4.6225	1.46629	4.63681	2.65	7.0225	1.62788	5.14782
2.16	4.6656	1.46969	4.64758	2.66	7.0756	1.63095	5.15752
2.17	4.7089	1.47309	4.65833	2.67	7.1289	1.63401	5.16720
2.18	4.7524	1.47648	4.66905	2.68	7.1824	1.63707	5.17687
2.19	4.7961	1.47986	4.67974	2.69	7.2361	1.64012	5.18652
2.20	4.8400	1.48324	4.69042	2.70	7.2900	1.64317	5.19615
2.21	4.8841	1.48661	4.70106	2.71	7.3441	1.64621	5.20577
2.22	4.9284	1.48997	4.71169	2.72	7.3984	1.64924	5.21536
2.23	4.9729	1.49332	4.72229	2.73	7.4529	1.65227	5.22494
2.24	5.0176	1.49666	4.73286	2.74	7.5076	1.65529	5.23450
2.25	5.0625	1.50000	4.74342	2.75	7.5625	1.65831	5.24404
2.26	5.1076	1.50333	4.75395	2.76	7.6176	1.66132	5.25357
2.27	5.1529	1.50665	4.76445	2.77	7.6729	1.66433	5.26308
2.28	5.1984	1.50997	4.77493	2.78	7.7284	1.66733	5.27257
2.29	5.2441	1.51327	4.78539	2.79	7.7841	1.67033	5.28205
2.30	5.2900	1.51658	4.79583	2.80	7.8400	1.67332	5.29150
2.31	5.3361	1.51987	4.80625	2.81	7.8961	1.67631	5.30094
2.32	5.3824	1.52315	4.81664	2.82	7.9524	1.67929	5.31037
2.33	5.4289	1.52643	4.82701	2.83	8.0089	1.68226	5.31977
2.34	5.4756	1.52971	4.83735	2.84	8.0656	1.68523	5.32917
2.35	5.5225	1.53297	4.84768	2.85	8.1225	1.68819	5.33854
2.36	5.5696	1.53623	4.85798	2.86	8.1796	1.69115	5.34790
2.37	5.6169	1.53948	4.86826	2.87	8.2369	1.69411	5.35724
2.38	5.6644	1.54272	4.87852	2.88	8.2944	1.69706	5.36656
2.39	5.7121	1.54596	4.88876	2.89	8.3521	1.70000	5.37587
2.40	5.7600	1.54919	4.89898	2.90	8.4100	1.70294	5.38516
2.41	5.8081	1.55242	4.90918	2.91	8.4681	1.70587	5.39444
2.42	5.8564	1.55563	4.91935	2.92	8.5264	1.70880	5.40370
2.43	5.9049	1.55885	4.92950	2.93	8.5849	1.71172	5.41295
2.44	5.9536	1.56205	4.93964	2.94	8.6436	1.71464	5.42218
2.45	6.0025	1.56525	4.94975	2.95	8.7025	1.71756	5.43139
2.46	6.0516	1.56844	4.95984	2.96	8.7616	1.72047	5.44059
2.47	6.1009	1.57162	4.96991	2.97	8.8209	1.72337	5.44977
2.48	6.1504	1.57480	4.97996	2.98	8.8804	1.72627	5.45894
2.49	6.2001	1.57797	4.98999	2.99	8.9401	1.72916	5.46809

N	N²	√N	√10N	N	N²	√N	√10N
3.00	9.0000	1.73205	5.47723	3.50	12.2500	1.87083	5.91608
3.01	9.0601	1.73494	5.48635	3.51	12.3201	1.87350	5.92453
3.02	9.1204	1.73781	5.49545	3.52	12.3904	1.87617	5.93296
3.03	9.1809	1.74069	5.50454	3.53	12.4609	1.87883	5.94138
3.04	9.2416	1.74356	5.51362	3.54	12.5316	1.88149	5.94979
3.05	9.3025	1.74642	5.52268	3.55	12.6025	1.88414	5.95819
3.06	9.3636	1.74929	5.53173	3.56	12.6736	1.88680	5.96657
3.07	9.4249	1.75214	5.54076	3.57	12.7449	1.88944	5.97495
3.08	9.4864	1.75499	5.54977	3.58	12.8164	1.89209	5.98331
3.09	9.5481	1.75784	5.55878	3.59	12.8881	1.89473	5.99166
3.10	9.6100	1.76068	5.56776	3.60	12.9600	1.89737	6.00000
3.11	9.6721	1.76352	5.57674	3.61	13.0321	1.90000	6.00833
3.12	9.7344	1.76635	5.58570	3.62	13.1044	1.90263	6.01664
3.13	9.7969	1.76918	5.59464	3.63	13.1769	1.90526	6.02495
3.14	9.8596	1.77200	5.60357	3.64	13.2496	1.90788	6.03324
3.15	9.9225	1.77482	5.61249	3.65	13.3225	1.91050	6.04152
3.16	9.9856	1.77764	5.62139	3.66	13.3956	1.91311	6.04979
3.17	10.0489	1.78045	5.63028	3.67	13.4689	1.91572	6.05805
3.18	10.1124	1.78326	5.63915	3.68	13.5424	1.91833	6.06630
3.19	10.1761	1.78606	5.64801	3.69	13.6161	1.92094	6.07454
3.20	10.2400	1.78885	5.65685	3.70	13.6900	1.92354	6.08276
3.21	10.3041	1.79165	5.66569	3.71	13.7641	1.92614	6.09098
3.22	10.3684	1.79444	5.67450	3.72	13.8384	1.92873	6.09918
3.23	10.4329	1.79722	5.68331	3.73	13.9129	1.93132	6.10737
3.24	10.4976	1.80000	5.69210	3.74	13.9876	1.93391	6.11555
3.25	10.5625	1.80278	5.70088	3.75	14.0625	1.93649	6.12372
3.26	10.6276	1.80555	5.70964	3.76	14.1376	1.93907	6.13188
3.27	10.6929	1.80831	5.71839	3.77	14.2129	1.94165	6.14003
3.28	10.7584	1.81108	5.72713	3.78	14.2884	1.94422	6.14817
3.29	10.8241	1.81384	5.73585	3.79	14.3641	1.94679	6.15630
3.30	10.8900	1.81659	5.74456	3.80	14.4400	1.94936	6.16441
3.31	10.9561	1.81934	5.75326	3.81	14.5161	1.95192	6.17252
3.32	11.0224	1.82209	5.76194	3.82	14.5924	1.95448	6.18061
3.33	11.0889	1.82483	5.77062	3.83	14.6689	1.95704	6.18870
3.34	11.1556	1.82757	5.77927	3.84	14.7456	1.95959	6.19677
3.35	11.2225	1.83030	5.78792	3.85	14.8225	1.96214	6.20484
3.36	11.2896	1.83303	5.79655	3.86	14.8996	1.96469	6.21289
3.37	11.3569	1.83576	5.80517	3.87	14.9769	1.96723	6.22093
3.38	11.4244	1.83848	5.81378	3.88	15.0544	1.96977	6.22896
3.39	11.4921	1.84120	5.82237	3.89	15.1321	1.97231	6.23699
3.40	11.5600	1.84391	5.83095	3.90	15.2100	1.97484	6.24500
3.41	11.6281	1.84662	5.83952	3.91	15.2881	1.97737	6.25300
3.42	11.6964	1.84932	5.84808	3.92	15.3664	1.97990	6.26099
3.43	11.7649	1.85203	5.85662	3.93	15.4449	1.98242	6.26897
3.44	11.8336	1.85472	5.86515	3.94	15.5236	1.98494	6.27694
3.45	11.9025	1.85742	5.87367	3.95	15.6025	1.98746	6.28490
3.46	11.9716	1.86011	5.88218	3.96	15.6816	1.98997	6.29285
3.47	12.0409	1.86279	5.89067	3.97	15.7609	1.99249	6.30079
3.48	12.1104	1.86548	5.89915	3.98	15.8408	1.99499	6.30872
3.49	12.1801	1.86815	5.90762	3.99	15.9201	1.99750	6.31664

N	N²	√N	√10N	N	N²	√N	√10N
4.00	16.0000	2.00000	6.32456	4.50	20.2500	2.12132	6.70820
4.01	16.0801	2.00250	6.33246	4.51	20.3401	2.12368	6.71565
4.02	16.1604	2.00499	6.34035	4.52	20.4304	2.12603	6.72309
4.03	16.2409	2.00749	6.34823	4.53	20.5209	2.12838	6.73053
4.04	16.3216	2.00998	6.35610	4.54	20.6116	2.13073	6.73795
4.05	16.4025	2.01246	6.36396	4.55	20.7025	2.13307	6.74537
4.06	16.4836	2.01494	6.37181	4.56	20.7936	2.13542	6.75278
4.07	16.5649	2.01742	6.37966	4.57	20.8849	2.13776	6.76018
4.08	16.6464	2.01990	6.38749	4.58	20.9764	2.14009	6.76757
4.09	16.7281	2.02237	6.39531	4.59	21.0681	2.14243	6.77495
4.10	16.8100	2.02485	6.40312	4.60	21.1600	2.14476	6.78233
4.11	16.8921	2.02731	6.41093	4.61	21.2521	2.14709	6.78970
4.12	16.9744	2.02978	6.41872	4.62	21.3444	2.14942	6.79706
4.13	17.0569	2.03224	6.42651	4.63	21.4369	2.15174	6.80441
4.14	17.1396	2.03470	6.43428	4.64	21.5296	2.15407	6.81175
4.15	17.2225	2.03715	6.44205	4.65	21.6225	2.15639	6.81909
4.16	17.3056	2.03961	6.44981	4.66	21.7156	2.15870	6.82642
4.17	17.3889	2.04206	6.45755	4.67	21.8089	2.16102	6.83374
4.18	17.4724	2.04450	6.46529	4.68	21.9024	2.16333	6.84105
4.19	17.5561	2.04695	6.47302	4.69	21.9961	2.16564	6.84836
4.20	17.6400	2.04939	6.48074	4.70	22.0900	2.16795	6.85565
4.21	17.7241	2.05183	6.48845	4.71	22.1841	2.17025	6.86294
4.22	17.8084	2.05426	6.49615	4.72	22.2784	2.17256	6.87023
4.23	17.8929	2.05670	6.50384	4.73	22.3729	2.17486	6.87750
4.24	17.9776	2.05913	6.51153	4.74	22.4676	2.17715	6.88477
4.25	18.0625	2.06155	6.51920	4.75	22.5625	2.17945	6.89202
4.26	18.1476	2.06398	6.52687	4.76	22.6576	2.18174	6.89928
4.27	18.2329	2.06640	6.53452	4.77	22.7529	2.18403	6.90652
4.28	18.3184	2.06882	6.54217	4.78	22.8484	2.18632	6.91375
4.29	18.4041	2.07123	6.54981	4.79	22.9441	2.18861	6.92098
4.30	18.4900	2.07364	6.55744	4.80	23.0400	2.19089	6.92820
4.31	18.5761	2.07605	6.56506	4.81	23.1361	2.19317	6.93542
4.32	18.6624	2.07846	6.57267	4.82	23.2324	2.19545	6.94262
4.33	18.7489	2.08087	6.58027	4.83	23.3289	2.19773	6.94982
4.34	18.8356	2.08327	6.58787	4.84	23.4256	2.20000	6.95701
4.35	18.9225	2.08567	6.59545	4.85	23.5225	2.20227	6.96419
4.36	19.0096	2.08806	6.60303	4.86	23.6196	2.20454	6.97137
4.37	19.0969	2.09045	6.61060	4.87	23.7169	2.20681	6.97854
4.38	19.1844	2.09284	6.61816	4.88	23.8144	2.20907	6.98570
4.39	19.2721	2.09523	6.62571	4.89	23.9121	2.21133	6.99285
4.40	19.3600	2.09762	6.63325	4.90	24.0100	2.21359	7.00000
4.41	19.4481	2.10000	6.64078	4.91	24.1081	2.21585	7.00714
4.42	19.5364	2.10238	6.64831	4.92	24.2064	2.21811	7.01427
4.43	19.6249	2.10476	6.65582	4.93	24.3049	2.22036	7.02140
4.44	19.7136	2.10713	6.66333	4.94	24.4036	2.22261	7.02851
4.45	19.8025	2.10950	6.67083	4.95	24.5025	2.22486	7.03562
4.46	19.8916	2.11187	6.67832	4.96	24.6016	2.22711	7.04273
4.47	19.9809	2.11424	6.68581	4.97	24.7009	2.22935	7.04982
4.48	20.0704	2.11660	6.69328	4.98	24.8004	2.23159	7.05691
4.49	20.1601	2.11896	6.70075	4.99	24.9001	2.23383	7.06399

N	N²	√N	√10N	N	N²	√N	√10N
5.00	25.0000	2.23607	7.07107	5.50	30.2500	2.34521	7.41620
5.01	25.1001	2.23830	7.07814	5.51	30.3601	2.34734	7.42294
5.02	25.2004	2.24054	7.08520	5.52	30.4704	2.34947	7.42967
5.03	25.3009	2.24277	7.09225	5.53	30.5809	2.35160	7.43640
5.04	25.4016	2.24499	7.09930	5.54	30.6916	2.35372	7.44312
5.05	25.5025	2.24722	7.10634	5.55	30.8025	2.35584	7.44983
5.06	25.6036	2.24944	7.11337	5.56	30.9136	2.35797	7.45654
5.07	25.7049	2.25167	7.12039	5.57	31.0249	2.36008	7.46324
5.08	25.8064	2.25389	7.12741	5.58	31.1364	2.36220	7.46994
5.09	25.9081	2.25610	7.13442	5.59	31.2481	2.36432	7.47663
5.10	26.0100	2.25832	7.14143	5.60	31.3600	2.36643	7.48331
5.11	26.1121	2.26053	7.14843	5.61	31.4721	2.36854	7.48999
5.12	26.2144	2.26274	7.15542	5.62	31.5844	2.37065	7.49667
5.13	26.3169	2.26495	7.16240	5.63	31.6969	2.37276	7.50333
5.14	26.4196	2.26716	7.16938	5.64	31.8096	2.37487	7.50999
5.15	26.5225	2.26936	7.17635	5.65	31.9225	2.37697	7.51665
5.16	26.6256	2.27156	7.18331	5.66	32.0356	2.37908	7.52330
5.17	26.7289	2.27376	7.19027	5.67	32.1489	2.38118	7.52994
5.18	26.8324	2.27596	7.19722	5.68	32.2624	2.38328	7.53658
5.19	26.9361	2.27816	7.20417	5.69	32.3761	2.38537	7.54321
5.20	27.0400	2.28035	7.21110	5.70	32.4900	2.38747	7.54983
5.21	27.1441	2.28254	7.21803	5.71	32.6041	2.38956	7.55645
5.22	27.2484	2.28473	7.22496	5.72	32.7184	2.39165	7.56307
5.23	27.3529	2.28692	7.23187	5.73	32.8329	2.39374	7.56968
5.24	27.4576	2.28910	7.23878	5.74	32.9476	2.39583	7.57628
5.25	27.5625	2.29129	7.24569	5.75	33.0625	2.39792	7.58288
5.26	27.6676	2.29347	7.25259	5.76	33.1776	2.40000	7.58947
5.27	27.7729	2.29565	7.25948	5.77	33.2929	2.40208	7.59605
5.28	27.8784	2.29783	7.26636	5.78	33.4084	2.40416	7.60263
5.29	27.9841	2.30000	7.27324	5.79	33.5241	2.40624	7.60920
5.30	28.0900	2.30217	7.28011	5.80	33.6400	2.40832	7.61577
5.31	28.1961	2.30434	7.28697	5.81	33.7561	2.41039	7.62234
5.32	28.3024	2.30651	7.29383	5.82	33.8724	2.41247	7.62889
5.33	28.4089	2.30868	7.30068	5.83	33.9889	2.41454	7.63544
5.34	28.5156	2.31084	7.30753	5.84	34.1056	2.41661	7.64199
5.35	28.6225	2.31301	7.31437	5.85	34.2225	2.41868	7.64853
5.36	28.7296	2.31517	7.32120	5.86	34.3396	2.42074	7.65506
5.37	28.8369	2.31733	7.32803	5.87	34.4569	2.42281	7.66159
5.38	28.9444	2.31948	7.33485	5.88	34.5744	2.42487	7.66812
5.39	29.0521	2.32164	7.34166	5.89	34.6921	2.42693	7.67463
5.40	29.1600	2.32379	7.34847	5.90	34.8100	2.42899	7.68115
5.41	29.2681	2.32594	7.35527	5.91	34.9281	2.43105	7.68765
5.42	29.3764	2.32809	7.36205	5.92	35.0464	2.43311	7.69415
5.43	29.4849	2.33024	7.36885	5.93	35.1649	2.43516	7.70065
5.44	29.5936	2.33238	7.37564	5.94	35.2836	2.43721	7.70714
5.45	29.7025	2.33452	7.38241	5.95	35.4025	2.43926	7.71362
5.46	29.8116	2.33666	7.38918	5.96	35.5216	2.44131	7.72010
5.47	29.9209	2.33880	7.39594	5.97	35.6409	2.44336	7.72658
5.48	30.0304	2.34094	7.40270	5.98	35.7604	2.44540	7.73305
5.49	30.1401	2.34307	7.40945	5.99	35.8801	2.44745	7.73951

N	N²	√N	√10N	N	N²	√N	√10N
6.00	36.0000	2.44949	7.74597	6.50	42.2500	2.54951	8.06226
6.01	36.1201	2.45153	7.75242	6.51	42.3801	2.55147	8.06846
6.02	36.2404	2.45357	7.75887	6.52	42.5104	2.55343	8.07465
6.03	36.3609	2.45561	7.76531	6.53	42.6409	2.55539	8.08084
6.04	36.4816	2.45764	7.77174	6.54	42.7716	2.55734	8.08703
6.05	36.6025	2.45967	7.77817	6.55	42.9025	2.55930	8.09321
6.06	36.7236	2.46171	7.78460	6.56	43.0336	2.56125	8.09938
6.07	36.8449	2.46374	7.79102	6.57	43.1649	2.56320	8.10555
6.08	36.9664	2.46577	7.79744	6.58	43.2964	2.56515	8.11172
6.09	37.0881	2.46779	7.80385	6.59	43.4281	2.56710	8.11788
6.10	37.2100	2.46982	7.81025	6.60	43.5600	2.56905	8.12404
6.11	37.3321	2.47184	7.81665	6.61	43.6921	2.57099	8.13019
6.12	37.4544	2.47386	7.82304	6.62	43.8244	2.57294	8.13634
6.13	37.5769	2.47588	7.82943	6.63	43.9569	2.57488	8.14248
6.14	37.6996	2.47790	7.83582	6.64	44.0896	2.57682	8.14862
6.15	37.8225	2.47992	7.84219	6.65	44.2225	2.57876	8.15475
6.16	37.9456	2.48193	7.84857	6.66	44.3556	2.58070	8.16088
6.17	38.0689	2.48395	7.85493	6.67	44.4889	2.58263	8.16701
6.18	38.1924	2.48596	7.86130	6.68	44.6224	2.58457	8.17313
6.19	38.3161	2.48797	7.86766	6.69	44.7561	2.58650	8.17924
6.20	38.4400	2.48998	7.87401	6.70	44.8900	2.58844	8.18535
6.21	38.5641	2.49199	7.88036	6.71	45.0241	2.59037	8.19146
6.22	38.6884	2.49399	7.88670	6.72	45.1584	2.59230	8.19756
6.23	38.8129	2.49600	7.89303	6.73	45.2929	2.59422	8.20366
6.24	38.9376	2.49800	7.89937	6.74	45.4276	2.59615	8.20975
6.25	39.0625	2.50000	7.90569	6.75	45.5625	2.59808	8.21584
6.26	39.1876	2.50200	7.91202	6.76	45.6976	2.60000	8.22192
6.27	39.3129	2.50400	7.91833	6.77	45.8329	2.60192	8.22800
6.28	39.4384	2.50599	7.92465	6.78	45.9684	2.60384	8.23408
6.29	39.5641	2.50799	7.93095	6.79	46.1041	2.60576	8.24015
6.30	39.6900	2.50998	7.93725	6.80	46.2400	2.60768	8.24621
6.31	39.8161	2.51197	7.94355	6.81	46.3761	2.60960	8.25227
6.32	39.9424	2.51396	7.94984	6.82	46.5124	2.61151	8.25833
6.33	40.0689	2.51595	7.95613	6.83	46.6489	2.61343	8.26438
6.34	40.1956	2.51794	7.96241	6.84	46.7856	2.61534	8.27043
6.35	40.3225	2.51992	7.96869	6.85	46.9225	2.61725	8.27647
6.36	40.4496	2.52190	7.97496	6.86	47.0596	2.61916	8.28251
6.37	40.5769	2.52389	7.98123	6.87	47.1969	2.62107	8.28855
6.38	40.7044	2.52587	7.98749	6.88	47.3344	2.62298	8.29458
6.39	40.8321	2.52784	7.99375	6.89	47.4721	2.62488	8.30060
6.40	40.9600	2.52982	8.00000	6.90	47.6100	2.62679	8.30662
6.41	41.0881	2.53180	8.00625	6.91	47.7481	2.62869	8.31264
6.42	41.2164	2.53377	8.01249	6.92	47.8864	2.63059	8.31865
6.43	41.3449	2.53574	8.01873	6.93	48.0249	2.63249	8.32466
6.44	41.4736	2.53772	8.02496	6.94	48.1636	2.63439	8.33067
6.45	41.6025	2.53969	8.03119	6.95	48.3025	2.63629	8.33667
6.46	41.7316	2.54165	8.03741	6.96	48.4416	2.63818	8.34266
6.47	41.8609	2.54362	8.04363	6.97	48.5809	2.64008	8.34865
6.48	41.9904	2.54558	8.04984	6.98	48.7204	2.64197	8.35464
6.49	42.1201	2.54755	8.05605	6.99	48.8601	2.64386	8.36062

N	N²	√N	√10N	N	N²	√N	√10N
7.00	49.0000	2.64575	8.36660	7.50	56.2500	2.73861	8.66025
7.01	49.1401	2.64764	8.37257	7.51	56.4001	2.74044	8.66603
7.02	49.2804	2.64953	8.37854	7.52	56.5504	2.74226	8.67179
7.03	49.4209	2.65141	8.38451	7.53	56.7009	2.74408	8.67756
7.04	49.5616	2.65330	8.39047	7.54	56.8516	2.74591	8.68332
7.05	49.7025	2.65518	8.39643	7.55	57.0025	2.74773	8.68907
7.06	49.8436	2.65707	8.40238	7.56	57.1536	2.74955	8.69483
7.07	49.9849	2.65895	8.40833	7.57	57.3049	2.75136	8.70057
7.08	50.1264	2.66083	8.41427	7.58	57.4564	2.75318	8.70632
7.09	50.2681	2.66271	8.42021	7.59	57.6081	2.75500	8.71206
7.10	50.4100	2.66458	8.42615	7.60	57.7600	2.75681	8.71780
7.11	50.5521	2.66646	8.43208	7.61	57.9121	2.75862	8.72353
7.12	50.6944	2.66833	8.43801	7.62	58.0644	2.76043	8.72926
7.13	50.8369	2.67021	8.44393	7.63	58.2169	2.76225	8.73499
7.14	50.9796	2.67208	8.44985	7.64	58.3696	2.76405	8.74071
7.15	51.1225	2.67395	8.45577	7.65	58.5225	2.76586	8.74643
7.16	51.2656	2.67582	8.46168	7.66	58.6756	2.76767	8.75214
7.17	51.4089	2.67769	8.46759	7.67	58.8289	2.76948	8.75785
7.18	51.5524	2.67955	8.47349	7.68	58.9824	2.77128	8.76356
7.19	51.6961	2.68142	8.47939	7.69	59.1361	2.77308	8.76926
7.20	51.8400	2.68328	8.48528	7.70	59.2900	2.77489	8.77496
7.21	51.9841	2.68514	8.49117	7.71	59.4441	2.77669	8.78066
7.22	52.1284	2.68701	8.49706	7.72	59.5984	2.77849	8.78635
7.23	52.2729	2.68887	8.50294	7.73	59.7529	2.78029	8.79204
7.24	52.4176	2.69072	8.50882	7.74	59.9076	2.78209	8.79773
7.25	52.5625	2.69258	8.51469	7.75	60.0625	2.78388	8.80341
7.26	52.7076	2.69444	8.52056	7.76	60.2176	2.78568	8.80909
7.27	52.8529	2.69629	8.52643	7.77	60.3729	2.78747	8.81476
7.28	52.9984	2.69815	8.53229	7.78	60.5284	2.78927	8.82043
7.29	53.1441	2.70000	8.53815	7.79	60.6841	2.79106	8.82610
7.30	53.2900	2.70185	8.54400	7.80	60.8400	2.79285	8.83176
7.31	53.4361	2.70370	8.54985	7.81	60.9961	2.79464	8.83742
7.32	53.5824	2.70555	8.55570	7.82	61.1524	2.79643	8.84308
7.33	53.7289	2.70740	8.56154	7.83	61.3089	2.79821	8.84873
7.34	53.8756	2.70924	8.56738	7.84	61.4656	2.80000	8.85438
7.35	54.0225	2.71109	8.57321	7.85	61.6225	2.80179	8.86002
7.36	54.1696	2.71293	3.57904	7.86	61.7796	2.80357	8.86566
7.37	54.3169	2.71477	8.58487	7.87	61.9369	2.80535	8.87130
7.38	54.4644	2.71662	8.59069	7.88	62.0944	2.80713	8.87694
7.39	54.6121	2.71846	8.59651	7.89	62.2521	2.80891	8.88257
7.40	54.7600	2.72029	8.60233	7.90	62.4100	2.81069	8.88819
7.41	54.9081	2.72213	8.60814	7.91	62.5681	2.81247	8.89382
7.42	55.0564	2.72397	8.61394	7.92	62.7264	2.81425	8.89944
7.43	55.2049	2.72580	8.61974	7.93	62.8849	2.81603	8.90505
7.44	55.3536	2.72764	8.62554	7.94	63.0436	2.81780	8.91067
7.45	55.5025	2.72947	8.63134	7.95	63.2025	2.81957	8.91628
7.46	55.6516	2.73130	8.63713	7.96	63.3616	2.82135	8.92188
7.47	55.8009	2.73313	8.64292	7.97	63.5209	2.82312	8.92749
7.48	55.9504	2.73496	8.64870	7.98	63.6804	2.82489	8.93308
7.49	56.1001	2.73679	8.65448	7.99	63.8401	2.82666	8.93868

N	N²	√N	√10N	N	N²	√N	√10N
8.00	64.0000	2.82843	8.94427	8.50	72.2500	2.91548	9.21954
8.01	64.1601	2.83019	8.94986	8.51	72.4201	2.91719	9.22497
8.02	64.3204	2.83196	8.95545	8.52	72.5904	2.91890	9.23038
8.03	64.4809	2.83373	8.96103	8.53	72.7609	2.92062	9.23580
8.04	64.6416	2.83549	8.96660	8.54	72.9316	2.92233	9.24121
8.05	64.8025	2.83725	8.97218	8.55	73.1025	2.92404	9.24662
8.06	64.9636	2.83901	8.97775	8.56	73.2736	2.92575	9.25203
8.07	65.1249	2.84077	8.98332	8.57	73.4449	2.92746	9.25743
8.08	65.2864	2.84253	8.98888	8.58	73.6164	2.92916	9.26283
8.09	65.4481	2.84429	8.99444	8.59	73.7881	2.93087	9.26823
8.10	65.6100	2.84605	9.00000	8.60	73.9600	2.93258	9.27362
8.11	65.7721	2.84781	9.00555	8.61	74.1321	2.93428	9.27901
8.12	65.9344	2.84956	9.01110	8.62	74.3044	2.93598	9.28440
8.13	66.0969	2.85132	9.01665	8.63	74.4769	2.93769	9.28978
8.14	66.2596	2.85307	9.02219	8.64	74.6496	2.93939	9.29516
8.15	66.4225	2.85482	9.02774	8.65	74.8225	2.94109	9.30054
8.16	66.5856	2.85657	9.03327	8.66	74.9956	2.94279	9.30591
8.17	66.7489	2.85832	9.03881	8.67	75.1689	2.94449	9.31128
8.18	66.9124	2.86007	9.04434	8.68	75.3424	2.94618	9.31665
8.19	67.0761	2.86182	9.04986	8.69	75.5161	2.94788	9.32202
8.20	67.2400	2.86356	9.05539	8.70	75.6900	2.94958	9.32738
8.21	67.4041	2.86531	9.06091	8.71	75.8641	2.95127	9.33274
8.22	67.5684	2.86705	9.06642	8.72	76.0384	2.95296	9.33809
8.23	67.7329	2.86880	9.07193	8.73	76.2129	2.95466	9.34345
8.24	67.8976	2.87054	9.07744	8.74	76.3876	2.95635	9.34880
8.25	68.0625	2.87228	9.08295	8.75	76.5625	2.95804	9.35414
8.26	68.2276	2.87402	9.08845	8.76	76.7376	2.95973	9.35949
8.27	68.3929	2.87576	9.09395	8.77	76.9129	2.96142	9.36483
8.28	68.5584	2.87750	9.09945	8.78	77.0884	2.96311	9.37017
8.29	68.7241	2.87924	9.10494	8.79	77.2641	2.96479	9.37550
8.30	68.8900	2.88097	9.11043	8.80	77.4400	2.96648	9.38083
8.31	69.0561	2.88271	9.11592	8.81	77.6161	2.96816	9.38616
8.32	69.2224	2.88444	9.12140	8.82	77.7924	2.96985	9.39149
8.33	69.3889	2.88617	9.12688	8.83	77.9689	2.97153	9.39681
8.34	69.5556	2.88791	9.13236	8.84	78.1456	2.97321	9.40213
8.35	69.7225	2.88964	9.13783	8.85	78.3225	2.97489	9.40744
8.36	69.8896	2.89137	9.14330	8.86	78.4996	2.97658	9.41276
8.37	70.0569	2.89310	9.14877	8.87	78.6769	2.97825	9.41807
8.38	70.2244	2.89482	9.15423	8.88	78.8544	2.97993	9.42338
8.39	70.3921	2.89655	9.15969	8.89	79.0321	2.98161	9.42868
8.40	70.5600	2.89828	9.16515	8.90	79.2100	2.98329	9.43398
8.41	70.7281	2.90000	9.17061	8.91	79.3881	2.98496	9.43928
8.42	70.8964	2.90172	9.17606	8.92	79.5664	2.98664	9.44458
8.43	71.0649	2.90345	9.18150	8.93	79.7449	2.98831	9.44987
8.44	71.2336	2.90517	9.18695	8.94	79.9236	2.98998	9.45516
8.45	71.4025	2.90689	9.19239	8.95	80.1025	2.99166	9.46044
8.46	71.5716	2.90861	9.19783	8.96	80.2816	2.99333	9.46573
8.47	71.7409	2.91033	9.20326	8.97	80.4609	2.99500	9.47101
8.48	71.9104	2.91204	9.20869	8.98	80.6404	2.99666	9.47629
8.49	72.0801	2.91376	9.21412	8.99	80.8201	2.99833	9.48156

N	N²	√N	√10N	N	N²	√N	√10N
9.00	81.0000	3.00000	9.48683	9.50	90.2500	3.08221	9.74679
9.01	81.1801	3.00167	9.49210	9.51	90.4401	3.08383	9.75192
9.02	81.3604	3.00333	9.49737	9.52	90.6304	3.08545	9.75705
9.03	81.5409	3.00500	9.50263	9.53	90.8209	3.08707	9.76217
9.04	81.7216	3.00666	9.50789	9.54	91.0116	3.08869	9.76729
9.05	81.9025	3.00832	9.51315	9.55	91.2025	3.09031	9.77241
9.06	82.0836	3.00998	9.51840	9.56	91.3936	3.09192	9.77753
9.07	82.2649	3.01164	9.52365	9.57	91.5849	3.09354	9.78264
9.08	82.4464	3.01330	9.52890	9.58	91.7764	3.09516	9.78775
9.09	82.6281	3.01496	9.53415	9.59	91.9681	3.09677	9.79285
9.10	82.8100	3.01662	9.53939	9.60	92.1600	3.09839	9.79796
9.11	82.9921	3.01828	9.54463	9.61	92.3521	3.10000	9.80306
9.12	83.1744	3.01993	9.54987	9.62	92.5444	3.10161	9.80816
9.13	83.3569	3.02159	9.55510	9.63	92.7369	3.10322	9.81326
9.14	83.5396	3.02324	9.56033	9.64	92.9296	3.10483	9.81835
9.15	83.7225	3.02490	9.56556	9.65	93.1225	3.10644	9.82344
9.16	83.9056	3.02655	9.57079	9.66	93.3156	3.10805	9.82853
9.17	84.0889	3.02820	9.57601	9.67	93.5089	3.10966	9.83362
9.18	84.2724	3.02985	9.58123	9.68	93.7024	3.11127	9.83870
9.19	84.4561	3.03150	9.58645	9.69	93.8961	3.11288	9.84378
9.20	84.6400	3.03315	9.59166	9.70	94.0900	3.11448	9.84886
9.21	84.8241	3.03480	9.59687	9.71	94.2841	3.11609	9.85393
9.22	85.0084	3.03645	9.60208	9.72	94.4784	3.11769	9.85901
9.23	85.1929	3.03809	9.60729	9.73	94.6729	3.11929	9.86408
9.24	85.3776	3.03974	9.61249	9.74	94.8676	3.12090	9.86914
9.25	85.5625	3.04138	9.61769	9.75	95.0625	3.12250	9.87421
9.26	85.7476	3.04302	9.62289	9.76	95.2576	3.12410	9.87927
9.27	85.9329	3.04467	9.62808	9.77	95.4529	3.12570	9.88433
9.28	86.1184	3.04631	9.63328	9.78	95.6484	3.12730	9.88939
9.29	86.3041	3.04795	9.63846	9.79	95.8441	3.12890	9.89444
9.30	86.4900	3.04959	9.64365	9.80	96.0400	3.13050	9.89949
9.31	86.6761	3.05123	9.64883	9.81	96.2361	3.13209	9.90454
9.32	86.8624	3.05287	9.65401	9.82	96.4324	3.13369	9.90959
9.33	87.0489	3.05450	9.65919	9.83	96.6289	3.13528	9.91464
9.34	87.2356	3.05614	9.66437	9.84	96.8256	3.13688	9.91968
9.35	87.4225	3.05778	9.66954	9.85	97.0225	3.13847	9.92472
9.36	87.6096	3.05941	9.67471	9.86	97.2196	3.14006	9.92975
9.37	87.7969	3.06105	9.67988	9.87	97.4169	3.14166	9.93479
9.38	87.9844	3.06268	9.68504	9.88	97.6144	3.14325	9.93982
9.39	88.1721	3.06431	9.69020	9.89	97.8121	3.14484	9.94485
9.40	88.3600	3.06594	9.69536	9.90	98.0100	3.14643	9.94987
9.41	88.5481	3.06757	9.70052	9.91	98.2081	3.14802	9.95490
9.42	88.7364	3.06920	9.70567	9.92	98.4064	3.14960	9.95992
9.43	88.9249	3.07083	9.71082	9.93	98.6049	3.15119	9.96494
9.44	89.1136	3.07246	9.71597	9.94	98.8036	3.15278	9.96995
9.45	89.3025	3.07409	9.72111	9.95	99.0025	3.15436	9.97497
9.46	89.4916	3.07571	9.72625	9.96	99.2016	3.15595	9.97998
9.47	89.6809	3.07734	9.73139	9.97	99.4009	3.15753	9.98499
9.48	89.8704	3.07896	9.73653	9.98	99.6004	3.15911	9.98999
9.49	90.0601	3.08058	9.74166	9.99	99.8001	3.16070	9.99500